D1236671

Defense Policy Formation

Defense Policy Formation
Towards Comparative Analysis

edited by

James M. Roherty

International Relations Series Number 6
Institute of International Studies
University of South Carolina

Carolina Academic Press
Durham, North Carolina

U A 11
D 39

Carolina Academic Press
P.O. Box 8795, Forest Hills Station
Durham, North Carolina 27707

Contents

Preface

There is a vast literature in the field of defense policy and military studies. Theoretical innovation and development of the field have not, however, been a match for the quantity. Too often writers have concentrated on superpowers and their relations, and have given inadequate attention to the role of the middle powers or to their military and defense establishments. The essays in this volume constitute a significant step in a new direction for defense studies by presenting timely and significant research on the policy making and security concerns of selected middle powers. They were originally prepared for the November 1978 Biennial Conference of the Section on Military Studies of the International Studies Association, held at Kiawah Island, South Carolina. James M. Roherty, the editor of this volume, was the Conference Chairman.

The Institute of International Studies of the University of South Carolina, a cosponsor of the Kiawah Conference, is pleased to offer this set of comparative defense studies as Volume Six in its *International Relations Series.*

RICHARD L. WALKER

Institute of International Studies
University of South Carolina

Contributors

Henry S. Albinski is Professor in the Department of Political Science, Pennsylvania State University.

Desmond J. Ball is Research Associate, Strategic and Defense Studies Center, The Australian National University, Canberra.

P. R. Chari is Director, The Institute of Defense Studies and Analyses, New Delhi, India.

Stephen P. Cohen is Professor in the Department of Political Science, University of Illinois–Urbana.

Richard Dale is Associate Professor in the Department of Political Science, Southern Illinois–Carbondale.

James E. Dornan is late Professor in the Department of Politics, Catholic University of America.

Diane Dornan, Hyattsville, Maryland.

Deon F. S. Fourie is Lecturer in Strategic Studies, Department of Political Science and Public Administration, University of South Africa–Pretoria.

Jean Klein, Institut Francais des Relations Internationales, Paris

LTC David P. Lohmann, USAF, Pacific Air Forces, Hickam AFB, Hawaii.

D. Bruce Marshall is Professor in the Department of Government and International Studies, University of South Carolina.

Stephen S. Roberts, Center for Naval Analyses, Washington, D.C.

James M. Roherty is Professor in the Department of Government and International Studies, University of South Carolina.

J. E. Spence is Professor in the Department of Politics, University of Leicester, U.K.

Taketsugo Tsurutani is Associate Professor in the Department of Political Science, Washington State University.

Defense Policy Formation

I. Introduction

Defense Communities: A Concept for Comparative Analysis

JAMES M. ROHERTY

I.

This volume grows out of two concerns. The first is the increasing complexity of defense policy issues now well recognized among those who may be said to make up the *Defense Community* and among the public generally. The second, more directly the concern of scholars who make "Defense Studies" their principal endeavor, is an increasing dissatisfaction with efforts to date to better comprehend defense policy formation. The present undertaking is a renewed attempt to deal with these concerns by elaborating upon a concept of *Defense Community*. At a minimum this effort seeks to be comprehensive where earlier work has focused on selected, albeit fascinating, aspects of defense policy. Likewise, it seeks to be comprehensive through the medium of nation-based studies, based on a common concept, which will lay the groundwork for comparative, cross-national analyses. Extending over a two-year period and involving scholars from seven countries this effort will be seen, nonetheless, as a modest one. In the academic world the realm of policy studies is strewn with its share of wreckage—monuments to ambitious, if not always elegant, attempts to "model" the policy process. We readily concede wariness on this score.

Some of the discomfiture of defense scholars in the United States may be explained in terms of two recently emergent hypotheses. The first of these is that the processes of American defense policy are not what they were thought to be. The accumulating evidence is that defense policy in this country is not marked by the free play of bureaucratic bargaining or by open processes which, if not altogether indispensable to the vitality of government, have been so regarded in the conventional *dictat*. Instead, what is more and more evident is (1) a concentration of authority at the top of government draining supporting structures of significant roles; (2) a concomitant doctrinal uniformity at the top, the persistence of which militates against intellectual initiatives either from within or from outside; and (3) this within a politico-

3

administrative system which not only seeks, but requires legitimization of decisions through elaborate processes of consensus building.

The discovery that certain characteristics, long associated with the formation of American defense policy, may be more apparent than real leads, in turn, to the second of the recently contrived hypotheses, namely, that the major features of the American process—such as they are—may be less than universal. There is the suspicion that, along with other colleagues in American political science, defense scholars have been victims of the "ethnocentric fallacy" of taking the American political experience (never mind massive evidence to the contrary!) as the archetype.[1] Now it is held for the first time in many quarters that defense policy formation may be highly idiosyncratic across national lines.

In a valuable study of "the peculiar problems" of weapons procurement in the United States. J. A. Stockfish suggests that they stem from an equally peculiar combination of American circumstances. Emphasizing the unique American experience of the past quarter century he draws the following conclusion: ". . . the rich and abundant experience of Western European countries provides only limited insight on how to manage military affairs in the present United States setting."[2] However, with deference, it may be pointed out that quite the opposite conclusion may be more pertinent, namely, that the "rich and abundant experience" of other defense communities, while found to be distinctive, will by that very fact illuminate the salient features of the American defense process and, thereby, center our understanding of it more in terms of its idiosyncratic character.

Michael Hobkirk provides a case in point. As an observer of the U.S. defense policy process, he has noted that "non-defense organizations" in the United States participate in the formulation of defense policy (which he neatly sorts out from "defense resource allocation decisions") to an extent and in a way unknown in the United Kingdom.[3] What Hobkirk does is make a

1. LTC Frank B. Horton, III, USAF took account of this problem nearly a decade ago in editing what must be regarded as a ground-breaking volume, *Comparative Defense Policy* (Baltimore: The Johns Hopkins University Press, 1973). As COL Horton has been the first to point out this volume does not altogether succeed in overcoming "ethnocentrism," nor does it provide an explicit concept for the direction of inquiries into the realm of defense policy formation. We are pleased to take note of a second edition of *Comparative Defense Policy* which will appear shortly and which, along with this effort, will attempt to take us a step father in comparative analysis. A useful attempt to devise a framework of analysis which will allow us to comprehend the "total process" through which the Soviet Union makes defense policy is Arthur J. Alexander, *Decision-Making in Soviet Weapons Procurement* (Adelphi Papers, No. 147) London: IISS, 1979.

2. J. A. Stockfish, *Plowshares Into Swords* (New York: Mason & Lipscomb, 1973), pp. ix-x.

3. Michael Hobkirk, "Defense Organization and Defense Policy Making in the UK and the USA," in Laurence Martin, ed., *The Management of Defense* (New York: St. Martin's Press, 1976), pp. 1–28.

notation about a point which quickly attracts his attention if only because it contrasts so sharply with the British process with which he is intimately familiar. Consequently, a point taken as commonplace by American scholars must now in the light of comparative analysis be seen as an idiosyncratic characteristic which goes much farther to "explain" the American system than was thought to be the case.

The contributions to this volume have a twofold objective: first, to provide basic, descriptive data concerning defense policy formation outside the United States and, secondly, to provide an initial base-line for analysis of other "defense communities" and, thereby, additional new perspectives on American defense policy formation. We do not prejudge the issue whether policy formation in different defense communities will be marked more by common features or by distinctive features. What must be remarked, however, is a growing awareness of the requirement for comparative analysis if we are to have a fully adequate understanding of both.

In what must stand as a "judicious" observation, Mattei Dogan notes that "one of the great difficulties of comparative analysis is securing agreement among scholars about concepts!"[4] Each of the contributors to this volume, in his own right, has pursued nation-based studies with a focus on defense questions. And each has relied upon his own concepts, observations, and his own judgments about levels of analysis. It is also the case that each shares the concerns that have been discussed up to this point. They concur in the requirement for practical, collaborative efforts pointing towards comparative analysis: thus, their presence here. Conscious of the difficulties of bringing scholars together in such undertakings and, most particularly, of the special difficulty at the root of Dogan's observation our starting point is an explicit concept.

The editor proposed the concept of *Defense Community* as a schema within the terms of which the "significant" features of defense policy formation could be identified. The contributors were invited to develop nation-based studies within this framework or, if you will, on the basis of these working-hypotheses. The initial task was seen as essentially descriptive; the task was one of "mapping" the terrain of the community for its major benchmarks. In the concept of *Defense Community* four sectors or elements (i.e., working-hypotheses) were emphasized:

4. Mattei Dogan, ed., *The Mandarins of Western Europe* (New York: Halstead Press, 1975), p. 1. Dogan's explanation of how his first-rate volume came into being we take as our own: "It is impractical for each scholar to try to understand the intricacies of the full range of political systems in which he is interested. It is practical to exchange knowledge with colleagues . . . our belief is that when a scholar participates in a panel or contributes to a symposium having a clearly defined topic, he is inevitably engaged in a collaborative effort of a team which has a common frame of reference and a set of working hypotheses generally considered worth investigating. In this way nation-based studies acquire truly comparative dimensions and parallel investigations do converge!" (*Ibid.*, pp. 1-2).

   a) *The Participants*—those who are attentive to and undertake to
      influence policy outcomes from inception through execution;

   b) *The Channels*—the interactive processes within the community,
      both formal and informal, from which policy issues;

   c) *The Constraints*—the political, strategic, and resource constraints
      which impinge on the process, including the role of "special
      constituencies";

   d) *The Functions*—the policy outcomes resulting from community
      functioning (defense policy, strategy, force planning).

Clausewitz has the nice phrase that "policy represents interests" to which one
makes the constant rejoinder to students: "would that it were so!" In his
effort to define policy (as a category) Clausewitz tries to guarantee that we
will not confuse it with the categories of strategy, force planning and the
like: "would that it were so!" Anguished practitioners in the American
defense community have suggested to the author that it is all well and good
to establish long-term imperatives i.e., delineate primary criteria for choices
at the Force Planning (Hobkirk: defense resource allocation) level. But, they
aver, this is the world of short-term imperatives where wholly secondary
criteria play a stubborn role. It is not difficult, they continue, to gain
agreement in principle that policy must be conducted strategically and that a
force structure is efficacious only in the degree to which it conforms to this
schema.[5] At the same time, we have the increasing prominence of the criterion of affordability and the ever present optimizations of the technologists
(the sub-community of defense contractors) driving choices not only at the
Force Planning Level but at the Strategy and Policy levels as well. In short,
we may take it that any adequate conceptualization of the complex, sometimes coherent, sometimes incoherent, and always highly political world of
defense policy formation can only arise from the closest empirical investigations of how it performs and what it produces.

   The *Defense Community* is the realm of defense policy formation. This
concept attempts to encompass not only the terrain of the community but its
functions as well. Figure 1 represents the functions "outputs" of the defense
community in what are at all events intellectually discrete categories of
Policy, Strategy, and Force Planning. This is not at all to suggest that
defense communities will always be found to be functioning in such a way as
to maintain categorical boundaries. More likely, all sorts of interesting hor-
rors will be discovered—the results of a failure to distinguish that which we

---

   5. For a compelling discourse on this theme see, Charles Burton Marshall, "Continuity
and Discontinuity: Dour Reflections on the National Security," *Journal of Politics,* 38 (August,
1976), 258–75.

are well advised to distinguish. In such cases we are likely to have evidence of imperfect performance but more importantly, it should be stressed, evidence of poor choices. At this point analysis can be valuable both for scholars and practitioners.

An example of a difficulty that, presumably, can be avoided through improved conceptualization is the taking up of significant defense issues either without regard to context or wholly out of context. Thus, the question "How Much is Enough?" is important in its own right and difficult enough to answer even within well defined Force Planning terms where, alone, this question has point.[6] No satisfactory answers are possible until answers to prior questions are in: "What is to be Done?" (Lenin!)—"What Interests are to be Supported?"—"How are They to be Supported?"—and, ultimately, "How Much is Enough?" Clearly implicit in the latter question is priority for the resource constraint. Putting it first, however, brings to the fore the criterion of affordability unaccompanied, as it were, by the more compelling criteria of policy and strategy. Such contextual problems can be revealed, if not remedied, through well designed analysis.

The not inconsiderable evidence of "short-term imperatives" at work in defense policy formation is largely responsible for the not inconsiderable effort to explain the entire realm in terms of "bureaucratic bargaining." This genre of analysis springs as well from the tendency to take "defense policy" to mean "defense resource allocation decisions." Our quarrel with this is widely shared today: because of a preoccupation with some interesting trees the forest is missed. Consequently, we learn very little about either the performance or the product of the defense community. More often than not this stance includes the contention that 'domestic processes dominate external necessities' in defense policy formation. Undoubtedly, then, it is essential to restate one's conviction that domestic constraints have their own significance before concurring with Laurence Martin that ". . . a universal and intemperate adoption of the myth that a defense policy is hardly ever more than the outcome of wrangling between domestic interests could dangerously encourage the belief that there are no real security interests at all, a delusion that would be all too welcome to the embattled guardians of national budgets."[7]

These difficulties have not gone unrecognized and efforts have been made to establish perspective. Not surprisingly, such efforts have not always achieved the intended result. Samuel Huntington, for example, emphasizing that "military policy cuts clearly across the usual distinction between foreign

6. Alain Enthoven and K. Wayne Smith, *How Much is Enough?* (New York: Harper, 1971).

7. Martin, ed., *The Management of Defense*, pp. xv.

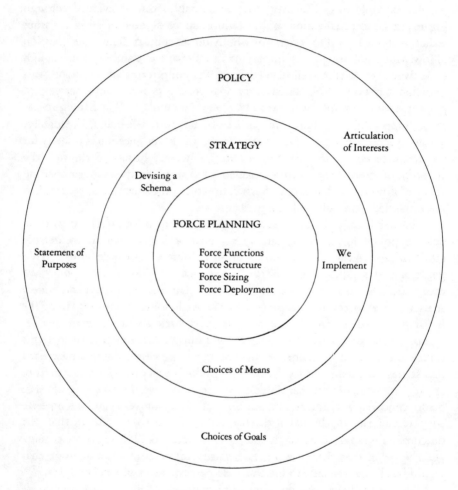

FIGURE 1. "Functions" of the *Defense Community*

policy and domestic policy"[8] (we shall come back to the point about *military* policy) attempts to come to terms with "this most troublesome aspect" through the device of a Strategy/Structure dichotomy. He suggests that "decisions made in the categories or currency of international politics may be described as *strategic* in character . . . *structural* decisions, on the other hand, are made in the currency of domestic politics."[9] There are countless objections to what is an extended and often tortuous argument, but we shall content ourselves with the following: a decision to extend the runway at Diego Garcia (or, *not* to extend the runway at Diego Garcia), for better or for worse, on the basis of all available evidence of the workings of the American defense community is as likely to be taken up in the currency of domestic politics as it is in the currency of international politics. In whatever *patois* the decision stands as unalterably strategic in character. *Strategic* decisions, of whatever they may be said to consist (and no matter how cavalier one is with the concept of strategy) are not, thereby, confined to any single decision-mold in the American defense community, or any other defense community one suspects. This device for the sake of analysis proves upon even casual investigation to be only that. Incidentally, once Huntington has his dichotomy in place he then contends that any major policy issue "inevitably has both strategic and structural implications."[10] It is difficult to be certain where he stands on the matter, but what is certain is that the Strategy/Structure device does little by way of enhancing our understanding of the complexities of defense policy formation.

It is necessary to say a word in defense of the term *Defense* in our title. We are bent, first, on taking the matter of defense policy beyond a consideration of "the military institution itself." It is not our purpose to focus on "the role of the military in politics," or to explore the sociology of the military. That academic enterprise thrives elsewhere and, apart from an occasional *tour d'horizon*, does not direct itself to defense policy.[11] The policy realm with which we are concerned is "the defense of the realm" in all of its present-day dimensions. It is at once inappropriate and imprecise to employ the limiting term "Military Policy." Our contention is that while recognizing the seminal

8. Samuel Huntington. *The Common Defense* (New York: Columbia University Press, 1961), pp. 1-12.

9. *Ibid.*

10. *Ibid.* The author hastens to note than another dichotomy from Professor Huntington ("objective civilian control/subjective civilian control") has served as the basis for his *Decisions of Robert S. McNamara,* A Study of the Role of the Secretary of Defense (Coral Gables: University of Miami Press, 1970).

11. Morris Janowitz, *Military Conflict, Essays on the Institutional Analysis of War and Peace* (Beverly Hills: Sage, 1975).

role of the military profession the *Defense Community* consists of numerous institutions and professions, both public and private.

Before proceeding to a brief discussion of the individual contributions to this volume, perhaps something more than a word is required concerning *Policy*. It is one of our objectives to underscore in what follows that *defense policy is public policy*. [12] It is a species of a genre that is defined in all essential respects by the polity (the *res publica*) at the center of policy formation. We do not envision a stateless society in which policy is the outcome of any process. The public/private distinction is critical: public policy formation and the policy making of the firm (e.g., the Chinese laundry) are qualitatively distinct. Moreover, defense policy as a species of public policy is to be distinguished from tax policy, education policy, agriculture policy and the like. Both the substantive character of the policy and the policy community in which it arises are critical factors bearing on the formation process itself. Clearly, however, the more important distinction is that between public and private sectors. Whether useful generalizations can be made across sectors of public policy (revenue, education, agriculture, defense) in our view has not been established on the basis of currently available work. It remains a task worth pursuing, however, in contrast with efforts to bring "greater precision" to public policy studies by focusing on "smaller policy making units." [13] The enormous difficulties attendant upon the effort to comprehend any public policy sector or community are not met by turning away from the public realm; any new found clarity in the private sector is illusion.

Let us be clear, finally, that we hold with Professor Lowi that a political science that forecloses analysis (criticism) of policy choices and their impact on the polity is essentially "technocratic and instrumental" and becomes merely Management Science. While we are concerned to look at both how the *Defense Community* performs and the choices it makes our purpose is not "decision analysis" under the rubric that "to improve the process is to improve the choices." [14] "Policy represents interests"; policy is a statement of what a polity takes to be its purposes and goals. If there is anything that cannot be mindlessly taken as "given" it is policy; nowhere is the critical function of political science required quite so much as in that particular policy realm which is our concern here.

12. Theodore Lowi, "Decision Making vs. Policy Making: Toward an Antidote for Technocracy," *Public Administration Review* (May/June, 1970), 314–25.

13. Ira Sharkansky, ed., *Policy Analysis in Political Science* (Chicago: Markham, 1970), p. 16.

14. Lowi, "Decision Making vs. Policy Making," 319.

II.

Upon editing a collection of British perspectives on defense policy formation, Professor Martin was inclined to remark that, perhaps, we ". . . should now move back . . . in careful case-studies to some older established lines of inquiry."[15] The point is well taken and will be reflected in this volume. Needless to say, the contributions pursue only a few among many lines of inquiry that must be followed. The four focal points in our *Defense Community* concept—"Participants", "Channels", "Constraints", "Functions"—will not all be taken up in each study that follows. What we shall find is that each does undertake the priority task of identifying critical elements in the total process of defense policy formation.

It is not our purpose to contend that from the standpoint of U.S. interests the five most important defense communities in the world are taken up in this volume. There can be little doubt, however, that the defense communities of Australia, South Africa, India, Japan, and France grow steadily in significance—and they do offer rich fare from the standpoint of comparative analysis. Moreover, their workings are not especially well-known at this juncture, another factor which particularly recommends them. Australia, South Africa, and India immediately present the common heritage of British "plantations," not to mention the common geo-strategic factor of location on the Indian Ocean littoral. Whether these shall prove to be decisive features in each instance remains to be seen; the idiosyncratic features may be more compelling. Japan offers the scholar what is, perhaps, an unprecedented opportunity of observing the growth of an "embryo" defense community to full maturity in the context of an advanced, industrial democracy. This evolutionary phenomenon is ordinarily seen in the context of new, developing states. France, on the other hand, exhibits in near classic dimensions the workings of a complex and sophisticated defense community which at the same time is notable for aspects which can only be styled as "singular".

Desmond Ball identifies in some detail those who participate in defense policy formation in Australia. Putting stress on the vitality of informal processes, he notes the extraordinarily "closed" nature of the Australian defense community—"more closed than any of the defense establishments in the West." Ball underscores the constraints entailed in the close relationship with the United States. Insofar as many significant questions have been

15. *The Management of Defense*, p. xv. For a perceptive statement of the need for "a careful comparison of how policy-making is conducted in other societies under a variety of circumstances" see, Michael Brenner, "Bureaucratic Politics in Foreign Policy," *Armed Forces and Society*, II (Winter, 1976), 326–32.

"effectively abrogated to the United States," in his view, the functioning of
the Australian defense community is, thereby, circumscribed.

Henry Albinski, nicely complementing the Ball study, examines the
Australian assessment of its defense concerns and the policy, strategy, and force
planning responses which are being fashioned today. Albinski finds Australia
attuned both to broad, international power relationships and to regional configurations. In the region, Australia is seen as supportive of efforts by
individual states to enhance their military capabilities; particularly welcomed
is the evolving Sino-American relationship. The sharpening focus is on the
Indian Ocean Area, however, and the extent to which the American partner
will be engaged there. While the "defense debate" within the Australian
defense community will continue to display various strands, Albinski concludes
that priority will be given to reinforcing an expanding American role in the
southern hemisphere. It is to be noted that an Australian observer (Ball) and an
American observer (Albinski) are inclined to highlight quite different aspects
of the defense community which both closely follow.

The three ensuing studies have a common thread that will be detected
immediately, namely, that in the Republic of South Africa a "defense community" is a very recent emergence. Not unlike Japan in some interesting
respects, a defense community is to be observed taking explicit form for the
first time. This development serves to emphasize, among other things, how
little prepared we are, conceptually, to analyze such phenomena. Two of our
authors (Dale and Fourie), by way of responding to this paucity, adopt a
historical perspective: one fascinating result is the revelation of a growing
"defense consciousness" in South Africa over a period from, let us say, the
Defense Act of 1912 to Cassinga in 1978.

Richard Dale utilizes the notion of "military institutional transfer" to
examine Anglo—South African links particularly in the period of the Union
Defense Force. He concludes that neither the present South Africa Defense
Force nor the broader complex of politico-military arrangements are "Imperial-
Commonwealth" artifacts as such. They are a richer blend that must be scrutinized in detail. At all events, historical perspectives are the indispensable
beginning point. Deon Fourie documents an almost unprecedented example of
disjunction between political and military elements throughout the history of
the Union and the Republic. A considered resort to the military instrument in
behalf of "policy" is a remarkably latter-day phenomenon in South Africa. In a
still young republic the conscious workings of an evolving defense community
is one of its newest dimensions. A new era is at hand in policy formation which
we must be prepared to assess through much improved analytical designs.

It is against this backdrop that J. E. Spence makes a current issue in the
South African defense community the focal point of his study. A new era
notwithstanding, Spence contends that at this date there is no inclination

towards "linkage" of a growing nuclear capability and growing defense concerns. At the same time there is little reluctance in moving towards a political exploitation of a considerable technical asset. Spence makes clear that the scientific-technological component in the South African defense community is already prominent and that its ultimate role may depend less on technological imperatives than on broader political currents defining South Africa's role in the world.

P. R. Chari and Stephen Cohen turn to yet different aspects of the defense community concept in their India-based studies. Chari is at pains to stress the continuity of administrative traditions deriving from the British experience. Inevitably, in the India of the late 20th century with increasingly complex economic, scientific, and industrial processes at work he finds the bureaucracy gaining in prominence as against other constituent elements in defense policy formation. The growing professionalization of the military is underlined. Chari puts in sharp relief a question implicit in most of these studies *i.e.,* whether the formation of defense policy will become increasingly the preserve of technocratic elements or whether it is a process that will continue to be understood as essentially political.[16] The resolution of this question will do much to determine the future configuration not only of India's defense community but others as well.

For his part, Cohen offers an intriguing look at the "strategic imagery" occupying the minds of defense principals in India and certain reciprocal images in South Asia. He puts forward the thesis that the "pictures" or "perceptions" of the regional security environment which the major participants carry with them, quite apart from whether they represent concrete calculations, become a major factor in the determination of Indian defense policy. Self-images as well as the images of potential adversaries combine to form a key psychological element in "defense consciousness." Is this the case elsewhere as well?

It is a matter of no small interest among scholars and practitioners alike to trace in Japan today the burgeoning of a defense community. Indeed, this may well be the "laboratory case" of the evolution of an "embryo" to maturity. That observers are not always in agreement as to the outlines or the direction of a developmental process will not be surprising. James and Diane Dornan identify public officials and private sector leaders in Japan engaged in a genuine defense debate and taking the lead in forging the "defense consciousness" called for nearly a decade ago by Yasuhiro Nakasone.[17] It is the

---

16. The author may be permitted at this point to note his raising of this question in the American context *viz. Decisions of Robert S. McNamara,* and "The Office of the Secretary of Defense: The Laird and McNamara Styles," in J. Endicott and R. Stafford, eds., *American Defense Policy,* 4th ed. (Baltimore: John Hopkins Press, 1977).

17. See the first of Japan's "White Papers" on defense, *Japan's Defense* (October, 1970), Japan Defense Agency, Tokyo. This paper received somewhat more attention than its successors and is the only one to address the question of building defense consciousness. One

contention of the Dornans that in the present day Japanese democracy the leadership and the public through an interactive process play prime roles in defense policy formation. Interestingly, Taketsugu Tsurutani discounts the idea that any significant defense debate is taking place within the nascent Japanese defense community. He argues that the discussion of "various options" represents little more than bickering among Liberal Democratic Party factions. While the LDP continues to be the dominant political instrument of the new democracy one must look to the traditionally powerful Japanese bureaucracy for definition of policy, strategy, and force planning options which, in turn, are accepted or rejected in the more visible "political process." LTC David Lohmann, USAF points out the extent to which the Japanese defense community has taken on both form and substance. In his phrase, "Japanese defense policy is maturing in process and content." A new realism evident among a broadening group of governmental, military, and industrial leaders (and *mirable dictu,* the press) is producing new frameworks within which defense issues are receiving extensive consideration. The structures devised and the agencies developed in recent years for enhancing U.S.–Japan defense collaboration stand in marked contrast to the dormant decades which preceded.

The difficulties of developing political and strategic consensus in a complex community, and translating agreed upon goals into specific programs become the central theme of three studies of defense policy formation in France. Jean Klein directs our attention to the French Left's treatment of defense issues in connection with the 1978 elections. It is clear that there must be some measure of common ground on defense questions—given their importance on the national agenda—among political elements that would undertake to govern France. Klein shows how "the Left" sought a credible "Common Program" on defense, but was unable to maintain what proved to be an awkward stance. Interestingly, however, there is a general acceptance of nuclear forces with future debates likely to turn on specific programmatic details.

Bruce Marshall details the extensive argument taking place throughout the French defense community on all matters of strategy, again, reinforcing the view that such matters are probably better attended to here than in most quarters around the world. The often conflicting strands of the continuing discussion of deterrence, the role of tactical nuclear weapons, and France's "vital interests" outside Europe are difficult to weave into a common piece.

---

of Mr. Nakasone's successors as Director-General, Japan Defense Agency, wished to make clear to this author that "that was Mr. Nakasone's paper!" Today, however, there would appear to be less reluctance to identify with it.

18. See the cogent observations of Professor N. Edwina Moreton in "Book Reviews," *Survival,* XXI (May/June 1979), 140–41.

The effort to do so is easily criticized and there is the suggestion that here too, "short-term imperatives" conflict strongly with the criteria of policy and strategy in the determination of ultimate outcomes. Stephen Roberts provides a detailed examination of a specific defense policy debate—"La Presence Maritime dans le Monde"—in his review of present and projected French naval missions outside of Europe. Roberts calls attention to the advancing technological capabilities of the French fleet, but more significantly his study points up the singular role of France. Here is a defense community that undertakes, at once, to work with the Western Alliance and follow an autonomous course.

What constitutes useful comparative analysis? To what extent is it possible, after all, to make meaningful assessments of "defense communities" across national lines? We remain more impressed with the questions than with such answers as have been provided to date. Clearly, it is the case that comparative analysis is difficult, indeed, impossible "when the basic political processes themselves are not understood."[18] Much of the wreckage referred to earlier is the result of having brought to an investigation elaborate conceptual apparatus for the purpose of organizing "data" when there is precious little "data" to organize. In the present effort we have sought to begin at the beginning, as it were, by developing some understanding of "basic political processes" at work in various places. This was done with the aid of some rudimentary "working-hypotheses." Yet more of this work must be done in our view before the application of complex, analytic categories can be expected to yield "useful" results.

II. Australia

Actors And Process

DESMOND J. BALL

Introduction:

Australian defence policy formation is in some ways a quite unique phenomenon. Two peculiar features especially stand out—the extraordinarily "closed" nature of the process and the degree to which Australian defence policy is one of dependence upon the United States. A discussion of these two features provides an introduction to the description of the actors in and process of Australian defence policy-making. The conclusion relates this discussion to the quality of the basic strategic guidance and its role in defence policy-making in Australia.

Australian defence policy has traditionally been one of dependence upon "great and powerful friends." Whereas before the Second World War this meant dependence upon Great Britain, the United States obviously emerged as the dominant partner in the 1950s and 1960s; World War II and its immediate aftermath represent an interesting period of transition from one big brother to another.

In consequence, a very large area of national security policy, including some of the most significant aspects, has effectively been abrogated to the United States; Australian defence decisions have to a large extent been relegated to the second-level questions.

Since about 1969-70, at least some elements of the Australian defence establishment have been moving away from this policy of dependence; notions of self-reliance and of independent operations in the defence of the Australian continent have become increasingly accepted.

But the capability for independent decision-making at senior levels remains somewhat deficient. Whatever truth there is in the adage with respect to the Australian military that its company and battalion commanders are first-class but that the general ranks are poor strategists and logisticians applies with similar effect to the Department of Defence. The lack of experience is certainly a major factor in this, and one which cannot be rectified overnight.

Moreover, the American connection remains strong. The ANZUS Treaty is still regarded by the Australian defence establishment as essential for any defence against "a fundamental threat to Australia's security."[1] This in itself is not extraordinary; many if not most countries today are dependent on allies for the ultimate guarantee of their security. What is curious in the Australian case is the relative lack of concern for the requirements of any independent defence effort.

Many undeniable benefits flow from the American connection. The US is apparently quite generous in the amount and quality of intelligence material which it shares with Australia; it also provides access to "defence science and technology, military staff contacts regarding tactical doctrine and operational procedures, and military exercising with forces using high technology which is not otherwise available."[2] But the discretion which the US has in deciding what material can be passed on to Australia obviously gives it great influence in Australian defence policy-making; the threat of cutting off the flow to Australia allows the US to bring great pressure to bear on Australian policy.

The most visible physical manifestation of the American connection are the various defence, communications, intelligence and scientific installations maintained on Australian territory. These installations have been involved in external military activities several times without the knowledge (or consent) of the Australian Government. The installations have also made it difficult for the government to pursue some policies aimed at greater regional coop-eration and regional arms control. And they have induced some serious differences in defence matters between Australia and our other closest ally, New Zealand.[3]

With respect to policy-making, then, a consequence of the American connection is that Australia's room for independent manoeuvre has been severely circumscribed; the connection goes a long way toward explaining the limited capability for effective and efficient strategic planning in the Australian defence establishment.

The second peculiar feature of the Australian defence policy-making process is the extraordinary degree to which it is closed. It is, for example, more closed than any other defence establishment in the Western world at

1. Hon. D. J. Killen, *Australian Defence* (A White Paper presented to Parliament by the Minister for Defence, 4 November 1976), p. 10.
2. *Ibid.*, p. 11.
3. For further discussion of the relationship between the American installations and Australian security, see my "American Bases: Some Implications for Australia's Security," *Current Affairs Bulletin,* October 1978.

least; and it is more closed than decision-making in other policy areas in Australia, including fiscal and budgetary policy.

Policy-making in respect to Australian defence is, to begin with, cloaked with the traditional bureaucratic secretiveness which characterises decision-making in all policy areas in Australia. As one study has argued, official secrecy "has become . . . a way of life, or a way of government" in Australia.[4]

Governments have supported this tradition with the arguments that the anonymity of public servants must be preserved at all costs, for otherwise the convention of an impartial civil service will be lost; and that freer release of official information is incompatible with the maintenance of the doctrine of ministerial responsibility.[5] As the Radcliffe Report of 1976 argued in the United Kingdom, the confidentiality of "all that goes to the internal formulation of government policy" is necessary and ought to be preserved.[6] The argument of the British Government in the Crossman affair in 1975 is also worth citing—viz.: that "details of discussions or communications between Ministers and between Ministers and advisers concerning the development and formulation of policies and their execution" must be kept confidential in order to give effect to the doctrine of ministerial responsibility.[7] Australia's interpretation of the secrecy requirements of this doctrine is even more stringent than that of the UK—even though, as some authorities have argued, the doctrine is "scarcely relevant in modern Australian government."[8]

Defence, of course, is even more closed because of the secrecy invoked in the name of national security. There are certain demands of national security where the case for secrecy is undeniable—for example, with respect to diplomatic negotiations, certain aspects of military capacity, specifications and performance details of some weapons systems, defence contingency plans, and details of some intelligence operations. There is, however, a natural tendency on the part of any defence establishment to identify the national interest with its own bureaucratic and political interests—and, if anything, this tendency has gone rather further in Australia than in other Western democracies. There are numerous examples of unnecessary secrecy, and of deception and misinformation directed at the Australian public, where no genuine element of national security has been involved.[9]

---

4. Enid Campbell and Harry Whitmore, *Freedom in Australia* (Sydney: Sydney University Press, 1973 edition), p. 340.

5. *Ibid.,* pp. 340-341.

6. *Report of the Committee of Privy Counsellors on Ministerial Memoirs* (Commonly referred to as the *Radcliffe Report*), 16 December 1975, (Cmnd.6386, HMSO, London, 1976), p. 19.

7. See Hugo Young, *The Crossman Affair* (London: Hamish Hamilton and Jonathon Cape, 1976), p. 48.

8. Campbell and Whitmore, *Freedom in Australia,* p. 341.

9. See, for example, Jim Spigelman, *Secrecy: Political Censorship in Australia* (Sydney: Angus & Robertson, 1972), chapter 7.

This is to some extent further compounded by the American connection. Much of the intelligence upon which Australian defence policy is based is derived from American sources and covered by extremely tight secret agreements. Much of this material finds its way onto the public record in the United States, but the exchange arrangements impose total secrecy at the Australian end.

The lack of any large informed or attentive public allows this extremely closed situation to continue unchallenged. There are no fulltime defence journalists in Australia, and only a handful of academics specialise in defence. The attentive public, measured in terms of those who subscribe to the few relevant journals and magazines or who are members of organisations such as the United Service Institutions, numbers about 3000 persons; by far the great bulk of these are Service personnel or officers of the Defence Department; very few of this attentive public ever attempt to influence defence decisions.

Virtually everything pertaining to defence policy in Australia is classified. There are fairly frequent, but invariably bland press releases; there is an Annual Report of the Department of Defence; and there have been two White Papers in the last two decades. However, these are most uninformative, even in their descriptions of current defence organisation, policy, and force structure; certainly, they make no attempt to describe or explain how the decisions underlying any of these facets of Australian defence have been derived. There is no equivalent of the American Congressional Hearings.

This extraordinary closed nature of the process does have one advantage for the student of Australian defence. This is that the participants in it are severely delimited and hence easy to identify. Of course, the particular actors involved in any given policy, and the particular process through which any decision is made, vary according to the particular decision. Some of the relevant factors are the strategic importance of the decision, its budgetary implications, whether the decision is innovative or merely supportive of accepted policy, whether the decision relates to equipment procurement, organisational matters, or substantive national security policy, etc. The policy-making with respect to the acceptance of American installations in Australia involved only the most senior Government and Departmental officials. Cabinet is most concerned when large financial commitments are involved. The military are the dominant actors in the weapons acquisition decision-making process.

Perhaps the best introductory way of describing the bounds of this generally closed process, and coincidentally mentioning some of the more important of the participants, is to provide some examples of the bureaucratic/political interactions which characterise Australian defence decision-making. The interactions are typically routine, often involving nothing more than passing paper. They are generally administrative, with little policy implication. Even where policy is involved, the relationships are cooperative as often as they are conflictual. The following examples relate to conflict only because the requirement for choice, or decision, is unavoidable in the resolution of the issue.

At the highest political level, there is the relationship between the Prime Minister and the Defence Minister. The most dramatic illustration of the politics of Australian defence is undoubtedly the confrontation in early 1971 between Prime Minister Gorton and Defence Minister Fraser which in turn derived at least in part from Mr. Fraser and the Defence Department's conflict with the Army. The confrontation was finally resolved only by the resignation of Mr. Fraser and the downfall of the Gorton Government.[10] Less dramatic, and more typical, was the argument between Prime Minister Fraser and Defence Minister Killen in August 1976 over the former's decision to cut nearly four percent from the civilian staff of the Defence Department.[11]

Just below this level are the relationships between the Defence Minister and Ministers of related Departments. Conflicts were much more frequent here before the Reorganisation of 1973-75 abolished the Service departments. More recently, the issue of the future of the aircraft industry has split the Defence Minister and his Supply-cum-Productivity counterpart.

Still at the ministerial level, there are the relationships between the Defence Minister and other members of Cabinet. The most significant clashes here in recent years have occurred in Budget Cabinet where, from at least 1973, the Defence Minister has had his public pledges cut from beneath him. A more specific example is Cabinet's rejection in October 1970 and again in July 1978, of Defence proposals for an Australian Defence Force Academy (ADFA), despite strong support for it from the Defence Minister (and, in July 1978, the Prime Minister as well).

At the heart of defence policy-making in Australia is the relationship between the Defence Minister and the Department of Defence. In practice this generally means that between the Minister and the Permanent Head of the Department, since the Minister rarely reaches down to contact other departmental officers.

The Minister also has relationships with the military. In early 1971, for example, open hostility developed between Mr. Fraser and Lt. Gen. Sir Thomas Daly, the Chief of the General Staff. In 1973, Mr. Barnard's decision against the DDL project—and against the strong recommendations of Admiral Peek—led to a bitter breach between the Minister and the Chief of

10. For a discussion of this episode, see Alan Reid, *The Gorton Experiment* (Sydney: Shakespeare Head Press, 1971), esp. pp. 416-446.

11. *Canberra Times,* 21 August 1976.

the Naval Staff. Again, rarely does the Minister relate to lesser officers, although during the 1973-75 Reorganisation there was much opposition to the thrust of the organisational decisions from the Colonel and 1-star levels.

At the departmental level, there is continuous working interaction between the Defence Department and other Commonwealth Departments. The Permanent Heads of the Treasury, the Department of Foreign Affairs, and the Department of the Prime Minister and Cabinet are members of the Defence Committee. Some 50 or more interdepartmental committees (IDCs) link Defence with virtually all the other Departments.

Within the Defence Department itself, there is an enormous range of cooperative and adversary relationships. Some of the differences within the policy planning areas, for example, emerge during the preparation of the strategic guidance; these typically seem to involve disagreement over how to characterise Indonesia in Australian defence planning.[12]

Finally, within the military there are various relationships both between the Services and also within each Service. During the period when Vice Admiral Sir Richard Peek was Chief of the Naval Staff, 1970-1973, decision-making between the Chiefs was bedevilled by his continued disparagement of the Army and Air Force. In the case of intra-Service relationships, decisional inter-action occurs between the regular and reserve components of the Australian Defence Force (cf the dissension among senior Army officers, and particularly Citizen Military Force (CMF) officers over the implementation of the Millar Report on the Army reserve forces); and between field units and organisations and staff officers in Canberra (cf differences in perspective between Naval officers at, for example, HMA Naval Dockyard, Williamstown, and those at Russell Hill).

Australian defence policy-making involves the resolution of the different views, interests and perspectives of these (and, to a somewhat lesser degree, other) participants, many of which have a quasi-autonomous power-political base, through a complex process of direction, bargaining, negotiation and compromise; in this resolution, the relative power of the participants is as relevant to the final decision as the cogency and wisdom of the arguments used in support of the decision taken. The following section surveys the principal actors and describes something of their interests, perspectives, and relative power bases.

The Actors:

As indicated in the preceding exemplification, the participants in Australian defence policy-making are, essentially, the Minister for Defence and various

---

12. See Brian Toohey, "Australia's Indonesia Dilemma," *Australian Financial Review*, 28 July 1978.

entities established to assist him on the one hand, and, on the other, the various elements of the bureaucracy of which the Department of Defence is itself by far the most important.

Formally, of course, the theory of Ministerial responsibility in the Westminster system holds that the Minister makes the decisions. This has substance both in the sense that the Minister selects, or at least endorses the recommendations of his Department, and also to the extent that he is held accountable for the decisions.

The Defence Minister's responsibility flows, in general terms, from his authority as a member of the Federal Executive Council as derived from Sections 62 and 64 of the Australian Constitution. His specific responsibilities are laid down in the Administrative Arrangements Orders, which lists the various enactments to be administered by him; although there are some 20 relevant Acts, the two key ones are the Defence Act 1903 and the Defence Force Reorganisation Act 1975.

Prior to the 1975 Act, the statutes were remarkably uninformative on the precise powers of the Defence Minister. Indeed, his particular authority flowed far more from a series of Prime Ministerial directives than from the statutes. The most important of these was that issued by Prime Minister Menzies on 11 December 1958, the principal point of which was that "the Minister and Department of Defence have the overall responsibility for the defence policy of the country."[13]

In the 1975 Act, the Minister's statutory authority is set out in Section 8:

> The Minister shall have the general control and administration of the Defence Force, and the powers vested in the Chief of Defence Force Staff, the Chief of Naval Staff, the Chief of the General Staff and the Chief of the Air Staff by virtue of section 9, and the powers vested jointly in the Secretary and the Chief of Defence Force Staff by virtue of section 9A, shall be exercised subject to and in accordance with any directions of the Minister.

The Act further provides that the Chief of Defence Force Staff (CDFS) and the three Service Chiefs shall in matters relating to their command "advise the Minister in such manner as the Minister directs."

The language of the Act is quite unqualified. However, the reality is much more complex as, in practice, there are some very powerful constraints on the Minister. First, there are constraints imposed by other Ministers and by Cabinet at large. It is not possible, and perhaps not even desirable, for the Defence Minister to have responsibility for every aspect of all factors imping-

---

13. Sir Arthur Tange, "Reorganization of the Control of the Australian Defence Force," (Strategic and Defence Studies Center, Australian National University, 1 October 1974), pp. 2-3.

ing on Australia's defence. Any division of responsibilities by administrative arrangements will always produce some over-lapping between portfolios; the large number of Ministries, each with their own infrastructures, makes this inevitable.

The policies and interests of such other Ministers as the Prime Minister, the Treasurer, and the Ministers for Foreign Affairs, Finance, and Productivity, impinge almost daily on those of the Defence Minister. And as Defence Ministers have increasingly found every year since 1973, and most particularly Mr. Killen in 1977 and 1978, budgetary restrictions can be a particularly constraining factor.

Second, as discussed further below, the Minister is constrained by the views, policies and actions of his own department. And, third, the Minister is constrained by his own predilections, interests and capabilities. Given the size of the Australian defence establishment, no single Defence Minister could possibly exercise his authority to the limit. In any case, few make the attempt. The demands of a Minister's other party, parliamentary and electorate responsibilities are simply too overwhelming. In the last two decades, only two Ministers, Messrs. Fraser and Morrison, have tried to fathom the murky depths where policy originates. The practice of the current incumbent of doing little more than signing departmental briefs is atypical only in its extremeness.

However, the Minister is not without non-bureaucratic forms of support. Indeed, in the last decade there has developed a variety of forms of Ministerial assistance which have impinged on the policy-making process.[14] This development received a particular impetus during the period of the Labor Government, when there was much concern to have available alternative sources of advice to that provided by the established bureaucracy. It is true that this concern is not shared by the current Defence Minister, but this does not presage the abandonment of the practice of Ministers seeking independent sources of informed review and analysis.

These various forms of Ministerial assistance include Ministerial staffs, Minister assisting Ministers, ad hoc advisers, consultants, committees, commissions and task forces, etc. of inquiry, and the establishment of independent groups to provide informed critiques of defence issues. Of these, the first has been the most important in the defence decision-making area.

The contribution to defence policy-making of committees, commissions, task forces, consultants, etc. has been of quite marginal overall significance. Rarely have they provided alternative advice to the Minister. They generally

14. This discussion of Ministerial assistance in defence policy-making is derived from chapter two, Part Three, of my *The Politics of Australian Defence Decision-Making* (Brisbane: University of Queensland Press, forthcoming).

work very much within the framework of the established system and with official personnel. Members of the Department of Defence are present on most of the committees; many of the committees are dominated by public servants; virtually all of them are dependent on Departmental officers for secretarial, staff and research purposes. Rather than doing their own research, most of the committees work by receiving submissions and requesting information from official and unofficial channels. The Department of Defence supplies most of the detailed information, conducts studies, and examines and appraises alternatives for the committees. And Departmental officers usually draft the final Reports of the committees. In those cases where the inquiry or study have attempted to begin from more fundamental premises or to work in a broader framework, little official cooperation is received. Indeed, such attempts have merely demonstrated the degree to which inquiries by outsiders lead to virulent opposition from individuals and groups within the system. [15]

The most significant form of Ministerial assistance has been the growing practice of attaching a group of advisers to the Ministers' private offices. This approach was widely adopted by Ministers in the last Labor Government, including Defence Ministers Barnard and Morrison, although of course it was not originated by them. Previously, however, Defence Ministers used their staffs for private secretarial assistance, for Departmental liaison, for electoral and party political duties, and for public relations. Under the Labor Government on the other hand, there was a general concern to strengthen the elected component of the machinery of government, and, in particular, to provide some "countervailing force" to the bureaucracy. As Prime Minister Whitlam expressed it, such a force was necessary if Ministers were to remedy the "remarkable lack of ministerial control over departments and over policy."[16] There was an explicit recognition that Ministerial staffs not only would, but should participate in the process.

The staffs of Defence Ministers Barnard and Morrison certainly had some impact upon policy; and, indeed, it is not difficult to find examples where these staffs had a significant impact, and were on occasion quite crucial. They were active with regard to the 1973-75 Reorganisation of the Defence Group of Departments; they played a significant role in Mr. Barnard's decision not to proceed with the DDL project; they were largely responsible for the Minister's attempts to get the bureaucracy to clarify Australia's basic strategic policy. More generally, they were important in attempting to widen the options which are delineated by the bureaucracy for Ministerial consideration.

15. See, for example, "Obstruction in Defence Study," *Canberra Times,* 4 April 1975.
16. Prime Minister E. G. Whitlam, "The Role of the Australian Public Service." (Sir Robert Garran Memorial Oration, 12 November 1973), p. 14.

However, these and other examples of cases and situations where staff members contributed to defence decision-making notwithstanding, the personal staffs of neither the Barnard nor the Morrison Ministries were able to act as a "countervailing force" to the bureaucracy. They were not atypical here. The fundamental reason for this lack of substantive impact is that the powers of Ministerial staffs are quite conditional, whereas they must operate in a polity of powerfully entrenched interests and individuals. This problem goes right to the heart of the present Ministerial system and, more particularly, the relationship between the Minister and the permanent bureaucracy. It is to this relationship that we now turn.

The bureaucracy is itself a conglomeration of disparate individuals and groups, each again with their own perspectives and interests, and some with very strong power-political bases of their own. The most important of these is, of course, the Permanent Head, the Secretary of the Department. The statutory responsibility of the Permanent Head of the Department of Defence derives principally from three enactments. The first is the Public Service Act 1922-1973, Section 25(2) of which directs that

> The Permanent Head of a Department shall be responsible for its
> general working, and for all the business thereof, and shall advise the
> Minister in all matters relating to the Department.

The second is the Audit Act 1901, which (together with related Finance Regulations) makes the Permanent Head accountable for all expenditure of the Department. The third is the Defence Force Reorganization Act 1975, which vests the Secretary (jointly with the Chief of Defence Force Staff) with responsibility for the administration of the Australian Defence Force. These enactments are complemented by a Ministerial Directive to the Secretary of 9 February 1976 which describes the Secretary as "the principal civilian adviser to the Minister for Defence" and makes him responsible, *inter alia,* for "advising on policy, resources and organisation," financial planning and programming within the Department of Defence, and financial administration and control of expenditure.

In addition to this legal authority, the Permanent Head in the Westminster system also has a large number of other sources of strength. There are, for example, those that arise from his length of tenure. Whereas Heads are "permanent", Ministers change every two or three years. (The current Permanent Head, Sir Arthur Tange, has served six Defence Ministers. The four Permanent Heads from 1937 to date served some twenty Ministers). Not only does this mean that the Secretary is likely to be more expert than the Minister in the subject matter of the portfolio, but it is also likely that the Secretary's loyalties extend beyond any particular incumbent.

The simple factor of time prevents any Minister becoming acquainted with the full range of his Departmental responsibilities and activities; the problem is especially great in an establishment as large and as technical as that of Defence. Hence, the Secretary must identify the issues to be brought to the attention of the Minister, determine their relative urgency, suggest the solutions and draft the briefs. Only the Permanent Head has the full range of technical expertise at hand, an extremely important factor in a portfolio as technical as Defence.

There are, further, a wide range of tactics which the Permanent Head can and does employ in his attempts to ensure that the Minister accepts his recommendations. Numerous of these are cited in the diaries of Richard Crossman;[17] they include such practices as manipulating the Minister's workload, putting important questions among less significant papers, presenting submissions only shortly before a "decision" is required, establishing, "off-limit" matters which the Minister must leave to the Permanent Head, reaching agreement with the Heads of other Departments so that no single Minister can overturn it, and presenting the Minister with *fait accompli*. Examples of all these practices have been experienced by Australian Ministers for Defence in recent years.

Other means of recourse are also available to the Permanent Head. It can be extremely damaging for a Defence Minister should it become known that, on an issue of national security, he rejected the advice of his professional civilian advisors. And, *in extremis,* the Permanent Head can threaten to resign.

In summary, the Permanent Head is clearly the single most important individual in Australian defence decision-making. He has extraordinary capability not only to influence the Minister but also to resist his wishes or even his demands. For example, despite requests from Defence Ministers in 1973 and 1975, there is still no official study of the specific defence requirements and actual force structure for defending continental Australia against foreign attack. On the other hand, the central and powerful role of the Secretary of the Department of Defence is limited to the extent of the power-political bases of other actors within the Defence establishment. In particular, the Secretary is circumscribed, both legally and in working practice, by the authority of the military.

The 1975 Act created the position of Chief of Defence Force Staff (CDFS), a four-star position at the pinnacle of the Australian Defence Force. Since 1958, there had been a Chairman, Chiefs of Staff Committee (CCSC), but the position lacked any statutory powers. The Tange Report of November 1973 recognised the serious weakness of this arrangement and its recommendations, which were the basis for the subsequent Reorganisation of the Defence Group of Departments, included a comprehensive set of responsibilities and functions

17. See, in particular, Richard Crossman, *The Diaries of a Cabinet Minister. Volume 1: Minister of Housing 1964-66* (London: Hamish Hamilton and Jonathon Cape, 1975).

for the CDFS.[18] Following the passage of the 1975 Act, the detailed functions were defined in a directive from the Minister to the CDFS on 9 February 1976, which begins:

> You are the principal military adviser to the Minister for Defence and, subject to the control of the Minister, you are to command the Defence Force.

The CDFS is responsible, *inter alia,* for the conduct of military operations by the Defence Force, for ensuring the effectiveness of military plans, training and organisation and the effectiveness of the Defence Force, and for tendering military advice on the size of the Defence Force and the balance within it in relation to the strategic requirements.

The three Service Chiefs were retained, of course, and together with the CDFS they form the Chiefs of Staff Committee. The revised functions of the Committee include responsibility for providing to the Minister "collective professional advice on military operations and on the military implications of defence policy and activities." Previously the Chiefs of Staff Committee had more restricted terms of reference. The individual Chiefs themselves are the professional heads of their respective Services, and are responsible to the Minister through the CDFS for the command of those Services.

As a result of the reorganisation of 1973-75, the military are thoroughly embedded in the departmental structure. On the formal side, they are well-represented on the committees through which, according to the departmental organisation charts, the decision-making process flows.

And, informally, the unquestioned technical expertise which the military can bring to bear greatly enhances its authority. There is no civilian group within the Australian Defence establishment which can challenge the Services in terms of knowledge of weapons system specifications or technical performance characteristics. It is difficult to over-estimate the "authority" which accrues to the military from this; most civilians would prefer to allow Service claims to pass rather than to demonstrate their technical ignorance. Moreover, the Services naturally make great play of the fact that they are the cannon fodder; they are the ones that have to go into combat with the ships, tanks, guns, aircraft or whatever. This is especially important in the case of decisions with respect to the acquisition of military hardware.

In the overall civil-military relationship, however, the military suffer one major disadvantage—that is, while the civilian chain is made up of career bureaucrats, the military posting system involves frequent rotation of serving officers. Given a three-year posting, an officer is really just beginning to

---

18. Sir Arthur Tange, *Australian Defence: Report on the Reorganisation of the Defence Group of Departments* (November 1973), pp. 35-37.

settle in at Russell Hill when he must begin preparations for handing over to his successor. This severely handicaps the military in their responding to the opportunities for co-equal participation opened up by the recent reorganisation. Consequently, as a former Defence Minister has pointed out, "there continues to be an imbalance between the Service and civilian imput in the development of defence policy."[19]

Although the Department of Defence is, of course, by far the most important Commonwealth Department involved in the making of defence and other related national security decisions, it is far from the only one. Indeed, to greater or lesser extents, and with widely varying frequency, most Australian Government Departments contribute to the defence decision-making process.[20]

Various legislative and administrative arrangements, together with some established practices of convenience, ensure that there is a constant inter-action between Defence and other Government departments. Despite the administrative arrangements, there is inevitably some overlapping of departmental responsibilities. There are also some areas of defence for which the Defence Department has consciously abjured responsibility—for example, the managment of Australian defence industries. There are issues of public policy which must be dealt with in a coordinating department, which in turn deals with Defence as simply one of a number of other departments, albeit one of the largest ones—for example, the role of the Finance Department and Treasury in defence budgeting. And there are some areas (such as transport, or science) where although the Defence Department has a legitimate interest, defence considerations are only one of many, and sometimes one of the least important, in the making of policy in that area, so that prime responsibility obviously must lie with the parent Department (such as Transport or Science). As the concept of national security becomes more widely defined, with viable national security policy requiring inputs from a whole range of economic, overseas trade and national development policy areas, these departmental inter-actions are bound to increase.

In the case of some Departments, the inter-action with Defence is both extensive and frequent, even continuous. In other cases, it is quite rare and invariably of little consequence. Some Departments have sections, branches, and even divisions dedicated to defence matters on a day-to-day working basis. Other departments deal with defence in a quite ad hoc way.

---

19. W. L. Morisson, in R. J. O'Neill, (ed.), *The Defence of Australia: Fundamental New Aspects* (Canberra: Australian National University, 1976), p. 77.

20. For a fuller discussion of the contribution of the non-Defence Departments in defence policy-making in Australia, see chapter five, Part Three, of my *The Politics of Australian Defence Decision-Making*.

However, virtually all the substantive inter-departmental inter-action with Defence comes from some five departments—the Departments of the Prime Minister and Cabinet, the Treasury, Foreign Affairs, Finance and Productivity. Each of these Departments has policy lines and interests somewhat different from those of Defence. The Departments of the Treasury and Finance, for example, are concerned with the costs and budgetary implications of defence programs; it is not difficult to imagine that these concerns could lead them into a conflict relationship with the Department of Defence. The Department of Productivity has the responsibility, *inter alia,* for munitions supply and for the Australian aircraft industry. It is much more concerned than the Department of Defence that defence industries have high and increasing workloads. This has led it on occasions to take positions at variance with those of the Department of Defence; sometimes, from the point of view of Defence, these positions of Productivity have seemed rather inconsistent. For example, in September 1972 and March 1974, as the Department of Supply and then as Secondary Industry and Supply, this interest in generating work for the aircraft factories prompted the Minister to lead Cabinet discussion of a Mirage replacement even though the Department of Defence itself considered such discussion premature; on the other hand, in mid-1977, officers of the Department of Productivity were most active in seeking postponement of a TFF decision on the grounds that the Australian Industry Participation (AIP) offered by the various contenders in their responses to the November 1976 RFP was in all cases inadequate.

All the participants in the Australian defence decision-making process described so far have been elements of the official Defence establishment. However, there are two other sets of actors which deserve mention.

First, there are those governmental and non-governmental actors external to Australia. Foreign governments have occasionally been known to have attempted to directly influence Australian defence decisions. In the case of the Mirage replacement, for example, many of the overseas companies have received formal assistance from their home Governments in their efforts to secure a favorable decision. The French Government joined with the French aircraft industry to offer a co-production and offset deal on the *Mirage* F-1 in November 1971. In December 1971 the Swedish Parliament enacted a new arms export policy intended to allay fears of war-time supply embargoes, and the Assistant Minister for Defence, Mr. Anders Thurnborg has outlined this new policy to Australian defence correspondents on several occasions, and to the Technical Evaluation Mission which visited Sweden in March 1973. And American Admirals and Air Force Generals have been quite forthright in pressing the F-14 and the F-15 with their respective counterparts in Russell Hill.

The Government-to-Government relationship is closest, of course, in the case of the American connection. This relationship has not only circumscribed

Australia's room for independent manoeuvre as discussed earlier, but has also led on some specific occasions to American intervention. (For example, the US Government made clear its objections to the Indian Ocean Zone of Peace proposals and its dissatisfaction that an ally should consider a course which the US had declared inimical to its interests).

With regard to the non-governmental external actors, the most influential group is clearly that of the arms manufacturers. In the case of the Mirage replacement, for example, some dozen overseas aircraft companies have been directly involved in attempting to influence the decision-making process. These companies are obviously enormously powerful in their own right. They command large resources and are adept at lobbying—courting the relevant technical experts (e.g. Northrop and the Technical Evaluation Mission in May 1973), the trade press, and even the actual decision-makers. All of the interested companies have representatives and consultants in Australia. That the Mirage replacement question went to Cabinet in September 1972 and March 1974 for decision on industrial grounds was due in no small part to the lobbying of the Dassault and the McDonnel Douglas representatives.

Finally, there are a variety of local actors from outside the defence establishment who nevertheless attempt to affect defence decision-making. These include the relevant parliamentary committees and interested back-benchers, the indigenous defence industries, pressure groups such as the Returned Servicemen's League (RSL), and defence journalists and academics. It is possible to cite instances where individuals and groups from this set have influenced decisions in Australia, sometimes in some quite crucial ways (such as the decision in late 1975 to establish the Defence Council), but the examples are very few and far between. The Australian defence process is simply too closed for outsiders to successfully penetrate and, in any case, there are no outsiders with anywhere near the strength of (say) their American counterparts. Allegations of a military-industrial-academic-bureaucratic complex in the Australian context are simply foolish!

The Formal Process:

Australian defence policy formation, then, takes place largely within the Australian Department of Defence. The responsible member of Cabinet (the Minister for Defence) is in practice much less of an actual decision-maker than his American counterpart (the Secretary of Defense). There is no Australian equivalent of the American National Security Council, of the President's Assistant for National Security Affairs and his subordinate staff in the White House, of the powerful Armed Services and Defence Appropriations Committees in the Congress, of "think-tanks" such as the RAND Corporation, or of the many powerful pressure groups, lobbies and interested observers and commentators.

The current structure of the Australian Department of Defence is essentially that recommended by Sir Arthur Tange in November 1973; his Report on the Reorganization of the Defence Group of Departments remains the fullest description of that structure. There are four general aspects of the formal structure and process which warrant special mention.

First, there is the diarchic structure of the Defence establishment. Section 9A (i) of the 1975 Act states that ". . . the Secretary and the Chief of Defence Force Staff shall jointly administer the Defence Force." This sharing of responsibility between the Secretary and the CDFS is reflected right throughout the Defence organization. The Department of Defence is an integrated department not just in the sense that the separate Service Departments have been reorganized into a centralized system, but also in the co-working of the civilian and military elements. The working operation of this diarchy should become apparent in the following discussion of the other aspects of the departmental structure.

The second aspect is the functional organization. As recommended in the Tange Report, the reorganized Departmental structure is built around the following seven functional groups:

(1) Strategic Policy and Force Development.

This is responsible for the formulation of the basic strategic guidance; the translation of this guidance, once it is approved by the government, into detailed force capabilities; and the preparation and submission of proposals for major equipment development and procurement.

(2) Supply and Support.

This is responsible for the very large and complex management task involved in the procurement of supplies, their storage and distribution, technical support, provision of facilities, and repair and maintenance.

(3) Manpower.

This organization is responsible for the deployment, training and utilization of all personnel, both civilian and military.

(4) Resources and Financial Programmes.

This is responsible for the financial and resources policy aspects of Defence requirements, activities and proposals, and their force structure implications.

(5) Organization and Management Services.

This is responsible for the development and implementation of policy in respect of the organization and management of the Department of Defence itself, and the coordination of the administration of the Defence Regional Offices.

(6) Defence Science and Technology.

The DSTO is responsible for the development and implementation of defence science policy; the provision of scientific advice on all defence matters; the analysis of weapons systems and equipment; the conduct of research and development, trials and evaluation of proposed and existing equipment; and the relation of Australian R & D to international programs.

(7) The Joint Intelligence Organization.

JIO is responsible for intelligence collation and assessment.

A significant military input is provided for in each of these functional groups. For example, in the Strategic Policy and Force Development organization there is a small military cell to assist in the development of appropriate Service inputs, as well as a Chief of Materiel (Two Star) for each of the Services to manage the development of major equipment proposals and the general new equipment programmes of his Service. These are "two-hatted" appointments—that is with responsibilities within Central Defence as well as in their Single Service. In the Supply and Support organization there are Service officers integrated directly into line management itself, while other "two-hatted" officers head sectors of the organization with dual Defence/Single Service responsibilities. In the JIO, one of the two Deputy Directors is a senior military officer; the Directorate of Joint Service Intelligence, JIO, is predominantly military; and military officers serve in other offices, such as the Directorate of Scientific and Technical Intelligence (DSTI), JIO.

The third noteworthy aspect of the departmental structure is the committee system. A full listing of all the standing and ad hoc committees is not available. The number is continually changing, and no central registry is maintained; the existence of some is apparently not meant to be public, especially if they involve inter-departmental representation; and many are little more than working groups with no formal basis. Altogether, however, they must number a few hundred. There are, for example, some 75 with not less than two-star (or Level 2 of the Second Division of the Public Service) status.

The committees are an integral part of Australian defence policy. As pointed out by the Tange Report, it is the committees "which accommodate the expertise, and the material interests, of different Services and of civilians drawn from different areas."[21] The resolution of these different interests is, of course, the essence of decision-making.

At the pinnacle of the committee structure is the Defence Council. Consisting of the Minister for Defence, the Minister Assisting the Minister for Defence, the Secretary of the Department of Defence, the CDFS and the three Service Chiefs, the Council's official function is "to consider and discuss matters relating to the control and administration of the Defence Force and of the respective Arms of the Defence Force, referred to the Council by the

---

21. Sir Arthur Tange, *Australian Defence*, p. 130.

Minister." The Council meets only infrequently, and limits its activities to general discussion; it is not a decision-making body.

The most senior decision-making committee is the Defence Committee. Chaired by the Secretary of the Department, and having as its members the Permanent Heads of the Treasury and the Departments of the Prime Minister and Cabinet and Foreign Affairs, the CDFS and the three Service Chiefs, the Defence Committee has quite wide-ranging responsibilities—it is to advise the Minister on:

the defence policy as a whole;

the co-ordination of military, strategic, economic, financial and external affairs aspects of the defence policy;

matters of policy or principle and important questions having a joint Service or inter-departmental defence aspect; and

such other matters having a defence aspect as are referred to the Committee by or on behalf of the Minister.

and carry out such investigations as it thinks fit for the purpose of advising the Minister on those matters.

The Chiefs of Staff Committee is the most senior military committee. Tasked with providing the Minister with collective professional advice on military operations and on the military implications of defence policy and activities, it is the only one of the senior Defence committees which does not include both military and civilian personnel.

In the area of force structure development, the two most important committees are the Defence Force Development Committee (DFDC) and the Defence Force Structure Committee (DFSC). Indeed, as the Defence Committee has declined in importance since the reorganization, the DFDC has come to play the pre-eminent role in Australian defence decision-making in general. The DFDC consists of the Secretary, the CDFS, and the three Service Chiefs; its formal function is, *inter alia:*

> To advise the Minister for Defence, in the context of strategic assessments and the most efficient use of resources, on the development of the Defence Force as a whole; and the inclusion in the Five Year Rolling Programme of major weapons and equipment capabilities.

This leads to the fourth significant aspect of the current defence decision-making process—the Five Year Defence Program (FYDP). Introduced into the Department of Defence in fiscal year 1971-72, the FYDP provides the programming basis for the flow of Defence proposals through to actual decision. The program is a "rolling" one in that, at least ideally, any proposal involving expenditure should enter as a Year Five project and "roll" forward until authorization for that expenditure is required in Year One, the fifth year of the Program under review—hence the associated acronym FYRP (Five Year Rolling Program).

Reconciliation of the Service requests with the annual budgetary allocation is done within the FYRP process. As Sir Arthur Tange has stated, this reconciliation is not easy:

> The process is a complex one of analysis and multiple-faceted trade-offs between years in the FYDP, categories of expenditure and between each of the Services. There is a requirement to ensure that the end programme is not in contradiction to the strategic guidance endorsed by the Government.[22]

Service bids are almost invariably greatly in excess of that which recent Governments have been willing to allocate to Defence. For example, in the 1973-78 FYDP, the relationship between the financial guidance and the service bids was as follows:[23]

Overall 1973/78 FYDP
$m (August 1972 prices)

	1973/4	1974/5	1975/6	1976/7	1977/8	Total 1973/78
Guidance:	1432	1427	1502	1493	1542	7396
Bids:	1439	1602	1634	1614	1574	7863
Excess of bids:	7	175	132	121	32	467

In the case of the current cycle, Sir Arthur Tange has stated that:

> the FYDP bids for new major equipment projects had to be more than halved over the 5 year period and in Year 1 had to be reduced from $69 million to $6 million. Service manpower bids also had to be halved over the FYDP and in Year 1 had to be decreased from 1300 to the Government's guidance of 600. Overall, the FYDP bids had to be reduced by some $2000 million and is still not within the Government's guidance given in October last year.[24]

As might be imagined, the squaring of the bids with the financial guidance is an essentially political process. Of course, the determination of the financial guidance is itself political. As Aaron Wildavsky has noted, if politics can be

---

22. Sir Arthur Tange, *Administration of the Defence Force* (Lecture to the RAAF Staff College, Fairbairn, 19 June 1978), p. 15.

23. Briefing to Minister for Defence on Five Year Defence Program 1973 to 1978, January 1973.

24. Sir Arthur Tange, *Administration of the Defence Force*, p. 14.

regarded as a conflict over whose preferences shall prevail in the determination of national policy, "then the budget records the outcomes of this struggle."[25] The fact that in Australia in recent years the Defence Minister has not done well in Budget Cabinet has made the politics of the intra-Defence allocative process even more intense. The struggle has been as much between the Services as between the military and civilian officers of the Department.

The Ratio of the Informal to the Formal:

In explaining actual policy outcomes, the nature of this political process is just as relevant as an understanding of the formal FYDP machinery, the functional organization, and the committee structure. For while necessary, neither organisational charts nor more detailed descriptions of formal processes are ever fully satisfactory explanatory tools. There are always, at the very least, some informal relationships and arrangements which impact substantively on decision-making outcomes, not to mention the inevitable political and bureaucratic-political factors.

Indeed, just as the power and authority of the various participants in the process is derived as much from informal as from formal sources, so the policy outcomes are products of informal factors as much as of formal factors. The interactions are, however, enormously complex—and the delineation of the formal from the informal is extremely difficult, if not impossible. At the theoretical level, there is, as James Kurth has pointed out,

> . . . the problem of alternative causes or the problem of *a posteriori* overdetermination. For nearly any interesting military policy (or indeed for any interesting policy generally), we can discover or invent, *a posteriori*, several alternative explanations each of which is logically and plausibly a sufficient explanation for the policy, is an exhaustive and therefore will seem an exclusive explanation for the policy.[26]

Nearly every defence decision can be explained or rationalized in terms of the formal process; equally, however, they can also be explained in terms of a variety of more informal, or even "irrational" factors.

It is rare for defence decisions not to follow the formal process. Of course, there are exceptions. Indeed, the chairman of the sub-committee on Defence Matters of the Joint Parliamentary Committee on Foreign Affairs and Defence recently stated that the Committee had received informed testimony "that our recent and current procedures . . . are excessively subject to government

25. Aaron Wildavsky, *The Politics of the Budgetary Process* (Boston: Little, Brown and Co., 1964). p. 4.

26. See James R. Kurth, "A Widening Gyre: The Logic of American Weapons Procurement," *Public Policy,* (Vol. XIX, No. 3), Summer 1971, pp. 377-378.

whim (as distinct from orderly government decision)."[27] (A recent example of government fiat was the dispatch of a RAAF overseas mission to evaluate two Beoing 727s for the VIP fleet; the RAAF had to very hastily write a requirement in order to persuade the Department of the Prime Minister and Cabinet to authorise the expenditure needed to send the team abroad).[28]

More generally, however, it may be that having to go through the formal motions of the committee structure and the FYDP machinery means only that bureaucratic-political and other factors take longer to work themselves out.

Empirical studies of Australian defence policy-making invariably show an inter-mixing of elements of the formal process with some decidedly more informal factors. Both are present, for example, in the relationship between the Department of Defence and other departments. Formally, the five principal non-Defence departments involved in defence decision-making (Prime Minister and Cabinet, the Treasury, Foreign Affairs, Finance and Productivity) are represented on numerous inter-departmental committees (IDCs) with Defence. The Department of Finance alone, for example, is represented on about 25 standing and ad hoc Defence IDCs at any given time.

Apart from this involvement in the Defence committee structure, the formal relationship between these Departments and Defence also involves routine memoranda, discussions with relevant Defence and other departmental officers involved in the defence function, and attendance at meetings.

On balance, however, by far the greatest and most important part of the relationships between Defence and these other Departments, including even the Department of Finance, take place at more informal levels. This is recognized as much by the Defence Department as by the other departments. A former Assistant Secretary, Policy Secretariat, was quite explicit on this: "The inter-departmental relationships are largely ad hoc; more time is spent on the telephone than at inter-departmental meetings."[29] This judgement is shared by the relevant responsible officers in the other departments.

It is also apparent that the factor of personalities is quite critical in these inter-departmental relationships. In terms of policy outcomes, in situations where there are differences of viewpoints between departments, the relative strengths of character of the persons involved in resolving the matter can be quite significant.

The factor of personalities will even determine to some extent the degree of interest a Department will take in defence matters. There is a more

27. The Hon. R. C. Katter, Press Statement, 2 July 1978, p. 3.

28. *Canberra Times,* 8 July 1978, p. 2.

29. For a more detailed discussion of the relative importance of formal and informal channels in inter-departmental involvement in defence policy, see the concluding section of chapter five of Part Three of my *The Politics of Australian Defence Decision-Making.*

particular factor involved in the case of the Department of Foreign Affairs, in that, since the late 1960s, the senior policy positions in the Department of Defence have come to be dominated almost completely by former career officers of Foreign Affairs. In 1977, for example, these included, besides the Secretary himself, the First Assistant Secretary, Policy Co-ordination Division; the First Assistant Secretary, Strategic and International Policy Division; the Assistant Secretary, Policy Secretariat; and the Director, Joint Intelligence Organization.

The sources of bureaucratic political power available to these departments for application in the resolution of any differences of interest or perspective between them are quire varied, and differ substantially from department to department. Of course, whether or not a department has the formal responsibility for a subject, based on legislation or Ministerial directive, is of principal importance in determining decision-making outcomes in these inter-departmental situations.

Representation on a senior Defence committee obviously confers some influence on a department, although only the Department of Finance has penetrated the Defence Department's committee structure sufficiently enough to make this a major source of its bureaucratic political power in defence matters. For other departments, the Defence committees are used more as a source of information or intelligence, enabling them to keep abreast of Defence thinking, rather than as an occasion for inputs into defence policy.

The size of the defence group or section within a department is also important in enabling it to affect defence decisions. Only the Departments of Finance and Productivity have large staffs dedicated to the defence function.

In some cases, the structure of a department in terms of its own decision-making processes can give it an advantage over the Department of Defence, particularly where the departmental responsibilities overlap or compete. The rather centralized, hierarchical structure which is required in Defence by the disparate backgrounds of the group of interests it now encompasses is sometimes counter-productive from a decision-making point of view.

Finally, the other departments are often able to have their most significant impact on defence policy at the political level. There is a general appreciation among the other policy departments that it is preferable from their particular points of view to take any contentious issues to Cabinet where, in their opinion, they are more likely to prevail.

The outcomes of this inter-departmental process are, then, principally determined through informal relationships and reflect such as personalities and the relative bureaucratic political power of the inter-departmental participants.

The same admixture of formal and informal factors operates with respect to decision-making within the Department of Defence itself. In the case of equipment procurement, for example, the formal process is invariably followed.[30] Service proposals begin with the preparation of the basic documentation (the Staff Objective, Staff Target, and Staff Requirement), are considered by the various relevant committees (the Defence Operational Requirements Committee, the Defence Force Structure Committee, the Defence Force Development Committee, the Defence Source Definition Committee, etc.), progress through the FYDP machinery, and are approved by the Minister or, if necessary, the Cabinet. Throughout this process reference is repeatedly made to the "strategic guidance." All the proposing documentation for a piece of equipment begins with a justification relating the proposal to the current strategic guidance. Before a project can be fed into the FYRP it has to be endorsed by the Defence Operational Requirements Committee (DORC), where compatibility of the project with the strategic guidance is the principal criterion invoked. And recommendations from the Defence Force Development Committee (DFDC) to the Minister must be framed "in the context of strategic assessment."

Despite this formal litany, it is clear that outcomes are often the product of other factors. The military is the dominant actor in major defence procurement; it is not only able to bring all its formal sources of power to bear, but also it is in this area that its informal authority is strongest. This position of strength allows the Services to generate outcomes which, while flowing through the formal procurement process in the appropriate way, are often not optimal from the overall perspective of the defence of Australia. The Services have obvious predilections, such as a disdain for local defence industries, and a preference for teeth at the expense of tail, and sometimes tend to follow some rather inimical practices, such as "gold-plating" and writing staff requirements around their preferred brand names. These outcomes are made possible principally because of the lack of clarity and coherence in the basic strategic guidance.

The Basic Strategic Guidance:

The problems of assessing the relative significance in Australian defence policy of the formal structures and processes on the one hand, and of the informal processes on the other, are very real. Empirically, the admixture is extraordinarily complex; and theoretically, Kurth's problem of *a posteriori* overdetermination pertains.

30. For a detailed outline of the formal defence procurement process in Australia together with a critique of the more informal factors, see my "The Role of the Military in Defence Hardware Procurement", chapter three of F. Mediansky, (ed.), *The Military and Australia's Defence* (Melbourne: Longman Cheshire, 1979).

Explanation is greatly assisted in the Australian case, however, by reference to the quality of the basic strategic guidance. For if this guidance, from which all subsequent decisions flow, is fundamentally inadequate, then the informal processes must prevail.

From the standpoint of defence policy formation, there are at least five major inadequacies of Australia's basic strategic guidance. First, the *Strategic Basis,* the principal relevant document, is filled with many qualifications; the compromises of bureaucratic language gloss over some basic contradictions in its strategic assessments; and its level of generality is too high for it to be anything more than vacuous as a basis for strategic planning. Very few pages of the document are actually addressed to the implications of the strategic assessment for "military requirements." The result is that, as a senior Army officer is reported to have said in 1976, "the *Strategic Basis* can be used to justify the procurement of any weapon system."[31] A similar point has been made by a First Assistant Secretary in the force planning area: "The *Strategic Basis* is the gospel; but it has as many interpretations as the gospel."[32]

From the military perspective, the resultant freedom from civilian "guidance" is attractive. Indeed, at this level, it is in the perceived interest of the military that the guidance be vacuous. As Admiral Peek, a former member of the Defence Committee, has said,

> In their contribution to the preparation of the strategic guidance, the individual Chiefs *deliberately* make it vague and woolly so that they can use it to justify the selection of any piece of equipment they want.[33]

A second, more particular, inadequacy is that the strategic documentation has a validity of considerably shorter duration than the perspective planning demands of defence, and particularly force structure, decision-making.[34] In the last decade, a *Strategic Basis* was produced in 1968, 1971, 1973, 1975 and 1976 (as the Australian *Strategic Analysis and Defence Policy Objectives,* or ASADPO). Although there were elements of continuity in each of these versions, the transition in basic national strategic policy from Forward Defence to Defence of Australia and the changes in Government in 1972 and 1973 have made for some significant differences in the "guidance."

Third, the strategic guidance has a rather restricted focus. In the case of the 1973 *Strategic Basis,* for example, low level contigencies were almost

31. Lt. T. P. Muggleton, *An Evaluation of the Analytical Infrastructure for Force Structure Decision-making in the Australian Defence Department* (B.A. (Honours) Thesis, Department of Economics, Faculty of Military Studies, University of New South Wales, Royal Military College, Duntroon, 1976), p. 36.

32. Interview, 24 February 1978.

33. Interview, 28 February 1978.

34. See Muggleton, *op. cit.,* pp. 30-31.

exclusively emphasised with the result that weapons systems pertaining to higher level contingencies lay outside the area of relevance of the document. As Admiral A.M. Synnot argued in 1976,

> At a time of low or intermediate threat strategic guidance cannot be expected to be sufficiently specific to enable us to determine the force structure.[35]

Hence, as a number of other senior officers involved in force planning have pointed out, the decisions to acquire such weapons systems as the FFG-7 patrol frigates and the *Leopard* tanks were made outside the justificatory realm of the *Strategic Basis*.[36]

Fourth, the strategic guidance does not address itself to fundamental defence questions. For example, it says nothing about the optimal defence posture for Australia to pursue—essentially maritime, ground, or whatever.

And, fifth, in recent years the strategic guidance has become overtly party-political. In March 1973, soon after assuming office, the Labor Government called for a complete re-write of the *1971 Strategic Basis*. In 1975, a further version was completed; this was still to be approved by the Government when it was dismissed from office, and the new Government did not even consider accepting it but, rather, called for another complete re-write.

Hence, defence policy in Australia derives, at its very source, from non-formal factors. And where the formal process is subsequently followed, it is often more a matter of rationalization than of rational decision-making.

This is not to say that if the Government provided clearer, more precise and less overtly political direction, complete rationality would be achieved. The closed nature of Australian defence policy-making notwithstanding, there are just too many participants—including politicians, bureaucrats, serving officers, analysts, etc.—for conflict and compromise to be removed completely. Indeed, it is being increasingly concluded in studies of the Australian defence process that "we must surrender the notion of the optimum," that outcomes will inevitably be determined by adversary processes.[37]

Defence policy formation is inevitably political. It will continue to be characterized by bargaining, negotiation and compromise—within Cabinet and within the higher defence organization, and between Cabinet, and more particularly the Defence Minister, and the higher defence organization. And

---

35. A. M. Synott, "The Changing Challenge of Our Defence Force," *Pacific Defence Reporter,* March 1976, Vol. II No. 9, p. 14.

36. See Muggleton, *op. cit.,* p. 32.

37. See Darcy McGaurr, "Defence Procurement: In Search of Optimality" (Paper delivered to the Conference on "Armed Forces and Australian Society," Royal Military College, Duntroon, May 1977), introduction; and Bernard Schaffer *The Administrative Factor: Papers in Organization, Politics and Development* (London: Frank Cass, 1973), Chapters 9 & 10.

this political process will continue to operate as much through informal channels as through formal structures and organizations. An alternative process, one dominated by a single influence (Minister, Secretary, Chief of the Defence Force Staff, or whoever) is not possible, at least in the Western democracies. What may be possible, however, is to open the process up to greater public scrutiny and to allow greater public debate. Positions of participants will still be reached subjectively, and resultant decisions "irrationally," but at least the positions would have to be articulated and justified, and the results would be subject to the attentions of a wider community.

Conceptions, Constraints, Policy Outputs

Henry S. Albinski

Fresh circumstances are shaping Australian security orientations. Significant implications are arising in the Asia-Pacific region out of the post-Vietnam era. The Sino-Soviet rivalry has sharpened. The United States, long regarded as the cornerstone of Australian security, elected a new administration in 1976, and has continued to reassess its defense role in Asia. In late 1975 Australia itself underwent a change of government, from the Australian Labor Party to a Liberal-National Country Party coalition headed by Malcolm Fraser. The new Government prided itself on its realism, arguing that Australia must "be prepared to face the world as it is, and not as we would like it."[1]

Our aim is to examine Australian defense during the Fraser Government under some broad, connecting rubrics. We will first try to reconstruct the Government's *conceptions* of the sources, character and importance of security concerns faced by Australia. We will then turn to the kinds of *resources* available to Australia in pursuit of its security objectives, and lead into the actual *policy outputs* that have emanated from the Government. We will conclude with brief thoughts about security-related *outcomes*.

How secure is Australia? Defense Minister Dr. J. Killen remarked in late 1977 that "Our major review of the international security outlook last year noted certain unfavourable developments and the uncertainty of the future,

---

1. Fraser, *Commonwealth Parliamentary Debates* (CPD), House of Representatives (HR), June 1, 1976, p. 2735. For a synthesis of L-NCP external policy conceptions while the coalition parties were in opposition, see Henry S. Albinski, *Australian External Policy Under Labor. Content, Process and the National Debate* (St. Lucia: University of Queensland Press, 1977), pp. 77-86. The L-NCP's last systematic statement on defense before leaving opposition was contained in *Defense Policy* (Canberra: Liberal Party Federal Secretariat, 1975).

but we judged our prospects on balance to be favourable,," and that assessment had not changed since then.[2]

Australia has certain, essentially invariant features that color its security position. Among these are its isolated, island-continent character, a relatively small population housed on a very large land mass with an enormous coastline and, as one of the world's foremost trading nations, exceptional dependence on open transport and communication lanes. Australia's location, size and configuration make it vulnerable to certain, especially lower-level forms of harassment and intrusion, but set formidable obstacles to successful high-level threats such as outright invasion. There foreseeably are no nations in Australia's environment capable of mounting a major military threat to it. Foreign Minister Andrew Peacock has in fact reasoned that "we appear to be leaving behind an era which was dominated by war and naturally our relationships with the area were focused on defence and security issues. Now I believe we are entering a period in which economic issues will become increasingly important with South-East Asia."[3] This perspective includes the Government's apparent agreement with its defense advisers that Asia's severe food and other resource claims are more likely to result in diplomatic and economic than in actual military pressures on affluent, food-abundant Australia.[4]

As it turns its attention in various directions, Australia finds little cause for alarm about any circle of unfriendly neighbors who in and of themselves constitute sources of threat. To the west stretches an essentially open Indian Ocean. To the south there is only an internationally controlled, demilitarized Antarctica. To the east lies friendly, socially and politically compatible New Zealand, plus a scattering of microstates. Only to the north can a potentially worrisome situation be imagined. Indonesia lies at Australia's doorstep. It is South-East Asia's largest state, the most powerful member of ASEAN, a member of OPEC, and for the present solidly anti-Communist. Its waters are, among other things, passageways for American submarines moving between the Pacific and Indian Oceans. Indonesia has a history of volatile

---

2. Killen, *CPD,* HR, September 22, 1977, p. 1478. Also see the Government's white paper on *Australian Defence* (Canberra: Australian Government Publishing Service, 1976), esp. pp. 1-9. Published excerpts from the "strategic basis" assessment prepared in the Defense Department at the close of the Labor period appeared in Brian Toohey, *Australian Financial Review,* March 12 and June 24, 1976, and Alan Reid, *Bulletin,* June 12, 1976.

3. Interview with Michael Richardson in Melbourne *Age,* May 17, 1977. Note the very considerable economic, North-South dialogue emphasis in Peacock's foreign policy review before Parliament, *CPD,* HR, May 9, 1978, pp. 2029-2043. Also see his address "Australia and the International Economic Order," Minister for Foreign Affairs *News Release,* No. M82, July 20, 1978.

4. See Peter Samuel in *Bulletin,* May 14, 1977.

politics, at one time of strong radical influence, and of unsettling neighborhood conflicts. Australia opposed Sukarno's seizure of West Irian (Irian Jaya) and his "confrontation" policy in Malaysian Borneo. More recently, Australia has been concerned about Indonesia's aggressive efforts to absorb East Timor. It has also worried about the impact on Papua New Guinea, Australia's former political ward, of Indonesia's problem of pacifying the insurgency on the Irian Jaya-PNG border.

Australia's security assessment becomes more agitated when the focus shifts to how surrounding areas are subject to disruption occasioned by great power conflict. South-East Asia has for years been an Australian security preoccupation. Earlier Liberal governments insisted that China in particular was responsible for inciting revolutionary ferment in the region. As individual states and then the entire region became weakened and then destabilized, as during the Indochinese troubles, Australia's own security was believed to be endangered. While all of Indochina became communized in 1975, the end of conflict was thought to provide an opportunity for regional relaxation. Australia has felt that, on balance, such expectations are plausible, but that it would be imprudent to be sanguine. Vietnam's own intentions toward non-Communist South-East Asia have not fully crystallized. Sino-Soviet competition among the states of Indochina is only one symptom of what Peacock, in a private letter to Secretary Vance, referred to as a "clash of national interests" of the great powers that could escalate into a major crisis.[5] Or, as the Government's white paper on defense speculated, regional rivalries and great power confrontation, especially if prolonged, "could lead the regional states to develop capability for conventional military operations on a regional scale." While such developments are not imminent, reference to them "can help to clarify the basis for our abiding concern regarding prospects in South-East Asia. . . . defence policy is concerned with contingencies and not simply demonstrable threats."[6] Strategically, South-East Asia is not only a chain extending downward from the Asian mainland into Indonesia and thereby into Australia's immediate vicinity. It is also a bridge between the Indian Ocean and East Asia, and a vital contact point for Japan, Australia's foremost trading partner and the nation viewed by Australia as critical to

5. Robert Haupt, *Australian Financial Review,* October 4, 1977. The account of Peacock's letter continues in the issues of October 5 and 6, 1977.

6. *Australian Defence, op. cit.,* p. 7. For a further exposition from an official source of low-threat problems in South-East Asia, see Peter Hastings in *Sydney Morning Herald,* June 22, 1978. For a broader assessment of Australia's interests in post-Vietnam South-East Asia, see Hastings, "The Changing Region," *Australian Journal of Defence Studies,* Vol. 1 (March 1977), pp. 10-14, and J. A. C. Mackie, "Australia and Southeast Asia I," and "Australia and Southeast Asia II," in Mackie, ed., *Australia in the New World Order. Foreign Policy in the 1970s* (Melbourne: Nelson, 1976), pp. 58-81 and 82-105, respectively.

assisting in the economic development of South-East Asia, and therefore in its political stability and security resiliency.

The Fraser Government originally took a pronounced, agitated view of potentially destabilizing tendencies in the South Pacific. The area had been generally free of major Communist power presence, and of American-Communist power rivalry. But Australia foresaw danger in rising Soviet diplomatic and aid/trade interest in South Pacific countries. These small countries might not be able to resist or even recognize Communist power blandishments and encroachments. As one great Communist power moved in, the other would likely be tempted to compete in kind, thereby transforming the region into another, prospectively destabilized site of the Sino-Soviet rivalry.

The Australian Government's 1976 apprehensions about security conditions in the South Pacific have been somewhat assuaged. But the Government in principle accepts the interpretation of a recent Parliamentary study that "To Australia the region is of strategic importance. Any potentially hostile power which could establish a military capability in the region could threaten or harass Australia and endanger its people, resources, lines of communication and supply across the Pacific Ocean."[7] A stepped-up Soviet fishing as well as naval presence imposes problems of adequate surveillance. It could also challenge American forces operating from the Guam/Micronesian island base complex.

Under the Fraser Government, the Indian Ocean has been regarded more anxiously than other neighboring regions. Australia has emphasized the importance of its lines of communication, transport and commerce across the ocean, which carry a substantial part of its petroleum requirements and over 50 percent of its trade by tonnage. Japan is overwhelmingly dependent on petroleum passing through the Indian Ocean. The ocean's north-west sector is the gateway to the Middle East, to the Mediterranean, and to Europe. Its north-east sector represents Australia's gateway to South-East Asia. The large but underpopulated state of Western Australia, which abuts on the Indian Ocean, contains a third of Australia's coastline and is extremely rich in natural resources.

---

7. Parliament of Australia, *Australia and the South Pacific*. Report from the Senate Standing Committee on Foreign Affairs and Defence (Canberra: Australian Government Publishing Service, 1978), pp. 14-15. Relatedly, see R. A. Herr, "Some Aspects of Regional Security in the South Pacific," forthcoming in *Pacific Islands Yearbook;* T. B. Millar, "Weapons Proliferation and Security Problems in the South Pacific Region," in Robert O'Neill, ed., *Insecurity! The Spread of Weapons in the Indian and Pacific Oceans* (Canberra: Australian National University Press, 1978), pp. 222-235; Robert G. Gordon, "Regionalism in the South Pacific," *Pacific Defence Reporter*, August 1977.

At first, Killen argued that Soviet behavior in the region constituted an actual and direct threat to Australia.[8] That viewpoint was amended, but the Government has insisted that the Soviets in the ocean and on its littoral have been menacing, symptomatic of their global efforts to compromise Western interests. Such manifestations are said to include a naval buildup, and the establishment of elaborate base and other facilities in the Horn of Africa/Red Sea/Gulf of Aden region. Further evidence is found in Soviet intrusions into various African trouble spots with the motive of consolidating a belt of sympathetic states on the eastern littoral of the African continent. The Soviets are believed preparing to introduce new weapons systems into the area, such as land-based Backfire bombers for an anti-shipping strike role. They fail to honor understandings designed to regulate a great power presence in the region, as when they augmented their naval strength in the area after a provisional, force-capping agreement had been reached with the United States. In sum, Soviet behavior is interpreted not simply as annoying; it is destabilizing the region, and engendering widespread danger for the security of Australia and of the West generally.[9]

The Government's appraisal of Indian Ocean security problems, and indeed of great power activity in other regions, reflects its wider formulations about international tensions. Although it has professed that the more strictly military aspects have been giving ground to socioeconomic aspects of international competition, and security, it has argued that "there is no substitute for a system of balances which will make resort to disruptive behavior an irrational act. If this seems an old-fashioned solution, it is well to remember that in power terms we are still living in an old-fashioned world of nation states."[10] The Government has definitely not translated this into anything like blanket anti-Communism. It sees the Soviets as bearing most of the responsibility for mischief. It construes the Soviet military buildup as unwarranted and therefore ominous. Soviet international interventions, alone or through surrogates, are more designed to confuse, frustrate and weaken Western resistance, and Soviet proclamations on behalf of détente are all too often spurious. As Fraser remarked in mid-1978, Soviet adventurism abroad

---

8. See passages from a Killen press conference in Brian Toohey, *Australian Financial Review,* July 1, 1976.

9. For a good summary of Australia's interests in the Indian Ocean, see Parliament of Australia, *Australia and the Indian Ocean Region.* Report from the Senate Standing Committee on Foreign Affairs and Defence (Canberra: Australian Government Publishing Service, 1976), esp. pp. 171-193. For the Government's Indian Ocean appraisal, see Fraser, *CPD.* HR, June 1, 1976, p. 2741, and Peacock, "Defence and Diplomacy in the Indian Ocean," in Minister for Foreign Affairs *News Release,* No. M74, November 12, 1976.

10. Peacock, Minister for Foreign Affairs *News Release,* No. M55, September 13, 1976, p. 5.

and persecution of dissidents at home have made it very hard to believe that the Soviet leadership intends to behave soberly and to live up to international understandings. The Soviets were bent on expanding their influence so as to achieve world primacy.[11] China, on its part, has been behaving sensibly and responsibly. It deserves to be encouraged in its resistance to Soviet ambitions. Its contribution will help to redress the destabilizing effects of Soviet machinations.

Australia has acknowledged that, within the context of its security conceptions, the familiar role of the United States has changed. Nixon's Guam Doctrine of 1969, embellished by the Ford and Carter administrations, foreshadowed the winding down of an American "offshore" security posture in Asia, some running down of force strengths, and a reluctance to take on new commitments. Australia's former "forward defense" posture lies behind, and Australians are very unlikely to face large-scale military involvement far beyond their immediate region. Australian needs to free itself of the "comfortable illusion" that it "can look to our major ally, the US, automatically to send military forces under all circumstances of military attack at any level upon our forces or territory."[12] Such self-admonitions notwithstanding, in its assumptions about international balance and dangers to that balance from the Soviets the Fraser Government has maintained that the United States is "the only power that can balance the might of the Soviet Union. If America does not undertake this task it will not be done. If it is not done the whole basis of peace and security is unsupported,"[13] and "the fact that . . . [the United States] attracts criticism in its international role is much less important than the fact that the task is done."[14] Australia therefore must plan for greater initiative and self-reliance in defense. For one, because the United States will be doing less and will not foreseeably be quickly responsive to Australian-defined concerns. Secondly, because America must be urged, guided, or persuaded to follow policies consistent with Australia's interpretations of balance and deterrence. It is in this context that we examine Australia's defense-related resources, and their linkage to policy outputs.

11. Fraser, electorate talk, Office of the Prime Minister *Press Release,* July 16, 1978.

12. Remarks of Sir Arthur Tange, Secretary, Department ofDefense, in *Sydney Morning Herald,* July 4, 1978. For sample assessments of Australia's changing international environment and options in the academic literature, see Robert O'Neill, ed., *The Defense of Australia. Fundamental New Aspects* (Canberra: Strategic and Defense Studies Centre, Australian National University, 1977) and, in brief compass, T. B. Millar, "The Defense of Australia During the Next Ten Years," *World Review,* Vol. 16 (March 1977), pp. 14-26.

13. Fraser, *CPD,* HR, June 1, 1976, p. 2738.

14. Fraser, White House dinner remarks, Office of the Prime Minister *Press Release,* July 27, 1976, p. 2.

We have indicated that Australia does not foresee any consequential threats to its own territorial integrity. Moreover, it acknowledges that the mounting of any such threats by antagonists would very likely require some years of preparation by them, and would signal their intentions. Low-level, short notice conflict in its neighborhood, such as guerrilla or terrorist raids, interference with its maritime and offshore resource claims, or interdiction of supply and communications routes, is of course not precluded. Understandably, Australian defense doctrine and planning hopes to anticipate contingencies rather than to await actual threats. This in itself requires a contextually meaningful defense establishment. The availability and utilization of defense resources has recently been underscored by the admission that Australia as well as its neighbors will need to be doing more for themselves, individually and cooperatively, instead of relying on Vietnam-style, side by side efforts with powerful allies such as the United States. Because Australia perceives dangers to regional and global balances, arising especially from Soviet behavior, because it still searches for reinsurance to manage various levels of conflict, it wishes to engage the United States in complementary strategies. But an implication of the Guam Doctrine is that America helps those who help themselves. Hence, in the language of Peter Sim, Chairman of the Australian Senate Standing Committee on Foreign Affairs and Defense, "The best way to maintain the United States interest [in Australia] is not by stressing dependence on the United States but by following policies that protect our national interests and showing that we are determined to the utmost of our ability to protect our own security interests."[15]

The Fraser Government entered office pledged to rescue defense from the allegedly neglected condition in which Labor had left it. In 1976 there was a promise to revitalize the armed forces through substantial financial outlays. However, despite efforts by Killen to salvage what he could, the 1977-78 defense budget was essentially standstill, representing planned expenditures of A$2.343 billion, or only about 2.5 percent of GNP. Defense estimates were calculated at 8.8 percent of total government spending, compared to 9.0 percent in 1976-77. The 1978-79 budget allocated A$2.501 for defense, which the Government portrayed as a 1 percent increase in real terms. The Government's reluctance to invest more in defense has been attributable to several factors. The single, most important factor has been the Government's preoccupation with domestic economic problems, and priorities that have led it to attack inflation by imposing heavy constraints on public spending.[16]

15. Senator J. P. Sim, "What Should Australian Foreign Policy Be?" *Pacific Defence Reporter*, July 1977.

16. For discussions of the economy-defense spending relationship, see for instance Frank Cranston, *Canberra Times*, August 18, 1977 and May 4, 1978; Andrew Kruger, *Sydney Morning Herald*, May 24, 1978; Greg Hartung, *Australian*, June 24, 1978.

Secondly, foreign and defense policy has not been an electorally active or profitable issue for several years, in part because the major party groups have found more mileage in domestic issues, in part because external policy issue differences have narrowed in recent years. In fact, it is Liberals who traditionally criticized Labor's alleged defense deficiencies, not the other way round. In the December 1977 federal election, under 1 percent of the electorate perceived foreign/defense policy as the key issue.[17] Although the Government acknowledges the logic of "self-reliance" in the present strategic environment, it feels that Australia's security objectives, including bringing influence to bear on American defense policies, can be accomplished by means other than a large-scale outlay for defense.

While there has been a leveling off of defense spending, Australia's military strength, at least by Asian-Pacific regional standards, is not negligible. Uniformed personnel number about 70,000. Although personnel costs consume most of the defense budget, much of Australia's equipment is impressive. The inventory includes *Mirage* 111-0 fighters, F-111C strike aircraft and the very sophisticated P-3C surveillance aircraft. It also includes over 100 *Leopard* main battle tanks, *Rapier* surface to air missiles, five modern *Oberon* class submarines, an aircraft carrier, a destroyer and frigate flotilla, plus new FFG-7 guided missile frigates and coastal patrol craft on order.[18]

So far, Labor and now L-NCP governments have favored a core force, maintenance of the "state of the art" approach to defense. Critical attention has increasingly been devoted to the appropriateness of the training, disposition, equipment mix, logistical and other features of Australia's defense forces. Very basic and expensive decisions, such as any sea-borne platform replacement for the aging carrier HMAS *Melbourne* and acquisition of air superiority planes, will soon be necessary. This rethinking has been prompted by strategic reorientations that focus on "neighborhood" (the Government dislikes the term "continental") rather than forward defense doctrine. It has also been prompted by need to respond to rapid changes in defense technology, including precision guided munitions and new classes of weapons systems.[19] The review has also been induced by rising concern about patrolling Australia's

17. See the results of the Melbourne *Age* polls, published in the December 1 and 9, 1977 issues. Also see essentially corroborative data in the *Morgan Gallup Poll,* No. 506, November 1977.

18. For a recent review of various defense resources, see Jolika Tie, J. O. Langtry and Robert O'Neill, *Australia's Defence Resources. A Compedium of Data* (Canberra: Strategic and Defence Studies Centre, Australian National University, 1978). Also see various portions of *Australian Defence, op. cit.*

19. For a good sample of this concern, see Ross Babbage, Desmond Ball, J. O. Langtry and Robert O'Neill, *The Development of Australian Army Officers for the 1980s* (Canberra: Strategic and Defense Studies Centre, Australian National University, 1978).

shores, both in military roles as such and to detect and/or apprehend poachers, drug runners, unauthorized refugees and other intruders, especially since the declaration of the 200 mile exclusive economic zone. There are nettlesome questions about how military resources can and should be diverted to civilian, coast guard-type surveillance tasks.[20]

Australian defense force capabilities are affected by available scientific and industrial backup, apart from what such resources provide by way of spinoffs for the civilian economy in ways such as broadening the employment base, introducing new skills and products, and contributing to savings on foreign exchange.

Evolving strategic conceptions have placed fresh attention on the state of defense industries. If Australia needs to become more self-sufficient, if in the future normally reliable overseas arms and munitions suppliers will not be able or might not wish to continue or to expand resupply, then there is a premium on indigenous Australian production. The same applies to repair, overhaul and retrofitting capabilities. Rising Soviet naval power in Australia's environment, plus Australia's relatively weak capacity to protect its own sea lanes, is seen to add to the argument. Self-supply of a range of sophisticated weapons technology not only seems to promise a greater capability as such, but suggests that a country of only 14 million may be able to economize on scarce military manpower. This, however, assumes Australia's ability to undertake a qualitative upgrading rather than simply expansion of defense-related industries and facilities.

Australia's record in the defense industry and technology domain is mixed. It possesses aircraft assembly and medium size ship construction capability. Although it partly relied on overseas components, Australia designed and produced pilotless target aircraft, an anti-submarine weapons system, a sonar system, over-horizon radar, and the *Barra* sonics system, which will be installed on the new P-3C aircraft being bought from the United States. Australia has also produced the *Nomad,* a versatile short take-off and landing (STOL) aircraft. Both to increase the nation's defense industrial skills and to promote the economy, successive governments have worked for Australian industry participation as tradeoffs in overseas defense purchase contracts. This has meant offset orders (such as producing certain components for all Boeing 727 aircraft against defense purchases from the United States), as well as manufacturing components and parts for Australian and export use for military systems purchased abroad. There nevertheless are major gaps in existing defense industrial capabilities, either for present military require-

20. For discussions of the coastal surveillance problem, see Peter Hastings, *Sydney Morning Herald,* June 30, 1978, and the interview with Killen by Peter Costigan in Melbourne *Herald,* March 1, 1978.

ments or for rapid retooling should defense emergencies arise. Moreover, Australia's defense R and D investment, both public and private, is slight by industrial national standards. Australian labor costs are high. The modest population and defense base raises hard questions of cost effectiveness, and technological capabilities cannot reasonably be expected to keep up with advanced weapons, avionics, communications and other systems that are in demand by the armed forces. As austerity and inflation erode annual defense expenditures, there is a temptation to save wherever possible, including buying overseas if the cost is less than for locally produced products. While standing by the principle of maximizing domestic defense production, the Government has simultaneously tried to maximize the dependability and comparability of overseas purchases. This has taken various forms. For instance, it was Australian perseverance and imagination that produced the formula wherein Australia, together with New Zealand and Japan and by indirection Israel—not just NATO nations—are exempt from ceilings on American overseas arms transfers. Following an Australian proposal extended at the 1978 ANZUS Council meetings, efforts will be stepped up to enhance cooperative supply and support, especially in circumstances requiring rapid Australian force expansion. Moreover, to reduce investment in local inventories of spare parts under peacetime conditions, Australia linked itself to the American Armed Forces Automated Digital Network.[21]

Australia is convinced that its security interests are served when its military resources are applied to assist and coordinate with other states in the region. Such aid is aimed at achieving immediate security objectives. It is also seen to contribute to fashioning a climate of national and regional self-reliance that will impress the United States. It will hopefully help to sustain American interest, capabilities and responsiveness. Before indicating the character of Australia's extramural military programs, its approach to American security policies needs to be reviewed.

We have seen that the Fraser Government has emphasized balance of power features in world politics, and that it has stressed the avoidance of regional and global disequilibriums that might redound to Soviet advantage. Theoretically, the announced Australian preference has been for equilibrium, without any single nation domination of regions such as South-East Asia, the South Pacific and the Indian Ocean. There nevertheless are strong intima-

---

21. For a comprehensive examination of Australian defense industries, see Parliament of Australia, *Industrial Support for Defence Needs and Allied Matters* (the "Hamer Report"). Report of the Joint Committee on Foreign Affairs and Defence (Canberra: Australian Government Publishing Service, 1977). For a summary, see Maurice Neil, "The Hamer Report," *Pacific Defence Reporter* August 1977. For useful shorter analyses, see Sir Arthur Tange's remarks in *Sydney Morning Herald,* July 5, 1978, and D. H. Eltringham in *ibid.,* 18 and 19 July, 1978; Frank Cranston, *Canberra Times,* August 3, 1977; Anne Summers, *National Times,* August 1, 1977.

tions that the Australian Government leans toward regional power configurations in which anti-Soviet forces predominate. Hence its enthusiasm for recent Chinese policies, and continued support for an active American role.

Australia did not directly try to dissuade the United States from withdrawing ground troops from South Korea, but pointedly imparted to Washington its concerns about potential spillover effects. Australia thought it most important that reassurance be extended to South-East Asian capitals that the United States was not indifferent to the regional balance of power, and that the Korean decision was not a prelude to the drawing down of military capabilities in the Pacific area generally. Such reassurances would also be welcomed in Peking and in Tokyo, and would remind the Soviets of America's commitment to fulfill an active, credible and unmistakably great power role.[22] Such considerations have caused the Fraser Government to encourage adequate American force levels in the region, as well as the necessary base and staging facilities. The dismantling or downgrading of the Philippine bases would impair American naval and air operational capabilities in South-East Asia, and would hinder reinforcement for the Indian Ocean. Should Guam and the Micronesian territories have to absorb many of the Philippine base functions, the United States could incline toward lowering its appreciation of the Western Pacific's inherent strategic importance.

Australia has also wished that regional states be encouraged to acquire adequate defense capabilities, including police and anti-insurgency measures, coastal protection and deterrence against external threats. Australia has visualized dangers in an overzealous application of military assistance sanctions against South-East Asian nations that may have failed to meet strict standards of human and political rights observance, and has strived to persuade Washington that human rights have to be adjusted to local realities. As Peacock outlined it in an address before the United Nations, human and political rights goals could not be expected to be realized rapidly, or had to await social and political stabilization, or had to be balanced against national or international security considerations.[23] Moreover, sharp human rights censure of states such as Indonesia could weaken their aptitude for mobilizing regional economic and political planning, as through ASEAN, and thereby undermine regional security. The withholding of military assistance as a human rights sanction could generate political reverberations in Indonesia and other areas where military establishments were politically prominent.

22. See Peacock's letter to Vance, in Robert Haupt, *Australian Financial Review*, especially issues of October 4 and 6, 1977, and Fraser's Washington press conference of June 22, 1977, transcript.

23. Peacock, United Nations General Assembly address of September 29, 1977, in Department of Foreign Affairs *Backgrounder*, No. 108, September 30, 1977, esp. pp. 20-21. Also see Creighton Burns' review in Melbourne *Age*, October 4, 1977.

Australia itself has for years provided military assistance to regional states. In 1977-78 the aid total was A$26 million, with the lion's share going to PNG. In addition to supplying training, arms and equipment, Australia has been involved in joint exercises with regional states, and has continued to station two Mirage squadrons and a company of training infantry at the Malaysian base at Butterworth. The Australian presence at Butterworth is designed to train Malaysian and Singapore air force personnel. It also is intended to contribute to Malaysian and Singapore air defense under terms of the Five Power Agreement, though the RAAF refrains from operations against Malaysian-based guerrillas. Overall, the arrangement is defended on grounds that it enhances self-defense capabilities, while providing a tangible yet low-keyed outlet for Australian defense contributions in a regional, mutual assistance context.[24]

Several rationales underpin Australia's military assistance efforts at large. If Australia did not help, others likely would step in, and Australia's professions of regional cooperation would lose credit. Defense aid affords Australia some leverage with recipient countries. Such programs provide valuable access to the defense establishments of recipient countries, and to their general strategic and political outlooks.[25] Moreover, incentives for regional state reliance on Australian defence industry capabilities appear to be rising. American arms transfers are being scaled down, and are being subjected to increased legal constraints and political scrutiny in Washington. Australia can help to fill some of the gap. In so doing, it can relieve recipient state dependence on great power largesse. Apart from Japan, Australia is the only regional power with the technological, industrial and related infrastructures able to make such contributions. Even China has expressed interest in defense purchases from Australia.

Australia also enjoys such advantages as proximity to recipient states, familiarity with tropicalization of defense equipment, and ongoing contacts and military and commercial relations with neighboring states.[26] Indeed, current strategic assessments point to foreseeable Australian military operations being confined to its immediate region, suggesting that Australia is a quite natural resource base for regional, defense-related matériel. To date, Australia has supplied its neighbors with surplus fighters, helicopters and

24. See the helpful summary of Australian military cooperation with Malaysia and Singapore in Hansan Dias Birhan, "Malaysian Report," *Pacific Defence Reporter,* June 1978.

25. See Peter Hastings in *Sydney Morning Herald,* June 23, 1978 and his "The Implications of an Australian Continental Defence Policy for Her Relations with Neighbours," in O'Neill, *The Defence of Australia, op. cit.,* pp. 89-95.

26. For a forceful exposition of this theme see remarks of Rollo Kingsford-Smith, reported in *News Weekly,* July 5, 1978, and the "Daedelus" article "Australia as a Regional Technology Centre," *Pacific Defence Reporter,* May 1978.

patrol craft from its own inventories, as well as with its domestically-developed and manufactured *Nomad* and a variety of smaller items. Hawker Pacific, formerly Hawker de Havilland Australia, has built up a considerable defense-related business in Asia. It orginally concentrated on civil and military aircraft engine and airframe overhauls in Australia, and then proceeded to establish facilities and to supply skilled personnel within Asian user states.[27]

Some special considerations impel Australian defense cooperation programs with particular regional states, even though these programs have occasionally created delicate policy problems for Canberra. We have mentioned Australia's assessment of Indonesia's significance. During the first half of 1976, the Ford Administration stopped arms transfers to Indonesia because, in contravention of American law, American-supplied equipment was being employed to suppress resistance on East Timor. The ban was rescinded, and not reimposed by the Carter Administration, though Australia was nervous that Indonesia's political rights record on Timor and on its metropolitan territory might lead to other curtailments of American arms shipments. The Fraser Government has consistently preferred a solution of Indonesian annexation of East Timor. But it has been plainly disquieted about the severity of Indonesian methods, the absence of a genuine expression of self-determination there, and the strength of critical, cross-party opinion within Australia. An understanding was reached that Australian-supplied military equipment would not be used by Indonesia in Timor. The Government has apparently been satisfied that Indonesia has abided by its promise.[28] In this respect the Australian Government has not had to face the question of whether to suspend further arms transfers, or to consider other sanctions that could severely strain relations with Jakarta.

In cooperation with Indonesian forces, Australia has provided men and equipment to map the area on the Irian Jaya-PNG border. An anti-Indonesian resistance movement in Irian Jaya has been creating complications both for Indonesia and PNG. The insurgents have moved across the border into PNG to elude Indonesian security forces. Indonesian forces have pursued across the border, and have bombed suspected insurgent positions very close to the border. The PNG Government does not sympathize with the insurgent movement, but finds it politically difficult to condone Indonesian border activity, or to employ its own security forces in sufficient strength to patrol the border. PNG remains overwhelmingly dependent on Australian economic assistance, and its defense force is Australian trained and equipped. A few hundred Australian service personnel continue on loan to the PNG defense

---

27. See a review of Hawker Pacific's Asian activities by Robert Murray, *Australian Financial Review*, January 4, 1978.

28. See Michael Richardson in Melbourne *Age*, April 25, 1978.

force in various training and specialist roles. There is no formal defense agreement between Australia and PNG. There are guidelines under which seconded Australian military personnel are as far as possible to be kept away from politically sensitive situations.[29] Still, serious irritations between Indonesia and PNG complicate Australian diplomacy. It has been reported that the Irian Jaya-PNG border issue caused the PNG Government to call in Australia under terms of the bilateral agreement that requires consultation when one party believes that a defense action could have an effect on the other.[30] The border problem has prompted Australia to step up its efforts to urge Indonesia to cool its military activities in the area, and to approach the United States on how to handle future arms transfers to Indonesia should Indonesia continue sorties by American-supplied aircraft.[31]

PNG faces a massive task of national integration and development. In this land of tremendous diversity, secessionist movements are barely below the surface. Effective police and defense force capabilities are required to supplement ingenious socioeconomic strategies if political stability is to be expected.

PNG's security importance to Australia includes its location to Australia's immediate north, its abutment on Indonesian territory via Irian Jaya, and its bridging position between South-East Asia and the South Pacific. We have seen that Australia has watched over security developments in the area. The Fraser Government's stated position is that no major power should dominate the South Pacific region. American naval and air capabilities there must be maintained. Hence the Government's forceful opposition to a nuclear-free zone in the Pacific, which would greatly complicate the mobility and effectiveness of American forces. Hence too Australia's concern for the integrity of American facilities on Guam and on what was the Trust Territory of the Pacific Islands, where access is provided from the American west coast through Hawaii and then either almost directly westward linking with the Philippines, or in a southerly direction linking with Australia. As the member parts of American Micronesia evolve toward various formats of political autonomy, the viability of United States defense facilities there will increasingly be affected by the viability of the new microstates. Their viability will in turn be furthered through intraregional, cooperative relationships with other South Pacific countries, bilaterally and through regional groupings. PNG assumes a special importance in this picture. Its potentially considerable leadership role derives from such factors as its large population and resource base, geo-

29. For a summary of Australia's defense relationship with PNG, see Tie, *et al, op. cit.*, pp. 51-54.

30. *Australia Financial Review*, July 18, 1978.

31. See Tony Walker, Melbourne *Age*, July 25, 1978; Brian Toohey, *Australian Financial Review*, July 26, 1978; Peter Hastings, *Sydney Morning Herald*, July 29, 1978.

graphic proximity to Australia and outlet to South-East Asia. For Australia, therefore, an orderly and stable PNG can contribute to a valued American defense presence in the South and Central Pacific. This raises the significance of assistance to PNG's defense force, and efforts to defuse distracting problems between Indonesia and PNG.

During its first year in office the Fraser Government was exercised about Soviet penetration of the South Pacific. For instance, it saw adverse security implications in the Soviet Union's offer to Tonga to assist in improving airport and fishing facilities in return for a servicing base for its South Pacific fishing fleet. Australia voiced concern that year at the South Pacific Forum, and then at the ANZUS Council meetings.[32] Australian apprehensions about security problems in the region were eventually moderated though by no means dispelled. There was Australian trepidation about the destabilizing effects of a Soviet and Chinese diplomatic presence, one of whose unwelcome effects could be the introduction of great power conflict in the area. In 1978, Western, and especially Australian lobbying helped to dissuade the PNG Government from allowing both Soviet and Chinese missions into Port Moresby.[33]

Australia is conscious that large scale military assistance is neither needed nor desired among the South Pacific states generally. The nations there wish if possible to avoid entanglement in great power rivalries and are too small and isolated to require substantial forces. As a neighboring middle power, Australia together with New Zealand finds itself more welcome in a defense cooperation role than the United States would be. There have therefore been training and joint exercises with assisted nation forces, gifts of arms and the like. In 1978, Australia provided arms and munitions for a battalion of Fijian infantry going on peace-keeping duty to Lebanon. The gesture seemed to confirm Australia's political compatibility with Pacific countries, its ability to serve in a responsible defense cooperation role with them, and to contribute to an important, conflict management task in a volatile part of the world.[34]

The Fraser Government had previously provided a helicopter detachment for peace-keeping service in the Sinai. That commitment was not, however, as significant for appreciating Australia's security calculations as was the prospect in mid-1978 that Australian peace-keeping troops might serve in Namibia, and possibly Zimbabwe. We thus turn our attention to Africa, and then to the Indian Ocean.

32. For some 1976 commentaries, see Russell Skelton, Melbourne *Age,* July 14, 1976, and *National Times,* July 26, 1976.

33. For one version of this episode, see *Post-Courier* (Port Moresby), April 14, 1978.

34. On the Fijian assistance program, see Peacock, Minister for Foreign Affairs *News Release,* No. 58, May 21, 1978, and *Fiji Times* (Suva), May 23, 1978.

Fraser's Government has from the onset exhibited conciliatory behavior on southern and central African issues. It has consistently deplored racist, non-popular political practices, has enforced various United Nations resolutions designed to isolate the Smith regime in Salisbury, has not encouraged trade with South Africa, and has been strict about sporting contacts with South Africa. It very early recognized the Cuban-backed Neto regime in Angola, allowed official aid to Mozambique, declined to make approving remarks about multinational efforts to prop up Zaire after insurgents had penetrated Shaba Province from Angola, and maintained a more restrained position than President Carter did about any pernicious Cuban role in southern African conflicts. It opposed the "internal settlement" arranged by Smith and moderate African leaders in Zimbabwe, and instead endorsed the Anglo-American plan for an all-party conference and solution there. It also favored the Western plan for self-determination for Namibia, and as of time of writing apparently stood ready to supply troops for peace-keeping service.

The previous Whitlam Labor Government had instituted a modest training program for Australian troops with Canadian forces, who were experienced in peace-keeping. The Fraser Government's seeming readiness to provide peace-keeping forces was testimony of Australia's acceptability in such a role; not only by the United States and Britain, but prospectively by African states as well.[35]

Australia's African policy has in part reflected the genuine, personal abhorrence of racial discrimination of ranking figures such as Fraser and Peacock. It in part has been inspired by Australia's wish to enhance its international image and influence. In part, it has stemmed from Australia's belief that its own, and the general international community's economic interests, including mature North-South relations, require deft handling of serious political problems and the avoidance of confrontational scenes in the region. But it also has been anchored in security considerations. The southern African area is exceptionally volatile. It could easily become combustible, create disorder that would compromise moderate elements as well as Western interests, and inject truly radical regimes as well as Soviet or Soviet proxy influence. The effects would be shattering for Africa. The reverberations would harm efforts to deter Soviet influence in the Indian Ocean region. A Namibian settlement, for instance, would greatly lessen Angola's rationale for hosting large numbers of Cuban personnel, advance rapprochement

---

35. On Australia's peace-keeping availability, see Brian Toohey, *Australian Financial Review,* June 19, 1978; Frank Cranston, *Canberra Times,* August 1, 1978, and Tony Walker and Stephen Nisbet, Melbourne *Age,* August 2, 1978. For general assessments of Australia's African policies see Christopher Ashton, *Australian Financial Review,* August 31, 1976, and Brian Toohey, *ibid.,* June 17, 1977, and June 13, 1978.

between Angola and Zaire, and lower chances for the fashioning of a Soviet belt of influence across the lower part of the continent. The Australian Government's expressions have been clear. On justifying aid to Mozambique: "the surest way to push southern Africa into the hands of communists and into increasingly radical tendencies is to refuse Western understanding and sympathy, and some assistance, in recognition of the plea of the black majority in Africa."[36] On opposing South African apartheid: Without peaceful change scores of thousands might die in armed conflict, and "If there were external intervention, the implications could be incalculable for Africa and for the international community."[37] On Zimbabwe: Some feel that the Smith regime should be supported because it is anti-Communist. But "If you want a door open to communism in Africa, people will then support a racist white minority regime that denies political equality for the great and overwhelming majority."[38]

This reasoning synchronizes with public Australian denunciations of chronically disruptive Soviet intentions in the Indian Ocean region. If the Government's strategic assumptions are granted, this is not inconsistent with advocacy of policies designed to check the Soviets in the Indian Ocean, particularly through a firm American posture. Indeed, conciliatory, pragmatic Australian policies on the continent are believed to add weight and credibility in Washington to Australia's tough Indian Ocean position.

Australia's formal position has been that there should be a military balance in the Indian Ocean at the lowest practical level. "Zone of peace" proposals are regarded as foreseeably premature and impractical, though Peacock has speculated that the concept itself could serve as a restraint on the great powers.[39] But, as previously suggested, the Australian notion of "balance" tends to translate into a Western and especially American capability advantage in the region. Carter's early, declared objective of a "demilitarized" Indian Ocean was especially unsettling to Australia, until assurances were obtained that the President has used the expression as a rhetorical gambit to induce the Soviets to negotiate seriously on Indian Ocean as well as other arms issues.[40]

36. Peacock, memorandum entitled "Notes on Southern African Issues," distributed to Liberal Government Parliamentarians, August 1977, transcript.

37. Peacock, address to World Conference for Action Against Apartheid, Lagos, August 23, 1977, in Embassy of Australia, Press and Information Office, Washington, *Press Release* No. 20/77, transcript.

38. Fraser, cited in Melbourne *Age,* August 30, 1977.

39. Peacock, "Dr. Camilleri and Australian Foreign Policy," *Current Affairs Bulletin,* Vol. 53 (March 1977), p. 8.

40. For instance, see Stephen Barber, *Far Eastern Economic Review,* April 8, 1977; Fraser's London press conference of May 31, 1977, transcript; Fraser's Washington press conference of June 22, 1977, transcript.

The Fraser Government's efforts at realizing its security objectives in the Indian Ocean have taken several forms. It has worked to keep its views fully explained to the United States, and has succeeded in obtaining exceptional access since the beginning of Russo-American Indian Ocean force negotiations. It has tried to elicit American promises that Australian and more broadly ANZUS alliance interests would be respected. Hence the July 1977 ANZUS Council communiqué was especially gratifying, in that it pledged that "any arms limitations agreement must be balanced in its effects and consistent with the security interests of the ANZUS partner."[41] A subsequent letter from Vance to Peacock promised that any arms agreement "will not in any way qualify or derogate from the US commitment to Australia or limit our freedom to act in implementing our commitment under the ANZUS treaty," that the Soviets had been so advised, and specifically that joint exercises in the Indian Ocean under ANZUS aegis would not be affected.[42]

Australia has desired the preservation of effective American nuclear strike, surveillance and other capabilities in the Indian Ocean. It therefore has cautioned against hasty and prejudicial force reduction bargaining concessions, and has been a firm supporter of upgrading efforts at the Diego Garcia facility. It has also tried to confirm the ability of Australia and American forces to maneuver in the Indian Ocean, of continued American access to Australia-based facilities, and to gain assurances that in time of emergency American forces could sail in strength into Australia's western and northwestern approaches. Australia was therefore delighted by the language of Vance's communication to Peacock. It was also very satisfied by Mondale's announcement in May 1978 that a major United States-Australian naval and air exercise would be staged in the Indian Ocean. It correctly understood the United States to have had a double motive for encouraging the exercise: To reassure Australia that the United States cared about the alliance, and to notify the Soviets that their Indian Ocean buildup was being answered.[43]

Throughout its term of office, the Fraser Government has taken concrete steps to enhance American capabilities in the Indian Ocean region, to involve America on Australia's broad, western flank.[44] Australia has for some time coordinated its antisubmarine and other surveillance in the South Pacific and in the Indian Ocean, but under Fraser tried to extend the principle to joint

41. ANZUS Council communiqué, in Department of Foreign Affairs *News Release,* No. D9, July 28, 1977. The 1978 ANZUS Council communiqué also reflected this sentiment.

42. Mike Steketee, *Sydney Morning Herald,* June 10, 1978.

43. See for instance Fraser *CPD,* HR, May 9, 1978, p. 2028.

44. For reviews of Australia's rationales, see F. A. Mediansky's articles in *Australian Financial Review,* August 9, 1977, and June 16, 1978.

surveillance efforts in sectors of the region. Australia's own naval presence in the Indian Ocean was scheduled for expansion. Very early in its tenure, the Government greatly pleased Washington by rescinding the standing ban on port visits by nuclear-powered vessels. It accelerated the building program at the Cockburn Sound naval base in Western Australia, and offered generous use of it to American vessels. Australian aircraft occasionally pass through Diego Garcia, and Australia has been eager to have continued use made of its Cocos Islands facilities by American aircraft flying in the eastern Indian Ocean.

Australia is a party to the NPT and shows no signs of moving toward a nuclear capability. It has taken a hard, anti-proliferation stand in world councils (including terms on which it is willing to sell its uranium), in its advocacy of stringent international nuclear controls, and in its recommendations for nuclear and general disarmament.[45] At the same time, in its desire that the great power nuclear balance not be tilted to Soviet advantage and that the United States maintain its strategic capabilities, Australia has continued to endorse the operation of American defense facilities on its soil. Among these is the United States naval communications station at the North-West Cape, Western Australia, whose ultra-low frequency transmissions are beamed to ballistic missile-equipped and other submarines. In Australia's interior are Pine Gap and Nurrungar, part of a space defense system concerned with monitoring Soviet and Chinese nuclear missile launchings, systems and tests. They contribute to an American strategic retaliatory as well as deterrent capability. In the context of a renewed search for strategic arms controls, they can serve in a conflict management role. To the extent that the capabilities of the various American facilities have over time been upgraded, their usefulness to the United States has risen.[46] In 1977, the Fraser Government extended the Pine Gap arrangement for an additional ten year period.

Australian security assumptions and policies under the Fraser Government have been subjected to considerable criticism from both academic and partisan quarters. Preferred alternative policy options fall beyond the compass of this study. At minimum, however, it is useful to notice some of the main areas where the Government has been challenged on its estimates of actual security conditions, on its assessments of great power interrelationships, and on the effectiveness of Australia's responses.

45. For a good summary, see Fraser's address to the Special Session of the General Assembly Devoted to Disarmament, June 5, 1978, transcript, issued by the Australian Mission to the United Nations.
46. See, for instance, Ian Reinecke, *Australian Financial Review*, May 19 and June 29, 1978, and Brian Toohey, *ibid.*, June 23, 1978.

The Australian Government has been especially chided for exaggerating the security significance of Soviet power, whether such power has been projected in basically non-military form (as in the South Pacific), or in military terms (as in the Indian Ocean). Obversely, complaints have been raised that the Government has *underestimated* the radical leanings and potential pro-Communist orientations of black African states and movements whom Australia supports precisely to reduce prospects for disorder and Soviet influence.

More generally, Australian assessments of great power relations have been alternatively described as confused or naive. In a changing international and regional Asian-Pacific environment, the Fraser Government has itself admitted that the American role will be less conspicuous, and that Australia's self-reliance requirements will be greater. But the criticism runs that Australia has not successfully forsaken traditional strategic assumptions about an American leadership role virtually tantamount to hegemony. Perhaps the Liberal Government cannot foreseeably manage this transition, since a central part of its displayed "self-reliance" is aimed at preserving American presence, reactive capability and will. From a different direction, it has been asked whether there is still another, basic, conceptual flaw in the Government's approach. The Government is seen to believe that the United States, Japan, China and Australia, states with quite different interests, can be brought together to thwart Soviet designs *and* to assure stability in South-East Asia. Only Australia, and perhaps China but in a very qualified way, are actually congruent in this respect.[47]

Australian policies as such have also been sharply questioned. An especially common complaint has been that not only has Australia failed to reconcile its ostensible preference for regional balances with its support for anti-Soviet responses, but that its responses are counter-productive to the overriding objective of stable conditions sought by Australia. Thus the observation of Bill Hayden, now Leader of the ALP Opposition, that the Government refuses to acknowledge a critical paradox in its approach to the Indian Ocean. Its "tactics, if successful, are guaranteed to create a sort of instability which would require a much larger permanent US presence. The balance the government says it wants in the Indian Ocean is really the launching pad from which great power rivalry takes off in an area previously free of this potentially deadly competition."[48]

47. See especially J. L. S. Girling, "Australia and Southeast Asia in the Global Balance," *Australian Outlook,* Vol. 31 (April 1977), esp. pp. 12-15.

48. W.G. Hayden, "The Soviet Naval Presence in the Indian Ocean: Implications for Australian Defence Policies," in *ibid.,* p. 198.

There is another line of objection to Australian policy that has been about for several years, but whose thrust is argued to be increasingly relevant. The view is that Australia has remained unduly preoccupied with South-East Asia, its traditional area of security concern. Instead, Australia should have been concentrating on threats posed to itself by great power competition. For Australia to enter into commitments with South-East Asian or South Pacific states, Hedley Bull has argued, "represents a net liability and not an asset." These countries cannot make much contribution to Australia's security, and "Regional involvement therefore cannot represent a basis for Australia's foreign policy."[49] As case in point, some would say that Australia's security-based infatuation with maintaining cordial relations with Indonesia repeatedly subjects Canberra to policy dilemmas, as respecting East Timor, the Irian Jaya-PNG border, and the human rights/arms transfer nexus. It has also been remarked that inadequate Australian defense budgets, and therefore adulterated military capabilities, are incompatible with desired security outcomes. This is said to apply whether defense capabilities are designed to impress and serve alongside the United States, or to reflect a genuinely self-reliant posture to deal with low and middle-level disturbances in the regional environment without invoking the assistance of the powerful American protector.

The Australian-American security relationship has been brought under especially close scrutiny. The long-standing argument that American defense facilities in Australia increase Australia's vulnerability to attack or to be held hostage continues to be heard. The Fraser Government is seen as refusing to act in a responsible, moderating role on Russo-American Indian Ocean force reduction negotiations. The net effect has not only been that the arms race has been fueled, but "to associate Australia with the most hawkish elements in the Pentagon and, in the event of war, to make Australian cities [as well as the American defense facilities] a surer target than ever before."[50]

The limitations of Australia's ability to bring about intended American security responses have been frequently mentioned, including by persons who basically favor continuing Australian security links with the United States. One line of argument has stressed an essentially episodic but no less important problem—that Fraser is basically out of step with Jimmy Carter's nationalist, economically-minded, moralistic approach, and that therefore Australia cannot expect a sympathetic reception in Washington.[51] Others, without necessarily

---

49. Hedley Bull, "Options for Australia," in Australian Institute of International Affairs, *Foreign Policy for Australia. Choices for the Seventies* (Sydney: Angus and Robertson, 1973), p. 148.

50. J. Camilleri, "Fraser's Foreign Policy—The First 12 Months," *Current Affairs Bulletin,* Vol. 53 (January 1977), p. 12.

51. Specifically, F. A. Mediansky, "An Assessment of the Fraser Government's Foreign Policy," *Pacific Defence Reporter,* June 1977.

challenging the Fraser Government's security assumptions and policies, emphasize the prudence of adjusting ANZUS, and the American alliance generally, to realistic proportion. Continuing alliance benefits to Australia, ranging from intelligence exchanges to an ultimate American nuclear security umbrella, are in various degree acknowledged. But the alliance's reliability as an "on call" mechanism to invoke American support for assorted and essentially Australian-defined security concerns is analyzed as weaker than before, reconfirming that Australia counts for less to the United States than vice versa.[52] Other critics have taken a much longer jump, choosing to write off or invalidate any meaningful security benefits of the alliance for Australia, and to treat the alliance as frankly an albatross round Australia's neck.[53]

It is not the purpose of this study to serve a protagonist's role. Hindsight will help to judge the wisdom and effectiveness of Australian policies and the validity of critiques. Most of the regional or global security-related outcomes of interest to Australia that have been emerging as the Fraser Government moves toward completing its third year in office only partially or not at all can be traced to Australian influence. Still, given its guiding strategic conceptions and assumptions, the Fraser Government can take reasonable satisfaction from the evolution of the policies of the United States, the great power on whose performance the Australian Government has predicated so much of its security thinking and behavior. We are reminded of the Fraser Government's misgivings about the general atmosphere of a post-Vietnam America letting slip some of its interest, will and capability, and about the directions of the Carter Administration in particular.

In another study, the present author concluded that, based on such indices as compatability of Australian-American outlooks, the putative utility of the alliance to the United States, and the likely American receptivity to Australian claims, current, Fraser Government-defined security interests enjoy good standing.[54] Succeeding events seem to confirm that judgment, for which a few illustrations would be helpful. For instance, Australia has been

52. Variants of this view have currency within the Australian defense establishment. For instance, see Sir Arthur Tange, "Defence Policy Making in Australia," *Pacific Defence Reporter,* February 1976; Admiral Sir Victor Smith, "A Military View on the Limitations of Australia's Future Defence Capabilities," *Australian Journal of Defence Studies,* Vol. 1 (March 1977), pp. 3-9; (Army) Capt. M. G. Smith, "The Australian-American Alliance: Some Possible Restrictions on a US Response," *Defence Force Journal,* No. 3 (March 1977), esp. pp. 19-21.

53. See the argument of a former senior Australian Diplomat, Malcolm Booker, in his *The Last Domino. Aspects of Australia's Foreign Relations* (Sydney: Collins, 1976), esp. pp. 214-238.

54. Henry S. Albinski, "American Perspectives on the ANZUS Alliance," paper delivered at the Australian Institute of International Affairs Conference on "New Directions in American Foreign Policy. The East Asia-Pacific Region," Canberra, April 1978, forthcoming in *Australian Outlook,* Vol. 32 (August 1978). For other commentaries on the state and prospect of the

eager that the United States not accord low priority to the South-East Asian region, and that it be mindful of the security concerns, morale, and requirements of the ASEAN states themselves. Arguments along these lines made by Peacock and other Australians to the United States have in fact been very close to ASEAN's own regional security perceptions, which in various ways have been communicated by the South-East Asians to Washington.[55] Like Australia, the ASEAN states have supported the continuation of an effective American security presence in the area. Particularly as of 1978, both in word and deed, the American Administration made clear such commitments. Apart from the rundown of ground forces in South Korea, the American military presence in Asia and the Pacific is not to be degraded. The Philippine bases are to be continued, and forces are to be kept quantitatively intact and qualitatively improved. To Australia's relief, the Carter Administration's human rights concerns have generally been adapted to local circumstances, and military assistance programs to nations such as Indonesia and the Philippines have not been shut down. These elements were given pointed definition by Vice-President Mondale during and after his 1978 visit to selected South-East Asian countries, Australia, and New Zealand.

There has also been general American agreement with the Australian assessment that it is Soviet behavior that requires special monitoring, and that China basically contributes to, not distracts from, the regional balance.[56] In the Indian Ocean region, the United States has not promoted a hurried "demilitarization" course, and Soviet actions in the Horn of Africa caused Washington to suspend the Indian Ocean force reduction conversations. As mentioned, Australian-expressed security interests in the Indian Ocean have been fully respected by the United States. The American rationale for joint exercises in the Indian Ocean suited Australia perfectly. We are reminded

---

US-Australian alliance, see Hugh Collins, "Australia and the United States: Assessing the Relationship, and Joseph M. Siracusa, "The State of Australian-American Relations: Some Impressions," conference papers in *ibid.;* F. A. Mediansky, "United States Interests in Australia," *Australian Outlook,* Vol. 30 (April 1976), pp. 136-154; John Edwards' articles in *National Times,* July 8, 1978.

55. For instance, see the summary of a report circulated among ASEAN heads of government at the August 1977 conference in Kuala Lumpur, in Michael Richardson, *Australian Financial Review,* December 29, 1977, and ASEAN reactions during the ASEAN-United States ministerial meetings in August 1978, in David Binder, *New York Times,* August 4, 1978.

56. See for instance Mondale's address at the East-West Center, Honolulu, May 10, 1978 in Office of Vice President's Press Secretary *Release,* transcript; Defense Secretary Brown's address in Los Angeles of February 20, 1978, in Office of the Assistant Secretary of Defense (Public Affairs) *News Release,* No. 85-78; address in Honolulu of June 16, 1978, by Assistant Secretary of State for East Asian and Pacific Affairs Richard Holbrooke, in Department of State, *Current Policy,* No. 24, June 1978. Also note reports of American military preparedness in the area by John Hamilton, *Auckland Star,* April 29, 1978, and Russell Spurr in *Far Eastern Economic Review,* June 2, 1978.

that this was to be a tangible manifestation of American support for the Australian alliance, and for the Soviets a remonstrance. A central Australian objective in southern Africa has been to deny strategic gains to the Soviets. The Government has concluded that this can best be achieved through accommodationist policies toward black African nations and liberation movements. American policy has therefore been welcome in Australia—in this instance because it has been accommodationist rather than protective of white and conservative interests. It is instructive that under a strongly anti-Soviet, balance of power-oriented Fraser Government, Australia seems to have earned acceptability to discharge a delicate peace-keeping function in southern Africa. Concomitantly, at home and in its neighborhood, Australian defense-related resources are being expended in support and encouragement of firm and reliable American security roles.

III. South Africa

The Legacy of the Imperial-Commonwealth Connection

RICHARD DALE

I. The Point of Departure: The Military Transfer Concept[1]

A cursory examination of the literature now available on the South African Defense Force (SADF) would suggest that such literature contains an embarrassment of riches. A more careful scrutiny, however, suggests that, in terms of nominal measurement, it can be grouped into fairly discrete categories covering the first (1880-1881) and second (1899-1902) Anglo-Boer Wars, World Wars I and II, the Korean conflict, and the growth of the SADF as a natural complement to the world isolation engendered by the pursuit of the policy of apartheid. The last category is more appropriately considered as part of the civil-military and foreign policy history of the Republic of South Africa because of the severance of the Commonwealth tie in 1961 and the declaration of the arms embargo against the Republic in 1963.[2]

Because of its ostracism by much of the world, the South African polity is regarded as *sui generis* and a glaring reminder of the potency of white power in

1. The author is most grateful to Southern Illinois University at Carbondale for financial and other support for his research work on, as well as in, Southern Africa. He is indebted to Rear Admiral Edward F. Gueritz of the Royal United Services Institute for Defense Studies in London, Brigadier Willem Otto of the Documentation Service of the South African Defense Force in Pretoria, Miss Jacqueline A. Kalley of the South African Institute of International Affairs in Johannesburg, and Mr. Christopher R. Hill of the Center for Southern African Studies of the University of York (England) for providing source materials, and he wishes to thank Professor Leslie C. Duly of the University of Nebraska-Lincoln, Professor James M. Roherty of the University of South Carolina, Professor Sam C. Sakesian of Loyola University of Chicago, and Professor Claude E. Welch, Jr. of the State University of New York at Buffalo for advice and encouragement. However, only the author is to be held responsible for errors or omissions in the presentation of the data in this paper.

2. As provided for in operative paragraph 3 of United Nations Security Council Resolution 181 (1963) of August 7, 1963 and operative paragraph 5 of United Nations Security Council Resolution 182 (1963) of December 4, 1963.

the deep south of the African continent. Far too often, perhaps because its policies are repugnant to so many, South Africa ends up as a terminal case study, and the literature on South Africa has a strangely configurative appearance. Such an approach is typical of the pre-World War II era of political science.[3] There is thus a patently obvious need to analyze South African defense data within a framework which will permit temporal and spatial comparison with other military institutions.

In order to focus on the legacy of the imperial-Commonwealth connection for South African defense policy, it is instructive to consider the Anglo-South African link from five selected perspectives which can be subsumed under the heading of the military transfer concept. Before enumerating these five categories, it should be stressed that the concept of institutional transfer has been used by historians, such as William B. Hamilton[4] and Richard A. Preston,[5] and by political scientists, such as David E. Apter.[6] An especially helpful utilization of the concept as applied to the post-World War II French and British military decolonization in Africa appears in the work of Chester A. Crocker, a work which does devote some attention to South Africa.[7] Crocker's study is commendable because it is comparative, rather than configurative, in terms of British and French postwar defense policies in Africa and because his formulation of the concept of military transfer[8] is sufficiently broad to encompass the South African experience.

3. See the classic critique in Roy C. Macridis, *The Study of Comparative Government* (New York: Random House, 1955), pp. 1-22. Samuel P. Huntington's pioneering work, *The Soldier and the State: The Theory and Politics of Civil-Military Relations* (Cambridge: The Belknap Press of Harvard University Press, 1957) does consider military forces other than the American ones and can properly be regarded as a work which is comparative in methodology and which illustrates the impact of British, French, and German military systems on the growth and development of the U.S. armed forces.

4. William B. Hamilton, "The Transfer of Power in Historical Perspective," in William B. Hamilton, Kenneth Robinson, and C. D. W. Goodwin (eds.), *A Decade of the Commonwealth, 1955-1964* (Durham, N.C.: Duke University Press, 1966), pp. 25-41.

5. Richard A. Preston, "The Transfer of British Military Institutions to Canada in the Nineteenth Century," in William B. Hamilton (ed.), *The Transfer of Institutions* (Durham, N.C.: Duke University Press; London: Cambridge University Press, 1964), pp. 81-107.

6. David E. Apter, *Ghana in Transition*. Revised ed. (New York: Atheneum, 1963), p. 9 and ftn. 3 on p. 9.

7. Chester A. Crocker, *The Military Transfer of Power in Africa: A Comparative Study of Change in the British and French Systems of Order* (Washington, D.C.: The Johns Hopkins School of Advanced International Studies, unpublished Ph.D. dissertation, 1969), pp. 9, 13, 17, 38, 42, 50, 57, 66, 109-112, 114, 116-117, 127, 130, 132-134, 137-138, 140, 142, 161-165, 167, 170, 178, 202, 213-216, 219-220, 222-227, 262, 302-303, 307, 312, 315, 317-318, 323, 329-335, 357-359, and 421-422.

8. He develops his model in *ibid.*, pp. 13-26, which includes a lucid diagram on p. 18. The basic themes spelled out in the above pages, in the abstract of the dissertation, and in the table of contents are the strategic redeployment by the metropolitan power, the utilization of African manpower, localization, Africanization, the definition of post-colonial defense roles,

The five perspectives in this particular study of Anglo-South African defense links during the half century in which the Union of South Africa existed have been selected in order to build on Crocker's excellent work and in order to allow students of comparative defense policy to analyze the South African experience in such a way that South Africa may be considered an African state (albeit under minority rule) and as a Commonwealth state. Such approaches would permit one to draw comparisons between the Union and African states formerly under British sovereignty, such as Ghana or Kenya, and those old and new members of the Commonwealth outside of the African continent, such as Australia and India.[9] Thus, one could have a solid basis for intra-African and intra-Commonwealth comparative military studies, and the crucial linchpin would be the Anglo-South Africa connection.

Consequently, the first perspective concerns the nature of the South African reliance upon British military institutions and personnel. Such a perspective is based on the assumption of technological dependence upon the metropole and draws attention to the transfer of professional skills, attitudes, equipment, personnel, and plans from the more sophisticated center of the periphery of the empire-Commonwealth. It does not, however, assume that the recipient of such aid is a military non-entity or a *tabula rasa.* In the South African case, one must take into account indigenous military traditions, particularly the Afrikaner ones. One of the most striking examples of Afrikaner prowess is the fact that quite a number of Western military observers and attachés were involved in the 1899-1902 Anglo-Boer War and their reports are now being translated and published in an official South African military journal.[10] The British public and their armed forces were sometimes chagrined at the quality of at least some elements of the British defense establishment in that particular war, which was followed by an attempt to improve its organization, leadership, and martial skills.[11]

---

and military development in the former dependency. These categories are broad enough to include South Africa, and other researchers have dealt with the topic of the utilization of non-whites in the South African defense establishment.

9. A companion study would be Stephen P. Cohen, *The Indian Army: Its Contribution to the Development of a Nation* (Berkeley, Los Angeles: University of California Press, 1971).

10. C. de Jongh and J. Ploeger, "Verslae van Neutrale Militêre Waarnemers tydens die Anglo-Boeroorlog," *Militaria* (Pretoria) vol. 4, no. 1 (1973), pp. 1-34 and vol. 4, no. 2 (1973), pp. 1-12; C. de Jong, "Verslae van Neutrale Militêre Waarnemers tydens die Anglo-Boeroorlog," *Militaria,* vol. 5, no. 1 (1975), pp. 46-56 and vol. 5, no. 2 (1975), pp. 54-65; C. de Jong and E. Foxcroft, "Reports of Neutral Military Observers during the Anglo-Boer War," *Militaria,* vol. 5, no. 3 (1975), pp. 1-21 and vol. 5, no. 4 (1975), pp. 49-61; and C. de Jongh, "Reports of Neutral Military Observers on the Anglo-Boer War, 1899-1902," *Militaria,* vol. 6, no. 1 (1976), pp. 52-56.

11. Consult Brian Bond, *The Victorian Army and the Staff College, 1854-1914* (London: Eyre Methuen Ltd., 1972), pp. 181-211 and Gwyn Harries-Jenkins, *The Army in Victorian*

The second perspective concerns South African defense cooperation within the empire-Commonwealth. This particular perspective does assume that the Union defense forces have the requisite capabilities to undertake military tasks on behalf of the imperial government in London or to participate in combined maneuvers or military campaigns. In other words, the part is assumed to be able to contribute something of worth to the whole. In this sense, there is reciprocity involved in the transfer of military skills and resources, especially as the technological gap between the center and the periphery of the empire-Commonwealth begins to close. It is well illustrated by Jan C. Smuts' membership in the British Imperial War Cabinet in the First World War and his elevation to the rank of Field Marshal in the Second World War.[12]

Imperial and Commonwealth defense cooperation, particularly in wartime do raise issues of political consent, and General Smuts had been dubbed a handyman of empire by his political foes in Afrikanerdom.[13] Such an epithet suggests a third perspective in the military transfer concept, namely, the external mission of the South African military forces. The Union of South Africa has had a long history of divisiveness within its white body politic about just where its armed forces should be engaged and how the military instrument can best be used to protect and advance South African national interests. Questions such as these are, in practice, inextricably bound up with the conduct of foreign affairs.

The fourth perspective, which is analytically separate, is the internal mission of the South African armed forces. Both the external mission and the internal mission are at the civilian-military interface and have a marked impact upon the conduct of foreign and domestic affairs, especially in terms of budgetary allocations and manpower needs. In addition, there is the nettlesome question of boundary maintenance between the armed and the police forces, a topic which is of considerable import to students of military intervention.[14]

Society (London: Routledge & Kegan Paul; Toronto and Buffalo: University of Toronto Press, 1977), pp. 2-3.

12. Perhaps more functionally, Jan C. Smuts served as Prime Minister, Foreign Minister, Defense Minister, and Commander-in-Chief in the Second World War, thus aggregating a huge amount of power not unlike his British counterpart, Winston Churchill. See William K. Hancock, *Smuts*. 2 vols (Cambridge: Cambridge University Press, 1962 and 1968), vol. 2, p. 350.

13. This phrase was one used by *Die Burger,* the leading Cape Town Afrikaans-language newspaper, according to T. Dunbar Moodie, *The Rise of Afrikanerdom: Power, Apartheid, and the Afrikaner Civil Religion* (Berkeley, Los Angeles, London: University of California Press, 1975), p. 16. Unfortunately, Moodie does not give the date of the relevant issue of *Die Burger*.

14. See Claude E. Welch, Jr. and Arthur K. Smith, *Military Role and Rule: Perspectives on Civil-Military Relations* (North Scituate, Mass.: Duxbury Press, 1974), pp. 10 and 68-69

Finally, one can investigate the topic of military transfer from the perspective of nation and institution building in the recipient state, in this case, the Union of South Africa. This perspective assumes that the development of the military institution in South Africa does have an impact upon the political development (or even decay) of the nation. To what extent does it involve a redistributive process, does its growth facilitate or impede the rapprochement between Afrikaans-speaking and English-speaking whites, and does it enable the nation to enhance its national bargaining position relative to other Commonwealth members? There is also the added question of whether the Union could be considered (by 1961, when it left the Commonwealth) what Harold D. Lasswell has termed a "garrison state"?[15]

Following a brief discussion of each of the five perspectives, it would be fitting to conclude with some tentative remarks on the state of the literature bearing on the topic of the imperial-Commonwealth legacy. Such tentative conclusions will concern areas that need more thorough investigation and data and areas that appear to hold considerable promise for the comparative study of defense policies particularly within the Commonwealth of Nations.

II. Reliance upon British Institutions and Personnel

Bearing in mind the fact that the basic corpus of legislation for the South African military establishment, the 1912 Defense Act, was placed on the statute books a decade after the termination of the second Anglo-Boer War and only two years after the formation of the Union of South Africa, it is not surprising that the British did maintain troops in the Union in imperial garrisons, such as in Natal Province.[16] Moreover, in the early years of the Union, British officers were seconded to South Africa, although the number seemed to be quite small, and the most senior of the British officers in the

---

and Eric A. Nordlinger *Soldier in Politics: Military Coups and Governments* (Englewood Cliffs, N.J.: Prentice-Hall, Inc., 1977), pp. 54-55.

15. See Huntington, *The Soldier and the State . . .*, pp. 346-350, 360, 391, and 461 and Morris Janowitz, *The Professional Soldier: A Social and Political Portrait* (Glencoe, Ill.: The Free Press, 1960), p. 440. Such comparative analysis could also involve the study of James H. Clotfelter, Jr., namely, *The Garrison State and the American Military: Public Attitudes and Expectations* (Chapel Hill, N.C.: University of North Carolina, unpublished Ph.D. dissertation, 1969).

16. In 1906, six years before the passage of the Defense Act, there were 20,370 imperial troops stationed in South Africa. Great Britain. Parliament. House of Commons. *Debates*, 4th series, vol. 153 (1906), cols. 655-657 as cited in Ernest M. Teagarden, *The Haldane Army Reforms, 1905-1912* (Cleveland: Western Reserve University, unpublished Ph.D. dissertation, 1962), p. 49 and ftn. 9 on p. 49. South Africa acquired the rights to imperial installations in the Union shortly after the end of the First World War, according to Eric A. Walker, "South Africa and the Empire," in Eric A. Walker (ed.), *The Cambridge History of the British Empire. Volume 8: South Africa, Rhodesia and the High Commission Territories* (Cambridge: Cambridge University Press, 1963), p. 787.

Union, General Aston, was involved in the establishment of officer education for both English-speaking and Afrikaans-speaking (or more exactly, Dutch-speaking at that time) aspirants.[17]

Drawing upon the literature concerned with Commonwealth African armies,[18] one would expect to find that at least some South Africans would have attended the prestigious Royal Military Academy at Sandhurst, as was the case for white Rhodesians,[19] but the readily available data suggest that this did not happen very frequently. The writer has so far not found any evidence that Sandhurst was relied upon by the Union Defense Force to train its junior officers. This topic requires further investigation.[20] At the upper echelon of the officer crops, it is known that South Africans did attend the Army, Air Force, and Imperial Defense Colleges in the United Kingdom, but the numbers of such South African officers and the frequency with which these officers were sent to British staff colleges needs to be thoroughly investigated.[21]

British institutions and personnel figured much more prominently in the naval sector. Although General Smuts noted the influence of Swiss military organization upon the drafting of the 1912 Defense Act,[22] the Royal Navy was the preeminent model for the embryo South African navy. Indeed, the naval forces of South Africa were considered to be an adjunct of the Royal Navy and to be incorporated in the Royal Navy in wartime. The disciplinary

17. See Great Britain. *Imperial Conference, 1911: Papers Laid before the Imperial Conference: Naval and Military Defence.* Cd. 5764-2 (London: H.M.S.O., 1911), p. 17 (Appendix A) as collated in Great Britain. Parliament. House of Commons, *Parliamentary Papers,* 1911, vol. 54 and R. H. Beadon, "South African Defence: A Resumé of the South Africa Defence Act of 1912," *Journal of the Royal United Service Institution* (London), vol. 57, no. 421 (March, 1913), p. 349.

18. See especially Crocker, *The Military Transfer . . .,* pp. 198, 270, 272-273, 276, 280, 393-394, 396, 398, 400-404, and 409.

19. *Ibid.,* pp. 281 and 407-408.

20. Both British and South African sources would need to be checked so that only those South Africans who attended Sandhurst (or similar institutions in the U.K.) and were commissioned in the Union Defense Force, rather than in British units, would be counted. For an example of a South African who attended Sandhurst, served with the British forces, and retired in his land of birth, see "Major Darrell D. Hall: The New Chairman," *Military History Journal* (Johannesburg), vol. 4, no. 2 (December, 1977), p. 74. A solid point of departure is F. J. Jacobs, "Die Suid-Afrikaanse Leëkollege," *Militaria,* vol. 4, no. 1 (1973), pp. 63-70.

21. See F. H. Theron, "The Union Defence Forces of South Africa," *The Journal of the Royal United Service Institution,* vol. 75, no. 500 (November, 1930), p. 754. Limited South African data may be found in "Officers Who Took Course at Camberley since Union, Returns," Annexure to Votes and Proceedings No. 828 of 1925 as cited in South Africa. Parliament. House of Assembly, *Index to the Manuscript Annexures and Printed Papers of the House of Assembly Including Select Committee Reports and Bills and Also to Principal Motions and Resolutions and Commission Reports, 1910-1961* (n.p.: author, 1963), p. 82.

22. Sourth Africa. Parliament. House of Assembly, *Debates,* 1912, cols. 624 and 630 (February 23, 1912).

codes under which the South African naval personnel operated were in fact those currently in force in the Royal Navy.[23] The extreme dependency of the Union Defense Force upon the men and ships of the Royal Navy was graphically illustrated by the German South West Africa campaign in the early years of World War I, an operation which had amphibious components in addition to land transportation.[24] The Union Government did initially provide for a subvention to the Royal Navy as a *quid pro quo* for its protective services, but this subvention was ended in the early 1920's.[25] The South Africans contend that their navy began in 1922, a point of national pride.[26] But even as late as 1930, the commander of the South African naval forces was a British officer on loan from the Royal Navy.[27]

The South African Defense Force depended heavily on the metropole for armaments and indeed had no arsenals and defense industries. Moreover, it counted on aircraft from the British to inaugurate its fledgling air force. The reasons for this dependence were rather obvious because the Union was slowly transforming itself from a pastoral, agricultural economy into an industrial and mining one.[28] Only much later in its history can one meaningfully write about any sort of military-industrial complex in South Africa.[29]

III. Cooperation with the Empire-Commonwealth

Within two years after the passage of the 1912 Defense Act, the Union Government under Prime Minister Botha found itself at war with the enemies of the British King, a traumatizing experience for those Afrikaners who remembered the two wars against the United Kingdom. A parallel situation would have arisen had Americans become part of an Anglo-American wartime coalition in about 1826, following the Revolutionary War and the War of 1812. The Botha Government, as a result of his Government's willingness to cooperate with the Empire in the German South West African campaign, found itself faced with a domestic insurgency launched by the more ardent

23. *Ibid.*, col. 629 (February 23, 1912, speech of Defense Minister Jan C. Smuts) and Theron, "The Union Defence Forces . . .," p. 747.

24. H. F. Nel, "Die Rol van die Seemag in Duits Suidwes-Afrika, 1914-15," *Militaria*, vol. 7, no. 2 (1977), pp. 56-69.

25. See the debate concerning that contribution in Africa. Parliament. House of Assembly, *Debates*, 1912, cols. 1407-1432 (March 26, 1912), 1459 (March 28, 1912), and 1754-1755 (April 11, 1912) and also Walker, "South Africa and the Empire," p. 787 regarding the termination of the subvention.

26. J. C. Goosen (compiler), *South Africa's Navy: The First Fifty Years* (Cape Town and Johannesburg: W. J. Flesch & Partners, 1973), p. 15.

27. Theron, "The Union Defence Forces . . .," p. 750.

28. *Ibid.*

29. The subject is explored more fully in David R. Lowin, *Causes and Aspects of the Growth of the South African Defence Force and the Military Industrial Complex, 1960 to 1977* (York, England: University of York, unpublished M. A. thesis, 1977).

Anglophobes in Afrikanerdom. The insurgency was defeated,[30] but the issue of South African neutrality in Empire-Commonwealth wars remained throughout most of the Union period of South African history. One respected scholar of South African politics has argued that the defeat of the Smuts Government in 1948 by the National Party (and its coalition partner, the Afrikaner Party) was not simply the attractiveness of apartheid doctrine to the white electorate but the decision not to remain neutral in World War II.[31]

Without going into detailed campaign histories,[32] the South African units acquitted themselves well in various theaters in the African continent and in Europe in World War I. Their contribution to the Empire defense effort was primarily in land, rather than naval or air, forces. However, General Smuts, who saw active combat in German East Africa against a superb German commander, took an interest in military aviation and has been regarded as one of the founding figures of the Royal Air Force and as an air strategist of some note.[33]

As a result of an agreement reached between Winston Churchill and General Smuts in 1921, the Royal Navy secured the use of the valuable Simonstown base near Cape Town, and the Union Defense Force assumed the responsibility for the security of the base.[34] Given the long primacy of the Royal Navy and the small South African naval establishment, which received marked budgetary cuts during the depression years, there seemed to be little latitude for cooperation between the Royal Navy and its Union counterpart.[35]

With the onset of the Second World War, the arena of naval cooperation was widened, with the principal pattern being the secondment of South

30. For a brief overview of the situation, consult S. B. Spies, "The Outbreak of the First World War and the Botha Government," *South African Historical Journal* (Bloemfontein), no. 1 (November, 1969), pp. 47-57.

31. Newell M. Stultz, *Afrikaner Politics in South Africa, 1934-1948* (Berkeley, Los Angeles, London: University of California Press, 1974), especially p. 157.

32. Such histories are enumerated by J. A. I. Agar-Hamilton, "The Union of South Africa War Histories," in Robin Higham (ed.), *Official Histories: Essays and Bibliographies from around the World* (Manhattan, Kansas: Kansas State University Library, 1970), pp. 443-449 and Neil D. Orpen, "Resources in the Dominions: Part I: British Military History in South Africa," in Robin Higham (ed.), *A Guide to the Sources of British Military History* (Berkeley and Los Angeles: University of California Press, 1971), pp. 321-329.

33. Hancock, *Smuts,* vol. 1, pp. 438-442 and Robin Higham, *The Military Intellectuals in Britain, 1918-1939* (New Brunswick, N.J.: Rutgers University Press, 1966), pp. 132, 149-151, and 195.

34. Nicholas Mansergh, *Survey of British Commonwealth Affairs: Problems of External Policy, 1931-1939* (London, New York, Toronto: Oxford University Press, 1952), p. 238. The matter is examined in greater depth in C. J. R. Dugard, "The Simonstown Agreement: South Africa, Britain and the United Nations," *The South African Law Journal* (Cape Town), vol. 85, part 2 (May, 1968), especially pp. 142-145.

35. Goosen, *South Africa's Navy . . . ,* pp. 16-19.

African naval officers and seamen to the Royal Navy.[36] The Royal Navy did furnish several vessels to the Union naval force, which it operated with its own men and officers, and the South Atlantic and Indian Oceans were a lively combat theater, particularly for German submarines, during the Second World War.[37] Although the Union did not officially develop a Marine Corps until after the onset of the Korean War, South African officers were attached to the Royal Marines during the Second World War.[38]

Although the Union Defense Force did contain an air element[39] and South Africa participated in a Commonwealth scheme for pilot training,[40] a number of South Africans entered the Royal Air Force and participated in the Battle of Britain.[41] Indeed, South Africans have accorded a place of honor to their air aces in World War II, such as "Sailor" Malan, who later became active in a veterans' group concerned about the political position of the Coloreds after the National Party assumed power in 1948.[42]

Aside from those South Africans who volunteered to join British units as such (in a manner similar to American fighter pilots who formed the so-called Eagle Squadron of the R. A. F. in World War II or the Lafayette Escadrille in World War I), the vexing question for the South African military establishment was the operational definition of the South African war zone. Whether a South African serviceman was obligated to serve his tour of duty beyond the land or sea borders of the Union was an extremely contentious issue in both World Wars and further strained ethnic relations within the white body politic.[43]

36. *Ibid.*, pp. 208-215 (Appendix 2) and W. M. Bisset, "New Light on South Africa's Naval Heritage," *Militaria*, vol. 7, no. 4 (1977), pp. 38-44.

37. Goosen, *South Africa's Navy . . .*, pp. 46-47 and 91-110.

38. Deon Fourie, "The South African Corps of Marines," *Military History Journal*, vol. 1 no. 1 (December, 1967), pp. 32-33 and 35 and "Editor's Letter Box," *Military History Journal*, vol. 2, no. 3 (June, 1972), p. 108.

39. See Jan Ploeger, "Belangrike Getuienis oor die Suid-Afrikaanse Lugmag," *Military History Journal*, vol. 1, no. 5 (December, 1969), pp. 1-3 and Sophia du Preez, "Vliegopleidingskool Langebaanweg," *Militaria*, vol. 5, no. 4 (1975), pp. 1-15.

40. According to W. C. B. Turnstall, *The Commonwealth and Regional Defence*. Commonwealth Papers No. 6 (London: The Athlone Press, 1959), p. 10.

41. D. P. Tidy, "South Africans of Seventy Four," *Military History Journal*, vol. 1, no. 1 (December, 1967), pp. 8-9 and D. P. Tidy, "South Africans in the Battle of Britain," *Military History Journal*, vol. 1, no. 7 (December, 1970), p. 37.

42. See the series of articles by D. P. Tidy usually entitled "South African Air Aces of World War II" in *Military History Journal*, vol. 1, no. 2 (June, 1968), pp. 30 and 32; vol. 1, no. 3 (December, 1968), pp. 11-18; vol. 1, no. 4 (June, 1969), pp. 19-22 and 30; vol. 1, no. 5 (December, 1969), pp. 5-6 and 37; vol. 1, no. 6 (June, 1970), pp. 7-13 and 40; vol. 1, no. 7 (December, 1970), pp. 24-26; vol. 2, no. 2 (December, 1971), pp. 57-59; vol. 2, no. 6 (December, 1973), pp. 198-203; and vol. 3, no. 6 (December, 1976), pp. 191-193 and 202.

43. This matter is very carefully examined in Kenneth W. Grundy, *Defense Legislation and Communal Politics: The Evolution of a White South African Nation As Reflected in the Controversy*

Following its participation in the Second World War, the range and intensity of South African cooperation with the metropole and the Commonwealth declined, particularly as the nature of the membership in the postwar Commonwealth changed and the process of British decolonization began to accelerate in Asia and Africa.[44] South African air power was brought to bear in the Berlin blockade and once again in the Korean conflicts,[45] but these two campaigns were not principally Commonwealth endeavors. Neither ground nor naval forces were committed in either campaign or operation, but Anglo-South African naval bonds were strengthened in 1955 by the so-called Simonstown agreement which provided a fillip for the development of South African naval capability because of British arms transfers and sales.[46] In addition, there was desultory consultation between the two governments regarding African continental defense issues, but nothing very concrete in the way of bilateral or multilateral agreements seemed to emerge from these African-based conferences.[47]

IV. The External Mission of the Union Defense Force

One distinguished student of British military policy has analyzed post World War II British defense policy in terms of "the defense of the realm."[48] In the South African case, the same phrase would be apposite, but it would need an operational definition. What was the South African realm the Union Defense Force (UDF) was supposed to protect? Did it have fixed, inelastic borders and to whom did it belong? Answers to these, and related, questions were crucial and were hardly an exercise in military pettifoggery. The answers

---

over the Assignment of Armed Forces Abroad, 1912-1976. Papers in International Studies, Africa Series No. 33 (Athens, Ohio: Ohio University Center for International Studies, 1978).

44. For a succinct analysis of Anglo-South African defense cooperation in the latter days of the Union, see Deon Geldenhuys, "The South African National Party and the British Government (1939-1961)," *Politikon* (Pretoria), vol. 5, no. 1 (June, 1978), particularly pp. 56-60.

45. For details, consult "Partners in Combat," *Backgrounder* (Washington, D.C.: South African Embassy), No. 7 [July] of 1978, pp. 4-8.

46. The text of the agreement is published in Great Britain. Ministry of Defense, *Exchanges of Letters on Defence Matters between the Governments of the United Kingdom and the Union of South Africa, June 1955.* Cmd. 9520 (London: H. M. S. O., 1955) as collated in Great Britain. Parliament. House of Commons, *Parliamentary Papers,* 1955-1956, vol. 45.

47. These conferences are discussed in Tunstall, *The Commonwealth . . .,* pp. 47-48 and in Sam C. Nolutshungu, *South Africa in Africa: A Study in Ideology and Foreign Policy* (Manchester: Manchester University Press, 1975), pp. 65-72 and 299.

48. Richard N. Rosencrance, *Defence of the Realm: British Strategy in the Nuclear Epoch* (New York and London: Columbia University Press, 1968).

one gave to such questions had a significant bearing on the force levels, morale, and equipment needed for the UDF. Difficulties would be encountered, as the British discovered after World War II,[49] if there were a discrepancy between the human and non-human resources, on the one hand, and the mission the UDF was expected to accomplish, on the other hand. The more ambitious the mission, the more the UDF needed in terms of logistical and transport infrastructure, arms, support units, headquarters staff, and trained soldiers, sailors, and airmen. The mission, moreover, would have a bearing on the level of readiness needed for certain types of units in terms of mobilization plans.

As noted earlier, the South African Navy became essentially a phantom organization during the depression, but an attempt was made by Defense Minister Pirow to improve the sad state of the UDF, a project he began in 1934.[50] One of the more controversial Ministers of Defense, who served in General Hertzog's Cabinet, Pirow has been regarded as a Germanophile and one who took a rather narrow view of his mandate as Defense Minister.[51] Following the declaration of war on Germany in early September, 1939, the Cabinet was reshuffled and Pirow's portfolio was taken by General Smuts, who had held that portfolio earlier from 1910 until 1920. Smuts' biographer has recorded the General's displeasure with the way in which Pirow oversaw the gradual rearmament of the Union during his tenure as Defense Minister.[52]

Yet, under General Botha's, Smuts', and Hertzog's premiership from 1924 to 1939, the Prime Minister traditionally held the foreign affairs portfolio, a practice ended only in 1954, when J. G. Strijdom became Prime Minister and Eric H. Louw assumed the title of Minister of External Affairs. Some pioneering research on the South African Cabinet and Parliament has shown that the defense portfolio ranked slightly below the foreign affairs one and neither portfolio was among the top three in the South African cabinet.[53]

---

49. Walter Goldstein, *The Dilemma of British Defense: The Imbalance between Commitments and Resources*. The Social Science Program of the Mershon Center for Education in National Security, The Ohio State University, Pamphlet Series No. 3 (Columbus: Ohio State University Press, 1966).

50. J. van Wyk, "Die Unieverdedigingsmagte op die Vooraand van die Tweede Wêreldoorlog (1934-1939)," *Militaria*, vol. 6, no. 4 (1976), pp. 24-32 and Donald Cowie, "Union of South Africa," *The Journal of the Royal United Service Institution*, vol. 84, no. 534 (May, 1939), pp. 262-268.

51. See Richard H. Young, *Die Omstrede Rol van Oswald Pirow as Minister van Verdediging (1933-1939)* (Cape Town: University of Cape Town, unpublished B. A. (Hons.) thesis, 1975).

52. Hancock, *Smuts*, vol. 2, p. 332.

53. Newell M. Stultz, *Who Goes to Parliament?* Occasional Paper No. 19 (Grahamstown: Rhodes University Institute of Social and Economic Research, 1975), p. 77 (table V-13).

Moreover, notwithstanding the British practice of retaining their military titles,[54] very few South African M.P.s or Senators have been professional military officers before their election to Parliament. Indeed, the backbenchers in Parliament, rather than the middle or top leadership in the chamber, were more likely to have been retired military officers.[55]

These findings, which need to be studied in conjunction with other Commonwealth legislatures and cabinets, would seem to suggest that the South African Defense Ministry was not an *imperium in imperio* and could well have been the poor relative of the more prestigious Office of the Prime Minister and/or Minister of External Affairs. Hence, the UDF could have had a role not unlike the one the French devised for their armed forces, the great mute force.[56] Whether such a doctrine was developed for the UDF and, if so, whether it was carefully observed, is a topic worthy of comparative investigation. Where *la grande muette* would go beyond the confines of the Union, what it would do once it got there, and in cooperation with whom (if anybody) appeared to be questions of *haute politique* best left to the Prime Minister in consultation with himself as Minister of External Affairs.

Perhaps the widest defense perimeter, with all that that implied for the external mission of the UDF, was drawn by General Smuts himself. Well known for his desire to extend the Union's political influence beyond the Zambesi in the wake of the First World War and the heyday of white settlement in Central and Eastern Africa,[57] his visions of a type of manifest destiny were readily transmuted into defense arcs. Speaking on a motion dealing with the conduct of World War II before the Senate in Cape Town, the Prime Minister said that

> Hon. Senators who like myself have travelled about this Continent and know its geographical features will admit that our own borders are singularly indefensible. The line of the Limpopo [River] cannot be held. . . .
>
> Our northern boundary cannot be held. If you want to defend this country you will have to proceed a great distance beyond it, and the

---

54. John Sabine, "Civil-Military Relations," in John Baylis (ed.), *British Defence Policy in a Changing World* (London: Croom Helm Ltd., 1977), p. 240 and ftn. 29 on p. 251.

55. Furthermore, such persons were found more often in the United, rather than the National, Party. See Stultz, *Who Goes to Parliament,* pp. 25, 30 (table III-3), 46 (table IV-4), 65, and 90 (table VI-5).

56. See the discussion of the *grande muette* model of civil-military relations in Welch and Smith, *Military Role and Rule. . .*, pp. 208-212.

57. One of the best documented and most recent studies dealing with this topic, which builds on some of the finest antecedent works, is Martin Chanock, *Britain, Rhodesia and South Africa, 1900-45: The Unconsummated Union* (Totowa, N.J.: Frank Cass and Company Limited, 1977).

question then arises how far beyond it. Those who know this continent know that the proper line of defence is in the highlands of Kenya and once you have lost that line, you have lost your best positions. . . .

Present forms of warfare make it necessary for us, if we mean to defend ourselves, to defend ourselves far to the north, far beyond our borders.[58]

Even though it did take in a huge chunk of the continent, Prime Minister Smuts' excursion into geopolitics was still considerably smaller than that of his British mentors or his (non-Vichy) French allies, who had global responsibilities. Whatever else the external mission of the UDF has been, it certainly was not one of a South African Foreign Legion poised to go anywhere at any time. It is doubtful whether the UDF could ever be regarded as an example of Professor Morris Janowitz's constabulary concept, which seems more appropriate for metropolitan or technologically advanced nations.[59]

V. The Internal Mission of the Union Defense Force

The nature of the internal mission of the UDF was, in the final analysis, a police force of the last resort once the frontier had been secured before the formation of the Union following the Second Anglo-Boer War. Much of pre-twentieth century South African history consists of skirmishes between Afrikaner mounted units (commandos) or British regiments stationed in the Cape or Natal Province, on the one hand, and Africans, on the other. Frontier wars were the expected concomitant of expanding white settlement in the southern part of the continent.

Stemming from these conflicts between the African and the Briton or Afrikaner, a principle developed among the whites that Africans should not be in a position, by virtue of military training and the possession of modern arms,[60] to challenge effectively the asymmetrical balance of power between Africans and whites. Such a principle was operative in the American West in the last century, and the U.S. Army made the West secure for the white settlers. The late Leo Marquard's observation that South Africa was an empire of its own, with the whites constituting the metropole and the Africans, Asians, and Coloreds the colony,[61] is applicable to the United States in the

58. South Africa, Parliament. Senate, *Debates*, 1940-1941, cols. 13-14 (September 12, 1940).

59. Janowitz, *The Professional Soldier* . . ., pp. 418-430.

60. For the military perspective, see W. L. Speight, "Gun-Running in South Africa," *The Journal of the Royal United Services Institution*, vol. 79, no. 516 (November, 1934), pp. 765-768 as well as Mr. Legum's reply to Commodore R. Harrison's question in Colin Legum, "South Africa," *The Journal of the Royal United Service Institution*, vol. 102, no. 607 (August, 1957), especially pp. 315-316.

61. Leopold Marquard, *South Africa's Colonial Policy* . . . (Johannesburg: South African Institute of Race Relations, 1957).

nineteenth century with reference to the American Indians. The parallel is only a rough one because of the different ratios involving the number of whites and the American Indians, on the one hand, and the South African non-whites, on the other hand, and the practice of migratory labor in South Africa, which did not characterize the American Indians. The U.S. Army points with pride to what is called "civic action" work among the Indians in the nineteenth century, not to mention the work it also undertook in the governance of Eskimos in Alaska for a short while in that century.[62]

Drawing upon the U.S. experience, it would be logical to inquire whether the UDF was involved in comparable work in the African reservations. There seems to be little evidence to suggest that the UDF in its half century of existence engaged in such activities, presumably leaving the governance of Africans to the civil authorities. Moreover, in the application of violence, the South African Police were more accustomed to dealing with African unrest in the post-1910 era. However, the UDF was involved in several instances of quelling domestic insurrection among striking whites in the Witwatersrand[63] and in cooperating with Police units in containing potential African insurgency.[64]

In addition to the maintenance of law and order in the Union, the armed forces did engage in typical engineering and exploring duties common to peacetime military units. The Navy was engaged in charting South African coastal waters,[65] while one Army unit known as the Special Service Battalion was developed during the depression as a means to effect employment of impoverished young South Africans, particularly Afrikaners.[66] This battalion was, to some extent, comparable to the American Civilian Conservation Corps which operated during the depression and which was managed with the assistance of the U.S. Army. During those times when it was not engaged in full-scale combat, as in both World Wars and the Korean War (which

62. Harry F. Walterhouse, *A Time To Build: Military Civic Action: Medium for Economic Development and Social Reform.* University of South Carolina Institute of International Studies, Studies in International Affairs No. 4 (Columbia, S.C.: University of South Carolina Press, 1964), p. 59.

63. On the 1914 Rand strike, see J. Ploeger, "Hoofstukke uit de Vooren Vroeë Geskiedenis van die SAW," *Militaria,* vol. 1, no. 3 (1969), particularly pp. 64-87. On the 1922 Rand strike, consult J. Ploeger, "Op Brandwag: Drie Eeue Militêre Geskiedenis van Suid-Afrika," *Militaria,* vol. 1, no. 4 (1969), especially pp. 28-29 and Norman Heard, *1922: The Revolt on the Rand* (Johannesburg: Blue Crane Books, 1966).

64. See, for example, Tom Lodge, "The Cape Town Troubles, March-April, 1960," *Journal of Southern African Studies,* vol. 4, no. 2 (April, 1978), p. 236.

65. Goosen, *South Africa's Navy . . .,* pp. 29-35.

66. See W. Otto, "Die Spesiale Diensbataljon (1933-1939)," in W. Otto *et al., Die Spesiale Diensbataljon (1933-1973).* Publikasie No. 2 (Pretoria: Sentrale Dokumentasiediens, S. A. W., 1973), pp. 82-83.

involved only the Air Force), or in acting as a support unit for the Police Force in quelling labor and/or African unrest, the UDF presumably spent its time in traditional military activities, such as parades, maneuvers, instruction, sports, and the other rituals associated with garrison life. Whether the UDF had any internal missions that were unique, aside from maintaining the structure of white power, remains to be seen.

VI. The Union Defense Force in Nation and Institution Building

With the onset of decolonization by the major Western powers in the decades following the termination of World War II, it has become increasingly important to examine whether and how the establishment of a post-independence military instrument has facilitated the process of growth by undertaking such tasks as inculcating loyalty to the nation, leaders, and symbols, teaching literacy and basic hygiene to its recruits, building roads, maintaining communication channels, and so forth. Although structurally geared for its ultimate mission of combat, the armed forces in fledgling states may be schools for political socialization, ethnic arithmetic (mixing the so-called martial groups with those noted for other arts), inculcating new attitudes regarding frugality, national honor, and a willingness to put the welfare of the military unit above that of oneself. Whether such a litany of virtues is actually operative in the new nations is the key question, and the rash of army *coups d'état* that has taken place in the last decade suggests that military institutions and political decay are not necessarily antithetical.[67]

Turning to the UDF, what observations might one make about its contribution to the building of the nation known as the Union of South Africa and to the military capabilities of that nation? Has the South African experience with British decolonization in the military sphere been similar to that of other African states now under majority rule? Or ought South Africa to be relegated to the *sui generis* category?

There are several approaches one can take in order to make some tentative assessments about the contribution the UDF has made in the field of nation building. First, as South Africa scholars point out, the Union was, to a large extent, the result of the labors of senior Afrikaner officers who had faced the British on the field of battle; it was "the age of the generals,"[68] namely Botha, Hertzog, and Smuts. Yet none of the three generals was a career military officer or a graduate of an accredited military academy. Two of the

---

67. Walterhouse, *A Time To Build . . .*, pp. 60-64.

68. Hendrik W. van der Merwe *et al., White South African Elites: A Study of Incumbents of Top Positions in the Republic of South Africa* (Cape Town: Juta & Company Ltd., 1974), p. 115 and D. W. Krüger, *The Age of the Generals: A Short Political History of the Union of South Africa, 1910-1948* (Johannesburg: Dagbreek Book Store [Pty.] Ltd., 1961).

three took to the field in World War I to conduct operations against the Germans in South West Africa and East Africa, and one of the three held the portfolio of defense for almost two decades, albeit at different times. Moreover, two of the three Defense Ministers who served in successive Hertzog cabinets held a military title (Mentz and Creswell). Indeed, of all those six men who held the defense portfolio, 1910-1961, only two (Pirow and Erasmus) had not seen active duty at some time in their life; those two were advocates (lawyers) by profession.[69]

It seems plausible to believe that the UDF at least had access to the Minister of Defense because of shared military experiences, but whether access could be equated with influence was another question. Professor Stultz's findings[70] would suggest, though, that the Defense Minister *qua* Defense Minister was not necessarily the gatekeeper to the councils of the greatest power in the Union. Yet this Minister of Defense appeared to have had enough influence to prevent an estrangement between the UDF and the civilian polity. Civilian control, in brief, did not seem to have been a problem for the South African Government. The tradition of Cincinnatus was the dominant one in Afrikaner culture and this meshed easily with the Swiss participatory tradition which was so attractive to the drafters of the 1912 Defense Act. Both such traditions in and of themselves seem highly conducive to nation building, and both traditions are geared toward ground, rather than air and sea, warfare.

The British tradition complemented the Afrikaner one by adding the naval dimension which might be viewed as one of the ironies of South African history because the British consistently wanted to deny the Afrikaner trekkers an outlet to the ocean. It seems reasonable to surmise that the notions of *noblesse oblige,* class consciousness, public school virtues, and stress on amateurism in the Victorian Army officer corps[71] were immiscible with regard to the UDF. If indeed such is found to be correct, then one might expect to find that the British influence was far greater in the naval establishment than in the ground units. Perhaps the air force would be the most evenly balanced of the three services in terms of national derivation.

During World War I and II, the South Africans were able to furnish a credible fighting force which performed with commendable skill and gallantry, but yet the use of the military instrument on behalf of the imperial power against a nation which sympathized with the Afrikaners in 1899-1902 was a

---

69. Data concerning the various Cabinet positions, 1910-1961 were obtained from *State of South Africa: Economic, Financial and Statistical Year-Book for the Republic of South Africa, 1969* (Johannesburg: Da Gama Publishers [Pty.] Ltd., n. d.), pp. 44-48.

70. See notes 53 and 55 above.

71. These are some of the themes that emerge in Harries-Jenkins, *The Army in Victorian Society,* chapters 2-7.

risky venture from the standpoint of intra-white harmony in the Union. Professor Grundy's monograph[72] shows quite clearly the centrifugal political forces unleashed by employing the UDF in combat beyond the borders of the Union. Given the emotional baggage associated with the 1899-1902 war, on the one and, and the persistent call of the Afrikaner nation and secular religion,[73] on the other hand, the UDF seemed to have had only a small role to play in the nation building process. There were, in effect, two processes occurring simultaneously: the creation of an Afrikaner nation restricted to members of the chosen people and the creation of a larger nation consisting of those members of both language groups who viewed each other as neighbors and potential friends. So long as the imperial power did not intrude on the difficult work of building coalitions between the more moderate elements of both ethnic groups by putting the UDF to the test of battle involving the metropole, one could expect that the UDF could be a very useful vehicle of nation building. One wonders just how high a political cost African armies would have to pay were they to join in coalition warfare with their former metropoles. The role of the UDF in South African nation building is one that needs greater study, but within a comparative framework. Perhaps the question can be more effectively analyzed by disaggregating the UDF and looking at the different combat arms and support units. The Special Service Battalion, noted earlier, could very well be the most functional military organization from the standpoint of forging national unity.

VII. The Point of Return: A Tentative Appraisal

This preliminary inquiry has centered about the concept of military transfer, a concept which was examined from five particular perspectives. In the course of the inquiry it was assumed that the transaction flows were not unidirectional and that the emerging South African military system represented a synthesis of both British and Afrikaner models and traditions. It is possible that the process of transfer is more complicated and that it could well have involved more than the two governments and their respective armed forces. For example, it is conceivable that the South Africans emulated more than just one model and that, like Black Africans to the north of them, they tried to maximize the number of military donors, thus reducing the dependence on one single donor. Such shopping on the international market is predicated on the grant of independence, so that South Africa has had roughly a three decade lead (counting from the date of the Statute of West-

---

72. See note 43 above.

73. Consult Moodie, *The Rise of Afrikanerdom . . .*, chapters 1 and 5-11 for a fuller exposition of the potency of Afrikaner nationalism.

minster of 1931) on its fellow states in Anglophone Africa. Consequently, it would be important to scrutinize the various postings of South African military attachés as an indicator of possible traffic flows in doctrine, equipment, education, and planning. The Swiss connection in the 1912 Defense Act suggests that the Afrikaners may have learned more from the neutral foreign observers in the 1899-1902 war than one would have originally surmised. Indeed, the Afrikaners were able to attract volunteers from many nations to aid them in their Second War of Independence (as they term it).

Following the same line of reasoning, it is possible that the transfer process was mediated by a fellow Commonwealth member, such as Australia, for example, or even Rhodesia (which was not a full-fledged member of the Commonwealth although it enjoyed some of the club benefits). Here again the nature of the possible communications network needs to be scrutinized.

A third strategy of inquiry would be to examine the three principal branches of the UDF to determine which had the highest and which the lowest local content, to use the idiom of automobile manufacturers in present day South Africa. What data are readily accessible would suggest that the Navy would have the highest British (or Commonwealth) content, while the ground forces would be a blend of both Afrikaner commando and British regimental traditions and models. Presumably, the Air Force would tilt more toward the British than the Afrikaner mold, if only for reason of industrial production and plant facilities. A subsidiary question would concern the research and development aspect of technology transfers to the UDF. South African weapons and engineering costs would depend to some extent on what development work the UDF was able to do on its own. One nation's capabilities may well represent the other nation's vulnerabilities.

In the fourth place, not enough is known about the origins, training, assignments, overseas travel and posting of the elite of the UDF officer corps. Such a study could be based on the methodology utilized by Professor Janowitz in his classical work, *The Professional Soldier* (1960). Presumably if the British or Commonwealth connection is valued, those with such credentials could logically be expected to reach the inner elite of the officer corps. One might also ascertain whether in the Union officer corps there was an Old Boy network resembling the British network.

A fifth area for further investigation concerns the type of work undertaken by Professor Huntington and Professor Stultz. The area of civil-military relations and the allied defense decision-making processes at both executive and legislative levels constitute new research frontiers for those interested in comparative defense studies. Were British models of civilian control part of the Westminster heritage or were the models taken from the nineteenth century Transvaal or Orange Free State? Are the findings of scholars such as Professor William P. Snyder, an acknowledged expert on the conduct of British defense policy in the post-World War II era, applicable to South Africa?[74] For those who are conversant with the literature on decision-making, why is so little written on the roles of the various South African Defense Ministers, who seem to be more neglected by the students of South African affairs than their opposite numbers in the Ministry of External Affairs? There is a growing body of literature on South African foreign policy and diplomatic history, for example, by such scholars as Professor Amry Vandenbosch,[75] Professor J. E. Spence,[76] Professor James Barber,[77] and Professor Sam C. Nolutshungu.[78]

Admittedly, research on defense establishments is difficult, particularly on the contemporary period. However, by reaching as far back as 1910 for data, one can engage in worthwhile and creative research. What appears to be needed is an awareness that comparative defense studies can build on a solid theoretical base and can equally profit from the concept of military institutional transfer. In the 1970s, the South Africans themselves appear to have taken a deep interest in their own military history and have devoted public and private resources in search of their own martial roots. What appears to be lacking, however, is a clear focus for such a search.

74. William P. Snyder, *The Politics of British Defense Policy, 1945-1962* (Columbus: Ohio State University Press, 1964).

75. Amry Vandenbosch, *South Africa and the World: The Foreign Policy of Apartheid* (Lexington: The University Press of Kentucky, 1970).

76. J. E. Spence, "South Africa and the Modern World," in Monica Wilson and Leonard Thompson (eds.), *The Oxford History of South Africa.* 2 vols. (New York and Oxford: Oxford University Press, 1969 and 1971), vol. 2, pp. 477-527.

77. James Barber, *South Africa's Foreign Policy, 1945-1970* (London: Oxford University Press, 1973).

78. See note 47 above.

The Evolving Experience

DEON F. S. FOURIE

1. An Approach to South African Policy

It is probably true to say that one cannot adequately comprehend the motives which have resulted in the South African government's using military force as a response to situations containing elements of crisis and heightened political tension without a prior knowledge of the experience of South African governments in similar situations in the past.

In assessing South Africa's resort to military action and also bellicose statements by politicians, people in other countries tend to assume that their own experience in dealing with crises and warlike situations as well as their own perceptions of military response pertain equally to the South African government and military leaders. There appears to be an absence of appreciation of the extent to which South Africa lacks a body of experience or even precedent for decision taking in times of emergency or crisis as a consequence of her former complete dependancy on the British government in such matters and as a consequence of the absence of any direct threats facing the country. Yet when one looks at the experience of the South African cabinets in the past it is indeed astonishing to see how little they were concerned with the conduct of the wars in which their forces were involved and the extent to which the taking of decisions was abdicated almost entirely.

What makes this interesting is that consequent to firstly, the build-up of South African forces since the 1960s and secondly, South Africa's participation in the Angolan War a perception seems to have developed abroad that the South African military authorities are bellicose and a source of aggressiveness on the part of the government.

Moreover it is clear that among some foreign authorities the view is held that the South African military authorities, always rather vaguely defined, tend to control or so strongly influence the actions of the government in certain of its international relations as to account for this newly discovered bellicosity.[1] In particular South Africa's military involvement in Angola in 1975 is taken as evidence of military control—ignoring the role of countries such as Zambia, Zaire and the United States in effecting the involvement. It is particularly interesting that the South African attack on Cassinga on 4 May 1978 is regarded as strong evidence of the authority of the military, particularly when it is argued on the South African side that military considerations such as the weather, the phase of the moon, deception planning, the use of Citizen Force troops (i.e National Guard) temporarily withdrawn from their civilian occupations and the expectation of a SWAPO incursion, may have had to determine the timing of the attack when certain Western diplomats were preening themselves on their ability to secure South African collaboration.

It is by no means intended to try to disprove these perceptions and it would be foolish to think that it could be done. It is intended however to consider South African experience as a member of the British Empire and of the Commonwealth in order to determine whether this may throw any light on the question of whether the military authorities have begun a dangerous trend or whether the apparent bellicosity derives from the government's lack of a tradition of reliance on the military establishment to resolve South Africa's own international disputes so that there is neither experience nor precedent available for carefully controlled employment of military force.

2. The South African Experience of War

The experience of South African governments in war was curious in that while the country became heavily involved in both World Wars and, to a smaller extent, in the Korean War in no case was South Africa directly threatened nor called upon to defend her interests. Moreover, but for one exception, the South African government did little more than provide the manpower for foreign field commanders and even governments to dispose over. For the most part, direct control over her own forces together with the experience in taking decisions in situations of wartime crisis, was abdicated by the South African governments. The reasons varied from political to reasons of geography. Whatever the reasons, the effect was was the same.

When the South African experience is reviewed it is convenient to recognize four principal phases. The phases are:

(a) The South West African Campaign and the Rebellion, spanning the period August 1914 until July 1915 when the German commander surrendered.

---

1. In this regard reference is made to opinions expressed by the foreign press and by foreign diplomats which have been reported in the South African press (notably *The Star* and *The Rand Daily Mail*) or which have been expressed to the Whites in private conversations.

(b) The campaigns in East Africa and on the European Western Front, to which the Egyptian and Palestinian campaigns should be added, covering the period 1916 to 1918.

(c) The Second World War, which was closer in its prosecution to the second phase of participation in the First World War. South African forces were involved in four campaigns under their own national identity:

      (i)   the Abyssinian (Ethiopian) campaign (1940-1941);

      (ii) the Western Desert campaign (Egypt, Libya and Tunisia) during 1941 until 1943;

      (iii) the occupation of Madagascar in 1942 when a Japanese threat appeared to reach the Indian Ocean;

      (iv) the Italian campaign, including participation in the Sicilian campaign and a contribution by the Air Force to the rising of the Polish Army in Warsaw (1943-1945).

(d) The period after South Africa left the Commonwealth in 1961 when she became aware of her military isolation and of the need to re-establish her armed forces and became involved in military operations close to home.

3. South West Africa and The Rebellion

The decision of the South African government not only to declare war on Germany, which was inevitable given the constitutional status of the Dominion at that time, but also at the request of the British government to engage in an invasion of the adjacent colony then known as German South West Africa plunged the government into a crisis. The situation was of a kind that bore perhaps a closer likeness to the period of the Angolan campaign in 1975 than to any other intervening situation.

The crisis derived from a variety of sources. Not only was it a shock to many Afrikaners to be asked to go to war on behalf of Britain a mere twelve years after the two former Boer republics had ended their three year war against that country, but to them the request to invade a colony that belonged to a country which had sided with the Boers even though the Kaiser had feared to match his words with any concrete assistance, itself smacked of an alliance with the imperialist spirit that had ended the lives of the republics. To many Afrikaners Botha's cause was incomprehensible. Moreover, so many South Africans were themselves of first or second generation German descent, and so many Germans had fought as volunteers in the international "legions" that had chosen to fight alongside the Boers that the actions now contemplated seemed to be quite deceitful.[2]

---

2. Indeed many Germans had been settled in South Africa by the British having been recruited for the Hanoverian Legion for service in the Crimean War and then settled along the Cape frontier as a buffer against the Xhosas.

In addition, since the *Defence Act* of 1912 made provision for compulsory military service "anywhere in South Africa, within or outside the Union" Botha seemed to take it for granted that he should mobilize the Active Citizen Force requirements and the Commandos under the terms of the Act, and there seemed to be no pretence of calling for volunteers, irrespective of the views that citizen soldiers might hold.

It is difficult to understand why so astute a politician as General Louis Botha should have chosen so precipitous a course, especially when one takes account of his very great capacity to understand the Afrikaner's mind and emotions.

It would seem that he had taken the decision to participate in an invasion of South West Africa well before the war. This view seems to be substantiated by the cable received from the British Secretary of State for the Colonies in response to the South African government's offer to relieve the British garrison of some 6,000 men still stationed in South Africa to enable it to be employed elsewhere. Not only did he accept the offer but he went further and asked that South African forces should seize the two German harbours and wireless stations on the coast and at Windhoek. The reason that he proferred however, was simply that it would be ". . . a great and urgent Imperial service".[3]

Paying regard to the alacrity with which Botha seems to have acceded to the request in the light of a reason that was so vague and lacking in argument, seems to support the view that his decision stemmed from considerations reviewed at the Imperial Conference of May 1911 when, according to Hankey, the Secretary of the Committee of Imperial Defence, the possibility that German colonies close to Dominions might be seized as hostages was discussed. Spies, however, discounts any assertion that agreements in principle that the Dominions would be at war, bound their governments actually to act even though Hankey says that Botha gave a categorical promise in 1911.[4]

The relevance of this point is that Botha succeeded by his readiness to undertake military operations at the British request in creating crises at home, the results of which bedevilled his party and its successsors for generations after. As Spies points out, the strategic significance of South West

---

3. Collyer, J. J., *The Campaign in German South West Africa 1914-1915,* (Pretoria: Government Printer, 1937), p. 6 and UG 46-16 *Report of the Judicial Commission of Inquiry into the Causes and Circumstances relating to the recent Rebellion in South Africa. Annexure C: White Paper containing correspondence between the Union and Imperial Governments regarding German South West Africa,* pp. 112-113.

4. Hankey, M., *The Supreme Command 1914-1918,* London, 1961; and Spies, S. B., "The Outbreak of the First World War and the Botha Government," *South African Historical Journal,* No 1, November 1969, p. 47.

Africa in a naval sense was dubious in the extreme.[5] As it happened, the delay in operations caused by the Rebellion, resulted in the coastal radio stations being bombarded by the Royal Navy and being abandoned by the Germans without the need for overland operations. Without their reports on shipping the supposedly powerful Windhoek station had no further importance for the German navy.

Nevertheless on 7 August Botha urged his cabinet to accede to the British request. Only one of his Afrikaans-speaking ministers, N. J. de Wet, supported his view and even the English-speaking Minister of Railways, H. Burton, apparently stated that ". . . were it not for the British request, they would not have contemplated such a step."[6] With only a majority of five to four, Botha could have been expected to have had second thoughts but after receiving a further cable from England succeeded in swaying all the members of the Cabinet on 10 August when, despite reservations still held, an unconditional agreement was cabled to England.

Again, Botha accepted political risks by engaging not to act before Parliament met on 9 September and then calling out the Active Citizen Force and commencing operations on 1 September 1914.[7] His actions were doubly surprising considering the extent of opposition to direct participation that was abroad in the country, even in his own party.[8] One cannot escape the feeling that a good deal of the opposition was beginning to result from the rather secretive way in which the matter was approached by Botha and Smuts. Nevertheless in Parliament he obtained the approval of 91 against 12 members of the House of Assembly and 24 to 5 in the Senate.[9]

A series of circumstances then developed which resulted in the tendency to rebel amongst the Afrikaners gaining momentum. For example, although the cabinet had been told that only volunteers would be used, until the Rebellion had developed no real choice was given to members of the ACF and Commandos, all of whom were subject to the compulsory provisions of the *Defence Act.*[10] Nor did Botha take the Leader of the Opposition, General J. B. M. Hertzog, into his confidence about the communications with the British government, and in fact, the official opposition complained that they were the only party not to have been consulted.[11] Finally the accidental shooting

---

5. Spies, *op. cit.,* p. 49.
6. *Ibid.*
7. Spies, *op. cit.,* p. 51 and Collyer, *op. cit.,* pp. 27-28.
8. Spies cites various indications of this attitude on pp. 51 and 56.
9. Spies, *op. cit.,* p. 52.
10. UG 42-16, pp. 132-133.
11. Spies, *op. cit.,* p. 53.

of General H. de la Rey by a police roadblock who were searching for a gang of armed robbers, gave rise to unfounded public suspicions that he had been assassinated on Botha's orders to prevent his taking the field at the head of a Rebel army. Although he was a senator representing Botha's party and no evidence has ever been produced that he would have rebelled, this incident affected the opinions of many. Within weeks 11,472 men had rebelled, including one battalion that had been despatched into South West Africa and the Commandant-General of the Citizen Force, Brig. Genl. C. F. Beyers, who had been Botha's Deputy during the Boer War. Before the campaign against the Germans could be prosecuted, the Rebellion had to be put down and Botha himself gave full attention to this. Making use of 30,000 men, of whom 20,000 were Afrikaners, Botha quelled the Rebellion between October and 8 December 1914.

Owing to his experience as a field commander and his apparent feelings about the desirability of using Afrikaners to put down the Rebellion as well as because of the strangely organised defence headquarters establishment which provided for no centralised commander, chief of staff or even operations staff, Botha not only took direct command but actually took to the field three times. In October he defeated the Transvaal rebels under Beyers near Rustenburg, then defeated De Wet in the Orange Free State in November then with 1,200 men Botha defeated the last rebels in the Free State on 8 December 1914. While 190 rebels were killed and 300 wounded, government casualties were 132 killed and 242 wounded.

Having disposed of the Rebellion the Prime Minister now turned his attention to South West Africa. Botha was a man of remarkable character, possessing great capacities as a leader and as a politician with a warm personality and military insight which had resulted in his becoming Commandant-General of the forces of the combined republics in 1899 when he was thirty-eight years old. Although he had but a rudimentary schooling he had a good appreciation of staff work and of the free relationship necessary to assist a chief of staff in the direction of the work of the staff. In a desert campaign characterised by trying staff problems, he proved to be an ideal commander much given to personal reconnaissance and giving his full confidence to his staff while retaining full command.[12]

Of all the senior officers in South Africa, only Botha had commanded forces larger than about 300 and he was the only commander there who had commanded large forces against a sophisticated European enemy. Under his direction the Boers, never more than 66,000 strong had fought for three years against 256,340 regular Bristish troops.[13]

12. Collyer, *op. cit.,* pp. 165-168.
13. Collyer, *op. cit.,* p. 169.

In spite of, or perhaps because of, his competence as a field commander, he now made the curious move of abandoning his post as Prime Minister in order to take the field nominally as Commander-in-Chief in South West Africa, although in fact he effectively only commanded the northernmost of the four military forces totalling some 67,000 fighting men.

Even stranger was the appointment in April 1915 of the Minister of Defence, General J. C. Smuts, to command the three other forces which were now organised as two divisions known as Southern Army.

With no military chief of staff in Pretoria the various headquarters staff officers normally worked directly for the Minister. There was no mechanism at all for coordination of staff work nor any supervision but for that exercised by the Minister. Strictly speaking, while he was absent in the field the headquarters responsible for maintaining the field forces and for exercising some control over operations and intelligence were left without a head. It was fortunate that the civilian Secretary for Defence, who was the chief accounting and budgetary officer of the Department of Defence, had himself been an officer and that the heads of the various staff sections took it on themselves to report to him.[14] But the cabinet that remained in Pretoria remained with neither its leader nor his righthand man and without day to day advice as to its own policies and procedures regarding the war. Moreover with the two generals in the field, Defence Headquarters could not take it on itself to give the orders which its central position often told it were necessary. That the campaign did not suffer from even greater logistic shortcomings than it did, was remarkable and was probably due in no small measure to the fact that the German Commander, Franke, was lacking in imagination and that after Botha's landing in the north the idea had taken root that escape to Tanganyika to join the German forces there might be the wiser course rather than to attempt a decisive battle with the South Africans.

However, this is not to denigrate Botha's generalship in the field. His movements were ideal, being wide and rapid, relying as far as the rocky, arid country allowed on motor transport as well as horses and animal drawn wagons, to force the Germans to give battle in the least favorable circumstances. By May the area south of Windhoek was occupied and ultimately by these moves he succeeded in cutting off Colonel Franke's withdrawal into Angola, compelling him to surrender in July 1915 at Tsumeb. The northern force had been in the field for 133 days. Of these the need for replenishment for man and beast, especially with water, at times brought from Cape Town, as well as the lack of adequate transport, meant that only 24 days were used for actual movements and operations. The fact remains that Botha's anom-

14. Collyer, *op. cit.*, pp. 19 and 160.

olous decision to deprive Pretoria of his guidance as well as that of his deputy for six months can be said to be ill-considered and harmful to the government of the country.

4. Europe and East Africa

Botha had now realized that he had made political mistakes in his handling of the entry into the war. Although he responded favorably to the promptings of the Governor-General, Lord Buxton, to send troops to East Africa and Europe, he decided against sending the South African army. Instead he merely agreed to recruit and equip soldiers who were then allocated to what were called Imperial Service Units. These were effectively British Army units bearing the words "South African" before their designation in order to show their origin. But they were to serve under British command and to be paid by the British government. The latter course was again to bring Botha into some political discredit, this time with the English-speaking Unionist Party, since the British pay was only one shilling per day while the South African's rate of pay was five shillings.

In part this was the beginning of the abdication of control over South African forces. The South Africa Aviation Corps, which had served in South West Africa was now absorbed into the Royal Flying Corps, as 26 Squadron—which it remains today in the RAF, although it served with the South Africans in East Africa for a period. The 1st Infantry Brigade and several unbrigaded artillery and engineer units were sent to Europe and Palestine. The infantry brigade served first in Egypt before being completely destroyed three times in France and Belgium where the South Africans suffered 4,454 deaths and 10,325 wounded having been fed by 30,719 recruits from 1916 to 1918. In addition 27,000 Blacks went to Europe in transport, logistic and labor roles in the rear areas.[15]

The South Africans in Europe became part of British formations and could in effect be disposed of as the British government wished. The brigade commander did in fact become commander of the Division in which the brigade served in 1916, but this did nothing to alter the relationship with the South African government.

The contributions to the fighting in German East Africa were organisationally far larger and initially they were intended to be commanded by British generals.[16] Two divisions made up of mounted and infantry brigades,

---

15. *Official Year Book of the Union*, No 5-1922 (Pretoria: Government Printer, 1923), p. 399.

16. Collyer, J. J., *The South Africans with General Smuts in German East Africa-1966* (Pretoria: Government Printer, 1939); General Staff, *The Union of South Africa and the Great War 1914-1918—Official History* (Pretoria: Government Printer, 1924); *Official Year Book of*

field artillery and service units began arriving from South Africa in late 1915. The two divisions were given to Maj. Genl. Japie van Deventer, and to Maj. Genl. Coen Brits, both Boer War veterans. The overall commander of the three division expeditionary force was to have been the British General Sir Horace Smith-Dorrien but because of illness on the way to Africa the post was offered to Smuts who accepted in February 1916.

For what might be called the conventional phase of the war, the whole of 1916, he remained as commander-in-chief until all railways and ports had been captured as well as a large area of the country. As he left in January 1917 to attend the Imperial Conference and then to join the War Cabinet the guerrilla phase of the war was beginning. Four months later he was succeeded by Van Deventer who until the war's end remained in command of the dwindling forces which were steadily decimated as were the horses, mules and oxen by the tropical diseases rife in the country.

Although the operations were largely the business of South African generals, their responsibility was not to the South African government at all. At the beginning of the campaign the government of India had sent forces to the British colonies abutting on Tanganyika. For this reason initial responsibility for operations was to the India Office in London and the general staff in India. In November 1914 the War Office in London took control of the operations and it was to the War Office that Smuts cabled for approval of his plan to occupy the Kilimanjaro area soon after his arrival in February 1916.[17] He continued to remain in close touch with the War Office, sending outlines of proposed campaigns for approval, as in May and September 1916, seeking permission to treat with the German commander when the time seemed appropriate for generous terms, or keeping them informed by way of periodical despatches.[18] Botha once visited the South Africans for four days during which time he and Smuts discussed the campaign but there was no question of his government exerting control over the employment of their own forces. When Smuts finally left to join the War Cabinet in London, it was certainly not to represent South African interests and he was occupied with matters very much the concern only of the British government.

5. The Second Experience of War

The stage was set during the years between the World Wars by the Hertzog government which succeeded Smuts' in 1924, partly because as the

---

the Union, No 5-1922 (Pretoria: Government Printer, 1923), p. 399. 60, 322 White soldiers and Black laborers served in East Africa of whom 1,611 lost their lives, 66% due to tropical disease.

17. Collyer, *op. cit.,* pp. 29, 33, 36, 42 and 62.

18. Collyer, *op. cit.,* pp. 122-123, 165, 168, 239, 241.

result of the experiences of the previous war, partly because of the economically depressed times and partly because of the general attitude of the age, there was a great disinclination to be interested in questions of defence beyond the maintenance of a very small Active Citizen Force of 8,100 and an even smaller Permanent Force. The Defence budget fell in 1932-33 to £736,831 ($3,684,155) and the Citizen Force's training camps were abandoned for two years. General Hertzog had also made it clear at various times that it was his belief that the Imperial Conference of 1928 had accepted the principle that a member of the Commonwealth was not obliged to participate in any future war in which Britain might engage.[19]

After the government of Hertzog formed a coalition and then unified with Smuts' opposition party in 1933 to form the United Party, however, the new government began actively to rebuild the defence force. Nevertheless, in his first annual report to Parliament in 1936 the new General Officer Commanding, Union Defence Forces, complained that since the establishment of the defence force no defence policy had ever been defined by any government. Not a great deal had been achieved by the time Smuts on 4 September defeated Hertzog's motion that South Africa remain non-belligerent while observing the obligation respecting Simonstown and membership of the League of Nations. There was little the country was capable of undertaking and little call for action until it became clear that the Italian government would be likely to enter the war. In March 1940, therefore the first British call for assistance came by way of a cable asking for a brigade to reinforce Kenya. Asking for volunteers prepared to serve anywhere in Africa, beyond the confines of the *Defence Act,* Smuts promised the War Office a brigade group by the end of June 1940. Smuts added in his reply that the brigade commander would be placed directly under the command of the Commander-in-Chief, Middle East.[20]

The full meaning of Smuts' concession became clear in November 1940 when the Headquarters, 1st South African Division arrived in Mombasa to find the 1st Brigade incorporated in the 12th African Division. Not only did Genl. Cunningham refuse to return the brigade but on his explaining that he felt that he should be able to move South African units and formations from division to division, he was given a free hand by Smuts to do so.[21] Three months later Genl. G. Brink was still fruitlessly trying to "borrow" back his brigade in order to carry out some wide ranging manoeuvres with three

19. Orpen, N. *East African and Abyssinian Campaigns,* South Africa Forces World War II, Vol 1, Purnell, Cape Town, 1968, pp. 331-338. Roskil, *Hankey—Man of Secrets 1919-1931,* Vol. 2 (London: Collins, 1972), p. 432.
20. Orpen, *op. cit.,* p. 7.
21. *Ibid.,* p. 63.

brigades in order to capture towns in Italian possession before the rainy season began in March. Moreover two artillery units were taken for the 11th and 12th African Divisions, the anti-tank batteries were dispersed as were the anti-aircraft batteries.

Other examples of the manner in which South African forces were placed at the disposal of a foreign government abound. The purpose of this study does not require minutae however. Sufficient evidence of an extensive degree of delegation of authority by the South African government is forthcoming from the Middle East campaign.

Smuts and his Chief of the General Staff, Lt. Gen. Sir Pierre van Ryneveld, flew to a conference in Cairo on the future deployment of the 1st and 2nd South African Divisions in March 1941. It was resolved to fill the void in Egypt, created by the campaign in Greece by bringing forward not only the divisions but also engineer units, armored car units and air force squadrons. At the conference Smuts authorized, apparently without reference to the Cabinet, their use ". . . 'anywhere in Africa' at the discretion of the Middle East Command. . . ." He also explained that he had no wish for a South African army corps but preferred the divisions to serve wherever the situation demanded. The official historian's comment was that the compensation was that South African gained a wide range of experience, in every operation of note and at every possible kind of headquarter and posting.[22] The one disadvantage which has been suggested was that this enabled one division to be isolated and captured at Tobruk.

In this regard the South Africans were in a position quite different from that of the Australians and New Zealanders who were organised into expeditionary forces. Their commanders were granted powers quite unknown to the South African generals. Both generals Sir Thomas Blamey and Sir Bernard Freyberg were given explicit powers. The Australian document constituted the Australian Imperial Force from which no part could be detached only by consent of the commander who had a direct responsibility to his government and ". . . the right to communicate direct with that Government". In an emergency the commander could take a decision on policy, merely informing his government later. Secondly, the AIF was allowed to be placed under operational control of the theatre commander-in-chief, while finally the AIF commander directed domestic administration reporting directly to the Australian minister, to the exclusion of the Chief of the General Staff in Canberra.[23]

22. Agar-Hamilton, J. A. I. and Turner, L. C. F., *The Sidi Rezeg Battles 1941* (OUP, Cape Town, 1957), p. 73-74.

23. *Ibid.*, p. 81.

In contrast, while Smuts took an interest in the course of the war and was consulted by the British Prime Minister on many subjects it was a foregone conclusion that South African forces were at the full disposal of the Theatre commander whose orders were to be obeyed. When it was reported that General Neil Ritchie had expressed a "hope" that one South African commander would help another with transport Van Ryneveld immediately asked the Prime Minister to authorise his cabling General Frank Theron in Cairo to tell the commander-in-chief that ". . . as 1 Div is under his command, orders and not 'appeals' are all that is required."[24]

This line of approach remained in force for as long as South African forces were employed abroad not only in the desert but also in Italy when they subsequently served in an American and in a Canadian corps and in the 5th U.S. Army.

The result was that real demands for decisions on the conduct of war, were never presented to the South African general staff in Pretoria nor to the Cabinet, while the questions directed at Smuts by the British prime minister, unlike the very real problems presented to him as a member of the War Cabinet in the First World War, were of a more academic nature with the possible exception of Auchinlek's dismissal by Churchill in 1942 when Smuts was present in Egypt and probably found that Churchill really needed advice or at least assurance about a decision already taken.

Even the disasters in the desert such as the destruction of the 5th South African Brigade and the loss of the 2nd SA Division in Tobruk were crises *ex post facto*. Although the evidence points to contradictory decisions by the British commander-in-chief regarding the holding of Tobruk, Maj.-Genl. H. B. Klopper apparently did not dream of turning to appeal to his government for instructions that might have enabled him to escape from Tobruk.[25]

If there were any exceptions to the absence of real war time crisis decision-making in South Africa, it might have been at the time of the Madagascar campaign in 1942 because of the closeness of the operations to home and also when between May and July 1942 the Japanese surface raiders

24. *Ibid.*, p. 82.

25. *Report of the Court of Enquiry: Operations in the Western Desert 27 May—2 July 1942,* Vol. I, Part II, "Detailed Report on circumstances which ended in the surrender of the fortress," pp. 23-24 UWH Tobruk 371, SADF Documentation Services, which states: "Para 13: The fact that Tobruk fell must undoubtedly be attributed to the eleventh hour reversal of policy leading to the decision to hold the fortress, regardless of the fact that the Eighth Army was then in full retreat in the face of an enemy who had been uniformly successful. . . . It was impossible in the time available to make adequate preparations for the completely new role imposed upon the garrison which up to then had only been concerned with the prevention of raids. . . ."

Hokoku Maru and *Aikoku Maru* were operating in conjunction with Admiral Ishizaki's submarine flotilla in the Mocambique channel and in fact flew several reconnaissance flights with seaplanes over Durban. Before the expedition ended early in July at a cost of 120,000 tons of merchant shipping—20 Allied ships—a considerable reorganisation of coastal and maritime defences had taken place in South Africa and the decision had been taken by the British government at Smuts' suggestion to occupy the whole of Madagascar in order to forestall possible Japanese landings. No documentary evidence of South African government conferences or any other decision-making at military command levels could be found, however. As it was, according to Orpen and Martin, Smuts tended to leave the Defence Force very much to Van Ryneveld and to concentrate on his own task as Prime Minister.[26]

When the National Party of Dr. D. F. Malan succeeded Smuts's government three years after the Second World War ended the Prime Minister's academic title symbolised more than simply the end of the age of the generals, as the historian D. W. Krüger has called the preceding half century. For the first time South Africa now had a Cabinet which included no experienced soldiers or veterans of any war, for even the Prime Minister who was old enough to have served in the Boer War, had been a theological student during those critical years. The only possible exceptions if unconfirmed newspaper reports could be credited, were the Minister of Economic Affairs, E. H. Louw, and the Minister of Lands, J. G. Strijdom, who was to succeed Malan, who were rumored to have served as private soldiers in the South West African campaign.

This government ushered in an era during which the Union of South Africa would for the first time come to face direct threats to her security both externally and internally. And yet it represented civilian rule over the military as no government could have before. Whereas, during the years from 1910 only one Minister of Defence had had no military background, in the years to come none of the three Ministers of Defence until 1978 had ever been a soldier.

Moreover, during this period the country, previously so dependent for direction in military affairs and even in part for its naval security on Britain, was to draw away from military association with its erstwhile ally and in fact become more isolated and dependent on its own resources for defence.

In keeping with the general post-war expectations of peace, the government tended initially to allow the defence machine to run down and to spend only what was required to keep a rudimentary defence establishment going.

26. Orpen, N. & Martin, H. V., *South Africa at War,* unpublished manuscript, Chapter XI.

Although the South African Air Force participated in the Berlin Airlift soon after Malan came to power the first major military undertaking after 1948 was the despatch to Korea of a fighter-bomber squadron to serve in an American wing as part of the United Nations force there. Altogether some 800 airmen and aircraftsmen served in the squadron until the end of the war. There were some 36 deaths either in action or as a result of being held prisoner by the Chinese. A small contingent of army officers, one of whom is the present Chief of Staff, Operations of the SA Defence Force, Lt-Genl. Jack Dutton, also served in various roles with the British Commonwealth Division.

Once again, the forces made available were completely under either American or British control and the South African government had no involvement in the disposition of the forces. And again the reasons were obvious: the size of the contribution and the geographical remoteness from South Africa.

The Korean War had the effect in South Africa as elsewhere of stimulating fears of military adventures throughout the world on the part of the Communist countries in Europe and Asia. This led the governing party, whose traditional attitude was to shy away from agreements which tied the country to committing forces to military operations in assistance to other governments, to look afresh at its traditional views. The fresh look led the government early in the 1950s to binding itself in the first instance once again to send forces to the Middle East in support of the British attempts to form a Middle East defence organisation. In pursuance of this the government bought *Centurion* and *Comet* tanks, *Saracen* personnel carriers and *Ferret* scout cars sufficient to equip an armored division which was earmarked for the Middle East, which was commonly expected in those days to be the future scene of a struggle with Soviet forces attempting to secure the oil wells of the area. Of particular interest is the fact that once again the South African government had made it clear that its forces would be subject to a British Middle East Command.[27] As circumstances dictated, primarily the consequences of the Suez debacle in 1956, the concept was abandoned and was replaced by the so-called Central Treaty Organization. Since the latter originated in a pact between Turkey and Iraq and later Pakistan, Iran and Britain, South Africa was never contemplated as a participant.

As the ambition to send an armored division to the old South African desert battle fields where Africa was linked to the northern land mass of Asia Minor evaporated, the South African government was occupied with an engagement to serve closer home.

27. Lawrie, G. R., "The Simonstown Agreement: South Africa, Britain and the Commonwealth," *SA Law Journal,* Vol. 85: 2, May 1968, pp. 157-177.

In spite of the departure of the last British garrison troops from South Africa in 1921, the naval base of Simonstown still remained in the hands of the Royal Navy. While it was the ambition of Malan's Minister of Defence, F. C. Erasmus, to establish what was then still called the SA Naval Forces on a more substantial footing he desired even more to see Simonstown, almost a last vestige of colonial status, in South African hands. To these ends he engaged in negotiations with Britain with a view to obtaining control of Simonstown which resulted also in South Africa's agreeing to accept greater responsibility for the defence of the trade routes around the Cape. This led to South Africa's buying a navy designed specifically as an anti-submarine flotilla adapted to complement the South Atlantic command of the Royal Navy. In addition South Africa, while taking over Simonstown, allowed Britain to retain the right to use the base at any time, even if South Africa herself was not at war. Significantly, South Africa agreed that were she to be involved in a war as an active ally of Britain's, the South African Navy as it now became would fall under the operational command of the British Commander-in-Chief, South Atlantic. To this end a joint headquarters with a joint operations room for the C-in-C and the Chief of the SAN was established. Even in her own waters, therefore, South Africa was prepared to play a subordinate role in decision taking. It seems that implicit in this attitude was the assumption that the more experienced power was better able to exercise the requisite judgement and command.

6. Outside the Commonwealth

Although the Simonstown Agreement remained in force until unilaterally terminated by Harold Wilson's second government in 1975, changes in South Africa's defence relationships began to develop in the early 1960s.

Despite the purchase of naval vessels, armored fighting vehicles and some modern aircarft, the South African Defence Force had gone into a general decline during the 1950s. Apart from the disinclination to spend on defence during apparently quiet periods, there were also unhappy consequences of political interference by the Minister of Defence, resulting in some mediocre appointments, a decline in morale and a reduction in numbers. When Erasmus was removed from his appointment in 1960 by Dr. H. F. Verwoerd, it was because of a realisation of the harm that had been done to the SADF. At the same time the government had become aware that developing external hostility was appearing to take on a far more threatening aspect than before.

Partly, this consciousness began in 1960 with the tragedy of Sharpeville which seems to have resulted from a complete breakdown in discipline and control in the South African Police. In the immediate aftermath of marches and demonstrations the Citizen Force and some commandos were mobilised in the expectation of some kind of organised uprising. Although the mobilisation worked well and rapidly, it was clear that the Minister of Defence had allowed the force to fall into neglect, reflected chiefly in the enormous decline in numbers in the Citizen Force, which as a part-time militia based on the Swiss pattern in 1912 was the first line of defence in need. Although the mobilisation was found to be unnecessary, it was useful for the impact it had on thinking at governmental level.

A further contributory factor to the awareness of threat was the fact that South Africa's application to remain in the Commonwealth as a republic was rejected at the 1961 Commonwealth Prime Ministers' Conference in London. Since Dr. Malan had long advocated a republic within the Commonwealth and had promoted the idea of the Commonwealth as a valuable connection for mutual defence, even proponents of the republican idea were taken aback at the rejection of Dr. Verwoerd's application which meant that South Africa was to be left to fend for herself in future.[28]

Then in December 1963 following a ban on arms sales to South Africa instituted by the Kennedy administration the United Nations Security Council passed a resolution calling on members not to supply arms to South Africa. Although the arms ban was not universally observed it was considered in a serious light in South Africa, especially when the only country to whom South Africa was bound by a defense pact, Britain, also joined in the ban in 1964 during Wilson's first ministry.

In 1963 the Organization of African Unity had been established and at its first deliberations it had gone into the question of taking action against South Africa. Being unable to act directly the OAU resolved to buy arms for freedom fighters and to train them with a view to launching under the direction of a Liberation Committee a guerrilla war against the remaining colonial regimes (the Portuguese and the Rhodesian) and against the White minority government in South Africa.[29] Also in 1964 an old hobbyhorse which president Kwame Nkrumah of Ghana had bestrode since 1961 was recommended to the OAU summit meeting in Cairo. That was the establishment of an African High Command and although the resolution failed to gain acceptance it was noticed in South Africa.

The South African government knew little enough about Africa at that time to have to take all these threats very seriously. In parenthesis, it may be added that so reliant had South Africa been on Britain until 1961 that no intelligence institution had existed except during the Second World War when it was concerned simply with conducting an information programme

---

28. As quoted in Barber, J., *South African Foreign Policy 1945-1970,* (London: OUP, 1973), p. 93.

29. Cervenka, Z., *The Organization of African Unity,* (London: Hurst, 1968), p. 17.

and looking after security. Otherwise all foreign intelligence came from Britain in the same way as all Commonwealth countries received intelligence. Obviously, Commonwealth countries did not spy on one another and so the British government did not circulate data on the military capabilities of the countries now threatening South Africa.

Coming as they did at the time that the covert leader of the South African Communist Party, Braam Fischer, was arrested and tried for conspiracy to set a large-scale guerrilla war "Operation Mayibuye" afoot in South Africa it was difficult not to see in these events an immediate threat developing.[30] It was very difficult for the rudimentary intelligence department of some twelve officers established in 1961, to sift chaff from wheat. Credibility was lent to various rumors simply on the basis of the test of the worst possible case. When press reports were circulated that President Kennedy had had a study conducted of the feasibility of invading South West Africa a garrison was placed in the South African enclave of Walvis Bay.

In due course the role that was being played by the Portuguese colonies of Angola and Mocambique and by Rhodesia as barriers to protect South Africa became clearer. This cleared the air to an extent but it was not seen as any reason to neglect the defences of the country. While the navy remained in its role as an adjunct of the Royal Navy, an air defence system was built to defend the country from the north and the army began a long process of rebuilding which was well handled by both the ministers who succeeded Erasmus, ie J. J. Fouché, later to be president, and P. W. Botha, now prime minister. At the same time South Africa began to re-establish an armaments industry in order to cope with the difficulties occasioned by the arms ban and also to provide for future eventualities.

Relations with the neighboring states were cordial and after the insurgencies commenced in the Portuguese territories and later Rhodesia, the South African armed forces took care to become acquainted with the situations and to try to learn from their experience. South Africa's first direct contact with a warlike situation came in late 1965 and early 1966 when guerrillas belonging to the South West African Peoples' Organization (SWAPO) crossed from Zambia via Angola into Ovamboland and Eastern Caprivi. From that time on a small scale operation of very low intensity, involving very small gangs who always sought to evade clashes developed.[31] Until about 1971 the situation was handled entirely by the police and it was chiefly because this prevented the police from carrying out duties elsewhere and because the army

30. De Villiers, H. H. W. *Rivonia—Operation Mayibuye* (Johannasburg: Afrikaanse Pers-Boekhandel, 1964).

31. Morris, M., *Armed Conflict in Southern Africa* (Cape Town: Jeremy Spence, 1974), pp. 3-24.

wished to become involved that a change was gradually made. Moreover, as the Ruacana dam scheme developed the need for larger forces to afford protection on the South West African side of the border became apparent.

In 1967 too, after the South African African National Congress had sent some guerrillas on an expedition into Rhodesia in the company of Nkomo's Zimbabwe African Peoples' Union the South African Police began to send contingents of men into Rhodesia to act in an infantry role. Several engagements involving such mixed groups were fought in Rhodesia but none of the ANC succeeded in ". . . fighting their way to strike at the boers themselves in South Africa" in the words of a joint communiqué issued in Lusaka.[32]

For the most part there was almost room for complacency in South Africa until 1974 when the Portuguese government fell and the military government which took over in Lisbon decided to rid itself of all Portugal's colonies. It was the actual process of decolonising Mocambique and Angola that brought the South African military face to face with more fundamental military problems than had ever faced them before. When the first developed, the attempt at a counter revolution in Mocambique, the South African government, for good or ill, chose not to respond to request for help and ultimately the revolutionary party FRELIMO was installed by the Portuguese high commissioner. In the intervening years, South Africa has sought to maintain good relations with FRELIMO and buys electricity from the Cabora Bassa powerscheme, sells food to Mocambique and runs the Maputo-Pretoria railway as well as the harbor of Maputo which is used by South African traders.

As the scheme for tripartie rule in Angola began to disintegrate in 1975 with fighting among the three parties breaking out all over the country, the South African forces found themselves drawn more and more into the conflict on the side of the FNLA and UNITA against the MPLA and the Cuban advisors who had begun to train and help the MPLA since March 1975. Whereas this began as a series of small operations resulting from aid and advisors, a variety of factors drew the South Africans into greater participation than initially intended. One was the good impression UNITA made of their capacity to administer the area they controlled. But the principal factors were the requests for substantial aid from Zambia, Zaire and the United States.— By responding to the extent of sending in some 1,200 artillery and armored car troops with a very meagre ration of equipment, the South Africans succeeded not only in driving the MPLA and the Cubans back to within about 250 km of Luanda, but they also succeeded in drawing a massive Cuban response, reported as some 15,000 by the campaign's end equiped with artillery and also tanks which South Africa was not prepared to commit.

32. *Ibid.*, p. 37.

After the failure of the US administration to obtain support in Congress the South African decision to withdraw seemed to produce a fresh crisis since the Cuban army began to follow the withdrawing forces. In order to prevent the routing of the columns as they left Angola, a Citizen Force brigade was mobilized for three months early in 1976. As it happened the Cubans experience of the fighting dissuaded them from following the columns into South West Africa and as the result of negotiations through a foreign government all fighting was ended.[33]

Realising that the new situation would result in a fillip to SWAPO having bases as it now did in Angola under the protection of the MPLA and realising the possibility of renewed fighting with the Cubans could not be discounted, the South African Defence Force continued from 1976 to maintain a far stronger force on the border than had ever been kept there or on any border before by the expedient of calling up Citizen Force troops for three months service annually and latterly because of the disruption to the economy, by extending the initial pre-Citizen Force National Service to two years.

This has placed a new means at the disposal of the government for until 1976, very few soldiers served in South West Africa. The means being available and the conflict with SWAPO's having tended to extend because of the very much greater numbers of recruits the pending independence has given SWAPO, the army has been in a position more than ever before to carry out not only actions in pursuit of SWAPO raiders who always return to Angola since they have had no bases in South West Africa, but also larger pre-emptive raids such as the one on 4 May 1978 on the bases code-named Vietnam and Cassinga. They were also far more readily able to respond in August to the bombardment from Zambia of Katima Mulilo in the Caprivi. But at the same time this capacity has tended to result in a certain kind of political response from elsewhere in the world, especially with the young generals in command of the Defence Force and the Minister of Defence's having become Prime Minister.

7. Conclusion

Certainly no lawyer would be prepared to accept that this brief study proves that South African generals and politicians are so naive as to be ignorant of the meaning of force. It does appear however, that there is evidence that there is really not a great tradition of crisis management nor of using military force as an instrument of South Africa's own foreign policy.

---

33. Press release on Operation Savanah by the Directorate of Public Relations, SADF, 1977.

Before any judgement can be made about the tendency of the military to dominate foreign policy or at least in certain directions, perhaps a closer look at the traditional employment of the military and of the experience of using the military could say something about whether South Africa now tends to militarise the solutions to its problems. In particular it should be borne in mind that the whole caste of thinking of the Defence Force about the problem of insurgency, wherever it may arise or have arisen, relates to the removal of frustrations, social upliftment and economic development. In no other department of government have color barriers fallen so completely. The role of the military is to fight. The South African Defence Force has the capability but it is still not clear that it regards its capabilities as the primary means of responding to the country's problems. [34]

34. Thanks are due to various people who assisted me in preparing this study, and in particular I am grateful for invaluable discussions with Lt. Genl. J. R. Dutton, Chief of Staff, Operations and Lt. Genl. H. Martin, retired Chief of the Air Force and co-author of *South Africa at War*. Refence has been made also to *Defence White Papers* WP-DD-1967, WPH-1969, WPE-1975, WPF-1977.

The Nuclear Option

J. E. SPENCE

Introductory

The 1960s witnessed a growing concern with the question of nuclear proliferation reflected in a large volume of literature devoted to both the technical and political considerations involved in trying to devise means of discouraging the spread of nuclear weapons to Nth powers. Until the 1970s however, South Africa was rarely the subject of any detailed discussion in this context: at best, it merited a passing reference or footnote as compared with the attention lavished on India, Israel, West Germany and Japan—the prime contenders for nuclear power status. This early indifference to South Africa's nuclear pretentions is explicable if we bear in mind that until the 1970's its potential capability was relegated to the second rank of those powers deemed likely to have the capacity and the will to develop both such weapons— powers such as Argentina, Australia, Belgium and Pakistan. This group had been traditionally regarded as requiring between 10 to 15 years to produce a weapon system once the initial decision to do so has been taken.

However, during the last two years there has been renewed speculation about South Africa's capability. In May 1976 there was news that an international consortium involving American, Swiss and Dutch firms was bidding for the contract to build the Republic's first nuclear power station. The contract was eventually won by a French consortium and despite claims by the French government that the sale would be subject to "normal" International Atomic Energy Board safeguards (i.e., inspection), the critics argued that South African capacity to produce a nuclear weapon had been considerably enhanced by the deal: the Republic—it was claimed—now had the means to build such a weapon by refining the plutonium by-product of the French installed reactors. The debate that these events stimulated was foreshadowed by a speech made in October, 1975, by Dr. A. J. Roux in the course of which he paid tribute to the American role in developing South Africa's nuclear technology:

We can ascribe our degree of advancement today in large measures to the training and assistance so willingly provided by the United States of America during the early years of our nuclear programme, when several of the western world's nuclear nations co-operated in initiating our scientists and engineers into nuclear science. Much of the nuclear equipment installed at Pelindaba is of American origin, while even our nuclear philosophy, although it was unmistakably our own, owes much to the thinking of American nuclear scientists.[1]

This statement acquires added significance when we consider the arguments advanced in May 1976 by Mr. Myron Kratzer, American Deputy Assistant Secretary of State for Scientific Affairs before the Senate Foreign Relations Committee justifying the State Department's endorsement of General Electric's participation in the U.S./Swiss-Dutch Consortium to build South Africa's first nuclear power station. He claimed that from 1961 the United States had shipped 229 lbs. of enriched uranium to South Africa for use in the Pelindaba reactor. He also pointed out that in 1973 his Government had approved the sale of two computers to the Republic to help operate a uranium enrichment plant outside Johannesburg.[2]

Interest in South Africa's nuclear pretentions revived again in February 1977 with reports in the American press that the Republic was within two to four years of manufacturing a bomb. Observers also noted the calculated ambiguity implicit in the statements by Dr. Connie Mulder, the Minister for Information and the Interior that: "If we are attacked, no rules apply at all if it comes to the question of our existence. We will use all means at our disposal, whatever they may be."[3] These more favourable assumptions about the Republic's nuclear potential must also be seen in the context of developments since the announcement in July 1970 that scientists employed by the South African Atomic Energy Board had been successful in pioneering a new process—"unique in its concept"—for uranium enrichment.[4] South Africa is, of course, a major producer of uranium in its natural state, but up to 1970 had lacked the means to enrich it and thus make possible the efficient production of weapons grade material.

There are in addition other reasons why South Africa's position has excited concern:

1. "South Africa within 2 years of the Atom Bomb," *International Herald Tribune,* 17 Feb. 1977.
2. *Ibid.,* 30 May 1976.
3. *Ibid.,* 17 Feb. 1977.
4. See Prime Minister's speech, South Africa Parliament. House of Assembly, *Debates,* Vol. 25, cols. 57/8.

1. The government has not signed the Non-Proliferation Treaty;

2. The heavy defence expenditure of the last 15 years, coupled with the increasing concern manifested over internal and external security has aroused speculation over the Republic's ultimate intentions in the nuclear field.

There is also the evidence supplied by Zdenek Cervenka and Barbara Rogers that West German Corporations (Steag and Ucor) were instrumental in helping South Africa develop its uranium enrichment technology.[5]

3. The fact that South Africa, unlike powers such as Italy or Belgium, has never enjoyed the protection conferred by alliance with a super-power. Moreover the ambiguity of its military relations with the Western Powers and the failure to obtain a degree of formal incorporation within the alliance structure of western defence, suggests an incentive to acquire nuclear weapons as both a symbol and practical demonstration of the state's capacity to stand alone against the strictures, and if need be, intervention, of the outside world.

4. We must consider too, the South African perception of the significance to be attached to the presence of Soviet warships and the role that nuclear weapons might play in the Indian Ocean;

5. The extent to which policy makers might regard nuclear status as enhancing the claim to be a hegemonic power in Central and Southern Africa, and

6. The fact that the Republic possesses a delivery system in the form of Canberra B-112 bombers, and a variety of Mirage aircraft, all of which have the necessary range for operations in the region.

It is considerations of this kind that suggest that a decision to opt for the development of a nuclear weapons programme is bound to involve a delicate balance of incentives and constraints of a kind not present to anything like the same degree for the small powers of Eastern and Western Europe, the majority of which have signed the NPT.

The South African Atomic Energy Board was established in 1948 and the first uranium plant opened in 1952. The Republic is the West's third largest supplier of uranium and its resources are estimated to be "350,000 tons in the economically exploitable price range."[6] The United States and Britain were, and still are, the major export markets for uranium concentrate and by 1966 sales abroad had earned South Africa some R1,000 million.

---

5. See Z. Cervenka & Barbara Rogers, *The Nuclear Axis—Secret Collaboration between West Germany & South Africa,* Julian Freedman Books Ltd., 1978.

6. *The Near nuclear countries and the N.P.T.* (New York: Humanities Press for the Stockholm International Peace Research Institute, 1972), p. 32.

During the early 1960s these exports began to fluctuate, due to a "fall back in constructing nuclear power stations."[7] But by the 1970s demand had begun to rise, although not sufficiently to prevent stockpiling taking place in considerable quantities.

By 1965, South Africa's first research reactor (Safari I) based at Pelindaba had gone critical. During the next five years the government was at pains to deny any suggestions that its nuclear research had military implications.[8] Instead, emphasis was placed on the following objectives of policy:

1. The development and exploitation of the country's uranium resources;

2. Research into the use of atomic energy as a cheap method of producing electricity;

3. Production of radio-active isotopes and the development of new uses for them.

The marginal interest shown by scientific and strategic experts in the Republic's potential as a nuclear power, sharpened with the announcement by Mr. B. J. Vorster, the Prime Minister, in July 1970 that the SAAEB had devised a new process for uranium enrichment. Describing this process in rather extravagant terms as "unequalled in the history of our country," Mr. Vorster asserted that:

> South Africa does not intend to withhold the considerable advantages inherent in this development from the world community. We are therefore prepared to collaborate in the exploitation of this process with any non-Communist country willing to do so, but subject to the conclusion of an agreement safeguarding our interests.[9]

The utility of the project was justified in economic terms[10]: by 1980 annual production of enriched uranium would reach 6,600 tons, constituting 14% of the West's output and worth about 290 million dollars in export

---

7. See Abdul S. Minty, "Apartheid Atomic Bomb?," *Sechaba*, Vol. 5, No. 7, (July 1971).

8. See e.g., the statements made by Dr. A. J. Roux, Director-General of the Atomic Energy Board, and Mr. P. Botha, Minister of Defence and quoted in the *Daily Telegraph* (London), 20 April 1965 and *Sunday Express* (Johannesburg), 22 December 1968 respectively.

9. House of Assembly, *Debates, op. cit.*, cols. 57/8.

10. Dr. Roux did, however, claim that South Africa was by virtue of the new process in a position to manufacture nuclear weapons and some elements of the Afrikaner Press were quick to emphasize the possible military and political implications: "Mr. Vorster has not yet said categorically that South Africa will never make an atom bomb. In view of this fact, people will have to look at us in a new light. South Africa now becomes an altogether different proposition if you want to tackle it. This bargaining power can be used in various fields in the difficult years that lie ahead. America, for example, would have to revise its strategy towards us." *Die Beeld* (Pretoria), 26 July 1970.

value. Secondly, the Republic's efforts to establish a substantial nuclear power programme would prove less expensive if enriched uranium was available.[11] Despite the official emphasis on the economic rather than the military potential of the project, it was plausible to interpret this development at the time as having a strategic significance in the more general sense of the means required to maintain and enhance the political and economic viability of the Republic and its bargaining power in relation to the external world. Indeed, several commentators (present writer included) argued in the early 1970s that the Republic's nuclear technology was perceived by Pretoria to have an economic and political utility rather than a military one.

Thus, given the assumption that a major objective of South Africa's foreign policy in the post war period was the consolidation and further integration of its economic and military links with the western powers, then the prospect of making an important contribution to the West's stock of nuclear technology became attractive to the extent that these ties would be therefore strengthened. This view was not inconsistent with a parallel determination to become self-sufficient in key raw materials (oil and rubber are obvious examples in this context) and thus reduce the Republic's vulnerability to external sanctions or cut-offs in supply. Thus, in the case of uranium, one commentator argued:

> The reason for Pretoria's willingness to take the costly route was plain: South Africa could not depend on the cooperation of those very few countries—United States, Britain, France, Russia, China—equipped to enrich the fissile component of uranium, the key to smaller, more highly rated hence cheaper nuclear stations.[12]

The claim to have a novel and relatively cheap enrichment process initially generated a degree of scepticism among informed commentators.[13] Their criticism stressed the fact that the project had only reached the pilot stage, while there was considerable doubt about South Africa's capacity to achieve at substantially lower cost a goal which in the United States and Western Europe had required extensive governmental financial support, a sophisticated technology, and a highly trained management and scientific elite.

---

11. The government had already decided to build a 350 Mwe nuclear power station at Melkbosstrand in the Cape Province. It was for this contract that the French successfully bid in May 1976.

12. David Fishlock, "Pretoria pursues the Atom," *Financial Times* (London) 18 February 1971.

13. See in particular the writings of David Fishlock in the *Financial Times* (London) and Aldo Cassuto, "Can uranium enrichment enrich South Africa," *The World Today,* Oct. 1970, p. 421.

These criticisms were not necessarily as condemnatory as might appear at first sight. We should bear in mind Mr. Vorster's offer to collaborate with other countries in the exploitation of the process—an ambition which might be interpreted as an attempt to make virtue part of necessity. The explanation for this lies in the fact that for many years before 1970 South Africa's scientists concentrated their research on nuclear powered generation by means of reactors using uranium in its natural state. This was regarded as a cheaper method and not dependent on an external or technological and capital input to the same extent that would be the case if a commitment were made to the production and subsequent use of the enriched variety, and it is in this context that a comment in *"New Scientist"* had particular relevance:

> Although popular reaction to the news of a South African enrichment process had focussed on the possible military implications, the real impetus for the project is economics. Like the Third World, South Africa is keen to process her raw materials before export. Enriched uranium could yield up to 10 times the export returns of the raw oxide concentrate. And with projections of a bottle-neck in enrichment in the 1980's the possession of enrichment facilities and raw uranium may be a valuable political bargaining counter.[14]

Attitudes to the Non-Proliferation Treaty

The claim to have developed facilities for uranium enrichment, coupled with South Africa's unwillingness to sign the NPT suggests that its government has been intent on maintaining the option to develop nuclear weapons for as long as possible. Yet, it could be argued (to repeat an earlier point) that South African policy in the 1960s was designed to impress upon the Western powers the positive contribution that South Africa's scientists could make to advance nuclear technology in the civil field, in the hope that new profitable economic and technological links could be forged with those states, whose goodwill and support the republic has traditionally attempted to win. Thus, over the long term, the choice has traditionally been construed as lying between a decision to opt for nuclear status in a military sense (regardless of the political consequences) or, signing the treaty following the conclusion of some mutually advantageous agreement with those powers willing to work with the Republic as partners in pioneering and developing new skills in nuclear technology. In the short term, the government's strategy has apparently been directed at creating an impression that its refusal to sign the NPT implies a threat to develop nuclear weapons at some unspecified time in the future and providing at the same time a bargaining counter to persuade

14. *New Society,* 25 April 1974.

Western governments to take seriously South Africa's offer of collaboration in the nuclear and other fields.

To date, politico-economic objectives have not clashed with strategic imperatives, insofar as the South African government has not felt obliged to make the choice between them.[15] (In passing, it should be stressed that it has always been difficult to see what possible advantages South Africa might gain if its government signed the Treaty "blind," i.e., without some significant *quid pro quo* of the kind described above. Signature would not especially enhance the government's standing in the world, unlike the case of states such as Canada or Sweden whose decision to do so was in a sense confirmation—both internally and externally—of a diplomatic image of "liberal" concern with the evils of war politics. By contrast South Africa's policies arouse no such expectation on the part of its critics.)

Here, the evidence of South Africa's role in the International Atomic Energy Agency is perhaps instructive insofar as delegates in the 1960s and early 70s continually stressed their government's unwillingness to do anything that might contribute towards an increase in the number of nuclear armed states. What in fact the delegates were at pains to deny was any suggestion that South Africa was selling uranium to buyers who might conceivably be diverting it to clandestine military purposes.[16] What is significant here is the evidence of the traditional concern of the South African government to demonstrate its commitment to observe the rule of law and in general maintain the properties of international behaviour—if only to point a contrast to the "illegal" demands made upon the Republic by its enemies at the United Nations and elsewhere. This emphasis on a "correct" posture was, and still is, especially noticeable at the I.A.E.A. and is combined with an insistence that the Agency concentrate on technical issues rather than become an organ of political and ideological debate. There can be no doubt that the government has in the past attached considerable importance to its standing

15. It is interesting, although perhaps no more than coincidental, that the announcement of the new process in July 1970 occurred at the height of the controversy over British Conservative's announcement that it proposed to sell arms to the Republic. Was this perhaps an attempt by Dr. Vorster to influence British thinking on the subject of military co-operation with South Africa? If we accept that the timing of the announcement was deliberate, might it not be plausible to argue that Mr. Vorster was in effect stressing South Africa's capacity to act independently, if need be, in defence field in general and in nuclear matters in particular? Alternatively (and the positions are not mutually exclusive), the Prime Minister's statement might have been calculated to suggest to the Western powers that his government had a positive contribution to make in the scientific and technological realm and that the price of South African co-operation (and its signing of the N.P.T.) was a greater degree of receptiveness to its aspirations on the part of London and Washington.

16. *The United Nations.* General Assembly. A/C. 1/PV.1571, 20 May 1968.

17. *Ibid.*

within the Agency, welcoming the opportunity to make a valuable contribution in terms which have not been available in other international forums.

An analysis of the reservations ruling out for the time being the signature
and ratification of the NPT and listed by South African spokesman during
the General Assembly Debate on the NPT in May 1968[17] supports the view
that throughout the early seventies the Republic was more concerned with
gaining tangible benefits in the political and economic sphere rather than
committing itself irrevocably to the achievement of nuclear power status—an
option which as we have already noted it could afford to keep open as a last
resort.

South Africa specifically objected to the NPT on the following grounds:

1. The Treaty is one-sided and discriminatory insofar as it does not
effectively commit the existing nuclear powers to take active measures to
reduce and ultimately eliminate their own stock-piles of weapons. This objection was hardly the core of the South African case against the Treaty. It
was cited by many other powers, but it is by no means self-evident that the
Republic shares the general interest of many small and medium-sized states
in a deceleration of vertical proliferation. It is at least plausible that the
resulting detente between nuclear powers embarking on massive measures of
arms control would seriously weaken the validity of the South African claim
to be indispensable to the security of the West.[18]

2. The Treaty is guilty of technological discrimination against the "have
not" powers who cannot be sure that the "potential benefits from any peaceful applications of nuclear explosions" would be passed on. As the South
African delegate remarked.

> In return for the restriction and impositions which we as non-nuclear
> weapon States are required to accept and which we would normally
> accept willingly, we are offered promises by the nuclear-weapon states
> of technical co-operation in the further development of the applications
> of nuclear energy for peaceful purposes. Promises seem hardly adequate.
> Experience has shown that technical information and material required
> for peaceful purposes are sometimes withheld, even when specific agree-
> ments make their provision contractually obligatory.[19]

This statement must be read in the context of my earlier remarks about
South African aspirations for closer nuclear ties with the West in terms of its

---

18. Indeed, it could be plausibly argued that the South African government has always
had an interest in the maintenance of Cold War tensions and there are few signs that the
present level of détente between the west and the Soviet Union is taken at face value. N.B.
The reaction of the South African government to the invasion of Czechoslovakia in 1968: this
was construed as evidence that the "leopard had not changed its spots." The Soviet incursion
into Angola was also perceived as providing evidence of the fallacy of détente.

19. *United Nations*. General Assembly A/C. 1/PV. 1571, *op. cit.*, pp. 53-55.

position as a major uranium producer and the expertise it has laboriously built up in the field of nuclear technology. It indicates at that the government's concern to enjoy partnership status through the pooling of nuclear resources rather than take on trust the promises of the nuclear club and risk relegation to the ranks of those powers which have little option but to accept the uncertain benefits accorded to non-nuclear signatories of the Treaty. Moreover, the Republic's experience of discrimination in other fields (the sale of arms for example) served to strengthen this mood of scepticism.

3. Yet another and perhaps the most important objection was related to the question of safeguards. As Mr. Botha, the South African delegate explained, his government was not prepared to put its mine and ore-processing plant under international inspection, a potential requirement, he argued, implicit in the wording of Article III, paragraph 1 of the Treaty. This was cited as a threat to sovereignty on the grounds that "the greater the production of uranium by non-nuclear weapon states, the more extensive and stringent the safe-guards to which they become subjected." Furthermore, such controls would hamper the development of peaceful uses of nuclear energy while inspection procedures would encourage industrial espionage and put at risk the technical advances pioneered by non-nuclear states. Nevertheless, his government was prepared to delay its final decision until the precise nature of the safeguard's provisions were decided upon by the I.A.E.A.[20]

This objection is partly explained in terms of the strong attachment the South African government has always exhibited to the sanctity of domestic jurisdiction and its deep antagonism to any attempt at external interference with its domestic arrangements. No doubt the desire to protect commercial advantage is the strongest motive in this particular context, but it is hardly surprising to find traces of its traditional "legalistic" attitude informing its position on nuclear matters.

4. Finally, the Republic's spokesmen expressed doubts about the security guarantees associated with the Treaty for non-nuclear power signatories.[21] Here again, there is evidence of South Africa's interpreting its present needs in terms of past experience. Given the hostility generated against its policies at the United Nations, given the isolation that has been a striking feature of its role within that organisation, the government has ample cause to be sceptical about the efficacy of any guarantees emanating from that quarter. The lack of any real guarantee deriving from United

20. *Ibid.* See also House of Assembly Parliament. *Debates.* col. 57, *op. cit.*

21. These are contained in the Security Council Resolution of June 1968 and the Declarations of the United States, the United Kingdom and the Soviet Union associated with this resolution. These oblige the great powers to seek immediate Security Council action to assist a non-nuclear signatory of the treaty that is subject to aggression or the threat of aggression by a nuclear armed power.

Nations declarations, together with the fact that the Republic has never enjoyed the benefits of protection conferred by membership of the Western alliance structure might suggest an incentive to acquire nuclear weapons to compensate for the status of being an outcast.

One might be wary of exaggerating the importance of such guarantees for South Africa. At present, no power aspires to threaten the Republic with nuclear weapons; nor is it likely that any of its enemies on the African continent will be in a position to do so for some time to come, if at all. Therefore the question of a formal guarantee from the great powers against such an eventuality remains a theoretical issue in a way which is presumably not the case with say India or Australia, both of which—it may be argued— have a greater incentive to acquire weapons to the extent that both have reason to fear Chinese nuclear aspirations.

The Political and Strategic Constraints

It would be foolish to accept uncritically the cluster of arguments put forward by South Africa in defence of its decisions to delay signature to the NPT. The emphasis on discrimination whether military or commercial, the fear that an extension of the safeguard system will erode the principle of domestic jurisdiction, the scepticism about guarantees—all these assertions might be taken as so much rhetoric disguising the real intention of policy makers determined to opt for nuclear power status at a time conducive to the achievement of maximum benefit both in a military and political sense.

On the other hand, the outside observer must guard against the temptation to impute "wicked" motives simply because in all other respects the policy of the state in question appears reprehensible. Thus by a curious logic, South Africa is seen as an "obvious" candidate for nuclear power status on the grounds that this is an inevitable course of action for a state which in the past has not shown a decent respect for enlightened opinion. This is not to deny—as I have argued earlier—that the government has in the past been interested in using its reluctance to sign the Treaty as a bargaining counter to make tangible economic and political gains. What must be stressed, however, is that in this respect at least, South Africa is not unique in having to calculate the advantages and disadvantages in developing nuclear weapons.

This view is strengthened if we examine the purely strategic arguments for and against the acquisition of a nuclear capability. Obviously these cannot be separated from a consideration of the political implications stemming from a desire to go nuclear or, alternatively, to maintain its present status as a non-nuclear power.

The first question to ask is whether the addition of nuclear weapons to the South African armoury will significantly enhance its security in a military sense.

The government's fierce anti-communist posture in the external realm derives from a variety of sources, not the least of which is the conviction that any attempt to employ the weapons of subversion and terrorism against the Republic is likely to be Communist inspired and actively supported by the Soviet Union and China. In the government's view, this threat would still remain, however amicable American-Soviet relations were to become and there would be the added disadvantages implicit in the development—remote as this may seem at present—of a coincidence of interest between the super-powers in bringing pressure to bear upon South Africa if only to forestall massive Chinese support for an accelerated campaign of insurgency by the African states. The need to cope with this contingency might constitute a strong incentive to acquire nuclear weapons, although it is doubtful whether in these circumstances the Republic could deter both a United States/Soviet "pre-emptive" intervention as well as the prosecution of a major insurgency by its enemies. Threats to destroy Lusaka, Maputo and Dar-es-Salaam with nuclear weapons might well provoke a crisis that would rapidly spread beyond the confines of the African Continent and South Africa's survival in its present form could not, therefore, be automatically guaranteed. In any event, this scenario assures a pattern of world order radically different from that which prevails at present, though this of course is not to deny the possibility that South Africa might deem it a wise precaution to stockpile both scientific expertise and material resources for the production of nuclear weapons at relatively short notice.

By the same token, the military utility of nuclear weapons might seem dubious given the government's perception of a threat confronting the regime. The latter has concentrated on developing an effective counter-insurgency capability and it is difficult to see how nuclear weapons could usefully add to it.[22] It is unlikely that such weapons would deter the promotion of wars of liberation by South Africa's enemies abroad and any attempt to use them in response to conventional invasion by the combined forces of the O.A.U. would run the risk of direct involvement of the great powers in the conflict and this, as we have seen, is the one eventuality the South African government is most anxious to avoid. Nor can there be any doubt that for the present the Republic has managed to contain successfully any threat of insurgency within its own borders—apart from the counter-insurgency operation being conducted against SWAPO guerrillas in the northern part of Namibia.

---

22. This assumption has received substantial confirmation in a closely-argued analysis by Geoffrey Kemp. His interpretations of South Africa's defence expenditure between 1948 and 1971 reveals that apparently "at least eighty per cent of the . . . defence programme budget is allocated for the landward threat," G. Kemp, "South Africa's Defence Programme," 14 *Survival* (1972), p. 159.

In this context we should note Mr. Vorster's periodic threat to strike directly at the homeland of those states providing sanctuary for African insurgents. This, however, would literally be a weapon of last resort to be employed only if the insurgents began to make significant inroads into South Africa itself. At present, however, neither Zambia nor Mozambique show any sign of being deterred from their supportive role in the Rhodesian struggle and one wonders how far either would reconsider their commitment if and when the insurgents began to make sizeable gains in the Republic and the latter threatened the use of nuclear weapons. This would presumably depend upon a range of factors such as the costs the Republic would incur in terms of heightening the likelihood of external intervention if nuclear retaliation was offered against targets in Zambia and Mozambique. There is also the *strategic* utility of such bombing to be considered and here the parallel of American air-strikes in North and South Vietnam springs readily to mind.

While this is speculative it is perhaps worth considering how far both African and South African calculations would be affected by the substitution of nuclear weapons for the conventional strength already possessed by the former. My guess—and it cannot be more than that in so speculative an area—is that a nuclear deterrence capability might well be even less credible than the existing conventional deterrent if only because of the opprobrium that attaches to any state (and South Africa is not just any state) brandishing nuclear weapons over the defenseless heads of its weaker neighbours.

It seems impossible that either the Soviet Union or China would be willing to back their present degree of support for wars of liberation directed against South Africa with nuclear threats. Furthermore, the attempts by a variety of freedom movements to provoke insurgency in South Africa squares with the emphasis in Chinese revolutionary theory on the idea of the protracted struggle using the classic techniques of guerrilla warfare. It is difficult to see how the threat of nuclear attack could be accommodated satisfactorily within this theory and what advantages would be forthcoming as a result for those engaged in wars of this kind against the white South.

On the other hand it could be argued that the presence of Cuban forces in Angola (and the increase in both Soviet interest and influence that this development represents) have strengthened the South African incentive to acquire a nuclear capability if only to deter further Soviet instrusion in Rhodesia, Namibia and ultimately the Republic. And in this context, the failure of the United States to back up South Africa's intervention on the side of the UNITA forces in Angola, has certainly raised doubts about the West's willingess to act decisively to forestall a further extension of Soviet influence in Southern Africa.

Whether such options are open to the Soviet Union in the wake of its Angolan success, is a matter of considerable debate;[23] it is doubtful, however, whether the guerrilla movements concerned with the liberation of the remaining white ruled states or territories as well as the host of states in Mozambique, Botswana and Zambia would welcome Russian/Cuban conventional support to achieve their aims. After all, an extension of the present scale of guerrilla war into a conventional struggle involving the massive deployment of Cuban forces would probably provoke South African intervention and have damaging effects on the stability of the political and economic systems of the "front line" states. In any case, the guerilla leaders believe that they can win without having to call on Cuban help in this way; the struggle might take longer, but having won, the victorious leadership would have any debts to pay to outside powers.

If this is the likely course of events over the next few years, the real threat to South Africa will come when it is entirely surrounded on its northern borders by black governed states, all of which might well be the products of long drawn-out revolutionary war. Their governments might be willing to offer sanctuary to liberation movements bent on destroying the last citadel of white power in South Africa. A withdrawal behind the boundaries of both the Orange and Limpopo rivers might in these circumstances be the prelude to the creation of a garrison state determined to deal with any threat from within and without. To do this effectively would require all the counter-insurgency capability the Republic could muster and it is, therefore, hard to see the relevance of nuclear weapons—either as a deterrent or a defence—given this definition of the Republic's security needs over the long run.

Nuclear weapons seem equally irrelevant if we assume a more hopeful outcome for South Africa, involving, say, the establishment of black governments in Rhodesia and Namibia by constitutional rather than violent means. In these circumstances, South Africa would presumably have an interest in trying to revive and foster a high degree of detente with its black neighbours and the acquisition of nuclear weapons in this context would profoundly disturb such governments and make the pursuit of co-existence extremely difficult.

Yet another interpretation competes for our attention, however: it may be that Soviet interests in the area as manifested, for example, by the deployment of warships in the Indian Ocean since 1968 is motivated by political

---

23. J. E. Spence "Detente in Southern Africa: An Interim Judgement," *International Affairs*, Vol. 53, No. 1, Jan. 1977, pp. 1-16.

rather than military considerations and designed to gain influence on the latter states to exert leverage in situations of internal crisis. If this proposition is accepted, then it constitutes a further argument against the Republic deriving any advantage from the acquistion of nuclear weapons. Such action would probably serve to enhance Soviet influence in East and Central Africa if only on the grounds that the leaders of states in those areas would constitute a receptive audience to Soviet propaganda that stressed the aggressive ambitions of a Republic armed with weapons of mass destruction.

Moreover, a decision to take up the nuclear option might have adverse diplomatic effects on South Africa's relations with the Western Powers: not only because of the latter's hostility to the proliferation of nuclear weapons in general, but because of the effect this would have on a relationship which is already sufficiently ambiguous and subject to periodic strains and criticism from third parties. The spectacle of a nuclear armed South Africa would inevitably call into question still further the morality of dealing with a country, the domestic policies of which arouse such widespread hostility. It may be that in the last analysis criticisms of this kind could be ignored with impunity in the knowledge that there are few if any effective sanctions that can be brought to bear on the Western powers to alter their policies towards the Republic. On the other hand, both Britain and the United States would come under severe pressure from the more militant of the African states and make more difficult the traditional justification of British Conservation leaders that the best way of achieving racial harmony in South Africa lies in a policy of conciliation and co-operation with Afrikaner Nationalism.

Given that Britain and South Africa have an interest in maintaining existing political and economic links, it is obviously to their mutual advantage that this relationship remains free—as far as possible—from any stress caused by external or internal criticism by those who aspire to embarrass both countries and cast doubt on the legitimacy of British economic involvement in South Africa. Nor can the question of sanctions be summarily dismissed: British interests in independent Africa are considerable and from time to time they are subject to threat by African leaders impatient with British unwillingness to take active steps to induce change in the Republic. Clear evidence that South Africa was developing nuclear weapons would thus strain British relations still further with independent states on the Continent and at the very least obstruct the attempt by both governments to keep their relations with each other on a "normal" footing.

These then are the restraints which might operate to preclude South Africa becoming a nuclear power in the near future. The belief that a nuclear capability will enhance national prestige may well be a factor influencing a decision of other would-be nuclear powers, but it is very doubtful whether this would be true for the Republic. The status which allegedly comes from acquiring nuclear weapons may well serve as an integrating factor in developing societies, but in South Africa's case the effect of such a development on the Black majority would hardly be similar. As far as the two white communities are concerned, their cohesion into a single white community has been helped by the criticisms launched at the Republic from abroad. Nuclear weapons might help consolidate this sense of white South African identity, but this would occur only as a by-product of a decision to go nuclear on the quite different grounds of national security and the needs of external defence. The aspiration to acquire 'respectability' in the eyes of its traditional associates in the Western camp is deep-rooted and foreign policy throughout the post-war period has concentrated on attempts to persuade these powers that South Africa is indeed indispensable to their security needs in the South Atlantic–Indian Ocean region. Adoption of a nuclear posture would cut across these efforts to tie the Republic more closely into the structure of western defence and equally run counter to a policy based on strengthening economic and political links with a view to enhancing the Republic's value as a trading partner and reliable ally.

It could therefore be argued that there are a number of political, strategic and economic considerations which militate against South Africa becoming a nuclear power, or at least openly declaring themselves to be one (as distinct from maintaining its present ambiguous posture). Such a step would damage long standing aspirations to enjoy increasingly co-operative relationships with traditional allies; in strategic terms, the potential increment to the Republic's security represented by nuclear weapons capability would seem to be outweighed by the inevitable distrust that would surround its intentions, especially in those regions of Africa where it has attempted to maximise political and economic influence. In the economic context, South Africa would appear to have more to gain from using its nuclear resources to strengthen commercial and technological ties with the advanced nations of the West, rather than branding itself as a nuclear outsider and adding considerably to the opprobrium which in the past has surrounded its role in international politics.

Two major qualifications remain however: first the constraints discussed in the preceding analysis assume a world in which the pressures in favour of non-proliferation tend to outweigh the incentives to join the nuclear club. In other words, South Africa is unlikely to be the sixth nuclear power; on the other hand, if gross proliferation[24] were to take place South Africa might

---

24. See R. H. Rosecrance, *Problems of Nuclear Proliferation*, Security Studies, Paper No. 7 (University of California, Los Angeles, 1966) pp. 42-44

have relatively little to lose in prestige terms by becoming, for example, the twelfth nuclear power.

Secondly, the Republic's decision-makers may come to feel increasingly isolated if and when the Western Powers decide that a fundamental shift in the Southern African balance of power requires that their governments substantially reduce the level of their present commitment to the maintenance of the economic and political status quo in South Africa. Such a policy of disassociation might well force the latter to acquire a nuclear capability as a symbol of its determination to stand alone on the principle of *fiat justicia, pereat mundus*. This might be described as the apocalyptic option—the choice of last resort—and possibly what Dr. Collie Mulder meant when he stated that—". . . if we are attacked, no rules apply at all if it comes to a question of our existence." How far this is rhetoric, designed to confuse the calculations of western policy-makers and make them hesitate about radical changes in their policy towards South Africa (and the ambiguities of the Israeli posture on nuclear weapons provides an apt comparison in this context), how far the possession of a nuclear deterrent would constitute a realistic and strategic political option are questions which the West would do well to ponder during the next and perhaps the most difficult phase of its relations with the Republic.

Conclusions

South Africa has the capability of becoming a nuclear power; resources and technology are both available in the form of uranium and the development of an unsafeguarded enrichment process, together with the longer term possibility of re-processed plutonium deriving from the operation of French installed reactors—the ostensible purpose of which is the generation of nuclear power for civil purposes. The Republic has also a delivery system which is adequate for its purposes.

Is the motive for not signing the NPT *still* the fact that South Africa hopes to use its non-compliance as a bargaining counter for gaining an even greater degree of economic and technological integration with the West? In this context, we should note the obvious commercial advantage deriving from being in a position to sell enriched uranium to states requiring the material to feed civil and/or military programmes.

If the answer to the above is positive, then the desire to persist with the traditional strategy of closer integration with the West might just constrain the Republic from an open declaration of nuclear weapon status in the knowledge that to do so would make it more difficult for the West to sustain its economic and technological linkages with South Africa. By the same token, such a declaration would weaken the credibility of the orthodox Western belief that co-operation rather than conflict with South Africa is the surest way to transform the institutions of that society over the long run.

On the other hand, what are the implications for South Africa as a potential nuclear power should Western governments move from a policy of implicitly supporting the status quo to one involving active disassociation in economic and political terms? There is evidence of a growing belief in both the United States and the United Kingdom governing circles (in contrast to the attitudes that prevailed on this issue in the 1960s) that the white minority cannot sustain itself in power indefinitely.[25] Furthermore, that pressures will build up both within South Africa and on its periphery and the combined effects of these will produce a degree of dislocation and violence difficult to contain, even by a government as well prepared for the worst as is South Africa. The prospect of guerrillas operating from the sanctuaries of the "front line" states, outbursts of urban violence, a possible involvement of Cuban conventional forces, have combined to compel Western governments (the U.S. and the U.K. in particular) to revise their strategies on the issues of change and its consequences in Southern Africa. One that does appear to have been decisively rejected is what might be termed the "minimalist" strategy: that is, a policy of waiting passively on events in the confident expectation that once the worst has happened (in this case, the destruction of white rule in the Republic by revolution and its replacement by a black successor regime), Western governments, investors and traders can simply "pick up the pieces" and resume previously profitable diplomatic and economic links. The successful regime would have little alternative but to return to the *status quo ante* since only the West has the necessary capital, skills and experience to develop the area's resources. The chief objection to this strategy is two-fold:

1. if violence does spread into the Republic, the resulting dislocation will probably be long and physically destructive of much of what constitutes existing Western economic interests in Southern Africa, and

2. the new regime may well turn its back on offers from the West, however seductive, and look to the Soviet Union and/or China for major assistance with the task of internal reconstruction.

Hence the case for a strategy which avoids the worst by applying such pressures as are available to induce significant change in Southern Africa. This is, after all, precisely what is happening in Namibia and Rhodesia where it is readily acknowledged that the West has nothing to gain from a transfer of power from white to black brought about by prolonged violence. The difficulty is to decide what pressures will be appropriate. We have little in

25. J. E. Spence, "The West and Southern Africa," Report of a Ditchley Park Seminar, *The Ditchley Journal*, Oct. 1977.

the way of historical experience to guide us when it comes to deciding on measures designed to promote desirable changes in a distant country. The traditional instruments are blunt and uncertain in their effects: war and/or occupation. Understandably, the West fights shy of employing such strategies; but the search goes on for more appropriate techniques for inducing change before the escalation of racial conflict makes peaceful resolution impossible. Economic sanctions, for example, no longer seem quite the utopian strategy suggested in the early 1960s.

It is this outlook that (assuming of course, that Pretoria reads the future in this way) may constitute a considerable incentive for requiring nuclear weapons. The basic assumption would be that the West was a weak reed not to be trusted to help when the Republic's security was really threatened. In these circumstances, a declaration of nuclear weapon status will *in advance* of this potential combination of events quite conceivably be seen as serving to complicate Western calculations about the desirability of exerting significant pressures on the Republic. Of course, the advantages to be gained from a dramatic step of this kind would have to be weighed against the damage that might be done to the traditional policy of maintaining links with the West in economic and technological terms.

Yet another possibility suggests itself: Pretoria might gamble correctly on the assumption that an open declaration of nuclear status could have positively beneficial consequences for its relations with the West:

(a) NATO might be moved to offer South Africa a degree of military co-operation on the grounds that a maverick nuclear state is better constrained within an alliance framework than outside it.

(b) That after an initial flurry of concern and disapproval at South Africa joining the "nuclear club," relations would return to normal, trade and investments would continue, the Republic would have earned a degree a grudging and wary respect in Western capitals for this obvious and dramatic improvement in its military capability.

One other constraint against following the above course remains to be taken into consideration: in this context we have to assume that South Africa still maintains an interest in developing co-existence relationships with its black neighbours; that détente remains an aspiration, indeed a necessity if and when black governments come to power in Namibia and Zimbabwe. Pretoria may be counting on these governments being willing and able to restrain freedom fighters wishing to use their territory (and that of Mozambique) as bases for guerilla infiltration and subversion of the black majority within the Republic. Thus an open declaration of nuclear status might be construed as damaging prospects for co-existence with both old and new "front line" states.

In the writer's view, the most likely short term outcome will be the adoption by South Africa of an *ambiguous* posture on the nuclear weapon issue, i.e., hints will continue to be dropped about the state's potential nuclear capabilities on the assumption that ambiguity about capability and intentions can create a degree of uncertainty in opponents' minds, and add, therefore, a margin of deterrence to one's general strategic position. This option would seem to be attractive for the following reasons.

(a) It would not adversely affect relations with the Western powers (assuming that those are still regarded as important and it is hard to see how the reverse could be true, given the value of trade and investment from the West for the maintenance of economic growth in the Republic).

(b) Attempts to achieve détente with black neighbours could be resumed, especially if governments in those states were prepared to offer economic advantages to South African capital and export industries.

(c) The option of an open declaration could always be taken up at short notice if the apocalypse threatened, and the development of nuclear weapons were to be seen as having a political and military utility which at present does seem difficult to justify.

IV. India

The Policy Process

P. R. CHARI

I. Introduction

In a fundamental sense, administrative processes in transitional periods, have the same problems of retaining continuity whilst allowing change which accosts other aspects of State behaviour. Bureaucracies are notoriously conservative and averse to radical change. This is most clearly evident in the sphere of security management, where the stakes are traditionally perceived as being too vital to permit large experimentation. The stronger emphasis is on continuity, the attitude towards change is cautious. Hence, bequeathed historical traditions in a post-colonial country like India assume great significance in policy mechanisms for the management of security.

Two characteristics of the Indian policy-making process for defense require special attention. First, the British legacy needs notice, which evolved over two centuries. Traditions were established which permitted the growth of a Westminister-type Parliamentary form of governance in post-Independent India. The other major tradition established was civilian control over the apparatus. It was the civilian government in Britain which actually asserted this supremacy — within the country the Commander-in-Chief of the British armed forces enjoyed a unique position. But the principle was established that the armed forces functioned within a system wherein ultimate decisions were made by the political executive.

The second characteristic worth emphasis is the continuance of the parliamentary, democratic form of government in post-Independent India, and the continued assertion of the principle of civil supremacy over the military. These traditions have, indeed, strengthened since Independence. The uniqueness of this situation arises because India is a developing country, and has serious problems of national integration, over-population, poverty, unemployment and so on which strain the governmental apparatus. Most countries in the developing world have governments exercising different levels of authoritarianism. Many have military dictatorships, others have military

127

establishments exercising a dominant influence over the decision-making process. This situation does not obtain in India.

A mention of the Emergency period is necessary here, which lasted for some twenty months, and was dramatically rescinded after the defeat of the Congress party at the polls in March 1977. During this interregnum the democratic process was curtailed, civil rights were circumscribed, censorship of the press existed and a form of personal autocracy obtained. But it needs pointing out that, even during this period, Parliamentary and legislative processes continued as provided in the Indian Constitution, although the fact that its spirit was violated is unquestioned. The armed forces could have played an important part in maintaining the Emergency but it is clear now that they were not utilized for this purpose. Even during this period the cardinal principle of civilian direction of the military apparatus was neither questioned nor in doubt.[1]

The policy-making process inherited by India, therefore, requires analysis to describe the changes wrought therein by administrative changes after Independence and the provisions of the Indian Constitution. The manner in which civilian supremacy is exercised in the security processes also requires attention. Thereafter, it is proposed to scrutinize the role — marginal or significant — of interest groups which influence the policy-making process. The nexus between foreign and defense policy would be examined to describe how threat assessments are made in India, which is cardinal to defense planning. Space only permits a discussion of one important problem which the defense decision-making process seeks to address viz. the linked issues of weapons selection, external procurement and indigenous defense production.

British Legacy:

It could be inferred that the position of the military in British India was predominant, since the armed forces were the ultimate authority upholding the colonial occupation of India. Indubitably, the Commander-in-Chief dominated the defense appartus. He was the executive head of the armed forces in India including the Royal Indian Navy and Royal Indian Air Force. He was an extraordinary member of the Viceroy's Council — second in position only to the Viceroy. An Army Department existed under the Commander-in-Chief. It did not perform any true Secretariat functions as it could neither initiate new proposals nor examine proposals mooted by Army Headquarters. The role of the Army Department was restricted to issuing orders only in the name of the Government of India. In fact, this Department was

---

1. For a discussion on the unlikelihood of military coups taking place in India see S. S. Khera, *India's Defence Problems* (Bombay: Orient Longmans, 1968), pp. 80-89.

headed by a Major General till 1921; after that a civilian was appointed as its Secretary. The Army Department was renamed Defence Department in 1936. Except for a few minor changes during the war years, the basic structure of defense administration remained unaltered.

Any inference, however, that the military dominated the defense apparatus would be incorrect for two reasons. First, the British Government in India functioned in total subordination to the British Cabinet. All major issues, especially those pertaining to sensitive defense matters were settled in London. Further, civilian and military functions were coordinated and major differences resolved by the Secretary of State for India in Britain. Second, all proposals with a financial bearing made by the Commander-in-Chief were scrutinized by an independent Military Finance Department. This was headed by a joint Financial Secretary, primarily responsible to the Finance Member in the Viceroy's Council. That an independent financial judgment eroded the Commander-in-Chief's powers, and was found irksome, is evident.[2]

A diagrammatic representation of the higher defense organization in India on the eve of Independence would be as under:

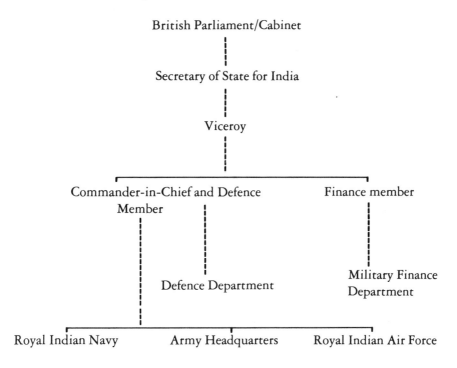

----

2. See, for instance, Stephen P. Cohen, *The Indian Army: Its Contribution to the Development of a Nation* (Bombay: Oxford University Press, 1971), p. 30 n.50.

A transitional period of about a year—Interim Government—preceded the ushering in of Independence on August 15, 1947. During this interregnum an Indian Defence Member was appointed to the Viceroy's Council. The Commander-in-Chief was simultaneously withdrawn from the Council, although he continued to head the three armed forces. A Defence Member's Committee was set up to consider important defense questions. It was headed by the Defence Member and had the Commander-in-Chief, the Defence Secretary and the Financial Adviser as its constituents. On the eve of Independence the heads of the Navy and Air Force were elevated to the rank of Commanders-in-Chief of their Services for the expressed reason that it was necessary to provide for a balanced growth of all the three Services.

Post-Independence Changes:

With the achievement of Independence the Defence *Member's* Committee was converted into the Defence *Minister's* Committee, and the heads of the Navy and Air Force were included therein. It became necessary for the fledgling Ministry to undertake tasks organic to higher defense management viz. external threat assessment, budgetary formulation, planning, weapons procurement, defense production and other allied matters. There was also the delicate problem of balancing the demands of the three Services for scarce resources. Such matters had been decided previously by either Services Headquarters in Britain or by Whitehall. It needs emphasis that the level of expertise available at that time on either the civilian or military sides of the decision-making machinery was nowhere equal to those exacting tasks. This paucity of expertise was made worse by the division of the civil services and armed forces between India and Pakistan consequent to partition of the country. The Defence Ministry had been a closed area of Governmental functioning for Indians during British rule; the few Indians who did serve in that Ministry before Independence had either worked in junior positions or in peripheral areas.

Some figures would reveal the experience available in the armed forces. There were only 93 officers of the ranks of substantive and acting Lieutenant Colonels. The Navy had only two regular Indian officers with over ten years of service, and the Air Force four officers with eleven years of service. Few Indians had the opportunity to familiarize themselves with staff work in General Headquarters; in any case the Indian General Headquarters was only a theatre command during the Second World War, and was not concerned with formulating or implementing national security policies. The dependence, therefore, on Britain continued. It is revealing that the first Indian Commander-in-Chief of the Army assumed charge on January 15, 1949, the first

Indian Commander-in-Chief of the Air Force was appointed on April 1, 1954, and the first Indian Naval Chief came into office on April 22, 1958.[3]

Despite these structural weaknesses, an attempt to assert civilian supremacy over the military is evident from the appointment of non-military personages as the first and subsequent Defence Ministers. Two other developments of symbolic significance need notice. First, and this aspect has attracted Western scholarly attention,[4] was the downgradation of military officers in the Warrant of Precedence. For instance, the Chief Secretary to a State had been ranked with a brigadier; after Independence he ranked with a major-general. The Chief Secretary to a State now ranks with a Secretary to the Government of India who ranks with a full general. All changes in the Warrant of Precedence, incidentally, are based on constitutional status, pay drawn and historical changes. In practice, it means little, and, only permits a rational seating arrangement at ceremonial functions. Second, the appelation Commander-in-Chief, with its colonial connotations, was dropped from the titles of the three Service Chiefs in 1955. Henceforth, they were designated as Chief of the Army Staff, Chief of the Naval Staff, and Chief of the Air Staff.

An overview of these developments would suggest a conscious and deliberate attempt by the Indian political executive to curtail the preeminent position enjoyed by the military apparatus in pre-Independent India. This can be explained as an unavoidable development, as the process of transition from colonial domination to parliamentary democracy proceeded. Considering this question I have noticed elsewhere: "The preeminence of the military apparatus in India expressed the fundamentally military occupational nature of British rule. The armed forces maintained law and order within the country and furthered British imperial interests abroad. The establishment of a parliamentary form of government rendered it axiomatic that the armed forces should be brought under effective administrative control and made an instrument of national policy. A reduction in the role of the military was inevitable within the historical process."[5]

Constitutional Position

Shifting our focus from civil-military relations to the decision-making process the relevant Constitutional provisions need attention. The Indian

3. K. Subrahmanyan, *Defence* (New Delhi: Publications Division, 1972), pp. 11-12.

4. As, for example, Stephen P. Cohen, *The Indian Army*, pp. 172-73; Lorne J. Kavic, *India's Quest for Security: Defence Policies, 1947-1965* (Berkeley and Los Angeles: University of California Press, 1967), p. 143.

5. P. R. Chari, "Civil-Military Relations in India," *Armed Forces and Society* (Chicago) Vol. 4, No. 1, November 1977, p. 11.

Constitution envisages a federation with unitary aspects, consequently subjects are reserved within the exclusive legislative competence of the Union Government and the State Governments—there is also a concurrent area where both can legislate. All matters relating to defense and security lie within the exclusive legislative powers of the Union (federal or central) Government, which would be abundantly clear from the following recital of items in the Union List of legislative subjects:—

1. Defense of India and every part thereof including preparation for defense and all such acts as may be conducive in times of war to its prosecution and after its termination to effective demobilization.

2. Naval, military and air forces; any other armed forces of the Union.

3. Delimitation of cantonment areas, local self-government in such areas, the constitution and powers within such areas of cantonment authorities and the regulation of house accommodation (including the control of rents) in such areas.

4. Naval, military and air force works.

5. Arms, firearms, ammunition and explosives. . . .

7. Industries declared by Parliament by law to be necessary for the purposes of defense or for the prosecution of war. . . .

9. Preventive detention for reasons connected with Defense, Foreign Affairs, or the Security of India, persons subjected to such detention. . . .

15. War and peace.

That the primary responsibility for ensuring the defense and security of India devolves upon the Union Government is evident.

Further, the Constitution makes clear that the executive authority of the Union Government, including that over the armed forces, vests in the President—the relevant provisions being:—

Article 53(1) The executive power of the Union shall be vested in the President and shall be exercised by him either directly or through officers subordinate to him in accordance with this Constitution.

Article 53(2). Without prejudice to the generality of the foregoing provision, the supreme command of the Defence Forces of the Union shall be vested in the President and the exercise thereof shall be regulated by law.

In view of the similar Constitutional position of the Indian President to a monarch in a democratic country, the authority available to him is exercised by the Prime Minister. This is envisaged in Article 74(1) of the Constitution which adumbrates: "There shall be a Council of Ministers with the Prime

Minister at the head to aid and advise the President (who shall) in the exercise of his functions, (act in accordance with such advice.)"[6]

The Decision-Making Process:

On the institutional side the Council of Ministers or the Cabinet exercises supervision over defense and security matters through the Political Affairs Committee of the Cabinet, of which the Prime Minister is the Chairman. Besides the Defense Minister, the Ministers for External Affairs, Home and Finance are its usual members; collectively this Committee constitutes the highest policy formulating authority in India for all matters relating to national security. During its deliberations the Chiefs of Staff are in attendance to provide any advice that may be required.

The routine functioning of the Ministry of Defence is overseen by the Defence Minister, who is assisted for this purpose by one or two junior colleagues. A separate Department of Defence Production was set up in 1962 to deal with research and development and the production of defense equipment. A Department of Defence Supplies was established in 1965 with the primary intention of achieving import substitution, and encouraging the indigenization of defense equipment. Generally these Departments are looked after by a junior Minister, but form part of the overall responsibility of the Defence Minister.

For purposes of administration and implementation of defense policy the Defence Minister has two major Committees. One of them is the Defence Minister's Committee, whose origins we have noticed. It concerns itself with the defense plan, important issues relating to the three Services and inter-Service problems. The other major Committee—the Defence Minister's (Production and Supply) Committee—regulates the defense production effort and coordination with civil industry. The Ministers in the Ministry of Defence, the Service Chiefs, Defence Secretary and Financial Adviser (Defence Services) are members of these Committees. In addition, there is a Defence Research and Coordination Council which directs and coordinates scientific research related to defense problems. There are, besides these, the Defence Minister's Appelate Committee on Pensions and other Committees at the apex of the decision making process reporting directly to the Defence Minister's Committee. Their names reveal their functions—Defence Electronics Committee, Principal Personnel Officers Committee, and Principal Supply Officers Committee.

6. Words in square brackets introduced by a recent amendment.

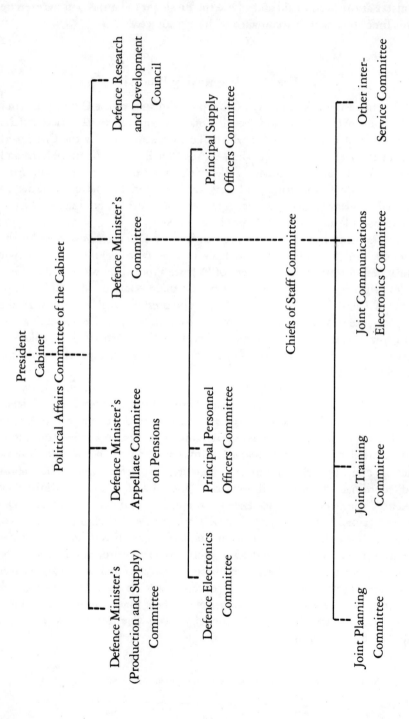

At the professional level the highest inter-Services Committee is the Chiefs of Staff Committee which is headed by the Service Chief who has had the longest tenure on this Committee. Not only does the Chiefs of Staff Committee decide inter-Service issues within its competence, and project other problems to Government collectively, it is the highest military adviser to Government on defense issues. The Chiefs of Staff Committee is assisted by sub-committees with specific functions like the Joint Planning Committee, Joint Training Committee, Joint Communications Committee and so on.[7]

The chart depicted on the opposite page explains the organizational framework in India for decision-making in the highest defense apparatus. An important innovation made in 1962 after the Sino-Indian border conflict was the institution called "morning meeting," which are held whenever the Defence Minister is in New Delhi, and average two a week. These meetings are held without an agenda, and discuss the latest developments on the border or in the country which have a bearing on defense. The "morning meetings" are attended by the Cabinet Secretary, Service Chiefs, Secretaries in the Ministry, and the Scientific Adviser to the Defence Minister; they provide a forum for policy review and also to bring up urgent operational or Service problems for quick decision. An equally important purpose is to establish "a kind of rapport, an interchange of ideas, and an understanding which makes for easy working, without much of paper work."[8] This description of the higher defense organization in India might give the impression that a formal and rigid hierarchical stratification through these Committees obtains. But this system of working through formal, informal and ad hoc bodies has many advantages. It permits the best military and political advice to be laid before the Minister; it enables the establishment of a sense of camaraderie between persons belonging to essentially different professions; besides, decisions obtained by consensus are calculated to have the greatest acceptability down the chain of civil and military administration. Over the years a convention has been established that purely operational matters lie within the domain of the Services. The operational directive issues from the political leadership. The interaction between Services Headquarters and the Ministries of Defence and Finance is concerned with providing the wherewithal for achieving the directions contained within the operational directive.

It would be useful to comment here on the general lines of criticism against this pattern of decision-making in the defense apparatus. These crit-

7. For more details on the Indian Defence Organisation, including the structure of the Defence Ministry, Army, Naval and Air Headquarters, see *Annual Report: 1971-72, Ministry of Defence* (New Delhi: Government of India Press, 1972), pp. 178-187.

8. Air Chief Marshall P. C. Lal, "Higher Defence Organisation" in *Defence of India* (New Delhi: Press Institute of India, 1969), p. 84.

icisms follow two streams. First, it is alleged that a consensus of opinion is generally projected by Services Headquarters by way of advice, or in the form of proposals. Inter-Service Committees, including the Chiefs of Staff Committee, are deemed to be no substitute for a unified joint command. Hence, it becomes necessary for the Minister to balance competing demands made by the three Services, particularly for scarce budgetary allocations, and take decisions which are compromises, but not the best ones for purely operational considerations. Second, and this line of criticism is more persistent, there is the complaint by the military that the Ministry of Defence acts as an unnecessary intermediary between Services Headquarters and the Defence Minister. All branches of Services Headquarters are replicated in the Ministry, which has powers to decide most issues apart from purely military questions. It is believed that: "this system is time-consuming, requiring elaborate and detailed preparation of a case and endless conferences. The Ministry being a step removed from the Service Headquarters has no executive responsibility but all the authority. Further, the Minister acting through a separate Defence Ministry will naturally tend to rely more on the civilians of the Ministry than on the Military experts."[9] A subsidiary argument here is that civilians only serve in the Ministry of Defence for a fixed number of years due to the operations of the "tenure principle," and are consequently unable to develop the expertise necessary to deal with complex security issues.

Consequently, the solutions offered to remedy this state of affairs are that an integrated Services Headquarters should be established, wherein civilian officials of the Ministry of Defence would work alongside their military counterparts, and the Minister would be advised through the Service Chiefs. In this system, which approximates the British pattern, only financial control would rest with the civilians. The other proposal mooted is that a Chief of Defence Staff should be appointed, who would coordinate proposals from the three Services, present them in an integrated form to the Government and also ensure that effective inter-Services coordination takes place. Such a personage could be nominated by rotation from the three Services.

The failure to establish an integrated Secretariat — it might have proved a more effective system for the higher direction of defense in India — is historical. Unlike Britain, the Chiefs of Staff preferred to remain outside the Government as independent heads of Services and did not merge with the Ministry of Defence to become principal advisers to the Defence Minister. This position was inscribed in the Army, Navy and Air Force Acts which were suitably amended in 1955 for this purpose. Consequently, the Services

9. Lt. Gen. P. S. Bhagat, *The Defence of India and South East Asia (Forging the Shield)* (Dehradun: E. B. D. Publishing and Distributing Company, 1967), p. 56.

Headquarters became separate entities as distinct from the civilian set-up comprising the Ministry of Defence.[10] Establishment of a Joint Chiefs of Staff Committee, therefore, would be subject to the liability that it would continue to function outside the Government, unlike the situation obtaining in other countries following this system. In fact, it was suggested by Jawaharlal Nehru to the Service Chiefs in 1955, before their designations were to be changed, that he was willing to consider establishment of Service Councils on the style of the Army Council in Britain, in which the Chief of Staff and Principal Staff Officers would be members. This suggestion was first accepted by the Service Chiefs, but they later changed their minds on the suspicion that the Army Council in England had been conceived and was set up, so as to reduce the power of the Duke of Cambridge, who was the Service Chief, and was Queen Victoria's brother (sic) [cousin]."[11]

The debate regarding appointment of a Chief of Defence Staff follows a desultory course. The arguments for and against the proposal are well-balanced. For the proposal it is argued that a single Service head would be able to plan, coordinate and integrate inter-Service functions more effectively, and that the present system of individual Service Chiefs functioning in a largely independent manner might lead to breakdown of inter-Service cooperation during emergencies. It is also argued that it would be advantageous for the Services to have a single channel focusing Service problems to the Government rather than the present essentially competitive system. Against the proposal it is urged that the Chief of Defence Staff would find it difficult to avoid bias towards his own Service, that the quality of his advice is unlikely to be markedly superior to that of the Service Chiefs, and that the Army, as the predominantly larger force in the Indian armed forces would dominate this arrangement, since a Chief of Defence Staff from the two smaller Services would lack credibility. The Government has repeatedly declared that this system is not under consideration. It is unlikely to find the proposal acceptable for the purely political consideration that it revives the Commander-in-Chief post in another form — which is anathema.

The criticism that civilians in the Ministry of Defence lack expertise is well-founded. Under present arrangements officers manning the Ministry serve for periods between three to five years and return thereafter to their parent Departments. There is no certainty that, in later tenures with the Central Government, they would be posted back to the Ministry of Defence. Consequently, the belief arises in Services Headquarters that examination of their proposals in the Ministry does not proceed with the knowledge or

10. K. Subrahmanyam, *Perspectives in Defence Planning* (New Delhi: Abhinav Publications, 1972), p. 121.

11. S. S. Khera, *India's Defence Problems* (New Delhi: Orient Longman, 1968), p. 16.

insight required to deal with complicated cases. This line of criticism can be overdrawn, because a fair degree of expertise has been developed, particularly by members of the Finance Ministry—there is a specific Service on the civilian side concerned with Defence Accounts. Besides, the generally non-transferrable civilian Armed Forces Headquarters Service and the Central Secretariat Service provide continuity, and perform the memory functions required for defense administration. Nevertheless, the basic reason underlying these criticisms is the perceived need for innovation in an essentially conservative administrative system, as also the belief that the importance of the armed forces in that system has eroded over the years since Indpendence.

Extra-Governmental Pressure Groups:

The role of interest groups outside the governmental decision-making apparatus relating to defense can now be examined. The most noteworthy influence is that exercised by Parliament, to which the Cabinet and the Minister for Defence are primarily responsible. A particularly severe judgment has it that India lacks the mature understanding to comprehend the complex problems of defense and security; it continues: "Witness the perfunctory manner in which our Parliament debates defence matters. The annual exercise of voting on Defence Estimates has been reduced to a mere ritual. Parliamentary excursions into the realm of defence sometimes generate heat but never light."[12] Explaining the role of Parliament in shaping foreign policy—equally applicable to defense policy—Krishna Menon believed: ". . . discussions in Parliament have the result of showing the world what we think and that we do think. . . . I think it [Parliament] performs a very useful function. There are speeches made. Some of the speeches made are a kind of routine opposition and often strong views are expressed. This enables the Prime Minister and the Government to feel that even if a thing has to be done for diplomatic or other reasons, Parliament should at least be told about it."[13] Such views would strengthen the belief that Parliament has a peripheral role in the defense decision-making process. Yet another opinion has it that Parliament's peripheral role stems from its being ill-equipped organizationally to investigate or supervise security affairs. Parliamentary Committees have little impact, because they bring little interest or expertise to bear on their tasks, neither have they seriously attempted independent examination of security problems.[14] All these are exceptionally harsh critiques of the influence of Parliament on defense decision-making. Its

12. P. N. Haksar, "Appearance and Reality," *Seminar* (New Delhi) No. 225, May 1978, pp. 39-40.
13. Michael Brecher, *India and World Politics: Krishna Memon's View of the World* (London: Oxford University Press, 1968), p. 262.
14. Stephen P. Cohen, "India's Security: Process and Policy," in Giri Raj Gupta Ed.

interaction with the Government must first be described before it is analyzed.

In conformity with the practice obtaining in other Parliamentary democracies a great deal of information about the working of the defense mechanism in India is elicited by Parliament through the device of questions, adjournment motions, calling attention motions and so on. This affords the opportunity, particularly for Opposition groups, to discuss specific aspects of defense policy, and ensure an element of responsiveness from the Government to public concerns. The entire working of the defense apparatus can be criticized during the annual debate on the Budget Demands. Besides, there are Parliamentary Committees which examine defense expenditure, and evaluate whether it is being properly incurred. The Public Accounts Committee scrutinizes past expenditure on the basis of the Audit Report prepared by the Controller and Auditor General, who is an independent authority under the Indian Constitution. The Estimates Committee examines the organizational set-up with a view to achieve economy and efficiency in the administration— it can also subject departmental estimates to a detailed scrutiny *before* they are presented to Parliament. The contention that these Parliamentary Committees only assess administrative performance *ex post facto* is not entirely correct.[15] In addition the Public Undertakings Committee examines the reports of the Comptroller and Auditor General on autonomous defense public sector enterprises to examine what economies, organizational improvements and so on can be effected.[16]

At the informal level a great deal of information is disseminated through the explanatory notes and appendices attached to the Defence Services Estimates presented to Parliament each year and the Annual Reports of the Ministry of Defence. There is a conscious effort to share more information with Parliament and the general public on defense matters in recent years, although there are influences within the defense apparatus which urge caution on the grounds that security might be jeopardized. The argument made is that Pakistan and China are notoriously reticent about their defense policies and security measures; why should India be more forthcoming? An attempt to associate Parliament more closely with the working of the Ministry is also made through the "Informal Consultative Committe," which is attached to each Ministry. The Committee has an all-Party character, and is

Cohesion and Conflict in Modern India (New Delhi: Vikas Publishing House Pvt. Ltd.; and Durham, N.C.: Carolina Academic Press, 1978), p. 250.

15. Raju G. C. Thomas, *The Defence of India: A Budgetary Perspective of Strategy and Politics* (Delhi: The Macmillan Company of India Limited, 1978), p. 80.

16. An account of the functioning over the years of the Public Acct. Committee, Estimates Committee and Public Undertakings Committee may be seen in S. L. Shakder, Ed., *The Constitution and the Parliament in India: The 25 years of the Republic* (New Delhi: National Publishing House, 1976), pp. 386-417.

designed to enable Members of Parliament to obtain a closer understanding of defense issues and programs, through discussions in a freer manner than is practicable on the floor of the Houses of Parliament.

Nevertheless, it is evident that the level of expertise available in the Indian Parliament regarding defense and security matters is hardly commensurate with either the levels of expenditure incurred or the military potential which it obtains for India. Three main reasons seem operative. First, the average Member of Parliament does not show much inclination to take interest in defense matters since, for obvious political reasons, domestic issues dominate his thinking. In other words, a Member would be more largely interested in Ministries which affect his local constituency in a material way. Consequently, parochial interests of the Members are reflected during defense debates. Issues such as recruitment from specific areas, the location of strategic communications, cantonments and defense installations, concessions to serving and retired Services personnel mainly interest individual Members. Concerns such as the defense of the borders, threats to security and defense preparedness are debated only in a general way. Second, a lack of expertise is due to the fact that the British system of "shadow cabinet" is yet to obtain in India—perhaps, this is a reflection of the fact that a clear-cut, ideologically polarized two-Party system has yet to emerge in the polity. Hence it is left to individual Members to develop interest and knowledge in whatever Ministry or Ministries they wish. With the growing complexity of the issues involved the level of expertise available is not sufficient to permit an incisive debate. Third, the system of Parliamentary democracy on the Westminster model is partly responsible for this state of affairs. There are no standing Parliamentary Committees charged with a continuous scrutiny of the defense budget and security issues. Such a Committee could develop expertise through knowledgeable persons associated with it, and subject the defense mechanism to closer supervision. But such a dispensation does not obtain, and is neither expressly provided for, nor envisaged, in the Indian Constitution.

The other pressure or interest groups outside Government can be noticed. First, the political parties have defined positions on security issues like the nuclear option, relations with adversaries, the source of defense procurements, the role of private enterprise in defense production sector and so on. But these positions are, more often than not, based on ideological predilections and political imperatives rather than any deep understanding of these issues. The same liabilities obtain as are operative in Members of Parliament developing necessary expertise in defense issues. No forums or organizations exist within the political parties for a continuous examination or analysis of security issues. Second, the press has taken a lively interest in current defense issues, and a vigorous debate proceeded recently on the purchase of fighter-bombers for the modernization program of the Indian Air Force, and the question of the Navy acquiring a blue-ocean capability. Most national and major newspapers have defense correspondents, usually retired Service officers, and devote at least a page each day to international affairs and security issues. Third, there is a growing consciousness in academic institutions, especially schools teaching international relations, that defense and security problems are worth analysis. To a small extent the Institute for Defence Studies and Analyses has helped create and foster this interest in the press and academic institutions through its publications and seminars. Fourth, the private sector is likely to gain greater influence in the decision-making process due to a larger association with defense production. This would be inevitable as the Government proceeds more swiftly towards it goal of achieving the greatest possible indigenization of defense production in the country.

It is dubious, however, if debate outside the Government, relating to security policy influences its thinking in any material way. At best these forums enable a sensing of the public mood to avoid or defer what might prove unacceptable. This is especially important, or so it is perceived, during internal crisis situations. There is some validity in the observation that: "Strong control and transformative pressure from the political executive alone could have taken India internally and externally on a different path. In practice the political executive, while laying down the broad contours of domestic, defense and foreign policies, has been excessively dependent on the bureaucratic elite, and made very little attempt at transforming its character and outlook."[17] In the somewhat esoteric realm of defense and security policies the influence of the civilian and military bureaucracies is overwhelming. This situation is likely to continue in the future as the defense and security questions with which India would be concerned increase in complexity.

Within the Government:

In this situation the nexus between the Ministries of Defence and External Relations or, more presciently, the bureaucracies in these adjuncts of the security planning process is worth notice. India's policy of non-alignment it is believed was intended to achieve full national independence, a stature of significance in world affairs, and the maintenance of a "third area" between the conflicting power groups.[18] The linkage of this policy with security considerations is not that well-recognized. In view of its military weakness

17. J. Bandyopadhyaya, *The Making of India's Foreign Policy: Determinants, Institutions, Processes and Personalities* (New Delhi: Allied Publishers, 1970), p. 78.

18. Charles H. Heimsath and Surjit Mansingh, *A Diplomatic History of Modern India* (New Delhi: Allied Publishers, 1971), p. 61.

and economic vulnerability non-alignment provided India with a foreign policy option to ensure its security through non-involvement in Cold War dynamics. But foreign military assistance was required to provide for internal and external security. Explaining these seeming anomalies, Nehru observed, ". . . when we say that our policy is one of non-alignment, obviously we mean non-alignment from military blocs. . . . Security can be provided in many ways. The normal idea is that security is protected by armies. That is only partly true; it is equally true that security is protected by policies. A deliberate policy of friendship with other countries goes further in gaining security than anything else."[19] Despite valid criticism that this policy did not protect India from the Chinese aggression in 1962, it is instructive to reflect that assistance was possible to be obtained thereafter from both the United States and Soviet Union to meet the new security threat from across the Himalayas.

Foreign policy has an obvious function to provide for the defense of India by securing external sources of material. Procurement of military stores is largely governed by political relationships between countries. India is still dependent, to an appreciable extent, on outside supplies. Consequently, she has to fashion her foreign policy to, among other requirements, keep avenues of defense supplies open. This aspect of foreign policy, and necessary inter-action between the defense and foreign affairs bureacracies, seems to have weakened over the years. The increasing number of external suppliers and fierce competitiveness between them makes it easier to procure defence equip-ment. Besides, it is clear that little effort is being made by the defense apparatus to blend procurement decisions into larger aspects of foreign pol-icy. For instance, the intended procurement of fighter-bombers and naval vessels—subject of much recent debate—does not appear to have respected sensitivities in the Foreign Ministry that such purchases might prejudice India's position in disarmament forums, or fuel an arms race in the sub-continent, or heighten suspicions among India's neighbors, or hamper on-going efforts to normalize relations with South Asian countries. To an extent this is reflective of the fact that the External Affairs Ministry no longer enjoys the predominance it enjoyed during the Nehru era, when the Prime Minister was also the Foreign Minister, and directed the overall security policies of the country.

Threat Assessment:

At the cardinal, functional level of threat assessment, interaction be-tween the two Ministries obtains in the Policy Planning and Review Com-

19. Jawaharlal Nehru, *India's Foreign Policy: Selected Speeches September 1946-April 1961* (New Delhi: Publications Division, 1961), pp. 79-80.

mittee (PPRC) set up in 1966 by the Ministry of External Affairs. The Foreign Secretary is its chairman, and its other members are the Commerce Secretary, Chairman of the Joint Intelligence Committee, and other Secretaries in the External Affairs Ministry. The Defence Secretary has been a permanent invitee since 1969. The functions of the Committee are "to examine important aspects of India's foreign policy in the over-all context of the changing world situation and in relation to developments within India and in the countries bordering India. The Committee will in addition examine current and anticipated problems and prepare long-term programmes for the achievement of India's foreign policy objectives . . . the Committee will give due consideration to the politico-military and politico-economic aspects of such policies."[20]

A sustained interaction between the defense and foreign affairs bureaucracies occurs in the Joint Intelligence Committee (JIC). This committee was under the Chiefs of Staff Committee until 1962 and comprised of the Intelligence Heads of the three Services and a representative each of the Defence and Home Ministries. It was headed by a Joint Secretary from the External Affairs Ministry. It is evident that the failure of Indian intelligence in 1962 occurred, not at the level of intelligence collection, but in correct evaluation of Chinese intentions. Hence the need was felt for a high-powered intelligence assessment body, which would function independently of the Chiefs of Staff. The Committee now functions within the Cabinet Secretariat. The Chairman of the Committee is an Additional Secretary in that Ministry. The members of the Joint Intelligence Committee are a Joint Secretary each representing the Ministries of Defence, Home and External Affairs, the Services Intelligence Chiefs and representatives of other intelligence agencies. The Joint Intelligence Committee is the highest evaluation agency in India relating to defense and security issues. It produces a large number of assessments either on its own initiative or on request from either the Chiefs of Staff Committee or the Ministries. The information required is generated by the Services and other intelligence agencies, although their individual assessments are respected the assessments of the JIC are an independent effort. A great deal obviously depends on the personality of the Chairman.

The basic weakness of both the PPRC and JIC is the absence therein of specialist staff. For instance the PPRC is serviced by the Policy Planning Division of the External Affairs Ministry which has no staff having knowledge of security matters. Similarly, the JIC has neither economists nor area specialists; its supporting staff is almost wholly drawn from the military.

---

20. Excerpt from report of the Pillai Committee set up in 1965 to review the Indian Foreign Service. Quoted in J. Bandyopadhyaya, *The Making of India's Foreign Policy*, pp. 205-206.

Quite obviously, trends in global economic, oil and nuclear politics influence security assessments, and the lack of such inputs must affect the quality of assessments made. Equally, the lack of relevant expertise makes it difficult to attempt long-term threat assessments. Neither can long range projections be attempted about the implications of technology transfers, new weapons systems, economic growth rates and so on which influence security evaluations.[21] The JIC has specifically been criticized for another shortcoming—that its members function as representatives of particular Ministries or Agencies and do not exhibit the objectivity, therefore, which is essential for impartial analysis. A possible solution, often suggested, is creation of a National Security Agency functioning directly under the Prime Minister.[22] No radical changes in existing arrangements for obtaining threat assessments are, however, under serious consideration by the Government. Even the relatively modest suggestion that outside consultants might advise the Policy Planning Division or the Joint Intelligence Committee has yet to gain favor. To a large extent the elitist character of the civilian and military bureaucracies is responsible—outsiders to the system are considered to be interlopers.

Weapons Selection/Acquisition Processes:

The manner in which the decision-making process operates with regard to weapons choices for equipping/reequipping the armed forces, by either external procurement or indigenous manufacture can now be examined. The main reason impelling such choices is the need for countermeasures against weapohs inductions by India's likely adversaries, or the need for modernizing her armed forces. The four options available here are:

a) Undertake symmetrical acquisitions, e.g., tank for tank, aircraft for aircraft and so on;

b) Undertake offsetting acquisitions, e.g., anti-tank missile against tanks, surface-to-air missiles against aircraft and so on;

c) Replace equipment as they become obsolescent by later generations, and

d) Induct weaponry reflective of latest state of the art by leap-frogging intermediate stages, e.g., laser-guided artillery.

These options are not mutually exclusive. Acquisitions, symmetrical or offsetting, might be undertaken, for instance, to develop counter-capabilities, which would also have the effect of replacing obsolescent equipment. Exam-

21. K. Subrahmanyam, *Perspectives in Defence Planning*, pp. 130-133.
22. P. V. R. Rao, *Defence Without Drift* (Bombay: Popular Prakashan, 1970), pp. 310-317; K. Subrahmanyan, *Perspectives in Defence Planning*, pp. 120-130; I. Bandyapadhyaya, *The Making of India's Foreign Policy*, pp. 209-210.

ined over a period of years India's acquisition of major weaponry, appears to have been reactive to inductions made by Pakistan, especially for the Army and Air Force. Thus procurement of T-54/T-55 tanks were intended to counter Pakistan's acquisition of Patton tanks. This pattern is more clearly evident with regard to aircraft. The induction of F-104s by Pakistan in the early sixties led to India seeking F-104s from the United States and the Lighting from U.K. Unable to obtain these aircraft India turned to the Soviet Union for procurement and licensed production of MiG-21 aircraft.[23] Despite official explanations that it is a replacement program, India's present interest in fighter-bombers is predicated by Pakistan's acquisition of Mirage III/V aircraft which have a longer combat radius than various MiG-21 modification with the Indian Air Force. The off-setting option does not seem to have been seriously considered here, although SA-2, SA-3 missiles and ZSU-23mm. A.A. guns are in the inventory, and interest is evident in later generations of Soviet surface-to-air missilry.

The replacement option is most clearly seen with regard to naval acquisitions. The Indian Navy was exclusively equipped with British vessels in the initial years after Independence. An effort is now proceeding to replace older ships with Soviet-built Petya-class and indigenously produced Leander-class frigates, and missile boats. Besides, Nanuchka-class missile corvettes and Kashin-class destroyers are reportedly on order.[24] It is unlikely, however, that India would pursue the option of procuring weaponry which are the most sophisticated available for budgetary reasons. Neither does this policy appear wise, due to attendant problems of absorption, maintenance, and logistics.

Weapons acquisition decisions in India are not, however, as simple as described above. Both policy and foreign exchange considerations require that the indigenous manufacture possibility be first investigated. Over the years India's defense production policy has focused on achieving the twin objectives of "modernization of Arms and Equipment and achievement of the maximum degree of self-reliance and self-sufficiency in the shortest possible time."[25] The difficulties in achieving these objectives are obvious. First, sophistication of defense production is broadly reflective of the general technological stage obtaining in the country. It is not possible for the defense production sector to be an island within the national industrial culture,

23. For details of India's negotiations with various countries preceding this agreement see Ian C. C. Graham, "The Indo-Sovet MiG deal and its international Repercussions," *Asian Survey*, Vol. IV, No. 5, May 1964, pp. 323-332.

24. Inder Malhotra, "New Vistas for the navy," *Times of India*, Sept. 23, 1977.

25. *Annual Report 1976-77; Ministry of Defence* (New Delhi: Government of India Press, 1977), p. 28.

without heavy investments therein, to the detriment of other sectors of national development, and attendant political and social costs. Second, the sophistication achieved by the defense production sector is seminally linked with investments in defense research and development. Here the problems encountered in the Indian situation are four-fold; paucity of resources, difficulty in getting a scientist of national eminence to head the establishment, lack of qualified personnel, and the familiar problem of "brain drain" to developed countries.[26] Third, the goal of total "self-reliance and self-sufficiency" is almost chimeric. Small quantities of infrequently required items would be cheaper to import, instead of establishing a new line of production for them. Further, if later generation weaponry are required, dependence on one or other of the major arms producing nations cannot be avoided. They are in the lead in sophisticated weapons technology. Their industrial economy and capacity for defense, R&D investments ensure a continued advantage. In essence, the area of indigenous manufacture can be expanded as the industrial economy grows in India, and develops greater sophistication. But a certain dependence upon imports would continue in the foreseeable future.

An important question in this connection is association of the private sector in defense production which, by statute, proceeds under Government auspices. There are some 32 ordnance factories and defense public sector undertakings supported by 32 major research establishments. The value of production is reaching $1.25 billion annually of which roughly 20% is for civil industry. Approximately 10% represents the value of spares and ancilliaries obtained from private trade.

The difficulties in transferring defense production entirely to the private sector is partly ideological, in that the Industrial Policy Resolution requires that control of strategic industries must rest in the state. The Government is also sensitive to criticism that a military-industrial complex might develop. Partly, difficulties arise because of the intrinsic nature of defense production in India. Production of large quantities of material for equipment/reequipment of the armed forces is followed by trickle production to keep the equipment in service. But this does not amount to a viable commercial operation to attract private industry. Besides, maintenance of strict quality controls, high rejection rate, uncertainty of future orders and so on inhibit the private sector.[27] Due to a renewed emphasis on achieving "self-reliance and self-sufficiency," and the enthusiasm of the private sector to enter the

26. P. R. Chari, "Defence Production in India: Import or Manufacture," *Strategic Analyses* (Institute for Defence Studies and Analyses Publications), Vol. I, No. 11, February 1978, pp. 1-5.
27. For an analysis of the private sector's role, and difficulties in the Indian defense production effort, and possible reforms see P. V. R. Rao, *Defence Without Drift*, pp. 231-248.

defense production area, it is likely that private industry would be more largely associated in future with the manufacture of sub-assemblies, spares and ancillaries.

Another question requiring brief examination is the policy towards external sources of military supplies which is singularly divorced from ideological overtones. Recent policy changes further require that all imports of weapons technology should be made with in-built co-production arrangements. India's initial dependence was on Western sources—notably U.K. and France—for both material and licensed production arrangements. It was basically the disinclination of the United States and U.K. after the Chinese aggression to supply the relatively sophisticated equipment required by India which led to her subsequent dependence on the Soviet Union. This situation was exacerbated by the Anglo-U.S. arms embargo laid upon the sub-continent in 1965, following the Indo-Pak war in that year. Major equipment purchases have been made from the Soviets for all the three Services, thereafter, which is broadly indicative also of an identity of Indo-Soviet interests in the political sphere.[28] It would, however, be facile to describe India's interests as subordinated thereby to Soviet global objectives. Despite the intimacy arising from an extensive military cooperation relationship, it bears reiteration that there are no Soviet advisers in the Indian armed forces, neither does the Soviet Union enjoy any especial naval facilities in India which are not available to other friendly countries. The fact that India is presently evaluating fighter-bombers from three Western sources and submarines from a number of countries in the Western alliance should disabuse notions regarding Soviet hegemonism over the Indian military apparatus.

Reverting to the actual decision-making process in India, weapons demand could be projected by the armed forces broadly describing their operational requirements and leaving it to the scientists to devise the equipment. This rarely happens in actual practice. More commonly, weapons demands are projected for the actual equipment required; its characteristics are assessed in the literature, and details obtained through Services Attachés posted abroad. Two difficulties arise with regard to weapons choices. First, the equipment has to suit Indian conditions, which involves performance over temperature variation, ranging between $-30°$ and $+50°C$, besides dust and humidity conditions. Second, taking into consideration the fact that these climatic variables influence all defense establishments, the problem was created by the Services changing requirements after their initial proposals were made.[29]

Once the administrative decision to obtain a particular equipment is taken other components of the decision-making process come into operation

28. For details see P. R. Chari, "Indo-Soviet Military Cooperation: A Review," *Asian Survey* (forthcoming).

29. This aspect is highlighted in P. V. R. Rao, *Defence without Drift,* pp. 217-223.

viz., budgetary factors involving the Ministry of Finance, and the possibility of indigenous manufacture involving the Defence Production Department and the Scientific Adviser to the Defence Minister. Quite obviously, no easy decisions are possible, since a number of opposing considerations enter into the picture viz., imminence of threat, weapons induction by potential adversary powers, budgetary and, especially, foreign exchange constraints, time-frames for indigenous manufacture, need for modifications to suit specific requirements, inter-Service priorities and so on. Trade-offs between these competing sets of considerations become necessary and, indeed, inevitable. The ultimate option chosen may, reflect, therefore, the best possible rather than the most ideal decision. Finally, the direction of India's modernization program would be evident from the goals laid down after the Sino-Indian border conflict which retain their relevance. These objectives were:

> a) building up and maintenance of a well-equipped army with a strength of 8.25,000 men;
> b) maintenance of a 45 squadron Air Force . . . and improvement of the air defense radar and communications facilities;
> c) phased program for replacement of average ships of the Navy;
> d) strengthening the defense production basis; and
> e) improving the organizational arrangements. . . .[30]

Space does not permit a critical analysis, of the manner in which the decision makers are achieving these objectives. But this would be clear in a gross manner from the three appendices attached to this paper. These display the allocations made over the seventies for defense, incremental annual increases therein, and its proportion to Central Government expenditure and G.N.P., percentage allocations to the three Services, and, production in ordnance factories/defense public sector undertakings as also allocations for defense R&D. It needs highlighting that the defense burden upon the economy is reducing. An emphasis upon the Air Force and Navy is evident, which is reflective of their on-going modernization programs. The increases in value of defence production may appear striking, but is partly due to increased unit costs due to inflationary factors.

Conclusion and Prospects:

The two characteristics distinguishing the Indian defense policy-making process are its civilian direction of the military apparatus, and the dominant role of the bureaucracy in that process. Both characteristics arise from historical premises, and have strengthened during the three decades following

---

30. *Annual Report 1964-65 Ministry of Defence* (New Delhi: Government of India Press, 1965), pp. 1-2.

Independence. As at present the main factor likely to induce change in this matrix of decision-making is the strain imposed by increasing modernization of the armed forces.

As the modernization process continues and decision-making becomes more complex the desire for innovation would become more acute. It can be reasonably anticipated that the present clear differences between purely civil and purely military functions would shade over, and that inter-postings of civilians and military officers between Service Headquarters and the Defence Ministry would become fairly common. Already this is taking place in research establishments, defense production units, inspection organizations, training institutions, and so on.

It may, however, be surmised that the centrality of the bureacracy in the formation of defense policy would increase as defense issues become more abstruse and more highly skilled persons are inducted into the bureaucracy. This assertion is made because of the weakness of extra-Governmental pressure groups and the inadequacy of expertise within them. Indeed, the increasing power of the bureaucracy is an inevitable trend as the complexities of problems facing most Governments require greater State intervention and direction.

Weapons acquisition decisions would require complex choices to be made, but would be increasingly important as the accuracy and lethality of conventional weaponry increases. A fresh set of decisions, impinging upon organizational patterns, logistics arrangements, tactics and so on would become necessary should the Indian armed forces have to cater for a P.G.M. environment. There is a growing awareness that existing military thinking would have to be revised considerably in these circumstances. Difficult decisions would also be required to grapple with entirely new tasks like protection of off-shore oil installations.

It needs mention, in conclusion, that India has been advantaged, as compared to other developing countries, in having internal stability, largely due to charismatic leaders having been at its helm of affairs. At present, a condition of turbulent politics obtains, which could have occurred during the earlier years since Independence. Older values are presently being questioned, difficult social challenges have surfaced, ideological cleavages have widened and political parties are in ferment. There is no dearth of dire predictions that forms of authoritarianism could arise. Nevertheless, the polity has acquired the maturity to sustain a parliamentary, democratic system of governance, and any radical changes in the political system are most unlikely. A slow change in defense policy processes can, therefore, be expected, but the stronger impulse would remain, as before, on retaining continuity of administrative traditions.

Table I

Year	Net Defense Expenditure (In crores)	% of Increase over Previous Year	% of Total Central Govt. Expenditure	% of Defense Expenditure to GNP
1971-72	1,525	27.2	23	3.9
1972-73	1,652	8.3	21	3.9
1973-74	1,681	1.7	20	3.2
1974-75	2,122	25.6	21	3.4
1975-76	2,410	14.1	20	3.9
1976-77	2,562	6.3	19	3.7
1977-78 (revised)	2,751	7.3	18	N.A.
1978-79 (budgeted)	2,944	7.0	16	N.A.

Table II

Year	Army (in crores)	% of Def. Expenditure	Navy (in crores)	% of Def. Expenditure	Air Force (in crores)	% of Defence Expenditure
1971-72	813	56	70	4	277	19
1972-73	826	53	70	4	305	20
1973-74	836	51	85	5	337	21
1974-75	1125	54	103	5	420	20
1975-76	1235	51	137	6	486	20
1976-77	1250	49	152	6	525	20
1977-78 (revised)	1303	48	175	6	551	20
1978-79 (budgeted)	1370	47	205	7	586	20

Table III

Year	Prod. in Ord. Facto- ries (in crores	Prod. in Defense Public Sector Units (in crores)	Exp. on Def. R&D (in crores)	% of R&D Expenditure to Total Budget
1971-72	178	174	18	1.26
1972-73	193	207	24	1.55
1973-74	182	252	30	1.86
1974-75	192	298	36	1.74
1975-76	249	346	48	1.99
1976-77	419	399	46	1.79
1977-78	N.A.	425	51	1.85
1978-79 (budgeted)			57	1.93

The Strategic Imagery of Elites

STEPHEN P. COHEN

I. Introduction

Every governmental policy is based upon a mix of calculation and intuition. While policy-makers claim that they possess the facts of a situation, closer analysis usually shows many of these facts to be informed guesses or hunches about reality. We cannot know everything, and most of us carry about in our heads sets of images and beliefs which allow us to fill in the gaps—or, at times, synthesize a new reality.

Our purpose is to examine some of the images and beliefs which help shape strategic policy in South Asia.[1] These can be grouped into "image clusters", related or linked images of the political environment, the causes of war, the conduct of war, domestic sources of security and insecurity, and so forth. In this study we shall examine two such image clusters, one group based upon the notion of state or regional vulnerability to outside penetration, the other based upon the linkage between domestic politics and foreign policy. We caution the reader against concluding that such image clusters are "operational codes" of state behavior, or that they lead immediately to predictive statements of the if-then variety. Yet, we believe, an analysis of defense policy formation is incomplete without a discussion of such images and perceptions, and that at a number of points a linkage *can* be established especially at the regional level between particular image-clusters and particular strategies and policies.

1. Research for this work has been supported by the Ford Foundation and the University of Illinois at Urbana.

II. The Shameful Image: Soft States in a Hard World

The first image cluster that we shall examine is derived from the assumption that South Asia is especially susceptible to outside penetration.[2] The fragility or weakness of one or more regional states is, according to this view, a strategic fact of life. Some include India in this category; most tend to assume a hierarchy of vulnerability, and these different views lead to different conclusions, but there is agreement that at least some regional states can be easily penetrated. We should note here that this is a quite different assumption than one discussed below: the influence of domestic factors (including the vulnerability of regional states) on foreign policy. Rather, these images tend to emphasize the *active* involvement of regional states in each other's politics, and of outside powers in the region and its constituent parts. There is an assumption of a predisposition to intervene, and that only by erecting suitable barriers (or raising the cost of such intervention) can it be prevented.

A vehement advocate of this view is Baldev Raj Nayar, who has called for a transformation of India's economy and political system in order to meet the challenge from the West, especially the United States. What he terms the "modernization imperative" has the compulsion of a law of the jungle:

> "Modernize or be subjugated." The subjugation need not always take the form of physical occupation but equally as well of political penetration and economic control. For the non-industrialized country there is no escape from the modernization imperative, there is no other alternative, there is no other choice. . . . The impulse for modernization emerges here then not internally . . . but externally from the threat to security from an industrialized country.[3]

Whether deliberate or not such intervention can take several forms. Some believe it to be primarily economic: dependency upon outsiders for technology, capital, markets, and resources. Others emphasize military alliances and interventions, and for some the importance of propaganda and "cultural imperialism" cannot be neglected. Finally, those who argue the vulnerability of the region to penetration have developed a variety of prescriptions to reduce or terminate that penetration. These can best be evaluated by examining the penetration image in the context of its two main variants: that of the smaller states surrounding India and of India itself.

The one image shared by the "garland" states of South Asia is that of a dominant, overbearing and oversized India inexorably encroaching on the sovereignty of a smaller, vulnerable state. The specific strategic implemen-

---

2. For a general statement of penetration see Andrew M. Scott, *The Revolution in Statecraft: Informal Penetration* (New York: Random House, 1965).

3. *The Modernization Imperative and Indian Planning* (New Delhi: Vikas, 1972), p. 81.

tation of such an image is tempered and conditioned by a number of factors, but the underlying premise is the same in Pakistan, Bangladesh, Nepal, and Sri Lanka.[4] Each fears cultural penetration, each is concerned about the domination of their economies by India; all have substantial minority or ethnic groups with links to India, or, in the case of Pakistan, feel that certain Indian minorities are de facto hostages.

The fear of penetration extends to other areas as well. Pakistan and Bangladesh are substantially dependent upon India for access to water; Nepal is critically dependent upon India for the trans-shipment of most of its external trade and India remains its largest trading partner. Before 1971 Pakistanis could not easily fly from wing to wing without overflying Indian territory.

This concern with Indian domination is genuine but is in each case tempered by other concerns. All of the smaller states of the region share with India a concern over foreign influence, especially by the superpowers. Even when their relations with the U.S., China, or the Soviet Union are close, they are wary of penetration by these states of their politics, their elites and their economies. This is so not only because of a natural desire to remain outside the spheres of influence of these states; with the exception of Pakistan, they are also worried that such close involvement might itself trigger Indian intervention.

Another facet of the image of Indian domination and penetration further complicates the situation. To the degree that none of India's neighbors have ever hoped to achieve great power status but that India can (or has), there is a grudging admiration for India's accomplishments. One encounters this attitude even in Pakistan. To the considerable degree that India's neighbors share with it a common cultural heritage they take pride in India's achievements even while suspecting its intentions and motives.

The strategic implications of these images are obvious. India's neighbors perceive it to be an inherent but not necessarily fatal threat. At the very worst some have believed that India would — if it could — destroy them as autonomous states, at the very best most believe that a strategy of balance and accommodation will suffice to keep the Indian giant at bay. Thus, at one extreme Pakistan has been the only one of India's neighbors to attempt to militarily balance Indian might; the others have been content with political strategies which involve the maintenance of ties with other important states (although not necessarily other regional states). They have calculated that

4. For a brief overview of regional relations see William J. Barnds, "South Asia," in James N. Rosenau et al., *World Politics* (New York: Free Press, 1976), pp. 501-527. A still-useful compilation of individual foreign policies of the region is in S.P. Varma and K.P. Misra, eds., *Foreign Policies in South Asia* (Bombay: Orient Longmans, 1969).

military resistance to India is not only technically impossible but would be highly provocative.

The Indian image of regional vulnerability has two components with linked strategic consequences. The first is that of the vulnerability of the "fringe" states, both to internal disorder and external penetration. To some degree (especially in the case of Pakistan) internal instability is strategically useful, but in other cases it can lead to external involvement or leak into India. A middle-rank Indian Foreign Service officer who has specialized in South Asian affairs makes the argument in these terms:

> I don't worry about a Pakistani attack on us, or even a joint Pakistan-China attack; we are now much better equipped than before and can defend ourselves in that way. No, what really worries me about Pakistan is that it is still tied into our internal weaknesses in so many ways. There is, of course, the problem of our Muslim population, and the temptation of Pakistan for them. I think they are loyal, but we must learn to treat them better. Then there is Kashmir, and a live territorial claim which also involves a large Muslim population. But finally there is also the question of separatism in the Indian states. This applies North and South. What if the Indian union were to be in trouble? What would Pakistan do? More importantly, what kind of example are they for our own separatists? Taking Pakistan back in would be worse, but there will always be problems with a separate Pakistan.[5]

This concern over the domestic religious, economic, and political implications of Indo-Pakistani conflict was earlier elaborated by the late Sisir Gupta, one of India's most distinguished scholar-diplomats:

> It is not difficult for any student of South Asian politics and of mass behaviour in this area to anticipate how serious the repercussion can be of another open conflict between India and Pakistan. . . . In the eighteen years of freedom one political lesson learnt in India is that it is beyond the capacity of the governments in the subcontinent to control mob fury generated by linguistic, communal, or religious passions.[6]

Much of the same argument could be made with regard to Bangladesh, Burma, Nepal, Sri Lanka, and Bhutan. These are all states with ethnic, religious, linguistic, or other minority groups which overlap with similar groups in India; disorder in any of these states can echo in India (and, as Indians tend to forget, vice versa). Part of India's strategic dilemma (and one with important implications for such arms control measures as reciprocal limits on forces close to international borders) is that by maintaining force levels adequate to contain or control such groups India may also be able to

5. Interview, 1977.
6. *Kashmir: A Study in India-Pakistan Relations* (Bombay: Asia, 1966), p. 473.

threaten some of its neighbors. And, most of these movements and ideas cannot be controlled by force. Pakistan faces exactly the same problem with several of its ethnic and tribal groups which have close ties to kinsmen in Afghanistan, Iran, and India (Pathans, Baluchis, and Kashmiris). Pakistanis, no less than Indians, have a deep anxiety about the loyalty of nationalist and tribal movements which transcend permeable borders. Leaders in both states thus have some hope that neighboring regimes be at least strong enough to restrain such movements.

However, a variant of the Indian image of regional penetration sees India itself as a target of external manipulation, both directly and indirectly through foreign support of its neighbors. Thus, regimes which are both capable and under the influence of foreign outside powers can present a major threat to India; hitherto only Pakistan has fallen into this category although there have always been profound Indian concerns over the penetration into Nepal of Chinese influence. The 1978 revolution in Afghanistan has raised similar concerns.

Indian perceptions of regional vulnerability are not dissimilar in broad outline from those of its neighbors. For most Indian elites, however, the risk of penetration comes not from within the region but outside of it. For example, Pakistanis regard the invasion of Islam from the 12th Century onward as a fruitful if not glorious period in regional history; many Indians see it as the beginning of the decline of an independent, strong subcontinent. Thus, the strategies of Nepal, Sri Lanka, and Pakistan inviting outside powers into the area (especially when it takes the form of a military connection) has always been seen by most Indians as a threat to the concept of a *region* free of outside interference. And when such a connection is military in character it is also assumed to have direct anti-Indian implications. It is hard for many Americans to appreciate the sensitivity of Indian opinion to such involvment, even in the case of the sailing of the *U.S.S. Enterprise,* and a small task force into the Bay of Bengal in 1971. One cannot overemphasize the intensity of the bitter Indian reaction to the *Enterprise* affair, and it is likely to continue to affect Indian perceptions of its own vulnerability (and that of the region's) for years to come, as well as adversely influencing Indo-American relations. Eight years after it occurred the sailing of the *Enterprise* is still invariably mentioned in discussions with Indian strategists, journalists, and other members of the foreign policy community. It had a major impact on military thinking and contributed directly to the present expansion program of the Indian Navy. Above all, it is remembered as a humiliating experience, all the more so because it occurred at just the moment of India's greatest military-political triumph.

These different perceptions of regional vulnerability have led to different approaches to regional collaboration in its various manifestations. All of the smaller states of the region prefer multi-lateral treatment of water resources; the Indian government has for several years insisted upon bi-lateral negotiations with each affected state. This is less because the Indians are trying to drive a hard bargain than an expression of their concern that outside agencies be excluded from regional matters. In fact, the terms of the settlements reached in a number of such negotiations in 1976-8 have been better for the smaller regional states than most observers had expected, as the Indian government has tried to demonstrate the attractiveness of bi-lateral problem-solving.[7] There has also been an active Indian program of military cooperation and training with those regional states that have been willing to utilize Indian services. India has bitterly and vehemently rejected U.S.-sponsored military pacts and arrangements which involve outside powers in the region, but it has also (if more cordially) refused to cooperate in Soviet plans for an Asian security pact. Indian diplomats have argued for many years that left alone the states of the region will settle their differences amicably; other regional states have not been persuaded of this line of argument nor of India's good intentions. Pakistan, Bangladesh, and in a lesser way, Nepal and Sri Lanka all seek reinsurance through the cultivation of outside powers, although the identity of these powers has changed over the years. India, in its turn, has judged such powers—the U.S., the Soviet Union, and China—largely in terms of their willingness to acknowledge in word and deed India's preeminent position in the region. The strategic consequences of this Indian view are complex.

If, as many Indians believe, the smaller states of South Asia represent a threat to India because of their vulnerability (either to outside penetration or internal fragility) then two alternative strategies present themselves. The first is to build up these states to the point where they are fully autonomous, and no outside power can influence them in a way that harms Indian interests. This might lead to neighbors which are not amenable to Indian influence, but will at least not serve as agents for others. The second strategy is quite the opposite: to dominate such neighbors to the point where they are under virtual Indian political control. The two strategies have been followed in varying degrees over the years, and have led to alternative periods of moderation, toleration, and toughness *vis á vis* Nepal, Sri Lanka, Bangladesh, and (to a lesser degree) Pakistan.

The Pakistani image of regional vulnerability is different than that of India and other regional states. Many Pakistanis have maintained that India—because of its size, diversity, and an absence of a unifying religion or

---

7. For an excellent survey see Shivaji Ganguly, "Continuity and Change in Indian Foreign Policy," *India Quarterly,* May, 1978.

ideology—is more fragile than Pakistan. This view is heard less often now than before 1971, but is still widespread, especially in the military. The strategic conclusion drawn by many who hold this image (and a conclusion reached at one time by many in the West) is that despite its smaller size Pakistan represents a more stable and secure platform for outsiders interested in the region than does India, and explains, to some extent, the conviction and success with which Pakistanis have pursued external alliances.[8]

Alliances have not been seen in Pakistan (as they are in India) as a sign of weakness, incompetence, or betrayal. Historically, most Pakistanis have viewed what are essentially dependence relationships as desirable, not merely necessary evils. There is thus a striking difference in the degree to which Indians and Pakistanis have subscribed to the image of dependency. This is a very complex relationship, but it essentially involves a voluntary two-party transaction. On the one hand, the smaller (or weaker) state gives up much of its autonomy and enters into a subordinate position in an alliance relationship. In doing so it may be called upon to make substantial sacrifices and run many risks. However, it receives material assistance and—even more important—the political and moral support of its ally. It thus places itself in a near-feudal relationship in which it accepts the status of dignified vassal. The relationship is *morally* and psychologically tenable only as long as the dominant partner provides continued evidence of its gratitude and is willing to "stand by" its ally in time of need, regardless of narrow strategic calculations. For, the essence of this relationship (and what makes it different from an ordinary alliance) is this psychological linkage between the two parties: it is a linkage which is supposed to transcend immediate self-interest because it is based not upon a calculation of gain and loss, but a commitment involving deeper, moral obligations between the two parties.

After Independence the predominant view of the Pakistani elite was that it needed such a relationship with one or more outside powers. The British, the Americans, and then the Chinese each in turn filled this role but seem to have "let down" Pakistan; more recently, Pakistan has again turned to other Muslim states in an attempt to utilize shared bonds of history and religion in its search for a relationship that is stable not only in its economic and military components but which is psychologically and morally tenable as well.

Pakistan is now torn between two images of itself *vis à vis* the outside world. The first is that it will play a major role in the geopolitical concept

8. It is peculiar that Pakistanis have regarded their state as "small," perhaps because it was—before 1971—surrounded by the world's first, second, and third largest states (in population it was then the sixth largest). If it were even today located in Latin America or Africa it would be regarded as a near-major power.

variously known as the "arc of danger" or "crescent of crisis."[9] In this formulation, developed by Anglo-American strategists and pursued vigorously by Pakistan until 1962, Pakistan is assigned a major role as protector and defender (against Soviet Communism) of the weak states of the Persian Gulf and South West Asia. As such, it stands in the front line of the Cold War and should be staunchly supported by the major Western Powers. An important asset of Pakistan is its Islamic character. Olof Caroe and others recognized this as an advantage that Pakistan had in serving as an intermediary between Western interests and the weak Muslim states of the region.

However, under Zulfikar Ali Bhutto's inspiration, many Pakistanis cultivated a quite different self-image of their state. It was Bhutto, first as a young Cabinet minister, then in opposition to the military government, and finally as Prime Minister, who led the way in a search for a *via media,* a policy which would accommodate what certainly was a changing reality. It is in many ways, a variant of non-alignment and even General Zia, the Chief Martial Law Administrator and President of Pakistan, now characterizes his country's foreign policy as "practically" non-aligned while still attempting to draw upon the benefits of various military pacts.[10] This aligned-non-alignment status grew out of Pakistani disillusionment with its role as the "most allied of allies" between 1963 and 1965. In 1963 Pakistan saw the Western powers rush to India's assistance after the Sino-Indian war of 1962; three years later Pakistan saw many of its fellow-Islamic states assume a non-aligned stance in its conflict with India. The two events led to increasing support for Bhutto's ideas, even though he was personally out of power, while the government persisted in its efforts to retain British and American military ties.

For Bhutto, the chief threat to Pakistan also came from the outside, but not necessarily from the Communist world. It was as much from the West as from India, and often from the two in collusion. *This* was the danger facing Pakistan, and he often accused the government of Ayub Khan of wrongly placing the Chinese ahead of India as a threat to Pakistan.[11] Bhutto divined in the policies of the West a successor to the old notorious "divide and rule" strategy: "unite and rule." If, as he argued, underdeveloped states could be divided into those that were pliable and those that were "non-pliable" to the

9. For a study of the origins of this concept see Selig S. Harrison, *The Widening Gulf* (New York: Free Press, 1978), pp. 260 ff.

10. Speech at Bahawalpur to officers and jawans, November 20, 1978. Pakistan has recently withdrawn from CENTO, but retains a bi-lateral military agreement with the United States.

11. While Prime Minister, Bhutto released a number of documents, including transcripts of conversations between Ayub and the British High Commissioner during the height of the 1965 war. These are gathered in *White Paper on the Jammu and Kashmir Dispute* (Islamabad: Ministry of Foreign Affairs, 1977).

West, then one could see the application of this Western formula of unite-and-rule:

> Most commonly, it is applied to the pliable under-developed nations, especially 'committed' states [e.g. Pakistan] with leaders who make their countries readily susceptible to economic and military exploitation. In the selection of the pliable states . . . the classification of aligned and non-aligned is no longer a yard-stick.[12]

He later went on to coin the term "bi-lateralism" to describe his foreign policy: it was essentially "non-alignment", but without subordination to the self-proclaimed leaders of the non-aligned movement whose pretensions in these directions were ridiculed by Bhutto, and, importantly, it did not exclude special ties with the Islamic movement. Thus, for Bhutto's followers, Pakistan is seen as a Third World state with special resources (Islam) and special problems stemming from its conflict with India. There was, as Bhutto pointed out, a practical side to "bi-lateralism", as it included an attempt to secure good relations with all of the major powers, and especially not excluding India's major supporters, the U.S. and U.S.S.R. Despite his flamboyance and world-wide diplomacy Bhutto did not forget that such a grandiose foreign policy was necessarily pursued for the sake of Pakistan itself and in harmony with more mundane interests and disputes:

> The importance of a universal, intercontinental understanding [between nations of the North and those of the South] is in no way diminished by the assertion that geography continues to remain the most important single factor in the formulation of a country's foreign policy . . . Territorial disputes . . . are the most important of all disputes . . . Many relations can be changed or influenced, but not the reality of the presence of a geographica neighbor.[13]

With the exception of the Kashmir issue, then, there is surprising agreement among many Pakistanis that *a* major threat to both the state and the region comes from efforts on the part of outside powes to intervene, meddle, or penetrate Pakistan. There is also agreement on the "collusion" against Pakistan between the Soviet Union and India, on the one hand, or the United States and India, on the other. The Sino-Indian border conflict of October 1962 removed all doubts as to America's complete support for India. It was now decided to support India even at the risk of alienating Pakistan. This was the opportunity for which the United States had been yearning from the time of Partition — its cherished dream was coming true.[14] And, finally, there is

---

12. Bhutto, *The Myth of Independence* (London: Oxford University Press, 1969), p. 11.
13. *Ibid.*, p. 28.
14. *Ibid.*, p. 62.

general agreement in Pakistan that some form of alliance, tie, or special relationship (whether it is with the United States or the Islamic world) is necessary for Pakistan's survival and the reclamation of Kashmir. All of this is quite different from the self-image of a self-reliant, non-aligned state held by many Indians. As we shall argue below, one of the major reasons for this striking difference in identity between two states similar in so many other ways pertains to their relative judgement about their own *internal* capacities.

III. Domestic Sources of National Insecurity

A second major image cluster is based upon the assumption of a direct link between external policy and internal, domestic considerations. Here the argument is either that external policies *should* pursue values generated within the state, or that domestic compulsions *necessarily* dominate foreign policy. This view has been articulated by an important figure in recent Indian politics, P.N. Haksar:

> Foreign policy is not an independent variable. It is a function of that hackneyed word called "interests" which, in turn, are governed by a country's internal political, economic and social structure perceived through its own history, tradition, and culture. There is thus a durability about perception of interests. It does not change with changing governments, except, of course, when there is a revolution. And even then geographical compulsions persist . . . and also national traditions.[15]

In this section we will examine images and perceptions of three such domestic factors. The first is the relationship between poverty and national priorities, the second is the relationship between state structure and national security, and the third is the linkage of communal conflict and foreign policy.

Scarcity, Security, and Self-Reliance

If there is one image of South Asia that crowds out all others in the developed world's collective imagination it is that of desperate poverty. For many, South Asia has come to stand as a metaphor of human degradation with such places as Calcutta representing a close approximation of Hell. Images of the starving child, the bloated corpse, the begging widow, are all familiar to the point of being cliches. Poverty on this scale implies a single, moral imperative: remove it. Any policy or act is justified if it contributes to the amelioration or elimination of such poverty; any policy which perpetuates it or which does not contribute to the elimination of poverty is immediately suspect.

---

15. In *Seminar* (New Delhi), May, 1978.

Jawaharlal Nehru certainly believed this and only reluctantly agreed to an expansion of the Indian armed forces just before the Sino-Indian war of 1962. General B. M. Kaul, at that time a confidant of Nehru, recalls the latter shouting to a group of generals: "You want more guns! There are people starving in India! Why should we give more money to fight war with!!"[16] But Nehru gave in, and his physical and political decline as a result of the disaster of 1962 has served as an object lesson to even his most unwarlike successors. While there are some in South Asia who hold that the government allocates too much to defense, there are more who see the issue from a quite different perspective. They recognize the absolute and relative poverty of their states on various measures and indices. They do not deny the existence of hunger, high death rates, and a relatively low per capita GNP. However, these elite groups do not draw the same conclusions from such facts as might a Westerner or Japanese or some of their own predecessors. The presence of poverty does not imply the subordination of security and defense expenditures to developmental programs; nor, for some, does it imply a necessary correlation *between* high defense expenditures and low growth rates. K. Subrahmanyam, a prominent writer on security affairs (and a senior I.A.S. official) has taken the lead in popularizing this view:

> The view of defense and development being mutually exclusive alternatives is popular in the academic world in India as well as abroad. Western academicians have had more success in convincing Indian scholars than in persuading their own governments of the truth of such theses! . . . Twenty years of fixed ideas . . . have convinced a whole generation of bureaucrats, academicians and even military men in this country that defense expenditure should be kept down to a minimum. Defense against mosquitoes, plague [or] rehabiliating "fallen women" is legitimate plan expenditure because it is social defense, but defense of the country against external threats is non-plan expenditure. . . .[17]

Subrahmanyam and others formulate the problem differently, in terms of scarcity and self-reliance. They see their nations as rich and powerful in certain resources: unskilled and skilled manpower, raw materials, and a sense of national purpose and identity which does not exist in many other new nations. For them, especially in India, their countries are not "poor" but quite wealthy, and it is only a question of pulling the right economic and strategic levers so as to maximize existing resources.

Thus, for many in South Asia the relationship between poverty and external policy (including military spending) is surrounded by a different set of images than for their Western or Japanese counterpart. Even before Nehru

---

16. Interview with Kaul, 1965.
17. *Defence and Development* (Calcutta: Minerva, 1973), pp. 6-7.

industrial might was closely correlated with military might, which in turn is seen as essential to protect the autonomy of new nations; while economic development remains the chief goal of the state national security is thought to be a necessary condition for achieving that goal. Further, there are those such as Subrahamanyam who have argued that there is a positive relationship between defense spending and economic growth, and who urge a defense-led strategy of development.[18]

While such arguments are relatively new in the region, they in fact draw from the same assumptions and beliefs as Nehru's antipathy to high defense budgets. This is the vision of "self-reliance", which is less of a policy than a desired state of existence, in which policy makers (and through them, the nation) are liberated from economic or military bondage to others. The only difference between Indian and Pakistani or Bangladeshi approaches to self-reliance is that in the former state there is some hope of at least partial autonomy in certain economic and industrial sectors, for Pakistan or Bangladesh there is very little.

This vision of self-reliance is critically linked to national strategy and security policies at every turn. Calculations of the duration of wars in the subcontinent are based not only on judgements about the ability of the economy to supply certain kinds of weapons, ammunition, and P.O.L. supplies, but on the anticipated cut-off of such supplies by external suppliers. The military in both India and Pakistan continually estimate the likely inflow of weapons from the outside, and attempt to build their own weapons inventories to meet and defeat not only the enemies existing weapons, but all weapons which *might* be delivered prior to or during a war. And they are not only concerned with military supplies but with manipulation from sources of food, energy, and even capital. From the perspective of outsiders, especially the superpowers, this is a form of arms control but in New Dehli or Rawalpindi it is a knife at the throat.

Decisions concerning the indigenous production of weapons are also heavily influenced by judgements about their contribution to self-reliance. If a weapons system can be linked with broader, economic capabilities (leading to increased autonomy) it immediately becomes more acceptable to a wide range of public opinion. During the Indian debate over acquisition of a "deep

---

18. Others have come to accept and expand this view. The Birla Institute of Scientific Research, "Economic Research Division," has advocated the development of a military-industrial complex, involving private manufacturers, along the lines of the U.S. What is of particular importance about the Birla study is that it indicates a renewed interest among private industry in acuqiring a share of the defense production sector, hitherto almost entirely government-dominated. See Rajesh K. Agarwal, *Defense Production and Development* (New Delhi: Arnold-Heinemann for the Birla Institute, 1978).

penetration strike aircraft" (DPSA) a senior government official made this point quite explicitly:

> We are not worried about Pakistan's Mirage [referring to one of the main arguments put forth by DPSA supporters]. Our concern is the long-run, and the acquisition of the technologies which would make us increasingly self-reliant, and some day we will reach the point where we can make our own "DPSA". That's why we are buying the Jaguar, not because of any present military threat. We need that aircraft to keep our own industry alive.[19]

This is true of both conventional *and* nuclear weapons, and public support for the nuclear programs in India and Pakistan is in part due to the early and sustained links between nuclear programs and economic self-reliance forged in the minds of nearly all politically attentive regional elites. In both states a popular and widespread image is that of peaceful nuclear programs which have enormous technological and economic benefits, and which contribute to national self-reliance; the symbiotic relationship between high technology and development has already been made with regard to conventional weapons, and can easily be extended to the nuclear field.

It is hard for many in the West to grasp this because they are overwhelmed by the problem of poverty in the Subcontinent. Regional elites are not overwhelmed by it: they have come to political maturity and power in societies which are—in relative terms, poor—but which for them are filled with resources, assets, and opportunities. This is not to imply that attitudes towards defense spending are promiscuous (especially in India). The historic juxtaposition of the images of India as a desperately poor country with enormous human and material resources has led to the development of an extraordinary security policy process. No other developing country (and few developed ones) have such exhaustive systems of fiscal and political control over military-related decisions, especially in the areas of force levels and weapons development and procurement. In India there is a long and respected tradition of critical budgetary analysis within the bureaucracy and some political parties. But the aassumption that most South Asians are obsessed with excessive defense spending because of the high priority they assign to economic growth is false. A strategy of growth plus security is pursued (especially in India) and there are hopes that in the long run this is, if not the shortest, then the safest route to self-reliance.

There are some differences between India and Pakistan in this regard if only because of their very different economic systems and historical circumstances. Pakistan's greater reliance upon alliance partners for weapons meant

19. Interview, 1978.

that it has deferred the question of developing an indigenous arms industry until quite recently. As we have seen, dependence was thought to be a way of ensuring support from alliance partners in time of crisis, until the unthinkable—that the U.S. would not come to Pakistan's rescue in time of war— actually did occur in 1965 and 1971. Zulfikar Ali Bhutto saw this danger before the military (with their institutional and personal ties to the U.S.) When he had the opportunity to do so, he diversified Pakistan's outside suppliers and made plans for an indigenous weapons manufacturing capability. Bhutto felt strongly that the Indian pattern of increased weapons autonomy was the only real guarantee of Pakistan's security. He recognized the difficulty of achieving such self-reliance quickly and toyed with both nuclear deterrents and the idea of a "people's milita" along Swiss or Chinese lines to serve as an interim measure.[20] Both of these strategies have not progressed very far, and Pakistan remains today totally reliant upon outsiders for weapons, totally vulnerable to their manipulation, and no closer than twenty years ago to "self-reliance".

To summarize, it is clear that proposals for arms control, restraint and limitation are not likely to be viewed wholly or even in large part from an economizing perspective. Unless an economic catastrophe strikes one or more of the major regional states or there is a persistent and extended decline in their economic productivity, decisions concerning levels of defense spending are likely to be made in terms of strategic, military, and political criteria. There is no rampant, overt "militarism" in India, but there are both interest groups supportive of defense spending and a belief that money spent on the military is not wasted. Indeed, one of India's most respected politicians and effective defense ministers, Jagjivan Ram, has argued in favor of high manpower levels on the grounds that there was no place to locate the thousands of officers and jawans that would be left unemployed by a reduction in force levels. In Pakistan major cuts in manpower levels are even more improbable, as senior generals seek to maintain support among important military and civilian constituencies.

State Structure

A second set of images linking domestic factors to the shaping of external policy emphasizes the importance of state structure. There is more concern over this in India than in Pakistan, and a more carefully articulated set of beliefs.[21] These are derived both from the liberal Western tradition of anti-militarism as well as India's own post-independence experience.

20. Bhutto, pp. 154 ff.
21. See Aswini K. Ray, *Domestic Compulsions and Foreign Policy* (New Delhi: Manas, 1975).

The essence of the Indian view has been for many years that a chief cause of war in South Asia is the domination of Pakistan by the military. A military regime cannot adequately represent the "true" interests of the people, and is more likely to seek war to resolve international disputes as well as to distract attention away from its domestic failures.

Complementing this distrust of the soldier is a strong Indian belief in the importance of following set procedures in reaching strategic and military decisions. Sound strategies are derived from sound processes, and there is an enormous skepticism within India of those who try to break the routines of established civilian or military bureacracies. And above all, this belief stresses the importance of a powerful civilian leader, centered in the office of the Prime Minister. This support of a centralized foreign policy process has, as a corollary, a distrust of "politicizing" security and foreign policy issues. There is a widespread belief that Indian democracy is fragile enough without introducing divisive, extraneous foreign policy issues. A number of India's most prominent centrist-oriented intellectuals, journalists and bureaucrats— including those who have supported and those who have opposed Mrs. Indira Ghandi — support this view.

Many Pakistani civilians and not a few in the military would agree in the abstract with this emphasis on civilian control through routinized bureacratic processes. However, they also argue that for states under seige, or whose territory is occupied by an alien power, normal "civilian" control is not feasible. Pakistan, they claim, is such a state, and the military of necessity will have a dominant voice in strategic decision-making. As President Ayub Khan believed,

> From the moment Pakistan came into being I was certain of one thing: Pakistan's survival was vitally linked with the establishment of a well-trained, well-equipped, and well-led army. I was determined to create this type of military shield. . . . Today I am convinced that without this army Pakistan could not have weathered the storms and attacks to which it was exposed; and the army behind the people of Pakistan is still a sure guarantee that our enemies will not be able to weaken us.[22]

This perception was inherited by at least some of the officers in the fledgling Bangladesh Army. One major (who has since achieved much higher rank) explained the behavior of his old army (the Pakistani) in this way one year after the creation of Bangladesh:

> Politics did not hurt the Pakistan army; they had to become involved for the good of the country; it was only when it lost its anti-Indian

---

22. Mohammad Ayub Khan, *Friends Not Masters* (New York: Oxford University Press, 1967), p. 21.

purpose, a clear goal, did it deteriorate [in fighting in East Pakistan/ Bangladesh]. No, I'm proud to have been an officer of the Pakistan Army even though they wouldn't want me back now! I'd like to see us do here what we did there, and stand up to the Indians.[23]

While a number of officers in Pakistan sincerely believe that a return to the barracks is necessary for both their professional well-being and the unity of Pakistan, many resist this, and are tempted by the prospect of a permanent military role in the political role in the political system. These men see "the politicians" (and the diplomats) as too willing to compromise, to sell out hard-won battlefield victories, and unable to generate the kinds of internal and external support required by the military. They believe, unlike most informed Indian (and some Pakistani opinion) that the complicated, pluralist state of Pakistan can be run by the military, or at least run by them better than the politicians.

During his years in power Zulfikar Ali Bhutto attempted to create a very different kind of civil-military structure (one, in fact, similar to the Indian model). He attacked the military for having led Pakistan into disaster in 1965 and 1971. He then sought to purge it, emphasizing both his own representativeness and strategic skills. Had Bhutto managed his other affairs it is possible he might have eventually changed the military-dominated politics of Pakistan; at the moment, however, the military's role is likely to be institutionalized behind a facade of civilian rule.[24]

These two sets of attitudes — India's distrust of military regimes, and the Pakistani military's suspicion of civilian ones — are further complicated by the religious-ideological differences between the states. For many Pakistanis the idea of democracy *in the context of South Asia* is repugnant, because it implies Hindu majorities and Muslim minorities. Democracy *among* Muslims is another question (on which there is some room for disagreement), but there is no doubt that when it implies a minority position for Muslims it is unacceptable. The creation of Pakistan eliminated this threat (which is still perceived as such, as can be seen in the absence of any pan-Bengal movement among East Bengalis). However, Indian or outside suggestions that the nations of the region form a common political, economic or defense arrangement, or suggestions of either a multi-lateral (regional) or bilateral economic, political, or military arrangement are viewed with extreme distrust. Not only because they might put Pakistan at a size disadvantage, but because

23. Interview, 1972.

24. As of 1979 the military rulers of Pakistan were groping towards a formula which would allow the restoration of civilian government but yet retain a "constitutional role" for the armed forces should the civilians be unable to govern. Speech of President Zia-ul-Haq, April 22, 1979.

they seem, to many Pakistanis, to be aimed at the very ethos or ideology of Pakistan. In the words of a senior Ministry of Foreign Affairs official:

> Pakistan presents a problem not only to India, but to the Soviet Union, and they would both like to see the break-up of Pakistan continue. They stand for secularism, linguistic, and cultural regionalism; we stand for Islam. They cannot dominate or change us; we stand in the way of their [India] becoming the leader of the Third World. I know we have trouble defining what "Islam" means in practice, I know we have trouble managing our own internal affairs, but in the end we stand for something quite different than they do, and our very existence is a challenge to them.[25]

What this official neglected to add, is that India's "existence" as a professedly secular state is no less a challenge to Pakistan itself. An enormous literature exists on this problem of competing or conflicting national identities, uch of it in relation to the Kashmir question, so we need only point out some salient features of the issue.

The trauma of Partition generated the strongest feelings about hostage or "lost" territories and populations in both India and Pakistan. Kashmir is a point of dispute between two states, but it is also a challenge to their self-image. Elites in all regional states are extremely sensitive to territorial disputes such as Kashmir, for in virtually every case what is at stake is not mere territory but identity. This is no different than European sensitivities to territories and "lost" populations, for in the age of nationalism borders assume more than economic or practical functions. They are seen as lines which *include,* not lines which *exclude.*

A classic juxtaposition of "whole vs. part" characterizes Pakistani and Indian perceptions of the nature of the Kashmir dispute. These two statements, by Ayub Khan and Jawaharlal Nehru are representative:

> Kashmir is keeping the two countries apart and unless this is settled, we would remain apart. So long as we remain apart, the solution of other problems stands in danger of being nullified. . . . The Kashmir problem is a result of other conflicts between India and Pakistan and even if the Kashmir problems were solved, well, not in a very friendly way, those basic conflicts would continue. If it were solved in a really friendly way, then, of course, it would help. But it is a friendly approach to the problem that is important, not a forcible solution which gives rise to other problems.[26]

25. Interview, 1978.
26. President Ayub on September 23, 1960 and Prime Minister Nehru, on June 13, 1956, both cited in Gupta, p. 439.

Is Kashmir the problem or the solution? Whatever it is, Sisir Gupta has argued, it is also composed of "the images that India and Pakistan had created of themselves on the eve of Partition." Indians regarded their state as the successor to the old British India, and that "what remained would be integrated into a stable, strong, secular, and unified state." Pakistanis, guided by the Muslim league, envisaged that "the Muslim majority areas in the northwest and east India, constituted into a separate State, would grow into a strong, strategically vital, Islamic State."[27] Pakistanis saw (in 1947) Kashmir as one of several states which might secede from India on the basis of Muslim self-rule, in or out of Pakistan; for the Indian leadership a predominantly Muslim Kashmir could be incorporated into India for both strategic and ideological reasons: Kashmir was and is the key to the defense of Ladakh and India, and any determination of population accession on the basis of religion might well cause instability among India's enormous Muslim population.

Virtually all proposals to settle the Kashmir conflict have foundered not for lack of imagination or ingenuity, but because they have been incompatible with the self-image of both India and Pakistan. The question has now resolved itself into the degree of Pakistani concern about Kashmir, as India possesses most of the region, including the strategically vital and symbolically determinative Valley. India is a status quo power, but Pakistani governments cannot or will not allow the issue to die. There is some indirect evidence that general concern over Kashmir has declined in Pakistan but it may take years until that altered perception is absorbed in official policy; no government in Pakistan is likely to *lead* public opinion in the direction of a settlement based upon anything like the status quo. If anything, images of Kashmir are stronger and more hostile in higher government and military circles than the rest of Pakistani society.

These images of state type and identity have a direct relationship to the propensity of India and Pakistan to subscribe to an arms control regime. Some images held by Indians and Pakistanis tend to downgrade what to many outsiders is the strongest motive for arms restraint, regional poverty. Other images imply the pursuit or irrational, or symbolic objectives, or stress the inability of a military (or democratic) regime to pursue and abide by a peaceful regional settlement, at least in the South Asian context. And, finally, the question of Kashmir looms as an issue which raises the most profound anxieties over security, territory, and national identity in both India and Pakistan.

27. *Ibid.*, p. 441.

The Eidetic Image: Communalism and Conflict[28]

This discussion of various images of national identity is not unrelated to a final image which links domestic and international politics in South Asia. This can be termed the "communal conflict with armor" model: it rests upon a belief that relations between regional states—especially India and Pakistan—are merely scaled up international versions of communal, religious, caste, or other domestic conflicts.

The "communal riot" is a set-piece in South Asian administrative history. A conflict between two recognizable ethnic, religious, or linguistic groups erupts because of both proximate and long-term considerations. The differences between the groups is substantive and real, but someone or some act precipitates violence. Both sides not only battle each other, they must keep one eye on outside forces (the police, administrative officials, politicians) who may or may not play favorites, and who may or may not act to speedily end the conflict. The riot does end but both parties are aware that it was only one episode in a long-term struggle and they prepare for the next round.

Many see in the wars between India and Pakistan of 1947-48, 1965, and 1971 a pattern resembling the communal riot: while both states have conflicting relations with other neighbors they appear to return again and again to each other. As in the riot, the causes of conflict between the two states run very deep and wars are thought to be as predictable as riots stemming from religious, linguistic, or caste hatreds. Outsiders, such as the UN, the superpowers, and interested states can influence the outcome of the conflict but they cannot prevent it. Nor can they be trusted, although they might be used.

This image or model of Indo-Pakistan relations as a communal riot can be based upon one or more of three different assumptions. At the crudest level it is motivated by a belief in the depravity and evilness of the other side. The imagery here is notorious and vivid. It includes sexual peculiarities, cow-worship (or cow-eating), hot tempers, and ingrained duplicity. What is of importance here is that when one side believes that the other is inherently evil or corrupt, the notion of cooperating or even negotiating with such a state is heresy. The communalist will argue that such cooperation can only lead to the contamination and degradation of your own state.

Secondly, the communal conflict model may rest upon a special interpretation of South Asian history. There are many in (and outside) the region

---

28. For an expansion of the following pages see my chapter in Shivaji Ganguly and M.S. Rajan, eds., *The Great Powers, World Order and the Third World: Essays in Honor of Sisir 12 Gupta* (New Delhi: Vikas, forthcoming).

who feel that religious systems must necessarily shape international politics and it is historical destiny that a Muslim Pakistan and a Hindu India face each other across a hostile border. "Secularism" in India is attacked by virtually all Pakistanis as a sham and by some Indians as well. In fact, many Pakistanis argue, "perhaps a conforming [i.e., orthodox] Hindu leader would have, in time, found it easier to live with Pakistan on a normal footing than did Jawaharlal Nehru, the exceptional [i.e., secular] Hindu."[29]

Thirdly, there are many in the region who personally do not hold communal interpretations of regional relations but conclude that because so many others do that Indo-Pakistan and Indo-Bangladesh relations will inevitably assume a communal tinge. These pessimist-realists argue that most subcontinental conflicts originated in Partition, or are a reprise of issues (such as the treatment of hostage minorities) which led to it. They claim that only a few of these issues are amenable to negotiation, and even then the politicians and volatile masses of the subcontinental states would disrupt arrangements. This image is widely held by civil servants and soldiers in the regional states and is derived both from experience and the administrative traditions which have been handed down from the days of the British.

An important strategic implication of the communal conflict image is that it supports both deterrent and action-reaction models of conflict.[30] In the short run an outburst of conflict is seen as a function of deterrence: when one side becomes weak or relaxes its vigilance the other is likely to strike; both sides must maintain a retaliatory or defensive capability to deter the eruption of conflict. Concessions, trust and compromise carry great risk, except as they might lull the opponent into carelesseness (a notion which implies the need to be vigilant against the day when the enemy will play a similar trick). Weakness invites pressure, negotiations can only take place from "a position of strength." However, since there is always some degree of uncertainty over enemy capabilities and immediate intentions, this 'position of strengh' is always a vague and uncertain goal. The requirements of deterrence are vague since the opponent is seen as motivated by communalist and emotional considerations. Thus, although major urban areas have *not* been systematically attacked in recent Indo-Pakistan wars, strategists in both countries know that in future conflicts—especially when and if nuclear weapons become available—the destruction of cities may enter into calculations of deterrence.

29. S.M. Burke, *Mainsprings of Indian and Pakistani Foreign Policies* (Minneapolis: University of Minnesota Press, 1974), p. 91.

30. See Robert Jervis, "Cooperation Under the Security Dilemma," *World Politics* 1, 2 (January 1978); 167-214.

Uncertainty over "how much is enough" contributes to the assumption of the communal conflict image that the present is rooted in a long history of violent attack and counter-attack, and action-reaction model. Both Indians and Pakistanis emphasize the regularity of their conflict and many on both sides argue persuasively that the crushing defeat of Pakistan in 1971 was an aberration, and did not usher in a stable imbalance of power. Those who hold the image of Indo-Pakistan relations as a communal riot tend to emphasize the historic inevitability of another conflict. They argue that it cannot be contained by mere manipulations of the level of arms or the temporary acquisition of effective deterrent capabilities by one side or another. This belief also contributes to the idea of (in India) and fear of (in Pakistan) putting an end to the escalatory process should another conflict break out, and it provides an additional rationale for the shift in Indian military planning to an "offensive-defense" after 1972. And, of course, there are a few on both sides who are attracted by the South Asian equivalent of "lobbing one into the men's room of the Kremlin;" they have an apocalyptic vision of a future nuclear holocaust in which the other side can be damaged so severely that it is unlikely to ever seek conflict again.

It is this element of unpredictability and uncertainty which is the most destabilizing contribution of the communal conflict with armor model. In the end it leads one to ask not whether Indians or Pakistanis can be trusted to fulfill their obligations in an arms control arrangement which lacked incentives for compliance, but whether, under the influence of a communal image of their relationship, they can be trusted in cases where it was in their self-interest to comply.

V. Japan

The Security Debate

TAKETSUGU TSURUTANI

One of the interesting phenomena in Japanese politics today is an increasingly lively debate on the issue of national security and military defense. For the first time in the postwar era, the Prime Minister's annual policy address to the Diet this spring contained a separate section devoted to defense problems. Again for the first time in the postwar period, the parliament is seriously considering the establishment of a committee on national defense in each of its chambers. There is talk about upgrading the Defense Agency (JDA) to Defense Ministry. Opposition parties that traditionally subscribed to the literal interpretation of the constitution's proscription of military power have shifted in the direction of at least implicitly endorsing the Self-Defense Forces (SDF). In parliamentary interpellation, the tone of opposition questions has changed from shrill pacifist idealism to a more subdued and inquisitive one. The current debate is not limited to party and parliament. The *zaikai* (the leadership stratum of the nation's modern economic sector) is making its views heard more aggressively than before, and the traditionally low-profile JDA is increasingly candid in expressing its views. The press, once a bastion of pacifist vigilance, also is showing signs of pragmatic concern in its approach and its tone on such matters. Our concern is with the character and substance of the ongoing debate in Japan. What are some of the more relevant alternative defense postures that are being debated? What are their respective rationales and motivations? Is it likely that a clear consensus on national defense will soon emerge?

A close observer of the current security debate in Japan is likely to be puzzled by its ambiguity as to substantive content, its lack of clear relevance to both the existing external environment and the most probable future contingencies, and the concomitant absence of any ascertainable strategic direction. What he witnesses is a strangely convoluted exchange of rhetorical exhortations and discreet circumlocutions which, upon clear scrutiny, would

175

prompt him to muse "So, what?" In an important sense, this is inevitable in that the debate is not entirely authentic. As in the past, the issue of national defense is still peripheral to politics. What motivates the current debate is the domestic political, partisan, institutional, and clientelist calculus of those who take active part in it. National security as an issue, in short, is treated as derivative from internal political competition. As we shall see, there are four major defense postures promoted by various sectors of what might be termed Japan's defense community, and they are four variations of one and the same theme, the theme of domestic political dynamics. Thus, within the policy spectrum that they presumably constitute, an advocate can, depending upon the turn of the domestic political dynamics (which includes intraparty competition), readily shift from one posture to another, for all are rooted in perceptions and expectations only marginally related to external events, and are mutually convergent in substance, and, in some empirico-logical sense, even mutually interchangeable. The fundamental criterion underlying the debate is, and has been, neither the constitutional permissibility (as two of the four approaches would publicly stress) nor external requirements (as the other two have us believe), but rather domestic (i.e., partisan, factional, etc.) political expediency.

The four alternative defense postures that emerge from the current security debate in Japan are: the permanent limits thesis, the basic defense policy, the requisite capability thesis, and the autonomous defense thesis. They share large areas of mutual convergence, thus making it difficult clearly to delineate where one ends and another begins, as well as to ascertain where a participant in the debate stands at a given moment. This is precisely because of the problem mentioned in the preceding paragraph. We shall first present the four alternative postures in a synoptic fashion and then discuss some difficulties with the way in which the issue of national defense and security is treated by the respective proponents.

Four Alternative Defense Postures

1. The Permanent Limits Thesis

Variously referred to as "the fundamental spirit thesis" (*kihon teki seishin ron*) and "the 'bounds' thesis" (*'waku' ron*), this represents an approach to national defense that underlay the past government policy and that still is most consistent with the pacifist inclination of the general public as well as most of the "progressive" opposition. It represents not so much a realistic concern about external military security as a captious wariness of domestic consequences of an activist defense policy. The "limits" (or "bounds") its proponents refer to are five: the spirit of the peace constitution, the principle of civilian control of the military, the exclusively defensive character of the

SDF, the three anti-nuclear principles, and the ceiling of 1% of the GNP for defense appropriations.

The issue of the SDF's constitutionality was once highly emotional, but the inevitable generational change in the population (over half of the population was born after August 15, 1945) plus a series of definitive court rulings (e.g., Sunakawa and Hyakuri) eventually led to a popular acceptance of the constitutional legitimacy of the SDF.[1] There remains, nevertheless, a quite strong feeling that the peace constitution is a unique national document. Thus, the proponents of the permanent limits thesis insist that the nation must remain faithful to its pacifist spirit ("fundamental spirit"), for it is this spirit, they argue, that makes Japan unique among nations.[2]

The principle of civilian control of the military assumes a great psychological magnitude because of the character and consequences of the prewar history of civil-military relations. There is an understandable apprehension on the part of many Japanese about the danger of resurgence of military influence in government and politics. As if to keep this apprehension alive, there appear from time to time inside stories about the pattern of interaction and relations between the uniformed and the civilian sectors of the JDA, alleging the dominance of the former over the latter and the latter's unquestioned deference to the former's "professional expertise."[3] There is also suspicion, which MPs themselves confirm, that most of the politicians remain indifferent to what is going on inside the JDA and to civil-military relations, thus in effect leaving issues of security and defense to military officers in the JDA and a handful of pro-military defense specialists within the ruling Liberal Democratic party (LDP).[4] Permanent-limits advocates fear that any activist defense policy would run the risk of increasing the power of the military in government.

The "exclusively defensive posture" principle is the empirical correlate of the "fundamental spirit." It dictates that the nation make judicious efforts to

---

1. Over 80% of the public view the SDF legitimate. See, for example, *Asahi Shimbun,* January 1, 1978, p. 9.

2. Thus, Hellmann notes that Article Nine of the constitution "gave legal sanctity and symbolic dignity to pacifism within the country and placed Japan in a *sui generis* category internationally." Donald Hellmann, "Japanese Security and Postwar Japanese Foreign Policy," in *The Foreign Policy of Modern Japan,* ed. by Robert Scalapino (Berkeley and Los Angeles: University of California Press, 1977), p. 323.

3. See, for example Osamu Kaihara, *Nihon Bōei Taisei no Uchimaku* (Tokyo: Jini Tsushin Sha, 1977), *passim* but esp. pp. 211-221. Kaihara speaks of "collective hypnosis" of civilian officials by the military brass and the rubber-stamping role they allegedly play in the agency's decision making.

4. See Sankei Shimbun, *Nihon no Anzen* (Tokyo: Sankei Shimbun Sha, 1976), vol. 1, p. 181; "Ronsō: Nihon o mamoru dōyū kotoka," *Chūōkōron,* January 1978, p. 84; and Mainichi Shimbun, ed.; *Kokumin to Jieitai* (Tokyo: Mainichi Shimbun Sha, 1969), p. 56.

avoid even appearing to increase its military power lest it cause fear and anxiety among neighbors. The government in the past went so far as to strip the F-4s (current mainstay of the Air Self-Defense Force acquired at enormous cost) of its key operational features (bombing and mid-air refueling capabilities) in order to keep them "exclusively defensive."

The three anti-nuclear principles (so-called *hikaku san gensoku*) were enunciated in 1967 by the then Prime Minister, in response to pacifist opposition and popular demands precipitated by China's nuclear explosions and the war in Vietnam. The Prime Minister pledged that Japan, as a matter of deliberate policy, would neither produce, nor obtain, nor permit the deployment of nuclear weapons. The principles have since been adhered to by the successive governments, although it should be noted that no LDP government has ever accepted that nuclear weapons are proscribed by the constitution.

The fifth "limit" or "bound" is the long-standing budgetary practice of limiting the defense appropriations to the maximum of 1% of the GNP. This limit came about by happenstance of earlier budgets quite unrelated to security requirements as such. The first year for which the SDF budget went below 1% of the GNP was 1959 when Japan had just launched a massive economic growth program. There is no evidence that the first "below 1%" defense appropriations were deliberate. In any event, the mere fact that the rate of annual economic growth in the 1960s generally exceeded 10% insured that 1% or less of the GNP for defense was sufficient to generate consistent increases in the SDF budget. That it was so, however, was purely a matter of statistical accident and not related at all to serious and comprehensive planning of national security requirements. In any event, the "1% limit" eventually became an operating rule for the nation's budgetary process, a rule to which all other sectors of government bureaucracy, their lateral policy counterparts within the ruling LDP and their respective client groups and institution in society became committed for their respective self interests. Its supporters argue, moreover, that 1% of the GNP is the maximum of what the public would tolerate for defense expenditure. In fact, in 1976, the cabinet officially accepted this argument, on the proposition that the annual rate of real growth in the GNP would average 6% into the mid-1980s.[5]

2. The Basic Defense Policy

Called *kiban teki boeiryoky kōsō* (literally, the fundamental defense capability plan), this constitutes the current defense policy of Japan. What is meant by

    5. *Asahi Shimbun*, October 10, 1977, p. 2 and Sankei Shimbun, Nihon no Anzen, vol. 2, pp. 156-9.

"basic" is that the SDF, and not the U.S. military, would be the "basis" of national defense and that the security arrangement with the United States would "supplement" them.[6] This is meant to contrast with the earlier government proposition that the SDF were to play a role "supplementary" to U.S. forces in case of serious military contingencies. Thus, under the current policy, Japan would prepare herself to cope, on her own (*dokuryoku de*), with an indirect aggression and a small-scale limited aggression, while repelling a large-scale aggression in cooperation with the United States.[7]

The basic defense policy rests, much as does its predecessor (i.e., the permanent limits thesis), on the basic reliability of the United States and the unlikelihood of a major war involving the nation's security. Its proponents thus point to the East-West detente, the Sino-American normalization, and the trend toward multipolarity and greater economic and political interdependence in the world.[8] The policy is also based on the proposition that the nation's military capability should be strictly defensive in posture.

Regarding the nation's domestic condition, the policy rests on the contention that "however powerful the SDF may become and no matter what sophisticated weaponry they may acquire, they could not constitute a genuinely effective defense capability unless it enjoyed the people's understanding, support, and cooperation."[9] Put differently, the policy clearly suggests the necessity of harmony between public opinion and military capability, and the lack of sufficient popular consensus in support of any significant expansion of the SDF. Moreover, it contends that the decline in the rate of economic growth militates against any notable increase in defense expenditure.[10] The policy regards the SDF as quantitatively adequate but needing qualitative improvement. Such improvement involves, in part, the replacement of the F-4s with the F-15s as mainstay of the ASDF and the acquisition of P-3C anti-submarine reconnaissance planes and helicopter carriers for the Maritime Self-Defense Force (MSDF). It must, however, be done with great circumspection and sensitivity toward neighboring states. A major proponent of the basic defense policy argued: "If Japan's peace-time defense capability is too large, it would arouse fear and alarm among our neighbors. On the other hand, if it were too small, it might create a vacuum in the Far East, thus causing instability in the region. We should therefore take care to limit our basic defense capability to the minimum necessary level as peace-time defense

6. See, for example, Prime Minister Fukuda's statement in the House of Representatives Budget Committee on February 6, 1978 in *Asahi Shimbun*, February 17, 1978, p. 2.

7. *Bōei Nenkan 1978* (Tokyo: Bōei Nenkan Kankō Kai, 1978), p. 603.

8. *Ibid.*, pp. 602-3.

9. *Ibid.*, p. 281.

10. *Ibid.*

capability."[11] The policy also emphasizes what one JDA official calls "a proper balance between the SDF capability and the 'home front support system' (*kōhō shien taisei*)."[12]

The basic thrust that makes the current policy distinct from its predecessor is that it purports to assume a greater share of national defense by preparing the SDF to deal with small-scale limited war contingencies with the security treaty with the United States as complementary to the task. To this extent, some analysts are tempted to regard the basic defense policy as moving away from total dependence upon U.S. forces, hence as demonstrating "an unprecedented realism and rationality in Japan's defense thinking."[13]

3. The Requisite Capability Thesis

This option is a loose distillation of various demands for a militant defense posture, such as the "as-required defense forces thesis" (*shoyō bōeiryoku ron*) and the "activist defense thesis" (*sekkyoku bōei ron*) that go as far back as the establishment of the SDF. Put simply, its various proponents argue that the level of Japan's military capability is woefully insufficient and that it should be determined not according to the constitution or to public opinion but by the magnitude of potential external contingencies and the extent of actual or potential adversaries' capabilities.[14] This "definition by situational contingencies" approach is presumably rendered increasingly plausible by a number of external developments in the present decade, such as the rise of petropolitics (not only of the Arab states but, more recently, of China and the Soviet Union), the lowering of America's politico-military posture in Asia and the Pacific, the expansion of the Soviet Asiatic Fleet, and the consequent exposure of Japan's vital life line to Soviet naval threat, the continuing instability of Southeast Asian nations through whose narrow waters Japan's life line extends, and the possibility of another violent outbreak on the Korean peninsula with the completion of American troop withdrawal. Moreover, proponents of the requisite capability thesis argue that the level of SDF capability conceived twenty years ago and more or less adhered to since then was based on calculations of trade requirements and military technology that have long ceased to be realistic.[15] In short, circumstances

---

11. Michita Sakata as quoted in Sankei Shimbun, *Nihon no Anzen*, vol. 2, p. 156.

12. Statement by the director of the Defense Bureau of the JDA at the House of Representatives Budget Committee, February 17, 1978, as reprinted in *Bōei Nenkan 1978*, pp. 104-5.

13. Makoto Momoi, "Basic Trends in Japanese Security Policies" in Scalapino, ed., *The Foreign Policy of Modern Japan*, p. 359.

14. *Asahi Shimbun*, February 3, 1978, p. 2.

15. For this argument, see, for example, Tadao Kusumi, "Japan's Defense and Peace in Asia," *Pacific Community* 4 (April 1973), pp. 431-2.

have long changed in the direction of requiring a greatly expanded defense capability for the nation.

Some proponents of this requisite capability option stress the necessity of acquiring deterrent as well as counterattack capabilities, and they speak even of engaging in a preventive attack, albeit in a circumlocutory fashion. Thus, one requisite capability LDP leader anticipates a contingency that would call for SDF forces to operate "hundreds of miles away [from Japan] in order to protect the merchant fleet or . . . to prevent intrusion into Japanese air space by hostile aircraft."[16] Early this year, the JDA director general exhorted SDF officers that their capability should be such that potential adversaries would "fear" them, for a nation whose defense forces could not be feared would be unable to deter aggression.[17] And the chairman of the Joint Staff Council in a widely debated article argued that only offensive capabilities would ultimately insure the nation's security.[18] The requisite capability thesis was also inadvertently reinforced by a 1977 court decision involving the constitutionality of SDF functions which stated in part that the constitution does not proscribe "the use of force for the purpose of *preventing* or repelling aggression."[19]

As mentioned earlier, the requisite capability thesis is not new.[20] What is new about it is the candor and aggressiveness with which its proponents now promote it. During the 1950s and the 1960s, the thesis (or any of its variations) was consciously downplayed in public. There were occasions when requisite-capability utterances were made by government officials, but they were made more by way of an aside or something akin to the slip of the tongue and were quickly qualified or explained away almost an soon as they were made. Officials were quite sensitive to what might be termed an "anti-military allergy" of the public and opposition parties. Thus, while the government never accepted the argument that a radical expansion of the SDF would be in violation of the constitution, it was always careful to point out the distinction it saw between what was constitutionally permissible (military

---

16. Yasuhiro Nakasone as quoted in Robert Osgood, *The Weary and the Wary: U.S. and Japanese Security Policies in Transition* (Baltimore and London: The Johns Hopkins University Press, 1972), p. 54.

17. Tarō Akasaka, "Bōei Rongi no juruizaki," *Bungei Shunjū,* March 1978, p. 164.

18. *Asahi Shimbun,* January 25, 1978, p. 2.

19. Quoted in *Bōei Nenkan 1978,* p. 97. Emphasis added.

20. To cite a few examples over the period: in 1954, the director general of the Legal Bureau (the highest legal office of the executive branch) stated that the nation should have whatever forces that would be needed for self-defense. In 1956, the Prime Minister observed in the Diet that the Constitution did not intend it for the Japanese people to just sit and be killed when attacked and that, in the absence of effective alternatives, it was in his view within the legal definition of self defense for Japan to attack enemy bases. In 1963, the Prime Minister noted that what should constitute self-defense capability could not be dogmatically

expansion) on the one hand and what was politically desirable (nonexpansion) on the other and to stress the latter over the former as its criterion of policy. For example, in 1959, the then JDA director general observed: "It is not the intention of the Constitution that we acquire weapons that would threaten other nations." In 1967, the Prime Minister noted: "The self-defense capability of our nation ought not to be such as to pose an aggressive threat to other nations."[21] Early in the current decade, the government decided to strip the F-4s of their bombing and midair refueling capacities on the grounds that it was "desirable" in view of the spirit of the constitution not to have an ability to bomb other nations.[22] Until recently, therefore, any statement smacking of the requisite capability thesis was commonly hedged with the qualifier of "not posing an aggressive or offensive threat." That constraint, however, seems to have gone out the window. And one commentator speaks of Japan's basic defense posture evolving from an exclusively defensive one to one of "tactical offense" (*senjutsu teki kōsei*).[23]

4. The autonomous Defense Thesis

The so-called *jishu bōei ron,* this alternative, on the surface at least, arises from any, or any combination, of three generalizable motives: national pride (nationalism), the nation's responsibility commensurate with its capability, and mistrust of the United States.[24] The general thesis itself is even older than the requisite capability thesis, dating back to early postwar years. Originally promoted by former Imperial military officers, the nationalist motive of the thesis has it that an independent national defense capability is an indispensable mark of a sovereign state.[25] Many influential members of the defense

---

or arithmetically determined but that it should instead be defined in terms of national resources, domestic condition, international environment, and levels of scientific and technological progress. Two years later, his successor viewed the nation's resources and conditions as defining the level of its defense capability. The 1970 Defense White Paper (the first of the kind ever) contained the following: "in the legal and theoretical sense, possession of small nuclear weapons, falling within the minimum requirements for a capacity necessary for self-defense . . . would be permissible" under the Constitution. See Kaoru Murakami, *Bōei Chō* (Tokyo: Kyōiku Sha, 1974), pp. 29 and 34; Momoi, "Basic Trends . . .," p. 346; Hiroshi Osanai, *Nihon no Kakubusō* (Tokyo: Daiamondo Sha, 1975), pp. 136-7; and Kunio Muraoka, *Japanese Security and the United States* (London: International Institute for Strategic Studies, Adelphi Papers No. 95, 1973), p. 24.

21. Both quoted in *Sekai,* April 1978, p. 116.

22. *Asahi Shimbun,* March 13, 1978, p. 1.

23. Kaoru Murakami, *Nihon Bōei no Kōsō* (Tokyo: Simul, 1976), pp. 150-152.

24. Ivan Morris, *Nationalism and the Right Wing in Japan: A Study of Postwar Trends* (London, New York, and Toronto: Oxford University Press, 1960), pp. 240-248.

25. For example, one former Imperial admiral lamented that "it is disheartening to place deterrent power in the hands of another country, even though it is an allied power,"

community argue that Japan is not a full-fledged nation but remains a semi-nation so long as her security is underwritten by "tax payers of the United States and South Korea."[26]

While, before the decade of the 1960s, the nationalist craving for independent military forces was not matched by the recovering nation's economic capability to meet its expectations, it came to be whetted as the nation entered the period of rapid growth, providing an additional argument (motivation) that the nation should assume a defense responsibility that is commensurate with its growing economic power. The "commensurate responsibility" argument need not be recounted here, for it is self-explanatory, except to note that it is compatible, albeit for a not entirely same set of fundamental reasons, with the desire of the United States since mid-1960s for Japan to increase her defense capability, and that it inevitably promotes the idea of self sufficiency in arms research, development, and production as well.

A third putative motivation underlying the autonomous defense thesis is an allegedly increasing doubt about America's resolve and will to come to Japan's aid in case of serious military contingencies. The lowering of America's politico-military profile in Asia through the Nixon doctrine, the end of the Vietnam War, and the decision to withdraw U.S. ground combat troops from Korea has strengthened the misgiving about the ultimate reliability of the United States as a security partner.[27] Some within Japan's defense community contend that the relevant events of the past several years suggest that the United States is reverting back to the "Europe first" policy.[28] Moreover, in their eyes, events within the United States in the past decade or so indicate a serious decline in internal discipline and political will of that country. Under these circumstances, Japan has no alternative to building sufficient military forces of her own to defend herself from external threat and aggression.

In one sense, the autonomous defense thesis is apparently consistent with both the intent and letter of a number of key official documents and authoritative statements of the past regarding the role of the SDF. As early as 1955, the JDA announced that its efforts were "directed at establishing a proper

---

Former Vice Admiral Fukudome as quoted in John Endicott, *Japan's Nuclear Option: Political, Technological, and Strategic Factors* (New York: Praeger, 1975), p. 63.

26. Murakami, *Nihon Bōei no Kōsō*, p. 142.

27. Consider, for example, President Nixon's statement: "we are not involved in the world because we have commitments; we have commitments because we are involved. Our interest must shape our commitments, rather than the other way around" as quoted in Hellman, "Japanese Security . . .," p. 333.

28. Masamichi Irie, "Shin jōseika de Nihon gaikō o kangaeru," *Jiyū* 20 (May 1978), p. 31.

The four alternative defense postures summarized in the preceding pages may be illustrated as follows:

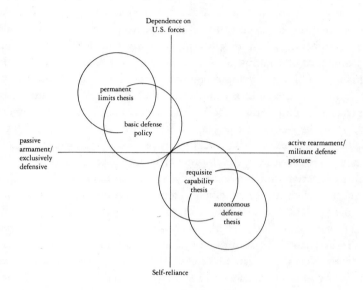

and appropriate self-defense system *necessary for an independent nation . . .*"[29] The Basic Policy of National Defense formulated by the National Defense Council and approved by the cabinet in 1957 stipulated a gradual increase of the nation's effective defense potential *"in keeping with the national strength and national conditions* within the limits necessary for self-defense."[30] The revised Japan-U.S. security treaty of 1960 in its third article provided: "The Parties, individually and in cooperation with each other, *by means of continuous and effective self-help* and mutual aid will maintain and develop . . . their capacities to resist armed attack." (Emphasis added) In 1970, the Prime Minister told the Diet: "We will build up our defense capability and will rely on the security treaty *to supplement* whatever is lacking."[31] Thus, proponents of autonomous defense could contend that the implementation of their approach is warranted not only by the changed and changing external environment but also by the promise contained in past government policies and the security treaty with the United States.

29. Quoted in Momoi, "Basic Trends . . .," p. 345. Emphasis added.
30. Kusumi, "Japan's Defense and Peace in Asia," p. 421. Emphasis added.
31. *Ibid.* Emphasis added.

Cause and Character of the Security Debate

On the surface, the four alternative defense postures may seem plausible. In fact, they are treated as worthy of serious attention by a press that has long been a bastion of pacifist vigilance.[32] Beyond the fog of verbiage surrounding the current security debate, however, they turn out to be essentially specious. And this for at least two reasons. First, none of them has any ascertainable relationship to the actual external circumstances of the nation. If there are any concrete situations to which any of the arguments address themselves, they are rather fatuous. Second, none of the alternative arguments presents a realistic picture of the level and type of defense capability it presumably pursues. This, of course, is a logical concomitant of the first.

The permanent limits thesis is both irrelevant and irresponsible in its apparent motive: irrelevant in that the external environment cannot be defined by domestic ideological, psychological, and political preferences; and irresponsibile in that it ultimately abdicates the sovereign duty of national defense and turns it over to another country. The focus of this thesis is not on national security but on the purity of a certain putative spirit and, in so focusing, the thesis renders national security and the purity of its concern mutually exclusive. Its practical utility consists, as has been demonstrated in the past, solely in its ability to resist U.S. pressures and pressures from activist-defense proponents to increase the nation's defense capability. Key assumptions that the thesis logically requires are closely interrelated and also either mutually indispensable or interchangeable. Among them are: (1) that there will be no major military contingency that would threaten the security and integrity of the nation; (2) that the United States would faithfully adhere to and honor the provisions of the existing security pact regardless of internal political change in the United States and vicissitude in its multiple external relations and commitments; (3) that the geopolitical as well as economic position of Japan within the international system will remain basically unaltered; and (4) that Japan will be able to resolve any serious external problem by cultural, economic, diplomatic, and political means. These assumptions would be tenable only so long as Japan continued to enjoy a most felicitious combination of fortuitous circumstances, a prospect that is ardently to be wished but not seriously to be expected. The permanent limits thesis, therefore, is a rationalization for not tackling the issue of military security and for not making any defense policy. It is a non-policy, or nothing

32. Consider, for example, the 15-part series of special commentary in *Asahi Shimbun* in February and March this year.

more than what Hellmann once characterized as a *māmā seisaku* (a stand-pat policy).[33]

The basic defense policy, to the extent that it is predicated on the dependability of the United States as security partner, constitutes little more than a rhetorical departure from the permanent limits thesis, for it adheres to all the "limits" contained in its predecessor. The only disagreement between the two is on the limit of some of those limits. Specifically, the limit the current policy places on the extent of the "defensive" character of the SDF is somewhat broader than the proponents of the permanent limits thesis would accept: for example, under the basic defense policy, the F-15s, as mainstay of the ASDF, would retain their bombing and mid-air refueling capacities, while their predecessors, F-4s, were stripped of those operational features in order to prevent them from appearing "offensive." (One ingenious rationalization offered in response to criticism that retention of those capabilities would render the F-15s offensive in character, was that they would cease to be the F-15s if their operational features were modified.)[34] Permanent-limits advocates also view any type of aircraft carrier as going beyond the limits of "exclusively defensive forces," but the supporters of the present policy contend that helicopter carriers fall within that limit. The significance of these disagreements, however, remains entirely obscure, precisely because the nation's defense requirements are never clearly spelled out by either.

Thus, the basic defense policy actually differs little from the permanent limits thesis. Its rhetorical novelty (including the reference to small-scale limited aggression to be coped with by the SDF on their own) is belied by the substantive continuation of the past nonpolicy, especially since the level of preparedness to which the SDF might be raised could not be substantially different from the existing level. Knowledgeable officials and observers have pointed out that, in case of a really serious contingency, the ASDF would be annihilated within one hour, the MSDF in a few days, and the Ground Self-Defense Force (GSDF) would immediately have to resort to guerrilla warfare in the event of enemy troop landing.[35] The current level of the nation's ability to defend itself from enemy incursion was graphically illustrated by the so-called MIG-25 incident. When a MIG-25 pilot defected to Japan in September, 1976, the ASDF, with its complement of electronic detection devices and F-4s, proved unable to intercept the plane, and before

33. Donald Hellmann, *Japan and East Asia: The New International Order* (New York: Praeger, 1972), p. 146.

34. *Asahi Shimbun,* March 5, 1978, p. 5.

35. See, for example, "Nihon no Senryoku," *Sandē Mainichi,* August 27, 1972, p. 20 an Martin Weinstein, *Japan's Postwar Defense Policy 1947-1968* (New York and London: Columbia University Press, 1971), p. 114.

it finally located the Soviet fighter's whereabouts the plane had already landed at a civilian airport right next to a major ASDF base.[36] This sorry state of the SDF could not change significantly under the present policy. Because of the budgetary "limit" imposed by the current policy and the continuing inflation, less than 20% of the defense budget can be spent for weapons procurement. (Personnel and food cost 50% of the budget, and the remainder is absorbed by maintenance.)[37] In 1976, for example, the total JDA procurements including such noncombat items as oil and food amounted to only slightly over $2 billion out of the total defense budget of $6 billion.[38] These procurements accounted for only 0.4% of the GNP of that year, well behind the share of color TV set production.[39] It is for these reasons that one is led to the conclusion that the basic defense policy provides the SDF with little beyond a few cosmetic and rhetorical changes. In short, the current policy represents another *māmā seisaku* disguised with a new label and a new verbiage.

The requisite capability and the autonomous defense theses presumably represent activist alternatives, but, thus far, the activism is only rhetorical. It is encouraged by what its proponents perceive to be a decline in the popular "anti-military allergy," a decline hastened in part by the MIG-25 incident, the contentious issue of 200-mile territorial waters, Washington's decision to withdraw troops from Korea, a resurgence of national consciousness, among others.[40] On the surface, the "definition by situational contingencies" argument of the requisite capability thesis sounds plausible, but, then, in an important sense, it is accepted by all other approaches. They differ in the extents to which they respectively contend the nation is threatened, though those extents are not entirely clear. The autonomous defense thesis, stripped of its nationalistic appeal, seems to dissolve itself into nonsense in that, strictly speaking, there is no such thing as autonomous national defense except perhaps for the United States and the Soviet Union.[41] Japan's geopolitical location, demographic and structural density, and insurmountably inferior level of armament vis-a-vis such neighbors as China and the Soviet

---

36. For a detailed discussion and evaluation of the incident, see Kaoru Murakami, "MIG-25 jiken kara nani o mananda ka" 1977 *Jieitai Neknan* (Tokyo: Bōei Sangyō Kyōkai, 1977), pp. 31-49.

37. See *Bōei Nenkan 1978*, p. 101; Murakami, *Bōei Chō,* p. 23; Sankei Shimbun, *Nihon no Anzen,* vol. 2, p. 158.

38. *Asahi Shimbun,* March 20, 1978, p. 1.

39. *Ibid.* Auer found that, in 1969, for example, the domestic defense procurement equalled in value the output of the leather industry. James Auer, *The Postwar Rearmament of Japanese Maritime Forces, 1945-71,* (New York and London: Praeger, 1973), p. 217. Also see John Emmerson, *Arms, Yen and Power: The Japanese Dilemma* (New York: Dunellen, 1971), p. 148.

40. *Asahi Shimbun,* March 13, 1978, p. 1.

41. Shūjiro Kotani, *Kokubō no Ronri* (Tokyo: Hara Shobo, 1970), esp. pp. 86-88.

Union, and the basic fragility of her economic system (far more fragile than it was before the war) all militate against any dream of genuinely self-sufficient defense of the country.

Presumably, both the requisite capability and the autonomous defense arguments are based, at least in part, upon a more "realistic," *realpolitik* assessment of the evolving external environment. What that assessment is, however, is not clear at all. Unlike Pentagon war-game players in the United States, JDA strategists have never even identified a potential or hypothetical enemy or enemies,[42] and, with the exception of the controversial "Three Arrows Plan" of 1963,[43] there apparently has never been serious and comprehensive strategic planning regarding the nation's defense. Proponents of the requisite capability and the autonomous defense theses vaguely allude to the Soviet Union attacking the country and landing troops on Hokkaido. This, however, is a most unlikely scenario, so unlikely, in fact, that its authenticity must be questioned. In the second place, even if we assumed the scenario to be credible, Japan could not hope to build up a military capability sufficient to cause the Soviet Union to "fear" her so it would be deterred from such an aggressive design. For example, the Soviet Asiatic Fleet today consists of a total complement of at least 1.2 milion tons, in contrast to Japan's 170,000 tons.[44] In air capability, the Soviet Union's deployment in the Far East enjoys a similar level of quantitative and qualitative superiority over Japan's ASDF. The extent of SDF expansion that would cause the Soviet Union to fear Japan, of course, is difficult to determine, but two things are certain: it would be impossible to achieve without fundamentally altering the domestic political, social, economic and cultural structures; and, if the Soviet Union indeed had a serious military design on Japan, any attempt that Japan might make to counter the threat would only prompt the Soviet Union to maintain or expand its vast superiority. In short, it would result in a bilateral arms race which Japan could never hope to win. Japan's acquisition of nuclear arms, which some argue would strengthen the effectiveness of her political, diplomatic and economic means in dealing with other states, would be dangerously counterproductive; it would make the country far more insecure by inviting the temptation of a preemptive attack by the Soviet Union (and perhaps by some

---

42. John C. Campbell, *Contemporary Japanese Budget Politics* (Berkeley and Los Angeles: University of California Press, 1977), p. 33.

43. A war plan prepared by staff officers of the JDA for a joint Japan-U.S. military operation in the event of a second Korean War. It was exposed in the Diet by opposition parties and the Prime Minister was compelled to fire some 20 top SDF officers. See Osanai, *Nihon no Kakubusō*, p. 136 and Albert Axelbank, *Black Star Over Japan* (New York: Hill and Wang, 1972), p. 51.

44. The figures are from Takuya Kubo, "Kaijō Bōei to Kaijō Kōtsū no Kakuho," *Kokusai Mondai* 217 (April 1978), p. 44.

others as well).[45] The desire to alter the existing balance of power in the Far East, which is quite explicit in the putative argument by the proponents of the requisite capability and the autonomous defense theses, then, is entirely un-realistic.

To the extent that Japan's security has been said to be predicated upon that of South Korea, it may be argued that the withdrawal of American ground troops from the Korean peninsula might lead to a contingency which would jeopardize Japan's security. But an attack on Japan by either Korea or a Korea unified under Pyongyang (assuming that such unification might take place) is as improbable as the Soviet attack. In any event, Japan's ASDF already enjoys an effective parity with its counterpart of either Korea. The same can be said of the MSDF. Should Japan acquire bombers (which neither she nor the two Koreas currently have), thus to cause either Korea to fear her? The GSDF would have to be nearly tripled in size in order to match the army of either Korea, but for what purpose? And what would be the political, economic, and diplomatic ramifications? Trade-offs between a military buildup for the purpose of causing these neighbors to fear Japan and its negative ramifications would seem distinctly unattractive.

The possibility of Japan's shipping lanes being subjected to harassment is frequently raised by proponents of the requisite capability and the auton-omous defense theses. One official observed that 80% of the nation's critical life line is threatened by the Soviet navy.[46] In fact, this concern is so strong that it constituted a prominent part of the 1977 Defense White Paper.[47] The apparent concern about the security of Japan's life line is not limited to the Soviet threat but extends to other contingencies especially regarding the Straits of Malacca which could be threatened by any number of states.[48] The credulity of this concern was strengthened this spring when the administrative deputy director general of the JDA, on his return from a Japan-U.S. conference on security in Hawaii, reported that "the United States entertains a strong expectation about Japan's ability to protect the East Asian sea lanes . . . and to provide her own aerial defense."[49] But, militarily to insure the safety of the nation's life line stretching through the Straits of Malacca would involve massive naval and air construction including submarines and aircraft careers.

45. Proponents of a militarily stronger Japan usually hedge on this matter, but some of their arguments, while rejecting the nuclear option in the short run, clearly endorse its ultimate political utility. See, for example, Ichiji Sugita, "Japan and Her National Defence," *Pacific Community* 5 (July 1974), esp. pp. 506-508.

46. Kubo, "Kaijō Bōei to Kaijō Kōtsū no Kakuho," p. 44. Also see Murakami, *Nihon Bōei no Kōsō*, pp. 70-73.

47. See its summary in *Asahi Shimbun*, July 29, 1977, pp. 1-2.

48. See, for example, Kaihara, *Nihon Bōei Taisei no Uchimaku*, pp. 131-4.

49. Quoted in *Asahi Shimbun*, March 1, 1978, p. 2.

Considering the most likely kind of reaction such a major endeavor would engender from a range of nations concerned and the impact it would have upon the nation's relations with them, the proposition cannot but be viewed as a bit absurd, for, in the end, Japan's life line would be no more secure than before.

In the end, then, neither the requisite capability thesis nor the autonomous defense argument provides a persuasive and realistic contingency for which it presumably argues that the nation should expand its military power. Neither, moreover, suggests the extent to which it seeks to expand the SDF in order to cope with such contingecy as it claims to fear.

The apparent argument of each of the four alternative approaches to the issue of national defense and security is essentially specious. To the extent that the activism of the requisite capability and the autonomous defense theses is rhetorical, it might be argued that these seemingly activist theses are little more than means of political challenge not against the basic defense policy or the permanent limits thesis but rather against their proponents. The real source of these arguments is neither public opinion nor the spirit of the constitution (as the permanent-limits and the basic-defense proponents would have us believe), nor the probability of external military threat (as those espousing the requisite capability thesis or the autonomous defense posture contend). The security debate currently taking place in Japan is a security debate only in a peripheral sense. What, then, is it about? What is its motivation?

Every major issue becomes an instrument of partisan competition, intra-party factional struggle, and bureaucratic jockeying in Japan. To a certain extent, this is true in every country. In Japan's case, however, the tendency has been maximized and exacerbated by the very fact of effective insulation of the nation from the slings and arrows of perilous fortune of international politics behind the protective shield of American military might throughout the postwar period. To compound the matter, the fragmentation of opposition into first three, then four and now five small, mutually contentious parties has thus far insured the semi-permanent supremacy of the LDP within which effective power is dispersed among mistrustful factions, thereby further encouraging the tendency to treat every issue as an instrument of narrowly partisan, factional, or sectional exploitation. It is thus that the issue of security continues to be obfuscated and instead treated as an object of those particularistic political calculations. And the factionalism of the ruling LDP prevents the emergence of relevant and forceful political leadership. The Prime Minister is a virtual figurehead selected through a series of bargaining and compromise and is surrounded by cabinet ministers and other leaders of the party many of whom are his actual or potential enemies or their surrogates for whom nothing would be more pleasing than seeing him (and helping him) stumble and fail and resign. In this rather unenviable predicament, the Prime Minister must avoid any risk of controversy either within his own party or with the parliamentary opposition. (At least four prime ministers were forced to resign as a direct consequence of intra- or inter-party controversy.) A genuinely new policy direction, especially for such a delicate issue as national security, then, is not compatible with the intra- and inter-party circumstances under which he operates.[50]

Another important factor relevant to the current security debate in Japan is the virtually sole emphasis the government has in the past placed on economy, which came to define effective policy and budgetary parameters for government bureaucracies and to institutionalize certain criteria and modes of decision making. In this process what the Japanese refer to as "economic ministries" (Finance, Intenational Trade and Industry, Agriculture and Forestry, Transportation, Construction, Economic Planning) have become enormously powerful (backed by wide ranges of influential client groups) and today virtually dominate the government. Their vast powers and extensive policy territories are the products of the politics of high economic growth and they brook no diminution of their influence. By and large, these ministries are the most resolute guardians of the "1% limit" principle and thus constitute a formidable impediment to any substantive change in the nation's defense policy.[51]

These intra- and inter-party and bureaucratic considerations are the bases of the character of the current security debate. They effectively militate against a significant change in the existing policy. What change that emerges, therefore, tends to be cosmetic and rhetorical rather than substantive. The formulation of the current basic defense policy illustrates these points.

The government policy that preceded the current one was in essence the permanent limits thesis. As years passed, there emerged considerable dissatisfaction with it among JDA officials (especially military) as well as among elements of the ruling LDP. One of those LDPers happened to become JDA director general when the agency was engaged in initial formulation of the so-called Fourth Defense Consolidation Plan. The new JDA director, Yasuhiro Nakasone, was determined, for his own political reasons, to incorporate his

---

50. For LDP intraparty factional politics and the predicament of the Prime Minister, see Taketsugu Tsurutani, *Political Change in Japan: Response to Postindustrial Challenge,* (New York: McKay, 1977), pp. 94-104.

51. For the condition of the JDA in the budgetary process, see Campbell, *Contemporary Japanese Budget Politics,* pp. 33-34; Hellmann, *Japan and East Asia,* pp. 146-8; and Angus Fraser, "Some Thoughts on the Resurgence of Militarism in Japan," *Pacific Community* 4 (April 1973), p. 445.

own view (essentially a requisite capability thesis) into the plan, thereby attempting to provide a new policy direction. Several relevant factors soon converged, however, to deflect what was then called the "Nakasone Plan." Nakasone was (and is) the leader of one of the five major LDP factions with a clear ambition to become party president and Prime Minister. The party's electoral popularity had been perceptively declining. While Nakasone and his supporters viewed the defense issue as an expedient means by which to revitalize the party (and thus to increase their influence in it), others in the party were either reluctant or opposed to further jeopardizing its electoral fortune by permitting an intraparty and parliamentary controversy to arise over a potentially explosive issue. They were also well aware of Nakasone's political ambition. Then there was resistance from the bureaucratic budgetary process. As may be clear from our preceding discussion, defense appropriations do not enjoy priority status in the budgetary process. The JDA does not have ministerial status; it is one of the "agencies" under the Office of the Prime Minister. Senior civilian officials of the agency come from other ministerial bureaucracies such as Finance, MITI, Interior. And the agency does not yet have a powerful and extensive constituency as does any of those other ministries or the DOD in the United States.[52] With the issue of national security effectively depoliticized by the traditional "stand-pat policy," therefore, JDA simply could not compete with those "economic ministries." With no issue and a marginal constituency, the JDA request would meet only with the Finance Ministry's relentless imposition of the "1%" doctrine. Nakasone's intraparty rivals had powerful allies in the government bureaucracy. These alone would have doomed the Nakasone Plan, but there emerged a number of other relevant events which tended further to strip the original Nakasone Plan of its expansionist thrust. (Nakasone in the meantime had been replaced in the perpetual game of musical chairs typical of the LDP.) The reversion of Okinawa, the so-called Nixon "shock," the Sino-American *rapprochement,* the Sino-Japanese normalization under a new prime minister, and a subsequent chill in Moscow-Tokyo relations, a further electoral decline of the LDP in the 1972 general election, the "oil shock" of the same year and

---

52. Unlike in the United States, no major firm, let alone no major segment of business and industry depends upon defense procurement for its sustenance. While there are close to 100 firms engaged in weapons production, defense contracts account for tiny fractions of their respective revenues. For the JDA-industry relations, see David Hopper, "Defense Policy and the Business Community: The Keidanren Defense Production Committee" in *The Modern Japanese Military System,* ed. by James Buck (Beverly Hills and London: Sage Publications, 1975), pp. 113-147. For an alarmist view of the military-industrial relations in Japan, see Axelbank, *Black Star Over Japan,* pp. 30-36 and *passim* and Jon Halliday and Gavan McCormack, *Japanese Imperialism Today* (New York and London: Monthly Review Press, 1973), pp. 105-111 and *passim.*

a sudden inflationary trend were among the events that variously affected not only the government itself but also the unpredictable fortune of factional politics within the ruling party, thus reinforcing the natural institutional and political pressure to repress the issue of national defense.

The ultimate result of the convergence and interplay of these and other factors, then, was the adoption of a policy (the basic defense plan) whose difference from its predecessor was largely cosmetic and rhetorical. It was a policy (or nonpolicy) conceived in response, not to any critical debate of the nation's security requirements and strategic considerations, but to intraparty factional political competition, bureaucratic budgetary politics, and partisan electoral misgivings. It was the same old policy in a new container.

The requisite capability and the autonomous defense arguments, which on the surface are based on a more critical and explicit concern with national security requirements in the changing international environment are also basically motivated by considerations other than military. They are, in one sense, *rhetorical* anti-mainstream arguments whose time their proponents feel is coming soon, perhaps sooner than they once thought, and which they could ride into power. Among their current adherents are a considerable number of younger LDP MPs whose leader, Nakasone, would challenge the aging incumbent mainstream policy leadership. (Nakasone is the youngest of the five major factional leaders.) The economic distress that has persisted since the initial oil shock of 1972 has given rise to expanding demands from certain sectors of business and industry and, more recently, from private-sector labor unions, for an expansion of arms production and for liberalization of government restrictions on arms exports. Big business and organized labor in Japan play a far more extensive and crucial electoral role than do their counter-parts in the United States. The sudden rise of the security debate and the more aggressive challenge by activist defense arguments against the current basic defense policy, then, is no accident. The requisite capability and the autonomous defense theses are thus responses on the part of those who wish to exploit the current economic predicament of the nation and the vague public anxiety as a spring board to power within the party and in the government.

In the past, the issue of national defense was in large measure treated as subordinate to, and a function of, the budgetary politics geared to growth and prosperity. Today, the newly active debate of the issue, in its basic motivation and purpose, is subordinate to, and a function of, intra-party power struggle and partisan electoral competition both of which are linked to clientelist economic and institutional calculus.[53] The issue, as such, remains

___

53. One former senior civilian official of the JDA and director general of the National Defense Council Secretariat complains the JDA/SDF is a football for intra-LDP power struggle, Kaihara, *Nihon Bōei Taisei no Uchimaku*, p. 47.

peripheral. It is precisely for this reason that the debate is conducted at a level of vague generalities and rhetorical obfuscations, devoid of specificity of content and clarity of context. National defense is yet to be subjected to a genuinely critical scrutiny.

The Domestic Factors

James E. Dornan*
and Diane S. Dornan

The future of Japan's defense policy has in recent years inspired considerable commentary among students of world politics in the United States. For more than a decade, scholars and journalists alike have called attention to the anomalous character of Japan's status as an "economic giant" and "military pygmy." Its emergence from the latter status has long been predicted.

During the course of the past year, a spate of reports has appeared in the Western press, asserting that the Japanese military awakening has begun. The postwar Japanese consensus on the desirability of a low-profile international policy, accompanied by low levels of defense expenditures and reliance on the United States to guarantee Japan's security, is said to be rapidly breaking down. Not only is Japan seriously considering rearmament on a major scale, but, in the words of one commentator, she has once again launched herself as a major Asian power.[1]

These reports deserve serious examination. If they prove to be correct, they presage one of the most important developments in post-World War II international politics. While it is somewhat of an exaggeration to label Japan a military pygmy, the description contains a large kernel of truth. Since the end of World War II Japan has played a role in world politics almost unique in history: possessing great—and growing—economic power, she has made

*This chapter was completed by Diane S. Dornan following the death of her husband. The editor wishes to express to her the gratitude of all who have collaborated in this volume.

1. See John P. Roche, "Japan Awakens on Security," *Washington Star*, August 30, 1978. See also Robert Whynant, "A Rising Military Sun," *New York Post*, February 11, 1978; Toshio Kojima, "Japan Begins to Think About Rearmament," *Christian Science Monitor*, April 25, 1978; William Sexton, "There's a Debate in Japan on Rearmament," *Philadelphia Inquirer*, July 30, 1978; Rowland Evans and Robert Novak, "Japan's Steady Rearmament," *Washington Post*, November 22, 1978; and Ernest W. Lefever, "Will Japan feel forced to rearm?" *Washington Star*, Jan. 14, 1979.

no effort to acquire military power commensurate with her economic status, and has thus been able to exert little direct influence over the course of regional and global international politics.

The reasons for Japanese acceptance of this anomalous international posture—which, incidentally, is sharply at variance with Japan's behavior in the prewar period, when she was deeply caught up in the imperialist power politics of East Aisa—have often been discussed. Principal among them has been the attitude of the United States. Stimulated by what one commentator has called "the messianic idealism" of General Douglas MacArthur and persuaded that among the principal causes of World War II in Asia was the authoritarian nature of the Japanese political system, the U.S. decided in 1945 both to change that system and, in the process, to prevent Japan from ever again possessing the military capability to threaten her neighbors. American policies were facilitated by the presence in Japan of a group of like-minded political idealists led by Kijuro Shidehara, as well as by the demoralizing effects upon the Japanese public of the nation's military defeat and of the Hiroshima and Nagasaki nuclear attacks.

Japan's acceptance of a "pacifist" role in the international political system after World War II was made easy by the political conditions which obtained in Asia during the postwar period. The attention of the United States and the Soviet Union was focused upon Europe, while China was torn apart by a civil war which totally absorbed its energies. Finally, particularly after the Korean War and the signing of the Japanese-American Security Treaty in 1952, Japan's alliance with the U.S. seemingly made unnecessary any concern with security questions.

For more than two decades, occasional Japanese restiveness with the American connection was kept in check by awareness within the ruling Liberal Democratic Party of the very real benefits, economic and otherwise, which Japan has derived from her relationship with the United States. Within the past several years, however, a combination of events has coalesced to encourage within Japan a fundamental re-examination of the nation's current international role.

The Influence of External Developments on Japanese Views on Defense Policy

One Japanese observer feels that the reversion of Okinawa to Japanese control in 1969 first stimulated the development of a new set of domestic attitudes on international security questions; for this was regarded by many in Japan as a key indicator marking the end of the post-World War II era of political dependence on the U.S.[2] Increased self-confidence and national pride has issued as well from continued Japanese economic success and consistent outperformance of most other world economies. Many postwar insecurities thus gradually yielded to growing self-assurance as the 1970s progressed. Meanwhile, two other trends were simultaneously undermining the postwar foundation of Japanese foreign and security policy: the power of the U.S.S.R. was rising, both on the global strategic plane and regionally, and the ability and desire of the U.S. to extend a fraternal protectiveness to Japan was declining.

Indeed, there have been certain underlying difficulties and recurrent stresses in the U.S.-Japanese alliance since its inception in 1952. While most U.S. policymakers have continued to believe that it is undesirable for Japan to become a major military power, since the Korean War more than one American defense official has voiced dissatisfaction with the level of Japan's contribution to security arrangements in Northeast Asia. Such officials argue that the U.S. has provided a nuclear umbrella which guarantees Japan's security, while Japan contributes nothing to the defense of the U.S. and is left free to concentrate totally on economic development. U.S. congressmen, moreover, often complain that Japan has shown little appreciation of the U.S. role in guaranteeing its security.

Many Japanese, on the other hand, appear to believe that the U.S. has been the chief beneficiary of the American-Japanese security relationship. There have been recurring complaints in Japan over the use of bases in the country to support U.S. foreign policy in other parts of Asia, as well as occasional controversies over the alleged presence of nuclear weapons on United States warships calling on Japanese ports. Finally, some political figures, principally those representing ultra-nationalist forces in Japanese politics, appear to feel that the nation's present degree of dependence upon the U.S. is unhealthy and prevents Japan from achieving its rightful place in world affairs.

In the early years of the Nixon Administration, several events considerably aided the emergence of a "new spirit" in Japan on foreign policy questions. The Nixon Doctrine itself was interpreted in some circles in Japan as presaging a U.S. disengagement from the Pacific. The so-called "Nixon Shokku" of 1971, involving the "opening" to Peking and various unilateral

---

2. Tadae Takubo, unpublished paper prepared for meeting of Japanese and American analysts at the Strategic Studies Center of SRI International, Washington, D.C., November 14, 1977. Mr. Takubo is Director of the Foreign Affairs Department of JiJi Press and a leading figure in the just-established private research institute, the Japan Center for Study of Security Issues.

initiatives on important economic issues, made it clear to Japanese leaders that the United States would attend to its own interests regardless of the impact on Japan. The collapse of the U.S. position in Southeast Asia in 1975 and the announcement by the Carter Administration early in 1977 that United States ground combat forces would be withdrawn from the Korean peninsula over the course of the next several years dramatically reduced confidence on the part of the Japanese public and many opinion leaders in American power and in America's reliability as an ally.[3] Another source of disagreement has been the Japanese desire to acquire enrichment and repro- cessing technology in connection with its nuclear power industry, which goals have conflicted with recent U.S. nuclear proliferation policy. And in the past decade, as Japan became more affluent and competitive whilst the American economy languished, recurrent and increasingly bitter clashes over economic policy have also soured the Japanese-American relationship. Prime Minister Ohira recently went so far as to indicate his belief that U.S. demands could be attributed to ignorance, not just misunderstanding, of the Japanese economy, and that difficulties in the relationship were deep- rooted.[4] It should be emphasized, however, that despite all these adverse factors Japanese elite and public opinion continues to attach great importance to retaining American friendship and cooperation.

If the eagle no longer soars so high as once it did in Northeast Asia, the bear looms increasingly large and menacing. For the past several years, dismay on the part of Japanese officials over the growing military power of the Soviet Union has been increasingly steadily,[5] and leaders have been troubled by the apparent U.S. unconcern over this perceived trend.

3. As one commentator has observed, "the common reaction, propagated and magni- fied by the press, is that Carter is cutting Japan's lifeline." Susumu Awanohara, "Will Harsher Criticism Mean Knee-Jerk Reaction?" *Far Eastern Economic Review,* June 24, 1977, p. 38. Public confidence was shown to be badly shaken as well in a poll taken by the *Yomiuri Shimbun* early in 1978, in which only 19% of the Japanese people expressed confidence that the United States would come to the defense of Japan in the event of external aggression, a figure similar to that of another poll taken in the fall of 1978 which is cited below. The 19% figure, reported in *Indianopolis News,* May 25, 1978, represented a decline from the 35% of the population which expressed confidence in the U.S. military commitment in a late 1976 poll. See *World Opinion Update* I (September, 1977), p. 4.

4. "Ohira says U.S. does not know Japan very well," *Japan Economic Journal,* March 20, 1979. Mr. Yasuo Takeyama, editor-in-chief of the pro-U.S. *Japan Economic Journal,* has declared that ". . . U.S.-Japan relations are unfortunately culminating into an explosive point." See *ibid.,* Mar. 20, 1979, p. 27.

5. See Hideaki Kase, *Northeast Asian Security: A View From Japan,* paper presented at SRI International's Symposium on Northeast Asian Security, June 20-22, 1977; "Japanese Envoy's Remarks on Troop Question Cited," Jan. 16, 1977, Foreign Broadcast Information Service, *Asia and Pacific,* Jan. 28, 1977, p. E-4; "KYODO Report on Japan-ROK Legislators'

In releasing the 1976 Japanese Defense White Paper, Takuya Kubo, then Secretary-General of the National Defense Council, asserted that "the U.S. has been replaced by the Soviet Union as the predominant military power in the Far East." Soviet air and sea power in the region, he said, are "vastly superior" to similar U.S. forces, and constitute a growing threat to the security of the non-communist states in the Western Pacific.[6]

The 1977 Defense White Paper treated such questions even more thoroughly. Pointing to Soviet deployment of "large land-based ICBMs with massive yield warheads," the White Paper concluded that "the strategic arsenal of the Soviet Union is now numerically superior in almost every indicator to American weaponry." As a consequence, the document continued, "there is growing anxiety that such Soviet efforts might lead to the relative superiority of the Soviet Union in mutual nuclear deterrence, thus placing the Soviet Union in a politically advantageous posture over the U.S." "Such a development," the White Paper concluded, "could affect the trust of the Western powers in the U.S."[7]

American officials continue to insist that the SALT treaties will deny the Soviet Union any strategic advantage over the U.S., but many Japanese elites nevertheless remain uneasy and question the ability and willingness of the U.S. to apply extended deterrence to the Far East. Even Europe has had its doubts on such protection for itself, and Japan is painfully cognizant that cultural and historical factors have bred in Americans a greater affinity for Europe and appreciation of its importance to the U.S. than is the case with the U.S.-Japan relationship; moreover, with regard to the Far East the U.S. has never developed a doctrine of "flexible response."

Equally alarming to Japan has been the deteriorating balance of conventional weapons in the area, particularly in naval forces. As an island nation Japan is heavily dependent upon sea lanes for importation of 70% of her raw materials and for the trade essential to her export-based economy. She has thus been disquieted by the surge of Soviet naval power in the immediate vicinity as well as in the farther reaches of the Pacific and in the Indian Ocean, particularly since much trade must pass through several narrow and vulnerable straits. U.S. naval forces are declining in number and America has reduced its aims to a "1-½ war" capability, concentrating on protection of Europe and the Middle East. As exemplified during the recent

---

Statement," Feb. 17, 1977, *ibid.,* Feb. 17, 1977, p. C-2. Concern over growing Soviet military power was repeatedly expressed by Japanese officials interviewed by the author in Tokyo in January 1977 and February 1978.

6. Ronald Yates, "Japanese White Paper Says Soviet Power Tops U.S.," *Chicago Tribune,* June 5, 1976.

7. Japan Defense Agency, *The Defense of Japan, 1977,* pp. 8-10, 15.

Iranian crisis, ships must be withdrawn from the Pacific and Indian Ocean areas to meet any extraordinary demands in other regions, leaving the Far Eastern balance more tenuous still. The 1978 White Paper noted that "both in Europe and in the Far East, the strength of Soviet forces now surpasses that of the U.S., and the safety of the sea and air lanes from the U.S. mainland is being jeopardized."[8] The White Paper was presented to the press by Ko Maruyama, Vice Minister of the Defense Agency; Maruyama specifically called attention to the Soviet naval buildup in the Pacific, and forthrightly labeled that buildup a direct threat to the security of Japan—a clear departure from prevailing Japanese practice.[9]

The Report also noted Japanese "apprehension" over the planned U.S. withdrawal of ground combat troops from South Korea, observing that the withdrawal "not only may affect the actual military balance but, still worse, may give an impression that the U.S. commitment to the defense of South Korea is being eroded."[10] It stressed as well the need for continued Japanese reliance on the Security Treaty with the United States, but asserted that "nebulous expectations and one-sided reliance" upon the U.S. should be ended, and called for more efforts by Japan to provide for its own security.[11] Recently Mr. Yamashita of the Japan Defense Agency expressed worry that the Soviet Union had established a military air base in Viet-Nam; he noted that certain evidence to that effect coincided with the possible assignment of the new Kiev class aircraft carrier *Minsk* to the Pacific and with reports that the Soviets might deploy new *Backfire* bombers in the Far East.[12]

But in the past several years such worries have received a somewhat unsympathetic hearing in Washington, although the U.S. has been anxious for Japan to increase its defense spending so as to lighten the American burden. The United States persisted in its announced determination to withdraw troops from Korea, albeit at a later date than originally proposed. Secretary of Defense Harold Brown has on several occasion refuted the legiti-

---

8. Japan Defense Agency, *The Defense of Japan, 1978,* p. 13.

9. Maruyama's statements received far less attention in the U.S. than they deserved. He was quoted at length, however, in the *Los Angeles Times,* July 29, 1978. *The New York Times* gave some attention to similar remarks by Atsuyuki Sassa of the JDA, who headed the team which prepared the report; see the issue of July 29, 1978.

10. See Foreign Press Center, *Summary, Defense of Japan, 1978,* p. 6.

11. Quoted in *Los Angeles Times,* July 29, 1978. To be sure, such references have occasionally appeared before in JDA statements; the 1970 White Paper argued that "we must stop being imitators, and we must stop following the wake of others; we must move on toward our own aims of our own choosing." Japan Defense Agency, *The Defense of Japan, 1970,* pp. 2-3.

12. William Chapman, "Japan Picks Up Signs of Soviet Bases in Vietnam," *Washington Post,* April 14, 1979.

macy of Japanese fears, moreover.[13] While Japan has pointed out the numerical and tonnage advantages of the Soviet Pacific fleet, Brown has stressed U.S. plans to upgrade quality by introducing new weapon systems into the Pacific threatre, and has declared that the U.S. fleet remains dominant in the western Pacific, where Soviet naval and air power are no match for their U.S. counterparts. Acknowledging that there has been a major increase in ground forces and air power by the Soviets, the Defense Secretary reiterates the Carter Administration's conviction that this buildup is directed at China and not other countries. In his recent statement concerning the possible Soviet base in Viet-Nam and the potential deployment of the *Minsk* and *Backfires* in the Far East, however, Yamashita specifically stated that he did not believe Soviet motivations were limited to concern over the China–Viet-Nam clash.[14]

Japanese officials have indicated that their fear is not so much that the Soviet Union actually will launch an attack upon their islands, but rather that the Soviets will attempt to use their new strength for political influence and to insist upon their own demands. Already a growing number of confrontations with the U.S.S.R. over the past several years has increased Japanese trepidation and encouraged the anti-Soviet sentiments latent in the populace.

The unencumbered landing of a MiG-25 by a defecting pilot at an air base on Hokkaido in September 1976 not only glaringly exposed the inadequacy of Japanese air defenses but created tensions between Japan and the Soviet Union as well. At that time a small front page article in the *Asahi Shimbun* speculated, for the first time since World War II, on the possibility that the U.S.S.R. might actually attack the Japanese nation.[15] In general there has been an increasing number of incidents of Russian intrusion into Japan's air space; whereas there were virtually no such occurrences a few years ago, there were 60 in 1976 and 96 in 1977. Similarly, the Russian naval presence and maneuvers off Japanese coasts have been growing,[16] with inten-

13. See Bradley K. Martin, "Soviet Pacific Buildup Not Worrisome to U.S., Brown Says," *Baltimore Sun,* Nov. 10, 1978; and Stephen Barber, "Brown's Asian Assurance," *Far Eastern Economic Review,* March 3, 1978.

14. Chapman, *op. cit.*

15. *Asahi Shimbun,* September 7, 1976. The *Tokyo Shimbun* recently carried a similar story, noting that the only foreign power which might consider invading Japan is the U.S.S.R., and suggesting that Wakkanai and Ishikari Bays on the Island of Hokkaido might be possible landing sites. See Henry Scott-Stokes, "Defense Increases Urged by Japanese," *New York Times,* May 14, 1978.

16. See the discusson of these and related issues in Japan Defense Agency, *Defense of Japan, 1977,* pp. 30-33. Shin Kanemaru, former Director-General of the Japan Defense Agency, recently observed that "Russian warships and other vessels make such frequent appearances in the Sea of Japan these days that we might as well refer to those waters as the Sea of Russia." Quoted in *Indianapolis News* editorial, May 25, 1978.

sification of activity during fisheries negotiations with the Soviets and while Japan was preparing to sign a treaty with China which the U.S.S.R. opposed.[17] Bitter negotiations over fishing rights led to the dispatch of a Japanese delegation to Moscow (the delegation including representatives of all political parties for the first time since the war) to condemn the Russian position in face-to-face meetings. Increasingly, the U.S.S.R. has begun to accuse Japan of militarism; in October 1978, for instance, the Soviet branded Japanese defense officials "the successors of the Samurai," accusing them of violating the Japanese constitution through the unlawful and excessive build-up of military strength.[18] On the heels of signing of the Japan-China Treaty of Peace and Friendship, the Soviet Union announced in November 1978 the conclusion of a 25-year treaty with Viet-Nam; this was quickly followed by the Vietnamese invasion of Cambodia and the subsequent invasion of Viet-Nam by China, events which left Japan's Asian policy in tatters. And while the Soviets have counted on large-scale Japanese aid to develop Siberia, these projects have lagged as Japanese businessmen grew disenchanted and even came to favor the opportunities presented by the market of the U.S.S.R.'s arch-rival, China.[19]

The most serious outstanding issue between the two nations continues to be that of the four islands off Hokkaido, which the Soviet Union seized in the final days of World War II and has since steadfastly refused to relinquish, while the Japanese have just as adamantly demanded their return before agreeing to sign a friendship treaty with the Soviets. After Japan signed a treaty with China despite frequent Russian threats of retaliation if it did so, the Soviets built up arms, personnel and installations on the two islands of Etorofu and Kunashiri.[20] Japanese protests were met with the customary brusque Soviet denial that there was any outstanding territorial issue between Japan and the U.S.S.R. The vulnerability and helplessness of the Japanese could scarcely have been highlighted in any more dramatic fashion: the four

17. Consider footnotes 18 and 19.

18. "Soviets Hit Japanese Policy," *Washington Post,* October 9, 1978.

19. Tracy Dahlby, "Japan cools its Moscow fever," *Far Eastern Economic Review,* Mar. 2, 1979, pp. 92-93.

20. The first signs of activity in the area had occurred when the Soviets strengthened their 6th Airborne Division stationed at Khabarovsk as well as other units; in May 1978 the 6th Airborne participated in military maneuvers in and around the Kuriles which involved nearly 5,000 troops. In January 1979 it was revealed in Japan that the Soviets had increased the numbers of troops stationed on the island from 2,000 to 5-6,000; deployed 50 tanks and armored vehicles; introduced radar installations; many large-caliber guns and some anti-aircraft weapons; erected dozens of new buildings; and built a 3,500-meter runway capable of receiving the Soviets' largest military aircraft. The Soviets then proceeded to test missiles in the waters off Etorofu.

northern islands are so close as to be visible from Hokkaido, and an amphibious or airborne assault from the Kuriles could be accomplished with little or no warning time. Faced with embarrassingly few options, the Ohira government reluctantly conceded to the public the existence of a buildup, minimized its extent, and stressed its defensive nature. Defense Agency Director-General Yamashita insisted that Japan's northern defense plans need not be revised in light of these new developments, but there is opposition to this view, and the whole affair has contributed to an increased sense in Japan of the existence of a Soviet threat and of Japan's military weakness.

Although the U.S. has refrained from encouraging such feelings, Japan's long-time Asian rival and ideological enemy, the Peoples Republic of China, has issued insistent warnings to her about the power and perfidy of the Soviet Union, and has urged Japanese rearmament to meet the danger. In September 1977, Vice Chairman Teng Hsiao-P'ing reportedly told a visiting member of the Diet that "we support the strengthening of Japan's Defense Forces."[21] During 1977 and 1978 a lengthy list of retired Japanese military officers and defense officials visited Peking. These included: retired admirals of the Imperial Japanese Navy and of the Maritime Self-Defense Force; Professor Hisao Iwashima, an influential strategist in the Japan Defense Agency; Hidao Miyoshi, former Chief of Staff of the SDF; and Osamu Kaihara, former JDA bureau chief. During these visits the Chinese exhibited great interest in the military capabilities of the Japanese Self-Defense Forces, and on several occasion urged their visitors to do what they could to alter the pacifist orientation of Japanese public opinion.[22] In September 1977, for example, the head of the China-Japan Friendship Association, Hua Sun-Ping, urged Yohei Kono and other New Liberal Club members then visiting China to do what they could to change Japanese opinion on defense matters. "China respects Japan's Peace Constitution," he said. "We understand that Japan does not have the military power for aggression abroad, but we do not take the attitude that it excludes military strength needed for defense. On this point we cannot agree with the Japanese Socialist Party."[23] In October 1977, Teng Hsiao-P'ing met with a group of former officers of the Ground Self-Defense Forces, including Kenji Mitsuoka, former commander of the SDF 9th Division, and said, *inter alia,* that "the preparations against war by Japan

---

21. Quoted in Nathaniel B. Thayer, "Changes in Japanese Foreign Policy in East Asia," paper presented at mid-Atlantic regional meeting of the Association of Asian Studies, Princeton University, Oct. 28-30, 1977.

22. See, e.g., the reports on the visits in the *Asahi Shimbun*, April 30, 1977; *Tokyo Times*, April 30, 1977; *Hokkaido Shimbun*, May 5, 1977; *ibid.*, June 20, 1977; and *Mainichi Shimbun*, June 27, 1977.

23. *Asahi Shimbun*, November 14, 1977.

and the U.S. and Europe are vital factors in postponing the outbreak of World War III."[24]

Such statements, sharply at variance with PRC positions of several years ago, has already helped make Japanese rearmament more respectable, particulary among that segment of the political left which has historically been Peking-oriented.

Attitudes of the Government and Opinion Leaders

There seems little doubt that the above-described external influences, together with growing Japanese self-confidence, have definitely influenced domestic views about Japan's international role in general and its defense policies in particular. Many surface indicators and isolated statements can be found to support the view that there has been a significant movement in attitudes, but the extent and depth of such movement should be examined closely; it would appear that the attitudes of government officials and the defense intelligentsia and of some businessmen have altered most noticeably, followed by certain shifts in the stated views of some political parties and trailed by a still-dubious but more quiescent public opinion. Any such changes must be viewed in the perspective of the unique, extreme pacificism and sensitivity which has characterized the Japanese political character since World War II. The highly emotional indignation which was aroused until very recently even by a discussion of defense options has subsided at least temporarily, but massive further shifts in outlook would be required before the country might undertake the sizeable rearmament predicted by some.

Growing self-assurance, the desire for a greater international role for Japan and the wish to distance itself somewhat from the position of the U.S. manifested itself in the stirrings of a more independent foreign policy several years ago. Prime Minister Fukuda, who assumed office at the end of 1976, greatly abetted this trend by consciously, if cautiously, encouraging a domestic re-examination of Japan's international and military posture. Mr. Fukuda enthusiastically assumed sponsorship of an "omni-directional" or "all-directions" foreign policy. He sought initiatives and an identity independent of U.S. foreign policy and strove to maintain an "equidistance" between the major powers, eschewing involvement in their quarrels and proclaiming

---

24. *Sankei Shimbun,* August 10, 1977. Cheng Tsai-chien, Deputy Chief of the General Staff of the PLA, paid a six-day "informal visit" to Japan in September 1978 to meet with ranking Japanese defense officials. Although reports on the visit have thus far been sketchy, Cheng and Gen. Takehiko Takeshima, chairman of the Joint Staff Council of the SDF, apparently agreed in principle on future exchanges of visits among military personnel of the two countries. See Foreign Broadcast Information Service, *Asia and Pacific,* "PLA, Japanese Military Officials Agree on Military Exchanges," Sept. 11, 1978, p. C4.

friendship for all.[25] This was supplemented by a drive to develop a Japanese policy toward Asia embodied in the so-called "Fukuda Doctrine" envisioning closer ties with ASEAN, accompanied by the treaty with China and cultivation of relations with Viet-Nam. Under some prodding to reduce its balance of payments surplus, Japan recently increased its development assistance and indicated its intention to expand aid to Turkey and the Middle East, including to countries which do not support the U.S.-arranged Egyptian-Israeli settlement.

Likewise Mr. Fukuda seemed to go out of his way to stimulate a re-thinking of Japan's defense posture. The debate over security within the government and in political cirlces generally has been rapidly broadening, both in scope and in nature. Fukuda himself played an important part in extending that debate in his public utterances and apparently in private as well. In his initial address to the Diet in January of 1977 he directly asserted that Japan needed to increase its defense capabilities — the first time since the War that a prime minister of Japan had proposed such a policy in a speech before Japan's parliament.[26] As noted earlier, the White papers issued during the past three years[27] by the Japan Defense Agency have been increasingly assertive in their references to the danger to the security of the Western Pacific posed by the growth of Soviet military power, and commentary on the White Papers by defense officials has become even more outspoken.

Following the surprise defeat of Prime Minister Fukuda in a limited LDP primary election, Masayoshi Ohira became Prime Minister of Japan on November 27, 1978. Although earlier polls had indicated surprising strength for Yasuhiro Nakasone, the outspoken conservative and defense-minded "hawk" whose serious candidacy alone bespoke changes in the Japanese body politic, Nakasone trailed a poor third behind Ohira and Fukuda. Mr. Ohira, in contrast to Mr. Fukuda, has been considered well within the traditional "dovish" mainstream of Japanese opinion with regard to defense matters. He has been a prominent spokesman of the view that Japanese security rests primarily on its internal strength as determined by economic factors rather than on military preparedness, and advocated no change in traditional post-war defense policies. For political reasons he was forced to appoint members of other LDP factions to his cabinet, however. Among them number four known to be loyal to Fukuda and two followers of Nakasone, including the

25. Some commentators remain skeptical that Japan's foreign policy has yet progressed beyond the stage of "resource diplomacy."

26. Foreign Broadcast Information Service, *Asia and Pacific,* Feb. 1, 1977, pp. C11-C15.

27. The first Japanese Defense White Paper appeared in 1970; the next was not published until 1976.

Seirankai group's ambitious Michio Watanabe. As of this writing it is too early to determine whether recent events may have markedly altered Ohira's status quo views on defense. His cancellation of a summit with President Park of Korea may reflect his liberal leanings; so too may the minimization of the Soviet buildup in the Kurile Islands and its implications for Japanese security by his new Director-General of the Japan Defense Agency, Mr. Ganri Yamashita. On the other hand, the Ohira government has indicated its distress over evidence of further Soviet military buildup in the region, and it has not opposed certain limited defense initiatives largely begun under Fukuda. Ohira has also persisted in the unpopular demand that procurement of the E2C airplane be included in the FY 1979 budget.

It has been an unwritten but heretofore seemingly iron-clad law of Japanese politics that the defense budget should not exceed 1% of the nation's gross national product; policymakers have kept well within this guideline, the budget having wavered between .84 and .90 percent of GNP during the past four fiscal years. The Defense Agency is now proposing a 5-year plan which would raise this percentage from .90 in FY 1979 to 1.0 by FY 1984.[28] Such figures may be somewhat misleading,[29] but it is clear that a projected rise in the military budget of only .1% of GNP over five years belies any dramatic change in attitudes toward defense with Japan. Proponents of this increase note that to succeed in their aims they will have to ensure that the defense budget is treated separately from the rest of the budget, and they hope to achieve the support of Ohira in this matter. It should be pointed out that the JDA itself is only an agency, having never been given ministerial rank and importance in postwar Japan, and has thus ranked very low in the bureaucratic pecking order. Policy-making within the JDA is primarily the function of the comparatively liberal civilian bureaucrats rather than of the more defense-minded officers of the armed services. Any new defense policies requiring financial implementation, moreover, must go through one or more ministries, which have often been hostile to increased defense spending; the powerful Finance Ministry, for instance, apparently reduced proposed acqui-

---

28. See, "Guidelines for Japan-U.S. Defense Cooperation," adopted by the 17th Japan-U.S. Security Consultation meeting (November, 1978).

29. These figures understate the amounts spent on defense according to NATO and U.S. standards, since the Japanese do not include certain expenditures such as military pensions and housing in their figures, which would raise the projected total by about 50% to approximately 1.5% of GNP. Moreover, it should be noted that since these figures are percentages, and because the Japanese economy has been growing rapidly with a relatively low level of inflation, the amount spent on defense has actually been growing considerably. For instance, the defense budget has increased sevenfold since 1970, and form FY 1978 to FY 1979 it is projected to rise by 10.2% even while remaining constant at .9% of GNP. Japan is now ranked seventh in the world in spending on defense, although as a percentage of GNP it spends far less than U.S. and NATO nations.

sition of new F-15 airplanes in 1978 from 123 to 100.[30] Reflecting on the history of debate in Japan over the F-15, one commentator declared that

> The agonised acquisition of these aircraft, the drawn-out debates, the irritating checks and balances from a host of interested parties, should give food for thought to any Americans still harbouring the hope that Japan can be railroaded into hasty rearmament.[31]

The Ministry of Foreign Affairs, which tends to be more internationalist in outlook than others, has traditionally been one of the less powerful of the cabinet posts, far less influential than MITI and Finance, for instance. On the other hand, since the Finance Ministry has the responsibility for drawing up the defense budget and thus for the cautious increase which is scheduled, as well as having input into the content of the Defense White Papers, it might be said that some movement and a new consensus of sorts has taken place as a result of a perceived increase in the Soviet threat.

Some public figures have openly begun to call for the allocation of a greater percentage of GNP to military purposes. Early in 1978 Dr. Masamichi Inoki, the influential then-President of the Defense Academy known as a past supporter of a low-profile defense effort for Japan, publicly urged the government to increase defense expenditures to at least two percent over the next decade.[32]

Moves to somewhat increase the defense budget have clearly been conditioned by the increased sense of Japanese vulnerability. In mid-1978 Japan's then top-ranking general, Hiroomi Kurisu, declared that Japanese planning was inadequate, and that in an emergency military commanders would have to take extra-legal action. These remarks provoked a furor, and Kurisu was fired. However, debate upon the adequacy of emergency planning has since been taken up in the Diet with only comparatively mild protests from the opposition, the JDA is conducting a study on the matter, and the proposed 5-year budget plan seeks to remedy some of the major deficiencies in emergency preparedness. Most notably, priority is reportedly being given to upgrading early warning and initial defense systems through acquisition of a new computerized radar system, E2C airplanes, F-15 fighters and updated or new surface-to-air missiles, and through replacement of obsolete destroyers. Proposals for the purchase of certain new aircraft, particularly the E2C, have faced much opposition in the Diet, partly because revelations of bribery

30. Russell Spurr, "F-15 victory in the air," *Far Eastern Economic Review,* Mar. 3, 1978, p. 27.

31. *Ibid.*

32. Masanori Kabata, "Defense Academy President Calls for Increased Spending to Beef-up Japan's Military Strength," *Japan Times* Jan. 4, 1978. Inoki has been named Director of a newly-formed semi-official research institute dealing with security issues.

in the procurement of contracts for JDA airplanes have attached a political onus to an affirmative vote.

Heightened government concern with security questions is also reflected in the new attention being devoted to long-range planning within the agencies concerned with defense. Former Defense Agency Director-General Shin Kanemaru in 1978 instructed the Joint Staff Council of the SDF to prepare a plan for joint military operations in the event of a foreign attack. This would be the first such detailed study undertaken by the Japanese armed forces since the so-called Mitsuya or "Three Arrow" plan, which stirred a wide debate over civilian control of the military in the mid-1960's.[33]

The National Defense Council, a planning agency established nearly two decades ago to deal with security problems, has in fact exercised only marginal influence over government policy. It was proposed both in 1972 and in mid-1978 that the NDC be upgraded through reorganization and expansion of its membership; recently, certain of the proposed measures were in fact enacted, but only on a very limited scale.

The Fukuda government also sought to upgrade Japan's ability to defend itself against an attack by undertaking a campaign to improve coordination with U.S. forces in the Pacific. Institutional arrangements for such cooperation have been widely regarded in Japan as inadequate. The Joint Japanese-American Security Consultative Committee established in 1960 at the time of the revision of the security treaty has in the main failed to address central Japanese concerns, particularly as perceptions of the emerging Soviet military threat have grown more acute. Japan's Foreign Minister Sonoda, after first suggesting that the membership of the Committee should be changed to include the defense ministers of both countries, recently proposed that a new, higher-level consultative organ be created at the Cabinet level, with members including the Japanese Foreign Minister, the Director-General of the Defense Agency and the Secretaries of State and Defense from the U.S. The U.S. however rejected this proposal, telling Japan it would be logistically impossible. Thus the only formal consultative mechanism which includes Washington-level participation remains the Subcommittee of the Security Consultative Committee, which meets annually.

There also exists under the SCC a joint Subcommittee for Defense and Cooperation, established in 1976 to discuss ways of achieving the purposes of the Security Treaty. This committee also had failed to live up to Japanese expectations, primarily because it had not seriously worked toward the devel-

33. For Kanemaru's mandate to the Joint Staff Council see Foreign Broadcast Information Service, *Asia and Pacific,* June 22, 1978, p. C5. George E. Moore, "Japan's Shifting Attitudes Toward the Military: Mitsuya Kenkyu and the Self-Defense Forces," *Asian Survey* (September, 1967), pp. 614-25, discusses the controversy over the "Three Arrows" study.

opment of a detailed combined plan of defense in the event of an attack on Japan. The 1978 White Paper called upon it to do so,[34] and in late November the Subcommittee did take some steps in this direction by approving general guidelines whereby Japan would be assigned a defensive role while the U.S. would take the offensive during a prospective attack on Japan. The guidelines called for further study and also for consultations between the two countries in the event of an emergency in the Far East which threatens Japan's security. The two countries' forces would still maintain a separate command structure under the guidelines, and there was no provision for the standardization of weapons, but Japan committed itself to provide more bases for the quick redeployment of U.S. troops in an emergency. "Official recognition" is also given to U.S.-Japan military consultations on joint operations, whereas the dicussions of such matters was previously considered politically taboo. The guidelines were rapidly approved by both the Cabinet and the National Defense Council of Japan. Even before they had been formally agreed upon, it was announced that the Japan Air Self-Defense Forces and the U.S. Air Force would soon conduct 4-day joint combat drills, the first such air exercises ever.

Japan's new interest in the expansion of mechanisms for formal cooperation with the U.S. on defense is highlighted also by reports that former JDA Director-General Kanemaru directly proposed to U.S. Defense Secretary Brown during their meeting in June of 1978 a joint plan for the defense of sea lanes around Japan in the event of war in the Pacific; neither the details of the plan nor the U.S. reaction to it have been discussed publicly.[35]

These recent moves to raise slightly the percentage of GNP allocated to defense and to upgrade certain of Japan's weapons systems, as well as to increase coordination with the country's main source of protection, the United States, have served as indicators of a somewhat altered view of defense within Japanese circles; particularly in this true when these actions are considered in conjunction with official statements on defense. The change of outlook is illustrated further by the fact that even the especially sensitive question of a possible nuclear capability for Japan is now discussed more openly than has been the case recently—by Government officials as well as others.

Official discussion of "Japan's nuclear option" has, of course, occurred in the past. As early as 1957 Prime Minister Nobusuku Kishi, in an appearance before a House of Counselors Cabinet Committee, stated that "it is not

34. See the discussion in Russell Spurr, "Japan Digs In," *Far Eastern Economic Review,* August 22, 1977, p. 22, and Foreign Press Center, *Summary, Defense of Japan,* 1978, pp. 21ff.

35. See "Brown-Kanemaru Discussion on Sea Defense Plans Reported," *ibid.,* July 5, 1978.

impossible for Japan to possess nuclear weapons if they are defensive in nature."[36] Eight years later, Mr. Masami Takatsuji, then Director-General of the Cabinet Legislation Bureau, argued in testimony before the Upper House Special Committee on Japan-Korea Affairs that in his view, under the Constitution Japan can possess any weapons—nuclear or non-nuclear—if they are designed to serve the purpose of protecting Japan against an armed attack by a foreign power. Takatsuji conceded that large-yield nuclear weapons deployed on long-range delivery systems did not meet this standard, but he argued that if technological developments in the future made it possible to manufacture nuclear weapons which were rather unambiguously defensive, these would not be prohibited by Article IX of the Constitution. As have all Japanese public officials in the postwar period, however, he reiterated that, as a matter of national policy, Japan had no intention of acquiring nuclear weapons. Takatsuji's statement was later endorsed by Prime Minister Eisaki Sato who, when asked if Takatsuji's statement was the official position of his cabinet, replied: "It has not been endorsed by a cabinet meeting as such, but as Prime Minister I find nothing in it that I feel I should correct." This position was reiterated in the 1970 White Paper of the Japan Defense Agency, and again in March of 1973 by Prime Minister Kakuei Tanaka.[37]

In January of 1968, however, Sato had announced the Three Non-Nuclear Principles, by which he pledged that Japan would not manufacture, possess, or allow the importation into Japan of nuclear weapons; these principles were incorporated into a formal resolution of the Diet in November of 1971, as part of an agreement between the LDP and several of the opposition parties to resolve the controversy over the Okinawa Reversion Agreement with the U.S. The Non-Nuclear Principles rapidly became powerful political symbols in Japan.[38] Japan is also constrained from acquiring nuclear weapons due to her signing of the Non-Proliferation Treaty.

Between 1973 and 1978 there were no official references to the possibility that Japan might acquire "self-defensive" nuclear arms. Public opinion polls taken during this period showed a significant increase in the number of

36. Kiyoaki Murata, "Japan and Nuclear Weapons," *Japan Times,* Mar. 3, 1978.

37. See Japan Defense Agency, *The Defense of Japan, 1970,* p. 29, and Kiyoaki Murata, op. cit.

38. For recent analyses of the debate in Japan over nuclear weapons see John E. Endicott, *Japan's Nuclear Option* (N.Y.: Praeger Publishers, 1975), chap. 2; Herbert Passin, "Nuclear Arms and Japan," in W. Overholt (ed.), *Asia's Nuclear Future* (Boulder, Colo.: Westview Press, 1977), pp. 67-109; T. J. Pempel "Japan's Nuclear Allergy," *Current History* (April, 1975), pp. 169-73; Daniel I. Okimoto, "Japan's Non-Nuclear Policy: The Problem of the NPT," *Asian Survey,* XV (April, 1975), pp. 313-27; and James E. Dornan, Jr., "The Prospects for Proliferation in Northeast Asia," *Comparative Strategy,* I, nos. 1 & 2 (1978), pp. 71-82.

Japanese who expected that their country would one day acquire nuclear weapons, although all such polls continue to show an overwhelming majority of citizens opposed to such a policy.[39]

One possible sign of changing attitudes in Japan toward the nuclear weapons question during this period, however, occurred during the campaign for governor of Tokyo in 1974. In a television appearance with his Socialist opponent, LDP candidate Shintaro Ishihara (later State Minister and Director-General of the Environment Agency) suggested that "Japan ought to have at least one nuclear weapon, so that she will be respected in the world;" despite the criticism which he received for that remark from Socialist party leaders and media commentators, Mr. Ishihara lost by less than 300,000 votes in an area normally a Socialist stronghold.[40]

The debate over nuclear weapons at the official level was resumed in 1978. On February 18, Keiichi Ito, Director of the Defense Bureau of the Defense Agency, told the House of Representatives Budget Committee that, in his view, there were no constitutional obstacles to Japan's possession of "defensive tactical nuclear weapons."[41] Although Mr. Ito's remarks stimulated the usual criticism from members of the opposition parties in the Diet and in certain segments of the media, the criticism was quite mild in comparison with that generated by similar remarks in the past.[42] Four days later, Takako Doi, a Socialist member of the House of Representatives Foreign Affairs Committee, asked Foreign Minister Sunao Sonoda if it were not true that Japan was forbidden to possess even defensive nuclear weapons as a consequence of having signed and ratified the nuclear nonproliferation treaty. Sonoda agreed:

> If we confine the issue to the interpretation of Article IX, there might be some theoretical argument in favor of our possession of nuclear weapons. But this is in fact forbidden by the NPT and Article 98 of the Constitution which provides that we must faithfully abide by all international treaties. Therefore, constitutionally, we cannot possess nuclear weapons regardless of their size [i.e., whether they are offensive or defensive in this perspective, it doesn't matter].[43]

39. See, e.g., Endicott, *op. cit.*, pp. 91-101.

40. Ishihara's first foray into politics came in 1968, when he ran in the national constituency for the House of Concillors and won more than 3 million votes, the largest number even obtained in a Japanese election. He doubts the reliability of the U.S. guarantee to Japan, and is alarmed about Japan's vulnerability to Soviet military pressure. For discussions of his views see Endicott, *op. cit.*, p. 61, and John K. Emmerson, *Arms, Yen and Power: The Japanese Dilemma* (New York: Dunellen, 1971), pp. 351-52.

41. Murata, *loc. cit.*

42. See, e.g., *Mainichi Daily News*, February 23, 1978, and Tokyo KYODO, March 7, 1978 in Foreign Broadcast Information Service, *Asia and Pacific*, Mar. 8, 1978, pp. C4-C5.

43. Murata, *loc. cit.*

Mr. Ito also accepted this view, although later observing to reporters that if in the future Japan should cease to be a signatory of the NPT, then she could acquire tactical nuclear weapons without violating the Constitution.[44]

Thus, while recent official statements have strengthened the traditional government position that Japan will never acquire a nuclear weapons capability, the pros and cons continue to be discussed. Almost all observers agree that drastic changes in the international environment could force a change in Japan's attitudes toward the desirability of acquiring such weapons.

The evidence presented above suggests a heightened concern within Japan over security issues. Stimulated by this atmosphere and encouraged by a new receptiveness to defense issues within government circles, the Japanese national security community has been growing rapidly in numbers. During 1977 and 1978 the formation of at least a half dozen research institutes devoted to the study of security issues was announced. Most of these are small and without extensive funding; nonetheless, their appearance is yet another sign of the emergence of defense as an important issue in contemporary Japan. Two among them seem to be of particular significance.

The first, named the Institute for Research on Peace and Security, will be funded by both the Japan Defense Agency and private business circles; 112 million yen already has been raised to launch its operations. Its first director will be former Kyoto University professor and President of the Japanese Defense Academy Masamichi Inoki. While, as noted above, Inoki has recently suggested that the ceiling for Japanese defense spending should be increased to 2 percent of GNP, he is basically a supporter of a low-profile international policy for Japan, at least for the present. In a recent interview in *Jiryu Shimpo,* the party organ of the LDP, he set forth his basic position as follows:

> Basically Japan should continue to be lightly armed. If Japan should decide to arm heavily, with the current national economic power and with its past economic accomplishments, it would seriously affect the balance of power in the world. The United States, China and the Soviet Union would all view such a development as a threat. Such an eventuality would be automatically followed by an ABCD-type encirclement. Hence the only way to prevent such an unfortunate circumstance is for Japan to remain faithfully lightly armed.[45]

Reports from Tokyo have suggested that the highly respected Takuya Kubo, who has served as Secretary-General of the National Defense Council,

---

44. *Ibid.*

45. *Jiryu Shimpo,* October 3, 1978. *The Japan Letter,* August 15, 1978, p. 2, has a brief discussion of the organization and funding of Prof. Inoki's Institute. The fear of an "ABCD encirclement," meaning the containment of Japan by the Americans, British, Chinese and Dutch, was often expressed in Japanese military circles before World War II.

would join Dr. Inoki's institute as its second in command. Mr. Kubo is well known in the United States, having participated in many academic conferences here in recent years and having published in scholarly journals here and elsewhere.[46] He too is known as basically a centrist on defense issues, although he has advocated surrender (perhaps only "strategic accommodation," depending on the translation) in the event of a nuclear attack on Japan.[47] Recently he wrote that it wuld be quite unlikely that Japan's defense budget would considerably exceed 1% of GNP and that in any case there would be no need for it to do so. Japan could enhance her security through concentration on economic assistance and trade in its dealings with communist and noncommunist neighbors, he suggested, in the process encouraging the development of a more economically and politically stable Asia. Japan should also "reduce the nation's potential threat to its neighbors," he argued, applauding the recent treaty with China. While deploring Soviet condemnation of the China treaty as well as the U.S.S.R.'s buildup in the Kuriles, he declared that Japan "will have to constructively deal with its northern neighbor. . . . It will not be able to continue sticking indefinitely to its position that conclusion of a peace treaty including the settlement of the territorial issue over the four islands off Hokkaido now held by the Soviet Union must come first."[48] Kubo also recently criticized Gen. Kurisu's contention that Japanese emergency preparations were inadequate and questioned the validity of the very concept of a surprise attack, given modern technological developments. Advocating that diplomacy be given a larger role in coping with international disputes rather than increasing reliance on defense forces, he also stressed the need for civilian control over the military, even at the expense of a more efficient defense. It is unlikely, therefore, given the outlook on defense issues of its leading figures, that the Institute for the Study of Peace and Security will assume a leading role in advocating a radically different defense posture for Japan.[49]

Of a somewhat different character is a second organization now forming under the name of the Japan Center for the Study of Security Issues. The leading figures in this group are Mr. Hideaki Kase, a well-known writer and defense commentator; Dr. Osamu Miyoshi, a former newspaper correspon-

---

46. See, e.g., Kubo, "The Meaning of the U.S. Nuclear Umbrella for Japan," in Franklin B. Weinstein (ed.), *U.S.-Japan Relations and the Security of East Asia* (Boulder, Colo: Westview Press, 1978), pp. 107-25.

47. See Endicott, *op. cit.*, pp. 92-94.

48. Takuya Kubo, "Defense Furor Shouldn't Lead to Big SDF Budget," *The Japan Times*, Oct. 29, 1978.

49. "Existing Laws Enough for Emergency Defense: Kubo" *Yomiuri Shimbun*, Oct. 17, 1978.

dent and editorial writer for the Mainichi newspapers and presently professor
of international relations at Kyoto Sangyo University; and Dr. Hitoshi
Hanai, also a professor of international relations at Kyoto Sangyo. Mr. Kase
has been active in conservative circles of the LDP for some years, and has been
particularly close to the Seirankei group, whose influence increased during
the prime ministership of Takeo Fukuda. The origins of the JCSSI can be
traced back to 1975, when Kase and Miyoshi, together with Asao Mihara and
others, created an informal discussion group to analyze security issues. In
1977 Mr. Kase helped organize a major conference on the security of Northeast Asia held in Tokyo as part of an ad hoc organization called the Committee on Defense Analysis. The success of the conference—which was
attended by several American scholars and a substantial number of Japanese
academics, Defense Agency personnel and retired military officers—led Kase
to the decision to form a permanent research institute. An organizing committee for the JCSSI was announced in February 1978, and includes such
notables as Mr. Takeshi Sakurada, the president of the Japan Federation of
Employers Association, and three former Directors-General of the JDA,
Masumi Esaki, Asao Mihara, and Michita Sakata. The Center is now seeking
funding, primarily from private sources; its leading figures are considered
close to the Nakasone faction of the LDP and it can therefore be expected to
advocate increased military preparedness for Japan and a more active military
role for the country in the politics of the Pacific Basin.[50]

Retired Imperial Navy commander and military commentator Hideo
Sekino heads a new group named the Strategic Study Association. In response
to the above-cited article in which Tokuya Kubo refuted the need for any
dramatic rise in defense spending, Sekino argued[51] that due to its increasingly tenuous security situation Japan required a "bold defense buildup" in
which expenditures gradually would rise to 2 to 3 percent of GNP and which
would enable Japan both to protect a large portion of its sea lanes and, with
U.S. cooperation, to repulse "a direct invasion of the largest possible scale."
Another of the new research institutes, the Japanese National Defense Study
Group, whose president is Hasegawa Saiji, the president of the Naigai news
company, has already published two lengthy reports advocating a vastly
expanded defense capability for Japan.[52] Other groups now being formed or

50. Author's interviews with JCSSI research staff in Tokyo, February 1978. For a
recent statement of Prof. Miyoshi's views see "The Growth of Soviet Military Power and the
Security of Japan: Why a Change in National Defense Policy is Essential," *Academic Review of
Kyoto Sangyo University,* September, 1978, pp. 1-36.

51. Hideo Sekino, "Defense Agency Seems to Work Backward," *The Japan Times,* Nov.
26, 1978.

52. For excerpts from the second of the two reports, which were prepared under the

in operation include: the Council on National Security Problems, directed by Tadao Kuzumi, a former Imperial Navy officer and a widely published military writer; the Research Institute for National Security, directed by Yozo Kato, former vice-minister in the JDA and later a member of the Diet from the LDP; and the Japanese Institute on Seapower, directed by Kazuomi Uchida, a submarine commander in World War II and Chief of Staff of the Maritime Self-Defense Force.

This swelling debate and activity on defense issues within the government and among the defense intelligentsia has been greeted favorably by many industrialists. There has been dissatisfaction within these circles because not only has the government itself been slow in procuring new defense systems, but it has also greatly restricted the export of weapons. Particularly during economic recessions, there has been some agitation by businessmen against such restrictions. In 1975, for instance, a campaign advocating expanded arms exports backfired because public sentiment continued to be strongly anti-military; restrictions were instead tightened when the Miki cabinet banned the export of machinery to produce weapons as well as the weapons themselves. Now businessmen, including the Japan Chamber of Commerce and Industry, have again been urging greater military spending in general as well as an increase in arms exports, having been spurred by an economic decline which persisted and became particularly severe in industries such as steel and shipbuilding. "The new factor this time," one author said, "is the lack of public outrage."[53] It is argued that development of the defense industry would provide considerable research and technological benefits to Japanese industry in general, and that arms exports would reduce Japan's balance of payments surplus and enhance her ability to obtain both an oil supply from the Middle East and raw materials from other areas. Japanese businessmen have also been lured by the potential arms market in China,[54] and several Asian countries have expressed strong interest in certain Japanese weaponry. In February of 1978 Mr. Hosai Hiyuka, Chairman of the Kansai Economic Association, told a group of foreign correspondents in Tokyo that it would be desirable for the government immediately to increase defense

---

direction of former Diet Librarian Jun Tsunoda, see *Asian Affairs,* V (March/April, 1978) pp. 199-215.

53. Susumu Awanohara, "Japan: once more into the breech," *Far Eastern Economic Review,* Apr. 7, 1978, p. 34.

54. A Japanese defense industry team recently visited China to explore the potential for weapons purchases, although the government thus far officially has discouraged such actions. Foreign Minister Sonoda has stated that although the Japanese government was not opposed to China's efforts to modernize her military capabilities, it would not assist these efforts. Foreign Broadcast Information Service, *Asia and Pacific,* "Sonoda on PRC Efforts to Modernize Defense Abilities," Oct. 13, 1978, p. C1.

expenditures to 1.5% of GNP; the U.S.-Japanese Mutual Defense Treaty, he asserted, was no longer adequate to protect Japan against all of the threats to its security which might arise in the future.[55] Nevertheless, there are no signs that a strong pro-defense lobby has already emerged among Japanese businessmen and industrialists. Many critics are vocal in expressing the fear that relaxation of export controls on peripheral hardware or "defensive" arms will be the hole in the dike serving to precipitate a flood of arms exports, and the government has remained unwilling to loosen such restrictions. However, the government's recent moves to increase domestic expenditures on defense have met with enthusiastic response and occasional fierce competition, particularly in the aircraft industry and the missile development and production field.

In the past several years, attitudes toward defense also appear to have become at least somewhat less antagonistic within the Japanese newspaper industry, which has been reputed to wield strong influence on policymakers. The idealism which was to varying extents applied to analyses of international relations by the different newspapers and reporters seems in general to have muted somewhat, yielding to "a more detached, or perhaps nationalistic, line."[56] Within the last year, major Japanese newspapers have begun to report regularly on issues such as the military balance and Soviet activities in the Pacific and their relationship to Japanese security.

It is clear, in short, that the changing international environment has produced noticeable movement in the views on military policy of many Japanese officials, elites and opinion makers. A certain uneasiness has been manifested in government circles, and public commentary on security matters during the past two years has been much more open and concerned, as well as less defensive, than was previously the case. But if the issues have been increasingly discussed, actions taken thus far have been quite limited. Japan's discomfiture was revealed in her attempts to partially disassociate herself politically, although not militarily, from the U.S. through a more independent foreign policy. Defense expenditures continue to grow in real terms as Japan's economy prospers, but as a percentage of GNP they are slated to rise only minimally, with concentration in qualitative rather than quantitative improvements. Certain obsolete or inadequate systems will be replaced or augmented, and a high priority is being given to better integration with and utilization of U.S. forces. Increased concern with defense and the more relaxed atmosphere now surrounding the discussion of military

55. *Korea Herald,* February 23, 1978.
56. *Asia 1977 Yearbook* (Hong Kong: Far Eastern Economic Review, Ltd., 1977), p. 203.

issues has also been reflected in the liberal-leaning media. As government interest has heightened and the stigma of association with military concerns has lessened, numerous fledgling "think tanks" have appeared within a short time, a number of which take a concerned view of the nation's security situation. In addition, some businessmen have supported greater domestic defense procurement and loosening of controls on arms sales for reasons that are mainly economic.

Political Parties, Public Opinion and Defense Issues

Significant as such developments are, they involve only a relatively narrow stratum of Japanese elite opinion, and thus may tell us less about the emerging climate on security issues in Japan than do shifts in the outlook of the leaders of Japan's major political parties. Here too, some movement is discernible.

The ruling Liberal Democratic Party has long been the most conservative party in Japan on defense issues as on other matters, although in the Japanese context this has heretofore meant not only that it has accepted and promoted the U.S.-Japan Security Treaty and the existence of the Self Defense Forces, seeking to expand the latter only gradually and within the limits imposed by Article IX of the Constitution. This, however, is but the general platform of the party, the situation being more complex than such a summary would make it appear.[57] Various factions exist on the issue of foreign and defense policy, some of them adopting a more "hawkish" approach than the relatively centrist position set forth above. The moderate "doves" within the party are represented in the Asian and African Problems Study Group (AA-ken) led by Ohira while the "hawks" have been associated with Yasuhiro Nakasone's Asian Problems Study Group (A-ken) and more recently have been represented also by the Seirankai (Blue Storm Group), formed by some of the younger LDP members of the Diet. Fukuda's positions have been somewhere between the two extremes of these groups on the conservative-liberal spectrum. Nakasone feels that Japan should not rely so much on the U.S., whose power is waning, but should undertake a comprehensive program to upgrade its military and related capabilities and even revise the Constitution to make unmistakably clear the legality of Japanese rearmament.[58] The first serious LDP candidate for premier to take such positions,

57. I am indebted to Hitoshi Hanai's as yet unpublished paper, "Japan's Defense Policies in Domestic Context," for a perceptive discussion of the views on defense of the various LDP factions.

58. For a report on Mr. Nakasone's views see "Nakasone Advocates Revision of Japanese Constitution," Foreign Broadcast Information Service, *Asia and Pacific*, Sept. 7, 1978, pp. C4-C5.

he aroused some attention by garnering more support than expected in some of the pre-election polls, but in November 1978 emerged in third place during the primary when the Tanaka faction threw its support behind Ohira. Nevertheless, some have felt that the center of gravity in the LDP has been moving toward the right;[59] if so, such a trend may be halted or slowed by Ohira's winning of the premiership.

The New Liberal Club, like the LDP from which it seceded, also advocates continuing the security connection with the U.S. and gradually improving the quality of the SDF. The other opposition parties, however, have historically rejected the entire defense policy of the LDP, including the U.S.-Japan treaty and the desirability and legitimacy of the Self Defense Forces, favoring instead pacificism, demilitarization and neutrality. The Japan Communist Party has not changed its position on these issues, but all the other major political groupings have announced definite shifts in a more moderate direction.

The Japan Socialist Party, largest party among the opposition and next to the JCP the most leftist, has reaffirmed its goal of unarmed neutrality for Japan, demanded that any buildup in the SDF be halted, and opposed plans for closer emergency military cooperation with the U.S. But as of November 1978 it markedly altered the tone of its policy draft to one of less idealism and greater recognition of power politics, and changed its stated views on a number of substantive issues as well. Rather than advocating the immediate abolition of the SDF, it is now calling for its gradual dissolution over a long period involving three stages; so too it now calls for a phased withdrawal from the U.S.-Japan security relationship rather than its immediate abolition. On the issue of the Kurile Islands, the JSP has proposed the adoption of a more nationalistic stance requiring the return of all four of them, rather than requesting the reversion of only two of them as it had previously, as a precondition to signing a peace and friendship treaty with the Soviet Union.

Even more dramatic steps have been taken by the Komeito Party, whose views have evolved over several years. Party leader Yoshikatsu Takeiri observed in early 1977 that "there are criticisms concerning the existence of the SDF, but it is an established fact . . . how to handle it within the framework of the Constitution should be left unsolved."[60] At the January 1978 party convention, however, he expressed as his personal view a belief that the treaty with the U.S. should be maintained and that "due recognition" should be

59. See Hanai, *op. cit.*, p. 6, for this theory; for this view and the contrasting view that the party may move leftward, see Derek Davies, "Japan '78: Overview," *Far Eastern Economic Review*, June 23, 1978, pp. 38ff., and Susumu Awanahara, "Stealing the ruler's clothes," *ibid.*, Feb. 3, 1978, pp. 12-13.
60. Quoted in "Japan Debates Defense," *Asahi Shimbun*, Feb. 17, 1977.

given to the role of the SDF in maintaining the security and independence of Japan."[61] Finally, in November 1978 a Komeito draft policy statement supported the maintenance of both the SDF and U.S.-Japan Security Treaty. Reportedly, the party has also considered cultivating ties with South Korea.

The Democratic Socialist Party, traditionally the most conservative of the opposition parties, for years campaigned for a phased abrogation of the treaty with the United States. Now, however, the DSP sees it as "an important element to keep the balance of power in Asia."[62]

The reasons for such shifts appear to be numerous. A significant factor has been Japan's treaty with China and Chinese encouragement of Japanese rearmament as well as its support for the U.S.-Japan treaty. All three of the above-mentioned parties were influenced by this factor since as socialists many of their members have been Peking-oriented. Indeed, the proposed changes, particularly over the Kurile Island issue, provoked hot disputes within the JSP between the pro-Peking segment and those oriented toward Moscow. Secondly, while the personal views of party officials may have undergone some alteration, a strong element of political opportunism has been involved in the shift of party policies. Komeito secretary-general Junka Yano said in an interview that his party had hoped for many years that the JSP would abandon its anti-military stance and adopt a more "nationalistic position;"[63] nevertheless, the move is clearly designed to facilitate the Party's new electoral strategy, in which it hopes to attain power through a coalition with the LDP or, more likely, with the more moderate of the opposition parties, particularly the DSP.[64] Komeito has in the process abandoned its long-time strategy of creating a coalition with the JSP, whose electoral fortunes have lately declined. Similarly, the JSP let it be known that the softening of its views on defense was expected to facilitate a coalition of opposition parties. The deeper reason for these shifts in fact appears to be that the opposition sensed a growing conservatism among its electorate and sought to adapt itself to this new mood so as not to lose the opportunity to attain power through coalition. The Komeito program openly stated that the current conservative trend in the country indicated a temporary period of reaction in the process of LDP collapse; while altering its views within the "action policy" draft designed to outline the permissible sphere of accommodation for coalition, in its "basic policy" draft it adhered to its traditional

61. *Japan Times,* Jan. 13, 1978.

62. *Mainichi Daily News,* Jan. 11, 1978.

63. William Chapman, "Japanese Socialists Losing Favor With Voters," *Washington Post,* May 5, 1979.

64. See Yoshiaki Kohzuye, "Democratic Socialist Party and Komeito tighten ties," *Japan Economic Journal,* Mar. 20, 1979.

policy of non-recognition of the SDF and the U.S.-Japan Security Treaty. JSP party sources acknowledged that there was overwhelming demand within the party rank and file that all four Kurile Islands be returned to Japan and that they took into consideration the public consensus on the matter; so too they confirmed that their platform was formed with a view toward the possibility of engineering a coalition.[65]

The significant "bottom line" therefore appears to be shifts in attitudes towards security issues which have occurred among the Japanese public at large during the past eighteen months. Indeed, polls taken by the government in late 1977 showed that 78% of those who supported the Japan Socialist Party and 55% of those who voted for Japan Communist Party candidates favored maintaining the SDF, even though the platforms of those parties still called for the abolition of the Japanese armed forces.[66] Takuya Kubo felt that polls showing rising support for the U.S.-Japan treaty and the SDF had a direct effect on the parties' behavior. Not only did the opposition "become more flexible on these issues," but also "they are no longer eager to drive the Government to the wall on defense issues through Diet questioning."[67]

Past survey research has shown that during the postwar period Japanese citizens by and large have not believed their nation to be seriously threatened by external enemies; as many commentators have pointed out, this outlook contributed to a low level of interest in security issues and in the state of Japan's military preparedness.[68]

In a series of polls taken in Tokyo between 1964 and 1971 designed to measure the public's interest in various policy issues, for example, the percentage of respondents expressing "great interest" in defense questions ranged from 18 to 35% (the peak year was 1969, when political leaders and the media were vigorously debating the renewal of the U.S.-Japan Security Treaty.) An additional 30-40% indicated that they had "some interest" in defense, with the total of those expressing strong and weak interest ranging from a low of 52 to a high of 70% over the years.[69] In a nationwide poll taken by the Japan

65. Consult "JSP Security Policy," *Mainichi Daily News*, Dec. 5, 1978; "JSP Drafts New Nat'l Security Policy Plan," *The Japan Times*, Nov. 9, 1978; and "JSP to Demand Return of 4 Northern Islands," *Mainichi Daily News*, Nov. 12, 1978.

66. See *Mainichi Daily News*, Jan. 11, 1978, and *Asahi Evening News*, Feb. 17, 1978. This poll reflects the deepening of a trend in attitudes among JSP and JCP supporters which has been evident for several years; in a 1975 poll 71 percent of the supporters of the JSP and 51 percent of those of the JCP expressed the view that the SDF should be retained.

67. Kubo, "Defense Furor Shouldn't Lead to Big SDF Budget," *op. cit.* Others have also commented on the increased reticence of the opposition and the greater confidence of the government when the Diet now considers defense questions.

68. See the discussions in Akio Watanabe, *op. cit.*, pp. 116-22, and Passin, *op. cit.*, pp. 74-78.

69. Watanabe, *op. cit.*, pp. 134, 139-40.

Defense Agency in September 1977 only 12% of the respondents indicated that they were "very interested" in defense and security issues, with 35% registering "some interest" and 50% little or none. Not surprisingly, interest in defense was lowest among youth and women.[70] This decline from a low of 18% expressing great interest and a minimum of 50% expressing at least some interest in such issues during earlier years to 12% and 47% respectively has now apparently been reversed. In the fall of 1978 an *Asahi Shimbun* nationwide survey indicated that in the intervening year there had been a sharp increase in such interest. Thirty-four percent expressed a relatively deep involvement in defense issues, while an additional 26% said they maintained at least some interest, for a total of 60%.[71] The upsurge in public interest in defense may well have been due to a growing perception of a Russian threat. For in the 1978 *Asahi* poll, the public registered great enthusiasm over relations with China, but by a margin of 62 to 13% they felt that relations with the Soviet Union were not good. When asked whether there was danger of a surprise attack on Japan, 30% replied in the affirmative (54% felt there was no such danger). A December 1978 poll conducted by the Prime Minister's Office which was worded somewhat differently found that 21% of the public predicted Japan could be attacked or become involved in war, 23% did not deny the possible outbreak of "emergency" cases, and 36% did not foresee any such dangers.[72]

That there is an increased sense of threat and insecurity would also seem to be verified by rising support for the Self Defense Forces. Surveys conducted by various government agencies during the 1960s showed a steady decline in popular support for the SDF, from a postwar high of 82% in 1962 to 77% in 1967, 75% in 1969 and 46% in 1971. Between 30 and 40% of the Japanese public was not well disposed toward the SDF during this period for a variety of reasons, especially due to lingering doubts over the constitutionality of the SDF and the growing cost of supporting it.[73] Recent poll data indicate a reversal in this trend. Mr. Kubo believes that "the Japanese people's awareness of defense needs began to undergo a gradual change in the early 1970s and took a more apparent turn after the fall of South Vietnam." He bases this assessment on a rise in support for the SDF as shown by government polls, from 71% in 1972 to 78% in 1975 to 83% in 1977.[74] The government poll of December 1978 showed another jump to a high of 86% who felt the existence of the SDF was necessary. Interestingly, the 1977 JDA poll registered an especially sharp increase in support for the SDF among young males,

70. Japan Defense Agency, *Defense Bulletin*, I (Jan., 1978), p. 2.
71. *Asahi Evening News*, Nov. 2, 1978.
72. "The Week," *Japan Economic Journal*, Mar. 13, 1979.
73. Watanabe, *op. cit.*, p. 141.
74. Kubo, "Defense Furor Shouldn't Lead to a Big SDF Budget," *op. cit.*

and the number of applicants taking examinations for admission to the Japanese Defense Academy reached an all-time high of 14,304 in 1978.[75]

There is difficulty in finding comparable data in polls measuring support for the U.S.-Japan Security Treaty, but it appears that attitudes are becoming more favorable toward it as well.[76] Government surveys showed a rise in support for a joint guarantee of Japan's security through the JDA and the treaty with the U.S., from 41% in 1972 to 74% in 1974, while those who wished to abandon the treaty and either reduce or disband the SDF decreased from 16 to 9%.[77] But if the public increased its support of the treaty in response to a growing discomfort over recent international events, it apparently had little faith that the treaty would provide effective protection: while the fall 1978 *Asahi* poll showed half the population to be willing to express support for the treaty, only 20% felt that in the event of an emergency the U.S. would "come and seriously attempt to defend Japan," while 56% replied in the negative.

Limited data such as the above obviously must be interpreted with some caution. However, polls would appear to substantiate a conclusion that the growing sense of threat felt among officials and elites due to the decline of U.S. power and will plus the increased strength and belligerence of the Soviet Union is shared by a significant amount of the population; this is implied by measures such as rising interest in defense, a feeling that relations with the Soviet Union are bad, fear of possible attack, growing support for the SDF and the treaty with the U.S., and lack of trust in the U.S. commitment to defend Japan. Such survey information is moreover reinforced by more informal observations of the Japanese scene on the part of political commentators, among whom there is widespread agreement of late on the "lack of outrage" over discussion of defense issues in contrast to the situation only a year or two ago and on an apparent increase in conservatism and nationalism among the Japanese public.

Nevertheless, the public's new concern with and receptiveness to defense matters is by no means comprehensive or wholehearted; many of the old pacifist ideas are still adhered to, and while there may be uneasiness, there is as yet little conviction that new policies are called for. Indeed, the polls indicate a great deal of inconsistency in the public's thought on defense.

There is some sentiment in favor of raising defense spending and thus expanding the SDF, and it appears to have increased at least slightly during 1978. The 1977 JDA poll found that 17% would favor an increase in defense

75. *Mainichi Daily News,* Feb. 12, 1978.

76. See Watanabe, *op. cit.,* pp. 135-39, for a dicussion of the problems involved in analyzing the data.

77. Kubo, "Defense Furor Shouldn't Lead to Big SDF Budget," *op. cit.*

spending, and the Prime Minister's Office discovered at the end of 1978 that 20% of people surveyed responded in favor of a military buildup, with 50% favoring a maintenance of the present situation, while the fall 1978 *Asahi* poll found 19% preferring a strengthening of the SDF and 57% favoring its maintenance at the present level.[78] The *Asahi* poll also showed that the adoption of Article IX of the Constitution prohibiting Japan from going to war or possessing military forces was felt to have been a wise idea by an overwhelming margin of 82 to 9% and that people opposed now revising that document to allow regular military forces in Japan by a margin of 71 to 15%. It would appear that the public does not believe the maintenance of the SDF in its current status and presumably with its current increases in budget along with the growth of GNP to constitute the maintenance of military forces. One commentator, however, feels that the widespread current support for the SDF as well as for Article IX, which has been reflected in other polls as well as those presented here, constitutes a surface inconsistency:

> The seeming contradiction can probably best be explained by the Japanese concern with form over content. It is increasingly apparent that a consensus of sorts has been reached on defense, and that if the government continues to cloak any build-ups in terms of national security [and is wise enough to retain the name Self Defense Forces for its ground, air and naval military arms] the violent protests of the 1960s will remain a memory.[79]

Other instances of apparent inconsistencies are obvious. The anomaly of increased enthusiasm for the U.S.-Japan treaty concurrent with the expression of severe doubts as to whether the U.S. would live up to its obligations under that pact has already been mentioned. In addition, the polls have reflected a general rise in the perception of threat and significant increases in support for the SDF and the U.S. security treaty as well as notable sentiment for increased spending on defense. Yet when the 1978 *Asahi* poll which reflected many of these trends asked respondents to identify the most important element in the defense of Japan, only 2% selected American support as a response and again only 2% cited the strength of the Self Defense Forces. The remainder selected responses associated with traditional postwar pacifism: 42% chose "peace diplomacy," 20% placed their trust in national economic power; 15% preferred reliance on the "Peace" Constitution.

78. A mid-1978 survey showed 30% supporting such an increase. See "The Japanese Re-arm," *Atlas*, Oct., 1978, p. 55.

79. John Lewis, "Japan sharpens the sword," *Far Eastern Economic Review*, Apr. 20, 1979, p. 28.

Conclusion

Thus while there has clearly been a more favorable outlook toward defense lately in Japan, strong popular aversion to any dramatic changes appears to remain; it appears in fact that the public has scarcely proceeded beyond an acceptance of the status quo in the form of accepting a treaty signed more than 25 years ago and registering support for the existence of defense forces established in 1954. When considered in historical context, moreover, the increases in support for maintaining the SDF and the Security Treaty are neither remarkable nor unprecedented; high levels of support for both have been registered before. In fact, it is surely rather extraordinary that at this juncture in the twentieth century a significant portion of the Japanese public doubts the utility of maintaining a defense establishment. The constituency for an expanded defense posture within Japan thus remains small. Should the international environment, particularly as reflected in Soviet military activities in Asia, change significantly, the renewed interest in the SDF and in the security connection with the U.S. could readily subside.

It is understandable, therefore, that even the Fukuda government, although itself obviously sympathetic to the idea of an increased defense capability for Japan, moved very cautiously. Mr. Fukuda succeeded in "desensitizing" public opinion on defense issues, as one person put it, so that at this point national security can at least be openly discussed. However, in response to suggestions that the government should relax its present policy against arms exports, for example, the Prime Minister on March 7, 1978, stated that existing restrictions on such exports would be maintained indefinitely.[80] The government moreover took pains to disassociate itself from those advocating an immediate increase in defense spending. Shin Kanemaru, Director-General of the Japan Defense Agency, repeatedly stated that Japan should keep military spending below 1% of GNP until the mid-1980s.[81] And there has been no move to upgrade the status of the Japan Defense Agency to a full-fledged ministry.

The debate over defense in Japan, in short, is thus far largely just that—a debate. It remains unclear when, and to what extent, it will become more than this. As the survey research data shows, there is not yet a broad popular consensus in favor of a substantial increase in Japan's military capabilities or the assumption by Japan of a greatly increased role in maintaining peace and security in Asia. Interest in defense issues remains low among the general public, and there is little disposition to believe that the SDF is a significant force in maintaining Japan's security. Popular opposition to the acquisition

80. Foreign Broadcast Information Service, *Asia and Pacific,* Mar. 7, 1978, p. C1.
81. *Japan Times,* Jan. 14, 1978, and *Mainichi Daily News,* Feb. 14, 1978.

of a nuclear weapons capability by Japan remains strong, as evidenced by the public outcry over remarks by U.S. Navy Secretary Claytor implying once again that U.S. warships entering Japanese ports do not off-load their nuclear weapons.[82] There remains significant political opposition to the use of U.S. bases on Okinawa and elsewhere in support of U.S. security interests in Northeast Asia.[83]

Japan today remains fundamentally a nation adrift, a nation without a clear strategy for dealing with international politics. For approximately the last 100 years, she has had a clearly identifiable goal, to "catch up with the West." In prewar days it was to be attained through the creation of a colonial empire. In the postwar era of American economic and military dominance, the goal was defined essentially in economic terms, and "catching up" was equated with acquiring a per capita income equivalent to that of America and the advanced European powers. During this period, rapid economic growth was pursued with a single-minded enthusiasm.

At about the time of the Meiji Centennial, in 1968, it became apparent that Japan was in sight of achieving its goal according to the terms by which it had been historically defined. Thereupon a very considerable policy debate developed centering on the key question, "what should Japan do next?" As a part of this debate, the possibility of seeking great-power status was first raised, and then firmly rejected in favor of continued emphasis on economic growth and development. At the time, however, the strategic and economic environment was very different from that prevailing today. The defense issue is now being raised again, as confidence in America is waning. When the debate over Japan's long-term future again becomes a central issue, which is likely to happen in the near term, it is almost certain to include a serious discussion of national security and of Japan's option to become a great power in fact as well as in potential.

An important question is whether Japanese statesmen, who are clearly more worried about the national security situation than the public and more disposed to rectify perceived weaknesses by building up military strength, will choose to speak and operate safely within the confines of known public tolerance, or whether they will act more boldy and gamble in the process on molding that opinion. Public opinion is very much in flux, torn between anxieties over international developments and preference for the assurances offered by postwar pacifist ideology. Increasingly there is great anxiety at the top, but no clear idea of what to do about it. There is fear of public opinion

---

82. See *Asahi Evening News,* Feb. 9, 1978, and *Japan Times,* Feb. 10, 1978.

83. See, e.g., *Okinawa Times,* in Foreign Broadcast Information Service, *Asia and Pacific,* Feb. 24, 1978, pp. C3-C4, and the media commentary and analysis in *ibid.,* Mar. 3, 1978, pp. C1-C4.

and hope for a revival of U.S. strength and involvement, as well as a reluctance to break openly with the U.S. in an assessment of the situation or of desirable remedies. Whether Japanese leaders decide upon a course of action, the U.S. takes the lead, or the present situation continues, the defense debate cannot be sustained indefinitely without striking some responsive chord within the public. It has often been said that public opinion in Japan is capable of erratic and sudden shifts. Indeed, this is precisely the fear of those who oppose any receptiveness to augmenting defense forces because they see it as a portent of militarism and of those who raise alarums over the slightest hint of increased nationalism because they feel it poses the danger of xenophobia (as in the case of the furor raised in April 1979 over the interment of convicted Japanese war criminals at a Shinto shrine). Since debate over defense in Japan has for so long been stifled by fear of hostile pacifist reaction, public opinion is woefully uninformed on defense issues and strategies; the potential for sudden shifts of mood and opinion would therefore appear to be greater than would normally be the case. Changes in opinion have thus far been gradual, although the pace of such changes and the pressures from external events on opinion noticeably accelerated recently, especially as of the concluding months of 1978.

There is clearly heightened interest in defense and security issues in leadership cirlces both in and out of government. This interest is basically a function of re-emerging Japanese nationalism and of changes in the international environment, and in particular of the shifting military balance, both globally and in the region, between the U.S. and the U.S.S.R. Should that shift continue, the constituency for rearmament in Japan will continue to expand as well and a steady enlargement of Japanese military capabilities will be highly likely.

Process and Substance in Evolution

LTC David P. Lohmann, USAF

Japan's defense policy is currently undergoing a period of active reevaluation. Precipitated by changing global and regional circumstances, and facilitated by an improved domestic climate for discussing defense issues, the current reevaluation presages an overall drive toward realism in content and modernization of process. This study attempts to describe the reevaluation process and suggest possible outcomes. The description is the perspective of an outsider, viewing Japan's defense policy from an American military vantage point. As such, it concentrates on those aspects that are most relevant to defense cooperation between Japan and the United States.

Some years ago Martin Weinstein put forth the notion that Japanese defense policy exhibited remarkable stability.[1] More recently he has noted that changing conditions in East Asia, principally those attributed to changes in U.S. defense policy in East Asia, could trigger fundamental changes in Japanese defense policy.[2] The spectrum of possibilities currently being discussed is broader than ever before, leading this writer to conclude that the putative stability of Japanese defense policy may warrant reevaluation also. The appearance of a dynamism in Japanese defense policy is widely read by analysts as indicative of an increasing possibility of the adoption of radically different policies. Discussions of rearmament, neutrality, total self reliance, and Finlandization are now popular. We subscribe to the view that defense policy determinations is a history of equilibrium when harmony and stability prevail, and of disequilibrium when controversy and change are required.[3] Japanese defense policy is now in the latter cycle. This does not mean,

---

1. Weinstein, Martin E., "Japan's Defense Policy and the Self-Defense Forces" in *Comparative Defense Policy,* ed. Frank B. Horton III et al., (Baltimore: The Johns Hopkins University Press, 1974).

2. *Defense and Foreign Affairs Daily,* October 28, 1977 p. 1.; and *Baltimore Sun,* 1 Nov 1977 p. 4.

3. Huntington, Samuel P., *The Common Defense* (New York: Columbia University Press, 1961).

however, that radical change must follow. In fact, there is basis for the view
that the current reevaluation is healthy, both from a Japanese and American
viewpoint, and that the defense policies that will emerge will be modern,
realistic, and conform with Japan's peace values.

Current Defense Capabilities and Limitations

To set the stage for the discussion of the current debate, a description of
current policy and force structure is in order. The 1977 Japanese Defense
White Paper says that within the context of the Japan-U.S. Security systems
and recognizing the stable global environment, Japan will base its force
structure upon a Standard Defense Force Concept. This somewhat elusive
concept sizes the force to be capable of performing adequate peacetime warning and surveillance, including actions to cope with territorial airspace violation; responding to domestic insurgency that receives external support;
countering limited and small scale aggression without U.S. assistance; and
rebuffing larger scale aggression until U.S. Force can be introduced. Forces
required to accomplish these missions are 13 Ground Divisions, 6 Brigades,
8 AAA Groups, 10 Surface Ship Divisions, 4 Escort Flotillas, 6 Submarine
Divisions, 2 Minesweeping Flotillas, 16 Squadrons of land based ASW Aircraft, 28 Groups of ACW Units, 14 Fighter Squadrons, 3 Air transport
squadrons, one early warning squadron and 6 Groups of High Altitude SAM
Units. With the exception of equipment modernization requirements, this
required force structure is remarkably close to the estimated actual strengths
at the end of the Fourth Buildup Plan. Equipment modernization requirements include modern air superiority fighter and ASW Aircraft.[4]

Depending upon the point to be made by the observer, the capabilities of
Japan's self defense forces are described in alternative ways. In answer to
critics of its large size, it is characterized as possessing nonthreatening,
defensive capabilities only which require less than one percent of the Gross
National Product. In response to the free ride critics, it is described as a
significant force possessing more aircraft in East Asia than the United States,
more tanks than South Korea and large enough to be allocated a defense
budget that is the tenth largest in the world, greater than that of Israel. Both
perspectives are factually correct. Neither are relevant if Kaihara's analysis,
which appeared in *Pacific Community,* is correct. He concludes that in any
scenario involving large scale forces, the self defense forces would be able to
fight for between one and seven days. They lack the logistics support and
survivable facilities to fight any longer.[5] The Kaihara critique is particularly

4. *Defense of Japan 1977* (Tokyo: Japanese Defense Agency) p. 73.
5. Kaihara, Osamu, "Japan's Military Capabilities: Realities and Limitations," in *Pacific Community,* IX (January, 1978), 129-142.

important to the current defense policy debate since it applies to the portion of the threat spectrum receiving the most attention today, in terms of structuring the self defense forces. The ends of the spectrum, strategic nuclear and internal aggression are not foci of the current debate.

For the Japanese fiscal year which began on the first of April 1978, the defense budget was Y1901 billion or $8.64 billion 220Y/$, a 12.4% increase over the previous year. As a percent of GNP the defense budget rose from 0.88% to 0.90% and as a percent to total government spending decreased from 5.39% to 5.54% from the previous year. The principal feature of this most recent defense budget is the commitment to two major modernization efforts (F-15 and P-3C) during the same year, and the continuing adherence to the policy of allocating less than one percent of the GNP to defense.[6]

Emerging Process of Defense Policy Formation

The Defense White Paper and the defense budget, documents frequently referred to by American observers, record the current state of the achievable consensus on defense policy within Japanese government circles. To the outside observer these documents convey the impression of a process of order and set procedure; but they hide the undercurrents of the current defense policy debate.

The defense policy making process is undergoing change. The evaluation of the situation, always an important part of policy making in Japan, has assumed even greater importance. American Defense policy, the key influence in the determination of Japanese defense policy is perceived to be changing consequently, there is intense activity to precisely define what American policy is. Constraints on a reasoned and open defense policy debate are receding, allowing evaluation of a greater spectrum of alternative security objectives and force structure options. The process itself is undergoing change as more parties pursue a legitimate role in the now politically acceptable area of defense policy.

Past Japanese defense policy was at best reactive and at worst unresponsive. It could hardly be characterized as dynamic and innovative. The sense of this criticism was captured in a *Korea Times* editorial cartoon at the time of the decision to withdraw U.S. ground combat troops from Korea. Under the title, "Japan Defense Plan" a Japanese standing on Mount Fuji is looking West and saying, "I think the GI's are leaving."[7] A more apt depiction in late 1978 showed a large cloud from which trial balloons periodically emerge. The process now evolving, however, appears to be one of greater

---

6. FY78 Defense Budget, Information Sheet by Public Information Division, Japan Defense Agency, Tokyo Japan.

7. Korea *Times,* November 28, 1977.

clarity and definition than in the past. While not yet approaching the formal procedural character of the U.S. system, the Japanese system appears to be gaining greater rigor to cope with the dynamic changes that are occurring.

Japanese defense policy is evolving today both in content and process. The assessment of the external situation and an evaluation of U.S. global and regional policies are central factors. The former is similar to the American threat assessment, though there is a significant difference. Included are analyses of the strategic balance, Soviet strategy in Asia, and other key strategic issues. The latter is an assessment of U.S. ability and resolve to cope with situations beyond the control of Japan to handle. A third key factor is the set of constraints derived from the domestic situation. These are reflected in current interpretations of the constitution and the status of forces agreement, Diet interpellations considered to be precedents, the state of current public opinion, financial limitations imposed by custom or fiscal policy, the apparent political strength of the ruling party, and any highly visible controversies which happen to be active at the time. All of these factors are melded to determine security objectives (*Policy*) and the reasonable range of force structure options (*Strategy-Force Planning*) which can be considered. Trial balloons can be used to more precisely define all of these variables. For example, uncertainty as to whether or not the current interpretation of constraints will allow consideration of a certain force structure option will probably lead to a trial balloon on the option or some approximation of it.

Following our description of these factors we shall turn to the process of consensus-building itself. This is the pattern of essential interrelationships among key participants and there is no more important factor here than the American input. The unique relationship with the U.S. calls for integrating U.S. views into the consensus-building process. This may be done by obtaining signs of U.S. support for particular points of view through informal consultation or formal consultation, or, again, through public trial balloons. Finally, we shall look at the outputs of the evolving Japanese defense process, both policy decisions and resultant operational force structure decisions.

Assessment of the Situation

Until recently, the situation in East Asia has grown more stable from a Japanese viewpoint. There is no war into which Japan can be drawn. China is no longer perceived as a military threat since her military power is tied down on the Soviet border, and Japan and China have established diplomatic relations. U.S.-China relations are improving and China has given tacit acquiescence to both the U.S. Japan Mutual Security Treaty and an enhancement of JSDF capabilities.[8]

---

8. *Asahi,* July 15, 1978 and *Washington Post,* July 10, 1978.

In the global arena, Japanese vulnerability to an unstable international environment was made clear during the oil crisis of 1973, and served to expand the theoretical definition of security in Japan. While another key development, Soviet military expansion in the Pacific, served to narrow it. The Soviet buildup in the Pacific and the collateral difficulties the Japanese appear to be having in negotiating with the bellicose Soviets seems to be the primary external change affecting Japanese defense perception. Quite simply the Soviet Union is now identified as the threat to Japanese security. In June of 1978 in response to a JSP questioner, JDA Defense Bureau Chief Ito stated that the Soviet Union is the object of Japan's efforts to strengthen her defensive power.[9]

The Soviet Pacific fleet is the focus of concern. It now has 750 ships including 10 cruisers; 125 submarines, including 50 nuclear powered; 80 destroyers, 300 smaller combatants and 240 support ships.

The fleet has exhibited steady qualitative and quantitative growth in recent years, probably as a result of the world-wide improvement in the Soviet Navy. The Japanese defense agency is predicting that the growth in the Soviet Pacific fleet will continue with the assignment of a Kiev class aircraft carrier in 1979.[10]

Perceptions of Soviet's Strategy in the Pacific are key to Japanese defense policy. Soviet capabilities are clear, and significant. Based upon public pronouncements, the Soviet's objectives appear to be to promote an eventual Asian security system centered on Socialism, and to facilitate their active involvement in East Asian Affairs, emphasizing political and economic relations, while maintaining significant forces in the region as a backdrop. Regarding Japan, the Soviets appear to be worried about two possible developments; a rearmed self-reliant Japan or a close effective defense relationship with the U.S. directed against them. Soviet threats and military posturing appear to be directed toward countering the former; appeals to Japanese nationalism the latter. A military relationship, between the PRC and Japan would be particularly disturbing to the Soviets. Soviet military maneuvers, for example, the Summer 1978 exercises near the northern territories and near Okinawa, remind the Japanese of Soviet military power, in this case as the Peace and Friendship Treaty negotiations got underway again. Izvestia announces that the Soviet Union cannot remain indifferent to the revival of the Japanese militarism again.[11] Soviet pronouncements condemning Japanese retired officers visits to China are harsh. Some Japanese writers have

9. *Sankai,* June 9, 1978.
10. *Yomiuri,* July 18, 1978.
11. *Izvestia,* February 5, 1978.

contended that Soviet power diplomacy already limits Japan's foreign policy choices.[12]

The identification of a threat is a significant change. Threat assessments and scenario building are necessary for rigorous requirements analysis.

U.S. Policies in Asia

Given the complementary nature of our two defense establishments necessitated by the Mutual Security Treaty, the Japanese antennae scan for shifts in U.S. policy, and significant changes have occurred in recent years. A new American administration came into office and made significant change.

In Northeast Asia, President Carter announced the gradual withdrawal of American ground combat forces from South Korea. Regionally, the statements of administration officials seemed to indicate that NATO would receive higher priority perhaps at the expense of East Asia, and that the U.S. was perhaps not as committed to maintaining the regional balance. In strategic nuclear areas, the new administration cancelled the B-1, failed to produce the enhanced radiation warhead and appeared to be less than firm in the Salt II negotiations. These developments caused concern in Japanese defense policy circles because they inferred fundamental changes in U.S. defense policy. They were not interpreted as adjustment pains. Subsequent events proved the Japanese concern largely unfounded. There was no shift in American defense policy; no withdrawal from Asia. President Carter decided that with the exception of the ground force withdrawal from Korea force levels will be maintained. The B-52's, the SSBN's, the nine tactical fighter squadrons, two aircraft carriers, two amphibious ready groups, twenty cruisers and destroyers, two-thirds of a Marine Division, and a Marine Air Wing would remain in the Western Pacific. Qualitative improvements would be made in U.S. forces including the addition of F-14's, F-15's, and AWACS.[13] Nonetheless, the Korea withdrawal decision primed the pump of the Japanese defense policy process. Some proponents of a stronger Japanese defense establishment welcomed the withdrawal as it reawakened the defense policy debate in Japan. They tried to prolong the effect by public statements alleging U.S. lack of resolve; for example, when a JDA official said that Japan cannot depend upon the Seventh Fleet in time of war.[14] Statements such as these provoked U.S. reassurances of resolve. In fact so much so that the U.S. was accused of protesting too much by critics. The trial balloonists them-

---

12. Miyoshi, H., "The Security of Northeast Asia in the 1980's: The Japan-Soviet Relationship," 1977 working note.

13. Speech by the Secretary of Defense Harold Brown before the Los Angeles World Affairs Council, Los Angeles, California, February 20, 1978.

14. *Yomiuri*, May 9, 1978.

selves were concerned that their efforts to continue the debate may have uncovered a true lack of U.S. resolve. In the fall of 78 most of this concern had disappeared. Secretary of Defense Brown's Los Angeles speech, Security Advisor Brzezinski's May 78 visit to Tokyo after Peking, Vice President Mondale's trip to Asia, the withdrawal slowdown decision as a result of Congressional delays in the transfer legislation, and Defense Minister Kanemaru's meetings with Secretary Brown dispelled the real concern among Japanese leaders and reduced the number of lower level statements questioning U.S. resolve for the purpose of continuing the defense debate in Japan.

The withdrawal decision by a new and unknown administration made Japanese policy makers more conscious than ever that U.S. Pacific defense policy *could* change. Should it change, Japan's options were obviously very limited. Events in other dimensions of U.S.-Japan bilateral relations, the trade talks and nuclear reprocessing for example, also seem to indicate that American basic policy toward Japan could be changing. The theme of lack of cultural affinity, with obvious racial overtones, reappeared in the Japanese press though it died quickly. The principal questions being asked were, "what does the U.S. wish of Japan, and why and what can we do about it?" The Japanese were particularly worried about the answer in the defense field until they had been reassured that U.S. policy regarding this dimension would be basically unchanged, i.e., the new administration understood the defensive nature of the JSDF, did not advocate a regional military role for Japan, and did not advocate rearmament for the purposes of aiding in the correction of the trade imbalance. U.S. policy continued to stress qualitative improvement of Japan's defensive capabilities, better defense cooperation and more financial support for the U.S. forces stationed in Japan. These old policies were finally reaffirmed, but the period of uncertainty over U.S. intentions provided an impetus to the defense policy debate in Japan. At the same time some of the constraints previously limiting both the debates and the policy at home were relaxing.

Constraints

The many boundaries around the Japanese military establishment limit its size, capabilities, operational stategy, and deployment, and interaction with U.S. forces in Japan. This section summarize the set of constraints during the 1978 Defense debate.

In Japan these constraints have received wide attention, since they result in a miniscule defense establishment in relation to the country's economic strength and population. The renunciation of force as a means of settling international disputes, and of the maintenance of land, sea and air forces, is contained in the Constitution. The prevailing sentiment in Japan is overwhelming support of this peace philosophy. Court interpretations and Diet interpellations, when trying to reconcile modern events to the Constitution do not attempt to change the basic sense of this peace philosophy. In keeping with the peace constitution and her active role in U.N. conventional arms limitations efforts, it is natural that Japanese arms export controls put a tight cap on the market for arms, and therefore the defense industry itself. Lethal arms exports are not permitted. Nonlethal items cannot be exported to areas of tension or to areas where such exports would contribute to arms competition. The implication of this policy of course is to limit the defense industry to only meeting the needs of the Japan Self Defense Forces, an unprofitable volume of business. In response to pressure brought by major business organization in 1978, Prime Minister Fukuda and MITI head Komoto both said in Diet interpellations there would be no change in arms export policy to relieve the effects of recession on certain industries. The decision has been made—strong arms export control will continue to be an important element of the GOJ policy.

Provisions of the laws establishing the Self Defense Forces govern their management at a detailed level. For example, small variations in authorized strength must be approved by the Diet. The limitations imposed place a tight rein on the Japan Defense Agency (JDA), and firmly impose civilian rule over the Uniform Services. These laws limit the JDA's ability to adapt to new circumstances. They must look to a lengthy process of Diet approval for relatively minor changes. These changes may become the focus of opposition party attacks on the ruling party, a prospect which makes even asking for the change a rare event.

Japan's nonnuclear principles place a theoretical constraint on the Self Defense Forces. Japan holds that she will not manufacture, or possess, and/or allow to be introduced into Japan nuclear weapons. Japan is a signer of the nonproliferation treaty and an advocate of initiatives to limit strategic arms and nuclear proliferation. Current policies clearly preclude the JDA from considering acquisition of a nuclear capability. In addition, geographic constraints keep Japan from developing a nuclear weapons capability. Population and industrial density preclude effective dispersion of nuclear delivery systems, and deployment at sea would require such a large investment as to eliminate this possibility. To be effective in Japan's environment and possible future scenarios any nuclear force would have to be so large that its cost would be prohibitive, even for Japan. Geographic constraints also severely limit Japan's ability to create effective war fighting capability. By constitutional interpretation, JSDF units may not deploy overseas. Unit training must therefore be accomplished in Japan where training/maneuver areas are small and where training is constrained by operational limitations imposed to minimize community frictions. Realistic training is not possible.

Not surprisingly, financial constraints also serve to limit JSDF size and capability. The JDA is the pauper in the castle. JDA budgets are tight with discretionary amounts very limited. Over one-half of the budget goes to personnel expenses, operational funds for training and equipment are scarce, and combat readiness sacrificed to funding at least some progress in equipment modernization.

As the constraints outlined above serve to limit the JSDF, so other limitations restrict what the U.S. can do to assist in the defense of Japan. The flexibility to adjust U.S. forces in Japan to meet changing circumstances is extremely limited. Article 24 of the Status of Forces Agreement assigns Japan the responsibility of providing, without cost to the U.S., facilities and areas for U.S. forces in Japan. The Ohira view, a determination resulting from Diet interpellation, laid out the position that Japanese responsibility under this provision included only construction to replace facilities and areas reverted to Japan. This view effectively capped the U.S. force presence in Japan. The Government of Japan would provide no new facilities unless old ones were relinquished. In addition, the GOJ held that they had no responsibility for the operations and maintenance costs of U.S. forces in Japan. Therefore, as inflation and wage rates in Japan far outstripped those prevailing elsewhere, U.S. forces in Japan began reductions in presence to accommodate to these pressures. Thus there is an inevitable downward bias in the U.S. force presence. From 1973 to 1978 the U.S. military population dropped from 65,000 to 48,000; and the number of Japanese workers employed dropped from 50,000 to 23,000. Nonetheless, the labor cost doubled at the same time.[15]

Consensus-building

From his assessment of the situation taking particular account of U.S. Policy and domestic constraints, the Japanese defense planner must evolve a reasonable set of defense policy objectives and force structure options which are logically consistent. Key to this is some general determination of what Japan's place in the world is to be. In this regard, it seems that some basic parameters can be identified. First, the relationship with the U.S. is so deep and mutually beneficial that it will probably continue to form the basis of Japanese foreign policy. This was underscored in Prime Minister Fukuda's speech before the Diet in January 1978. This relationship is not static, however, because adaptations to the changing relative position of both countries are necessary. Second, as the third largest economic power in the

15. GAO Report "The United States and Japan Should Seek a More Equitable Defense Cost-Sharing arrangement," June 15, 1977.

world and the second largest market economy, Japan must determine its role as a leader in the solution of regional and global problems and meld this role with its position vis-a-vis the U.S. It seems clear that Japan will play a more active diplomatic role and take on increasing responsibility. ASEAN is an example. Third, Japan must determine the direction of its relationship with the major communist countries. The Peace and Friendship Treaty, of course, gives new meaning to the term equidistance and the GOJ should perhaps consider adoption of the terms rough or essential equidistance.

Defense policy objectives that seem to be evolving from this synthesis are:

> As bound by the Constitution, Japan's defense posture will remain limited. Japan will have to suffer free ride criticism but as Prime Minister Fukuda said before the National Press Club of Japan. "In an interdependent world, the concept of maintaining peace through power balances will become more and more unrealistic. Japan's is the correct path. She can contribute to world peace and stability."[16]

> Second, The Japan-U.S. Security Treaty is indispensable to Japan and will be maintained.

> Third, Japan will improve its own defense capabilities to deter, and repel if necessary, either direct or indirect aggression.

> Fourth, Japan will contribute, within existing agreements, to the maintenance of the U.S. military presence in the Western Pacific.

> Fifth, Japan will strive to improve the military cooperation between forces of Japan and the U.S. for the defense of Japan.

The changing climate and the changing need allow consideration of a broader range of policies and force structure options, and trial balloons are frequently employed to explore the range limits. Testing on the policy range has included the following-redefinition of national security to include stockpiles of strategic materials as well as national defense, and allocation of 3 to 3.5% of the GNP for this purpose by 1985;[17] a shift from total dependence on the U.S. to autonomous defense in the context of studying the integrated means to defend against Japan in an emergency;[18] a recognition that deterrence requires the possession of a force feared by a potential aggressor[19] and

---

16. February 15, 1978 remarks by Prime Minister Fukuda before luncheon meeting of Nikon Kisha Club.

17. Nikon Keizai, May 22, 1978.

18. JDA Defense Bureau Dictor, Ito, before the Lower House Audit Committee, July 4, 1978; JIJI Press, July 5, 1978.

19. Defense Minister Kanemaru speech before 7th Division GSDF, June 1, 1978; Asahi June 2, 1978.

JSDF participation in the UN peacekeeping force.[20] Of these, only the idea of the SDF needing to pose a threat to be a deterrent raised so much as a murmur of protest and this objection subsided with a ritual wrist slapping criticism of its originator, General Kurisu, then Chairman of the Joint Staff Council.

The GOJ has also been exploring the feasible range for their force structure. Historically, a number of the Japanese defense policy debates have centered on weapons systems buys. Weapons systems procured must have charcteristics compatible with restrictions constrained in the SDF establishment law regarding offensive capabilities. For example, the McDonnell Douglas F-4, Phantom, is a multipurpose aircraft with air intercept, air superiority, interdiction and deep strike capabilities. As delivered to the JASDF, however, the F-4EJ does not have refueling or bomb carrying capability. These equipment restrictions keep the aircraft in a clearly defense mode.

Recent debates have gained general acceptance of the following views;

> Article 9 of the Constitution does not prohibit the possession of tactical nuclear weapons in the event Japan withdraws from the NPT[21]
>
> The JSDF can use cruise missiles.[22]
>
> It will be necessary for the JSDF to study having a killer satellite capability in the future.[23]
>
> Japan can possess large size aircraft carriers and tanker aircraft if the purpose is for defense.[24]

Little testing at the lower ends of the force structure spectrum has been done and there is clearly a bias in recent trends towards exploring the upper limits of the feasible range of defense policy and force structure options. At the high end the only systems eliminated out of hand were ICBM's and strategic bombers.[25]

The Key Participants

The range of possibilities is broader, the external environment changing and the domestic constraints lessening. In this flexible situation, Japan

---

20. Widely reported in Tokyo news papers during week of July 15, 1978.

21. Foreign Minister Sonoda before the Lower House Foreign Affairs Committee, February 22, 1978, termed by the *New York Post*—the first self-defense atom bomb, February 11, 1978.

22. JDA Defense Bureau Chief Ito before the Lower House Budget Committee, February 18, 1978.

23. JDA Vice Minister Maruyama Press Conference, January 26, 1978.

24. JDA Defense Bureau Chief Ito before the Lower House Budget Committee, February 8, 1978.

25. Interpellations before the Lower House Budget Committee, February 14, 1978.

must evolve a coherent defense policy using a process which itself has been influenced by new forces. New players are emerging, the positions of old players are changing and the interaction among them is producing new patterns. In this section, the key participants, their roles and apparent position will be described. The development of defense policy positions must consider all of these views and the proponent, usually the JDA, must obtain the acquiesence, if not always the approval, of all of the key players.

Organizationally the Prime Minister heads the collection of defense policy makers. Recently his involvement has been more public and major policy speeches, e.g., on the occasion of the opening of the Diet, now contain statements regarding Japan's defense policy. In recognition of the increased public awareness of defense issues the Prime Minister has a role in assuring the public that the government will deal with this issue both realistically and within the framework of the constitution.[26] He can also do so with reasonable expectations that his defense policy statements, which are general in nature, will not become the focus for controversy and become focal points for debates within the LDP or with the opposition parties. Defense issues no longer enjoy center stage in political competition.

While the LDP enjoys a majority in the Diet, it is slim. Most of the opposition parties, in anticipation of eventually joining in a ruling coalition or of functioning as a swing block in dealing with the LDP, and also in response to changes in public attitudes, have adopted positions more favorable to the JSDF and the MST. The Komeito and the Democratic Socialist Party now generally support both. The Socialists, the largest opposition party, continue to be concerned over the lengths to which any defense increase will be and continues to attack the LDP for not establishing firm limits.[27] Nonetheless, the JSP, in the draft of its new policy for national peace and security, admits the lack of reality in the long advocated JSP bid for "unarmed peace and neutrality."[28]

The defense policy interaction among the political parties is most visible when the Diet is debating the annual defense budget. The interpellation privilege permits the opposition member to question key officials at great length on any topic he chooses thereby tying the parliamentary procedure in knots, something the ruling party cannot afford if key legislation is pending. Concessions are required. The Spring 1978 discussion of the defense budget was unusual in the lack of concessions. Apparently the LDP judged that they had the strength to push the defense budget through intact and proceeded to take on all comers on issues of defense policy. They defended the retention of

26. *Sankei,* July 3, 1978.
27. JSP press statement, February 15, 1978.
28. Draft Statement of JSP Policy for National Peace Security, *Nikon Keizai* July 5, 1978.

a refueling and bombing capability on the F-15 and went on the offensive by suggesting that tanker aircraft were acceptable as well. As usual the public display was preceded by considerable quiet informal preparation. Each of the political parties now committees to deal with defense issues. Committees include the:

National Defense Committee (LDP)

Security Problems Research Council (LDP)

Parliamentarian League for National Defense (LDP)

Special Committee to Counter measure Japan-US
Security Treaty and Self Defense Force (JSP)

Special Committee on Counter measure Defense Issues (DSP)

Security Problems Committee (CGP)

A Diet defense committee was created on a nonpermanent basis last year. This year will probably see it become permanent.

Procedurally, the Cabinet level National Defense Council (NDC) heads the policy making apparatus. It currently includes representation from the Ministry of Foreign Affairs, the Ministry of Finance, JDA, and the Prime Minister. Additional representation proposed, in keeping with a broader definition of national security, would add MITI, the Transportation Ministry, the Science and Technology Agency and the Chief Cabinet Secretary. The JDA and elements of the LDP wish to see the NDC strengthened as well as broadened so that it can function much like the U.S. National Security Council. [29]

Theoretically, the JDA should be the leader in development of defense policy. Historically they acted more like the custodian of the JSDF rather than the agency in charge of security affairs. They want this changed and have proposed that they be designated as the government office in charge of security affairs and that the security division of the American Affairs Bureau of MOFA be abolished. [30] The proposal that the JDA be elevated from an agency to a ministry has resurfaced with greater acceptance and the JDA have initiated studies to modernize their internal organization. All of these reflect the growing awareness of the need for a structure which is capable of grappling with modern security issues, but also illuminate the debates now underway regarding the relative rights, bureaucratic duties and responsibilities of civilian and military leadership in Japan. Specters of past debates of this type are raised, but there are few similarities. There is little question that Japan's

29. *Sankei* of June 13, 1978, *Nikon Keizan,* April 2, 1978.
30. *Nikon Keizai* June 27, 1978.

military leaders of today are professionally committed to civilian control and to the peace constitution. The sensitivity of this issue was made quite clear, however, by the circumstances surrounding General Kurisu's dismissal in July of 1978. The outspoken general, when attempting to clarify rules of engagement, put forth the notion that field commanders should have the power to repel a surprise attack without waiting for orders from civilian officials. He added that this was not challenging civilian control, but merely trying to clarify what commanders should do before civilian leaders can exert that control in an emergency. The hint of "supralegal" actions was enough to lead the Defense Minister to remove the Chairman of the Joint Staff Council from his office.[31] Both the air SDF and the ground SDF Chief of Staff denied that such supralegal actions need be taken, noting that such authority could be prescribed if the situation became strained. Subsequently the LDP executive board decided to study the need for a law covering the situations described by Kurisu.[32]

More quietly, defense officials are undertaking studies to revise their organization and structure to modernize the JDA. The modality is a proposed revision to the twenty year old JDA establishment law and the SDF law, to be put before the Diet in 1980. The revisions would consolidate intelligence functions, increase flexibility in sizing and organizing components of the JSDF, strengthen the Joint Staff Council and give it joint operational coordinating powers in times of emergency.[33] Also at issue is the command arrangement between U.S. and Japanese forces in times of crisis.[34]

There appears to be general consensus on the strengthening of the Joint Staff office capability to act as the Defense Minister's Staff to coordinate, communicate and transmit orders to forces in an emergency. The relationships among the players in peacetime, however, are the source of significant disagreement over the roles of the JCS on the one hand and the Internal Bureau on the other. Most of the power struggle is behind the scenes although hints of it surfaced during the Kurisu dismissal when some of the Internal Bureau chiefs participated in asking for Kurisu's resignation.[35] Also, the struggle between the Internal Bureau and the JSO surfaced when the military and civilian interpretations differed on the Soviet activities near the Northern territory Etorofu Island in May 78. The JSO contended that there were large scale landing exercises. The JDA Bureau said it was not clear what the Soviets were up to. The newspapers reported General Kurisu had bypassed the

31. *Washington Post,* July 26, 1978.
32. *Tokyo Times,* July 26, 1978. *Sankei,* July 22, 1978.
33. *Sankei,* May 8, 1978.
34. *Nikon Keizai,* April 2, 1978.
35. *Nikon Keizai,* July 26, 1978.

Internal Bureau, infuriating its head who was at the same time briefing a Diet committee that the facts did not indicate a large scale Soviet maneuver. Kanemaru sided with the Internal Bureau head. The Asahi pointed out the evident communication and confidence gaps existing between the Internal Bureaus and the JSO.[36]

The Internal Bureaus are also caught up in the problem of resolving the relative responsibilities between themselves and MOFA's Security Division. In the past, the Security Division within the American Affairs Bureau was responsible for the security relationship with the U.S. and therefore implicitly for Japanese defense policy. As JDA confidence and capabilities grow it is apparent that the JDA wishes this responsibility shifted to them, something MOFA is reluctant to do.

The Foreign Ministry protests its primacy in dealing with other countries as a matter of principle, MOFA also is concerned that Japanese military leaders may not be as enthusiastic as they, in maintaining close (read dependent by military) security ties with the U.S. or in maintaining a purely defensive posture. MOFA appears to be worried about future directions of Japanese defense policy if they do not maintain control. The Foreign Minister has said to the Commander of U.S. forces in Japan, "If you have anything you want to tell to Japan, present it directly to the Foreign Office, instead of the JDA."[37] Apparently Mr. Sonoda does not like the prospect of contending with a politically powerful defense establishment in determining how Japanese defense policy should evolve. Parochialism is also not unknown in Japan, a fact that is painfully evident when trying to find logical consistency in the assessment of the regional situation found in the 1976 Defense White Paper.[38]

Confrontation cannot supersede consensus decision making however, and MOFA and JDA must jointly resolve security issues even if their relative responsibilities may be in a state of flux. Both are represented on the NDC; both answer defense policy questions before the Diet, although MOFA tends to answer those concerning the U.S. connection; both serve on the various consultative bodies with the U.S. The U.S. Department of State and Defense have similar problems in sorting out their relative responsibilities on certain security issues; we should not be too surprised if Japan has similar ones, nor should we read too much into this debate.

In addition to the government agencies described above there are a number of other key players, not the least of which is the very active Japanese press. The growing interest in defense issues within Japan is intertwined with the

---

36. *Asahi* and others, June 9, 1978.
37. *Sankei*, May 9, 1978.
38. *Defense of Japan*, (Tokyo, Japan: Japan Defense Agency 1976).

changing attitudes of the Japanese press. They have played a key role in increasing public awareness of security issues and at the same time, have increased their coverage in response to this demand. Specific elements within the Japanese press have close ties with particular ministries and are themselves involved in the decision making process. Their support is enlisted to help build the consensus or to fly trial balloons or to let a particular debate be exposed to the light of public scrutiny. In doing so, there appear to be tacit understandings on what will be released and when and the appropriate attribution. Editorial coverage is more balanced today since defense issues no longer hold as much potential for the favorite past-time of the Japanese press— sniping at the government.

Japanese press editorials now contain well balanced pieces asking critical questions on the future of Japanese defense policy including such issues as Article 9 and changing technology, new means of limiting defense power, the problem of sea lane protection, and the need for streamlined deliberation and decision mechanisms with the government.[39] This generally well balanced treatment of issues is a significant step in promoting the defense debate within Japan. Officials can proceed more confident that their views and decisions will be fairly dealt with by the press.

The growing interest in security issues has also spawned several research institutions much like American "think tanks." Most significant is the Peace and Security Research Institute created in October 1978 under the leadership of Dr. Inoki, formerly President of the National Defense Academy. The Institute is sponsored by the JDA and business to examine basic issues such as U.S.-Japan security system in the 1980's, and regional security conditions.[40] The role to be played by Japanese think tanks in the decision making process is yet to be determined. They will want to develop ties with similar organizations elsewhere in the world and could be used to exchange views on an international basis. They could research topics too politically difficult for the JDA to deal with in-house, or they could become lobbyists for interest groups. Their development could also affect the role of the National Defense College in long range strategy development.

Lastly there is the much discussed military industrial complex, such as it is. The unquestioned political clout of Japanese industry is felt even in their miniscule arms sector. They lobby for greater allocations to military research and development, larger military capital expenditures, maintenance of an arms industrial and technological base (mainly through licensed production inflow) and relaxation of arms export policies. Most active are the Defense

39. See for example, *Asahi,* July 20, 1978; *Yomiuri,* February 22, 1978; *Mainichi,* June 28, 1978.
40. *Asahi, Sankei,* July 15, 1978.

Production Committee of Keidanren representing approximately 80 companies, and the Japan Weapons Industry Association representing 100 companies, although these numbers are misleading since the industry is heavily concentrated. Based upon the current state of affairs one can conclude that influence of the arms manufacturers has been modest. The GOJ has, however, procured equipment and allocated funds to maintain the civilian industrial arms base, and the provisions for technology transfer in licensed production proposals are an important consideration in the acquisition decision. It is not uncommon to produce weapons systems in Japan at considerably greater cost in order to maintain a warm industrial base, and to obtain the technology transfer necessary to keep the industry near the current state of the art.

The American Involvement

The reliance on U.S. military power is evident in Japan's security policy pronouncements. In the process of developing defense policy this reliance finds practical expression in the frequent consultations with the Americans through the many mechanisms established for the purpose. The annual consultations between the American Secretary of Defense and the Japanese Defense Minister, begun by Schlesinger and Sakata in 1975, are next scheduled for November of 1978 in Tokyo. These consultations deal with strategic issues and initiatives concerning basic U.S.-Japan defense cooperation. Next in line is the Security Consultative Committee (SCC), established in 1960 to provide a forum for consultations on implementation of the Mutual Security Treaty and for formalizing arrangements and agreements regarding the treaty. As in all of the forums except the Secretary of Defense-Defense Minister Annual Consultations, the Ministry of Foreign Affairs leads the Japanese delegation. The SCC next meets in the fall of 1978 to consider the report of its subsidiary body, the Subcommittee for Defense Cooperation concerning bilateral planning. The Subcommittee for Defense Cooperation (SDC) was formed in 1976 to develop measures to facilitate joint actions in times of emergency. It normally meets every other month and has panels to develop guidelines in specific functional areas such as logistics, command and control and operations.[41] The Subcommittee of the Security Consultative Committee (SCC) was established in 1976 to provide a forum for information exchanges of views on basic defense issues. It customarily meets once a year, the last meeting being in Honolulu in January 1978. It is the only established committee mechanism which includes Washington level participants. The American delegations of the other mechanisms are headed by the U.S. Ambassador in Tokyo or his representative. Lastly the Joint Committee exists for implementation of the Status of

41. *Asahi*, July 5, 1978.

Forces Agreement (SOFA) and deals mainly with base-community interaction issues. Other inactive forums are still on the books.

The informal contacts are also extensive. Washington and Tokyo both see frequent vistors who travel to gauge moods in the other capital and to convey views, both personal and semi-official. They also come to validate what is being said in the more formal dialogues. Washington, like Tokyo, frequently speaks with more than once voice. Japanese visitors need to make sure, for example, that the people reassuring them on the U.S. resolve in Asia are, in fact, in a position to do so. They must gauge the power base of the Washington officials who are making statements of U.S. defense policy concerning Japan. They must also try to determine intent. For example, a large number of visitors came to Washington on the heels of the decision to withdraw ground combat forces from Korea. The number then dropped off, but picked up again as every high level American official visiting Tokyo made it a point to provide verbal assurances of the U.S. commitment. Perhaps they "doest protest too much." Based upon numbers alone, it would seem that the means to exchange views would be adequate to any consultative need. A number of them carry a legacy of form over substance, however, and may not be up to handling tomorrow's issues. Critic Kase has pointed to the need for a better mechanism to handle the more pragmatic and cooperative relationships he proposes.[42]

The Outputs

The output of the consensus mechanisms is a more realistic defense policy for Japan. While incompletely developed at the current time, the outline of a new policy for the future is emerging. Its key features appear to be identification of a threat for force planning, resolution of the issue of offensive versus defensive power, a commitment to a future force structure with deterrent and war fighting capability and reaffirmation of the close security relationship with the United States. It does not appear to consider changing the overall size of the Japanese defense establishment. Within the U.S.-Japan security relationship, it should be sized to the appropriate sharing of tasks as resolved in consultation and in keeping with Article 9 of the Constitution. An early definition of relative responsibilities and an agreed definition of the threat seems to be in order. The JDA is now actively discussing threat specification. For example, one scenario publicly hypothesized limited Soviet objectives leading to diplomatic negotiations rather than an all out war. In the scenario, the Soviet's scatter mines in the Tsugaru Straits, thereby blocking the sea lane between Honshu and Hokkaido, then conduct air strikes against radars

---

42. Kase, Hidgaki, "The new debate on defense," *Far Eastern Economic Review,* June 2, 1978, p. 29.

on Hokkaido to prevent opposition by Japanese aircraft. They follow with an amphibious assault near Wakkanai to capture limited objectives.[43] The Japan Defense Agency also announced in late June that they will begin an "anti-invasion" study cochaired by the JSO and the Defense Agency's internal bureau. The mild, almost indifferent, reaction to this announcement is a reflection of the change in public mood since 1965 when the "three arrows" study caused considerable negative reaction.[44] The 1978 White Paper briefing also publicly labeled the Soviet naval buildup in the Pacific as a direct threat to Japan.[45]

Regarding the persistent debate on offensive power, the relative nature of this concept has now been established. As explained by Cabinet Legislation Bureau Director Sanada, the definition of "threat of force" is dependent upon other nations' perceptions and the state of the art of military techniques.[46] It is interesting to note that PRC officials have told Japanese leaders that they do not consider strengthening of Japan's war capabilities as threatening.[47] Also during the Diet debate on the JFY 78 Defense Budget, Kanemaru defined the concept of defense threat as arming the JSDF to such an extent which would discourage foreign countries from the idea of invasion of Japan. He also attempted to deflect further debate away from the other defensive/offensive armaments theme pointing out that with today's technology, this is an impossible distinction. Nonaggression was found in policy, not in equipment.[48]

This argumentation of course, leads to a familiar policy, deterrence through maintenance of strong war fighting capabilities. As widely reported in the past, JSDF capabilities are deficient in readiness and sustainability. The JSDF has now begun to buildup those capabilities required to "be an effective organ in a real war." Studies of operational cooperation within the SDC, establishment of a centralized command structure, including a national command center emergency law legislation, correction of logistics deficiencies including stockpiling of ammunition, and establishment of a civil defense program are examples of steps taken.[49] The change in policy to focus military R&D on a few top priority projects instead of dissipating scarce R&D resources over the technology spectrum also supports this more pragmatic course of correcting deficiencies in war fighting capabilities.[50] Trial balloons on the

---

43. *Nikon Keizai,* July 7, 1978.
44. *Sankei,* June 23, 1978.
45. *Los Angeles Times,* July 29, 1978 p. 1.
46. Before the Upper House Budget Committee, January 30, 1978.
47. *Asahi,* July 15, 1978.
48. *Asahi,* January 20, 1978.
49. *Nikon Kuzai,* July 21, 1978 and 1978 Defense White Paper.
50. *Nikon Keizai,* June 22, 1978.

JFY 79 Defense Budget also contain important indications; for example acquisition of an unglamorous ocean survey ship to collect data necessary for ASW operations[51] and acquisition of HARPOON and SEA SPARROW for destroyer armament modernization.[52] The proposal for training of pilots in the U.S. is also an indication of JDA concern for its war capabilities as is the emphasis on more joint and combined exercises.

Lastly, Japanese leaders have gone to considerable lengths to reaffirm U.S.-Japan defense ties and to actively promote closer cooperation. At the same time they propose altering the relationship from one of total dependence to one of cooperation. The 1978 Defense White Paper says "nebulous expectation and one sided reliance" upon the U.S. should be ended.[53] As an example, securing the sea lines of communication to Guam and to Taiwan are mentioned as roles the JMSDF should consider assuming or extending the JMSDF operational area to 1000 nautical miles out to sea.[54]

The second dimension of promoting cooperation is the assumption by Japan of more of the cost of maintaining U.S. forces in Japan. Japan currently spends over $500 million dollars to provide bases, facilities and other support. The GOJ is currently considering raising this amount by some $100 million to offset the deficit caused in U.S. forces Japan budgets by inflation and yen appreciation during the last year.[55]

Japan's defense policy is maturing in process and content. Reacting to dynamic external events and a more rational domestic atmosphere, Japan is pragmatically addressing today's defense. What is being acquired is a new capability for the defense of Japan within the context of closer, more effective, and more equal defense cooperation with the United States.

51. *Tokyo Shimbun,* June 27, 1978.

52. *Nikon Keizai;* July 7, 1978.

53. *Los Angeles Times,* July 29, 1978, p. 1.

54. JDA Defense Bureau Chief I to before the Lower House Budget Committee, July 5, 1978.

55. *Yomiuri,* July 25, 1978.

VI. France

The Political Party Debates, 1976-78

JEAN KLEIN†

The French decision to go nuclear and to build a "force de frappe" in the early 1960s stirred up quasi-unanimous opposition within the country as well as among the allies. By contrast, today there is a consensus on the "reality" of this force, and the Atlantic Declaration of June 1974 recognized its contribution to the "global deterrent of the alliance." In addition, the withdrawal of France from the integrated NATO structure, which was hotly debated in 1966 and which gave Mr. Mitterrand the opportunity to indict "gaullist power," is considered ten years later as the cornerstone of an independent foreign policy and is supported by a majority of the French people. To be sure, this "anomaly" continues to bother the allied countries, but arrangements have been made to reduce the negative consquences of the French withdrawal from the military organization of NATO, and nobody thinks seriously that this move shook the security system of the West.

Paradoxically, the result has been that the opposition parties have become the most vigilant guardians of gaullist orthodoxy and they often have reproached the government for its "Atlanticist" complacency. This has induced some observers to suspect the sincerity of their adherence to the defense policy defined by General de Gaulle. In fact it would be hazardous to claim that the French Communist Party (PCF) and the Socialist Party (PS) agree on the role assigned to the nuclear force. The Left Radicals (the *Radicaux de Gauche* or MRG), like the PS, are reluctant to endorse an autonomous defense policy based on the nuclear deterrent and they cling to the classical model of collective security. The Radicals belonging to the majority changed their minds about nuclear weapons and are no longer hostile to a nuclear deterrent on principle. Nevertheless, their military experts are inclined to take advantage of the possibilities of small tactical nuclear weapons and they favor a

† Translation by D. Bruce Marshall.

selective response to an armed attack.[1] As far as the parties from the presidential majority are concerned, defense policy does not unite them either, and public differences appeared in 1976 about the nuclear strategy and about the slow-paced development of the nuclear forces.

The debate on defense policy within France is particularly interesting since the two main opposition parties, the PS and the PCF, signed a Common Program of Government and tried to adjust their programs to the requirements of a credible defense policy in order to form a Government of the Left. The talks on the updating of the Common Program, the crisis of September 1977, and the policies after the electoral defeat of March 1978 have underlined the discrepancies between socialists and communists, particularly in the area of defense and foreign policy. Today there is an open conflict between the two parties and the time of the United Left is over. Nevertheless, the views and declaratory policy of both parties on defense deserve a close study for at least three reasons: First, the debate shows that the nuclear force is becoming an integral component of the French defense system: nobody wants to give it away without compensations and any kind of unilateral nuclear disarmament is rejected. Second, defense issues were the main stumbling block in the talks on the updating of the Common Program, and they revealed deep misunderstandings on deterrence, alliances and foreign policy. Third, the talks between socialists and communists during 1977 and 1978 compelled them to clarify their views and to elaborate new proposals on defense policy which will survive the collapse of the United Left. Thus, it is necessary to analyze their content in order to gauge the limits of the consensus reached at the end of the inter-party talks and to speculate on the future alliance policy of the French political parties.

The Refusal of Nuclear Weapons

In his press conference of 23 July 1964, General de Gaulle gave a detailed explanation of his views on defense policy and stated that France was irreversibly committed to a policy of deterrence. Opposition to the French nuclear program appeared to him to be inspired by the usual alliance of "the eternal demagogy and the eternal routine"—an alliance which, in the past, had prevented the modernization of the armed forces and had been the cause of major disasters. But in the present case, the simple refusal of the reforms was not the only motivation of the foes of nuclear weapons. In reality it was inspired by two opposite sets of beliefs both leading to "the disappearance of

---

1. The proposals of the Radical Party were published together with an essay by Alain Bloch, *Et Goliath fut vaincu par David,* (Les dossiers du manifeste, No. 1). Chaumont: France Editions, 1977.

France under the tutelage of one or another foreign state." One group, he asserted, meant to establish a "totalitarian servitude" in our country and, therefore, wished to deprive us of the means to resist a threat coming from the East. On the other side were the partisans of the American protectorate, worried by the prospects of an autonomous France inside the alliance. De Gaulle concluded that the opposition was unlikely to "persuade the French nation" and that the atomic effort should be pursued.

This statement raised huge protests and during the budget debate in December 1964 all the non-gaullist parties opposed the national "force de frappe." Their arguments were the following: a nuclear deterrent is useless; it does not protect France and it duplicates the American guarantee; France cannot afford such a costly force and follow the superpowers in their arms race; the building of a nuclear force undermines the development of scientific research and diverts resources from more positive economic ventures. Finally, a small deterrent imperils its owner instead of preventing aggression, and complicates disarmament.

Upon closer examination of the statements of the political parties, one could discern a difference between the socialists, who were devoted to the Atlantic Alliance and/or inclined to conceive of the French nuclear effort within a European framework[2] and the communists, who were more attached to the national interest and more anxious to loosen the ties with the United States. These discordant views became visible when France withdrew from NATO: The socialists criticized the move, whereas, the communists hailed it with mixed feelings.[3] Despite these disagreements, the Communist Party and Mr. Mitterrand's *Fédération de la gauche démocratique et socialiste* published a joint statement on 24 February 1968 which was denounced by the Prime Minister of the day, George Pompidou, as a "program of anarchy leading to dictatorship." "How," he continued, "could the PCF and the Federation, who disagree on the alliance issues, possibly have a common attitude on European affairs which will be the main issue in the coming decade?"[4]

In the following years, the process of rapprochement between Socialists and Communists went forward and led to the signature of a Common Program of Government on 27 June 1972. Meanwhile, the two parties adopted their own separate programs: the PCF on 9 October 1971 and the PS on 11 January 1972. It is appropriate to examine their chapters on defense and security in order to see what base the compromise was built upon.

2. See the article by André Philip, "Pour une force de défense européene," *Le Monde*, 18 December 1964.

3. See the editorial by Yves Moreau in *L'Humanité*, 10 March 1966.

4. See Pompidou's speech to a luncheon of the *Association de la Presse ministérielle* as reported in *Le Monde*, 28 February 1968.

In the communist program, independence is the main aim. The French people should be able in all circumstances "to decide in full sovereignty on the conduct of national affairs." Therefore, France could not be encapsulated in any military bloc, nor subordinated to supranational insitutions which, in the "small Europe dominated by the trusts, would make progress on the road towards social welfare dependent on the consent of cosmopolite monopolies."[5] As far as defense and foreign policy was concerned, the PCF drew the following conclusions:

1) France should take an active part in the disarmament negotiations and should resume its seat on the Geneva Committee on Disarmament. It should also adhere to the other existing international arms control agreements and should support the convocation of a world conference on disarmament. Finally, France should refrain from selling arms to colonialist and racist governments like Portugal and South Africa.

2) France should disengage from the Atlantic treaty, since it was a political and military organization with aggressive aims and was dominated by the United States.

3) France should renounce the strategic nuclear force and tactical nuclear weapons.

4) She should also renounce the nuclear strategy, considering the dangers inherent in the balance of terror.

5) France should build a military force whose exclusive aim would be "the defense of the territorial integrity of the nation." This would be achieved by a conscript army, since a professional army would be out of the question.

After the congress of Epinay in June 1971, the new Socialist Party also published a program, but the proposals it contained were different from those of the PCF despite some similarities. Having recalled in the preamble the principles which inspire democratic socialism, Mr. Mitterrand stated that France would extract herself from "the diabolical cycle of the tests and the production of the atomic bomb" and would propose a disarmament plan which could be discussed during a special conference. Nevertheless, the PS which is "patriotic, being rooted in the people, would not leave the French defenseless agains the risks of an aggression."[6] These ambiguous statements could not conceal an embarrassment about the fate of the nuclear force if disarmament failed, and it did not say anything about how the national defense would be organized. Besides, it was claimed that a strictly national defense was impossible and that there was no alternative to collective security.

---

5. *Changer de cap: programme pour un gouvernment démocratique d'union populaire: Introduction de Georges Marchais.* Paris: Editions Sociales, 1971. See especially pp. 17, 221-22, 323, 234-36.

6. *Changer la vie. Programme de gouvernement du parti socialiste: Présentation de François Mitterrand* (Paris: Flammarion, 1972), p. 29.

A Government of the United Left would immediately adopt measures which could not be undone in the future, such as the signature of the Moscow Nuclear Test Ban Treaty of 1963, the cessation of arms sales to totalitarian or segregationist states (South Africa, Portugal, Greece) and the interruption of the build up of a nuclear strategic force. The long term objectives of the PS can be summed up as follows:

1) The European option is fundamental. The consolidation of European institutions must continue, but under conditions such that the Communities cannot become obstacles to the movement toward socialism. Some ten pages of the program were devoted to the measures to be taken to enlarge the competence of the community institutions and to move toward a "community foreign policy."

2) The two military blocs should be dissolved and in their place a system of collective security should be instituted, based on a progressive, balanced and controlled disarmament. The Government of the Left would not withdraw France from the Atlantic Alliance, but it would "denounce without delay the support which NATO has given to the dictatorships of Southern Europe and demand that this be stopped."

3) Support will be given to any initiative toward disarmament. In addition to participating in any disarmament conference, France would sign the Moscow Treaty and would propose to extend it to include underground tests, and would also adhere to the Non-proliferation Treaty. She would renounce chemical and biological weapons, and call for the holding of an international conference on the subject. Finally, she would reconsider the current policy of arms exports and take whatever measures were needed to reconvert industry from arms production.

4) The needs of national defense for a France "on the road toward socialism" will be provided for. The basis for defense would be, "the unanimous determination of all citizens who are prepared to resist with all the means at their disposal, so that an aggressor, no matter how strong he might be, would be dissuaded by the prospect of losses that would far exeed his gains." The nuclear strategy was condemned in favor of a collective security system in which France's European partners would participate. The program contained only a few hints about what type of military organization would replace the present system or about how the armed forces would be equipped. In any event, the PS refused to accept the "fact of French nuclear weapons" and once it was in office, the Government of the Left intended to stop the build up of the "force de frappe."[7]

7. *Ibid.*, pp. 193, 200, 204-5, 206.

Thus, despite a certain convergence of ideas on questions of disarmament and the renunciation of the nuclear force, the conceptions of the PS and the PCF on defense matters were quite different. While the Communists were insisting on the maintenance of national defense in the strict sense of the term, the socialists expressed doubts that France could defend itself and relied instead on collective security. While the former distrusted European community institutions, the latter saw them as closely associated with the coming of socialism in France. Finally, where one hoped to withdraw from the Atlantic Alliance, the other refused to question it. These contradictions in the original party programs were obscured by the ambiguous language of the Common Program of Government, but they resurfaced during the talks on the updating of that Program which began soon after the successful conclusion of the municipal elections in 1977.

The Common Program and Nuclear Revisionism

The Common Program of Government, which was signed on 27 June 1972, emphasized the points of agreement between the Socialist and Communist parties and sought to play down their differences, especially with regard to Europe and the Atlantic Alliance. Nevertheless, the fourth section of the Program, entitled "Contribute to Peace and Promote International Cooperation," was remarkable for the vagueness of its phraseology and the refusal to take a clear stand on defense issues. To be sure, there was consensus on the goal of disarmament, but there was nothing original about any of the measures envisioned, all of which had been proposed by one or another of the two superpowers during the preceding fifteen years. The renunciation of the nuclear "force de frappe" did not imply the destruction of the existing elements, but simply a halt to further construction, and tactical nuclear weapons were never explicitly mentioned. Still, one cannot help but wonder about the significance of a nuclear force whose development was frozen while the big powers continued to pursue qualitative improvements in their retaliatory systems and to equip themselves with counter-force weapons of greatly increased accuracy.

The Common Program proclaimed respect for existing alliances, but at the same time it affirmed a desire for independence from any politico-military bloc. The problems which might arise as a result of France's membership in the Atlantic Alliance, were to be resolved a step at a time as Europe progressed toward a true collective security system resting on regional disarmament. As far as national defense was concerned, it was to be assured by a conscript army, recruited on the basis of a six month universal military training period and given a "democratic status." In order to resist any eventual aggressor, that force would apply an "appropriate military strategy," which the Program's authors were careful not to define, but it could also be called upon to lend support to the operation of a European collective security system. Finally, the European conceptions of the PS were tempered to the extent that any extension of the Communities' powers and any participation in the definition of common policies was subordinated to the implementation of the political, economic and social program of the United Left Government.

The obvious weaknesses of the Common Program in the area of defense quickly drew stinging criticism from the majority and gave rise within the PS to doubts about the wisdom of any renunciation of nuclear weapons. Thus, for example, Mr. Michel Debré, then Minister of Defense, denounced the inconsistencies of the Common Program which, he said, "disarms France," and he regretted that the socialists, who had been in the Government at the time the first decisions were taken to build the nuclear force, had subsequently swallowed a policy of surrender.[8] These arguments were widely repeated and developed during the legislative election campaign of 1973, and the majority spokesmen emphasized the inconsistent positions of those political leaders who affirmed their desire to give up the principal means of national defense yet still maintained that their objective was to safeguard the country's integrity against any potential aggressor.

Within the PS, some members perceived these contradictions and publicly expressed their disagreement with the antinuclear line right from the beginning. In December 1971, Mr. Charles Hernu had made a proposal to the executive committee of the PS which favored maintaining the nuclear force in being and using it as bargaining chip in a general disarmament negotiation. In a speech to the Jacobins Club in Lyon in January 1972, he posed the alternatives of an effective defense policy or a policy of absolute neutrality. In that connection, Hernu declared that the real issue was not whether to maintain or to abolish the nuclear deterrent force, because, "no Government of the Left, confronted with the realities of power, would simply throw this force into the sea!"[9] Finally, one month after the signature of the Common Program he declared in a radio speech over "RTL" (28 July 1972) that the program remained open with respect to the question of defense and that a Left Government would not neglect "the security of France and of Europe caught between the two blocs."

8. *Le Monde*, 13 January 1973. Mr. Debré developed the same ideas in an article, "La Ve République continue," in *Le Monde*, 27 February 1973 and General Pierre-Marie Gallois referred to the responsibility of the socialist ministers in the decisions taken by the governments of the IV Republic to build atomic weapons during a debate broadcast by "RTL" on 15 May 1974. In his press conference of 27 September 1973, President Pompidou referred specifically to the role played by Pierre Mendes-France in the creation of the French nuclear force, a responsibility which Mendes-France promptly denied a statement reproduced in *Le Monde*, 29 September 1973.

9. *Le Monde*, 27 January 1972.

During the years that followed, the PS continued to challenge the defense options offered by the Common Program in an effort to win support from the armed forces by demonstrating concern for the issues that were troubling officers and enlisted men. Thus, personalities such as Gilles Martinet did not hesitate to characterize the recommendations of the Common Program on defense policy as "foolishness" and to propose instead, "a socialist language which would be a language of pride, rigor, and courage," which alone would be heard by officers and men disenchanted with the existing regime.[10] Later he went so far as to rely on advancements in military technology such as precision guided munitions and cruise missiles to create the core of an autonomous European defense system and to propose an interventionary force for the Mediterranean.[11]

The left wing of the PS which formed the *Centre d'Etudes, de recherches, et d'éducation socialistes* (CERES) under the leadership of Jean-Pierre Chevènement, followed a parallel path. It recognized as early as October 1973 that the provisions of the Common Program relating to defense matters needed to be spelled out in more detail and that the repudiation of nuclear weapons was inspired less by military concerns than by ethical and political considerations.[12] In April 1974, the CERES called for a concept of deterrence which justified the recourse to nuclear weapons, "as a support for the decisive component which is popular deterrence." According to its view, the Government of the Left needed an autonomous defense because it could not be satisfied with the American nuclear umbrella the way a social-democratic regime could, nor could it join the Soviet bloc in the fashion of the peoples' democracies of Eastern Europe. But a truly independent posture, "necessarily implied the capability to inflict upon anyone seeking to seize the demographic and industrial prize represented by France and the rest of Western Europe a level of damage sufficient to render him permanently inferior to the rival superpower."[13] Finally, toward the end of 1973, the PS was confronted with a report prepared by a high level civil servant writing under the pseudonym of Andre Riel, which expressed the views of the military experts in the party's national defense committee. After severely criticizing the defense provisions of the Common Program, the author of the report asserted that it was senseless to renounce nuclear weapons unilaterally. To have a defense policy without providing the means to implement it was, he asserted,

10. See his article which appeared in *Le Nouvel Observateur* and which was cited in *Le Monde*, 26 September 1973.
11. In an article that appeared in the socialist magazine *Faire*, as cited in *Le Monde*, 20 May 1976.
12. See the journal *Frontière*, October 1973.
13. *Frontière*, April 1974.

"suicidal," and "too often the attitude of the Left manifests a bad conscience in this respect which some would try to cover up by equipping the soldiers with sling-shots."[14] Thus, a heated debate began within the PS on a subject long considered taboo, and this change was considered by some as a decisive step forward for a party seeking to demonstrate its capacity to exercise power.

These different currents of opinion converged in April 1974 when the PS created three organizations for reserve officers: the *Convention des officiers de réserve pour l'Armée nouvelle* (CORAN) for commissioned officers, the *Convention des sous-officiers* (CSORAN) for non-commissioned officers, both of which were brought together into the *Confédération des cadres de réserve pour l'Armée nouvelle* (CCRAN) under the presidency of Charles Hernu. Its objective was to win over reserve officers whose affinities lay with the Socialist Party but who were reluctant to join the *Fédération des officiers et sous-officiers de réserve républicains* because it was considered too close to the PCF. However, that operation could not possibly succeed unless the party met the concerns of the military head-on, which meant making concessions on the nuclear force. That was exactly what General Becam, the president of the CORAN, did in a speech on 8 April 1974 announcing the formation of the three organizations. "We do not question the strategic nuclear force or the need for such a force," he declared. "The value of that force is clear and it in indispensable to our defense." Other speakers recalled that the Common Program did not specify what was to be done about the stockpiles of nuclear weapons or about tactical weapons, and Robert Pontillon, a vice-president of the CCRAN and national secretary of the PS, argued that, "socialism owed it to itself to elaborate a defense doctrine that was credible." Finally, Mr. Hernu let it be understood that, the Common Program was currently being updated with respect to Europe, economic questions, and questions of defense and security."[15]

A turning point was reached during the first national convention of the CCRAN at Colombes on 8 and 9 March 1975 when resolutions were adopted approving a concept of deterrence "which rests on at least two elements: the popular will to resist and the possession of modern armaments, and in particular nuclear weapons."[16] It was also explained, however, that these resolutions were designed simply to stimulate further thinking and study on the part of the parties and trade union groups on the Left, and in his speech to

14. See the news weekly, *Le Point*, 12 November 1973, "Les socialistes déterrent la bombe."

15. *Le Monde*, 10 April 1974.

16. *Le Monde*, 11 March 1975. The texts adopted at the Colombes convention were published in a collection of documents entitled, *Pour une réflexion ouverte sur la sécurité et la paix* (Paris: Les Conventions pour l'Armée nouvelle, 1975).

the convention on 9 March, Mr. Mitterrand emphasized that they were not binding on the PS. This was at least partly because opinions differed between the lower levels of the party and the leadership, many of whom had by then come to different conclusions from those set forth in the Common Program and had accepted the reality of nuclear weapons. It was not until 7 November 1976, however, that the executive committee was able to reach a consensus on the maintenance of the nuclear component of the national defense forces. Three reports were presented at that time, each representing the ideas of a different group within the party. Mr. Jean-Pierre Chevènement was firmly attached to the national character of the defense effort, while Mr. Robert Pontillon was more inclined to include the French military effort within the framework of an Atlantic and/or European system. Mr. Charles Hernu defended a position somewhere between the other two. Despite their differences, all three were in agreement about the need for France to maintain nuclear weapons, to preserve its autonomy, and not to let itself be drawn into conflicts where its vital interests were not at stake.

Although the debate on defense policy was well under way within the PS, the communists refused for a long time even to consider any revision of that part of the Common Program and, clinging to the old orthodoxy, the PCF reproached those socialists who took liberties with the charter of the Union of the Left. Thus, when Mr. Charles Hernu made a case for tactical nuclear weapons, which were not explicitly mentioned in the Common Program, *L'Humanité* reacted immediately, condemning such ideas as "contrary to the solutions proposed by the Common Program for the development and the security of the nation."[17] The statements issued by the leaders of the three *Conventions pour l'Armée nouvelle* which suggested that nuclear weapons were a reality and that their maintenance was consistent with the Common Program, led Communist Party leader, Georges Marchais, to tell the Central Committee that, "although it will furnish the armed forces of the nation the means necessary to assure the country's security, a democratic France would immediately put an end to the building of nuclear weapons."[18] Finally, while Mr. Kanapa denounced French nuclear weapons as a provocation in his report on international policy to the Central Committee of the PCF in April 1975, the CERES viewed them as, "an instrument of blackmail and reprisal within

17. See the articles by Mr. Charles Hernu, *Le Monde*, 21 July 1973 and *Le Figaro*, 5 November 1973 and the response of *L'Humanité* on 6 November 1973.

18. *Le Monde*, 12 April 1974. Mr. Marchais elaborated on his ideas in a speech at Orléans, 26 April, in which he said, "A democratic government will have every reason to renounce the maintenance of a 'force de frappe' which is ruinous, which has no effective deterrent value, and which is dependent upon American logistical support." (*Le Monde*, 30 April 1974). See also the article by Jean Marrane, "Luttes populaires et défense nationale," *Cahiers du communisme*, October 1973.

the panoply of weapons with which the Left will equip itself and which it would be a mistake to throw away."[19]

Nevertheless, over a period of several years, there were indications that a shift of emphasis, if not a change of attitude, was taking place among the Communists on matters of defense policy. After 1973 they constantly referred to the "tous azimuts" strategy and accused the Government of surreptitiously re-integrating France into NATO.[20] They also voiced increasing distrust of West Germany and fears that French armed forces would be used to serve German interests.[21] On 25 October 1975, the National Defense Committee of the PCF had decided to launch a campaign of discussion and explanation directed at the armed forces, and finally, Mr. Baillot, speaking to the advisory committee (*comité scientifique*) of the *Fondation pour les études de la défense nationale* on 8 April 1976, attested to the changes which were taking place within the party, even though the official line had scarcely been affected.[22] This is why the new orientation defined in the Kanapa Report and approved by the Central Committee of the PCF on 11 May 1977 was no surprise. Indeed, Defense Minister Yvon Bourges had admitted in an interview with the Paris daily, *Le Monde,* on 16 July 1976, that the opposition seemed to have accepted the existence of the national nuclear force and no longer challenged the need for it. He also pointed out the ambiguities and contradictions in the defense policy of the Left, however, and affirmed that on a number of critical issues they had left the public ignorant of their intentions. This assessment was shared by most analysts, including some of the experts in the PS,[23] and the new line of the PCF, far from dissipating the remaining

19. *Cahiers du CERES,* No. 22, Supplément.

20. For example, see the statement of Georges Marchais cited in *Le Monde,* 30 November 1973, and his declaration of 7 April 1975 on "Antenne 2" as reported in *Le Monde,* 9 April 1975. See also the interview of Mr. Baillot with the communist weekly, *France-Nouvelle,* extracts of which appeared in *Le Monde,* 18-19 April 1976.

21. See the *Report of Mr. Kanapa to the Central Committee* of the PCF dated 21 June 1976, in which he requests a renegotiation of the foreign policy options defined by the Common Program.

22. *Le Monde,* 18-19 April 1976. According to the stenographic notes of one of the participants, Mr. Baillot is reported to have said, "Under existing conditions, atomic weapons can be considered as an element of political independence. . . . The problem is more what mission should be assigned to the strategic nuclear force than whether or not it should exist. . . . We take account of nuclear weapons in two ways: in the Common Program it is definitely taken into account; and in actuality by virtue of its physical development and its international evolution."

23. Paul J. Friedrich, "L'union de la gauche et la défense nationale," *Esprit,* October 1975, and Jacques Huntzinger, "La politique étrangère du parti socialiste," *Politique Etrangère,* No. 2, 1975. Huntzinger, who was a member of the defense committee of the PS, let it be understood that if the Left won the elections of 1978, differences would still remain between the two parties, particularly on the future organization of national defense.

obscurities, gave rise to a number of new questions. Was it a tactical move in the context of the legislative elections of March 1978 or a real break with previous concepts which were poorly adapted to the requirements of defense in a changing international society? Was it linked to the idea of encouraging the development of a "socialism in French colors" or did it objectively favor the interests of the international communist movement? Finally, were the measures proposed coherent either with the logic of nuclear deterrence or with the foreign policy proposals of the Left Union? With respect to the latter, the PCF had advocated since June 1976, the opening of negotiations for the updating of the Common Program. Following the the publication of the Kanapa Report on defense policy, the need for revising the texts adopted in 1972 became obvious. The negotiations began in May 1977 in a working group of 15 members representing the three parties within the Left Union, and the questions of foreign and defense policy came under discussion on 21 July.

Revising the Common Program:

The Communist Party's decision to accept the nuclear deterrent strategy caught the Socialists by surprise, because, although they had discussed the matter at the meeting of their executive committee on 7 November 1976, no decision had been taken then. Moreover, the PCF proposals stemmed from a hard line conception of national independence that could only shock the sensitivities of some socialist leaders who were more inclined toward European or Atlantic ties. Finally, there were questions about priorities: How could the new defense policy be reconciled with a freeze on military expenditures and how could a middle power such as France renounce an anti-city strategy without reducing the credibility of its deterrent to zero? The general philosophy of the Kanapa report can be summarized as follows:

1) The nuclear force "represents the only effective means of deterring any threat of aggression which the country will possess for some time." Therefore, it must be kept in being, which means that it must be kept operational by "the inclusion of scientific and technological advances." That did not mean taking part in the qualitative arms race, but remaining at the minimum level required by "the security and independence of the country."

2) French strategy "would once again become a strategy of deterrence in the strict sense of the term," which implied that it would be a "tous azimuts" strategy in which the adversary was not designated in advance and it would not be directed against cities.

3) The credibility of the national deterrent force requires that it be equipped with "an independent system of detection in case of attack and of targeting for its ships. France had the technological capacity to build such airborne radar and satellite surveillance systems and should provide them."

As a corollary to that policy, all ties to NATO should be dropped and any sort of common European defense system rejected. "Not only would any such orientation simply aggravate the present involvement of France in an Atlantic strategy, but it would also open the way for West Germany to gain access to nuclear weapons. We say categorically: we will never agree that West Germany should have access to weapons of mass destruction in any form or under any pretext whatsoever."

4) The decision to employ nuclear arms would no longer be left in the hands of a single man but would be assumed by a high level committee composed of the President of the Republic, the Prime Minister and Minister of Defense, Ministers representing the Government coalition, and the Chief of the General Staff.

5) As far as disarmament was concerned, several new ideas were put forward including French participation in the Strategic Arms Limitation Talks and adhesion to the Convention of 22 June 1973 on the prevention of nuclear war. [24]

The about-face by the PCF on nuclear weapons and the authoritarian manner in which it occured—the Central Committee took the decision without the matter ever having been publicly debated [25]—aroused strong opposition among the leading figures of the leftwing parties and trade unions. A deep division developed within the PS making it necessary to seek a compromise among the various tendencies, and at the party Congress of Nantes (17-19 June 1977) it was decided that a special national convention would be convened before the legislative elections to deal with the problems of defense policy. [26] It was in this context that the working group charged with the updating of the Common Program began on 21 July 1977 to revise the defense policy of the Left Union. The PCF considered the matter a vital question which should be dealt with in clear language. The PS, on the other hand, could not take a definite position so long as its national leadership had not yet reached a decision. In addition, the first exchange of views between

24. See the Report of Mr. Kanapa to the Central Committee excerpts of which were published in *Le Monde*, 14 May 1977, and his article in *Foreign Affairs*, January 1977 entitled, "A New Policy for the French Communist Party."

25. The communist deputy, Mr. Fiszbin, admitted in an interview with the editor of *France-Nouvelle*, Charles Haroche, on 20 June 1977, that there had been questions and even challenges raised by some party militants concerning the manner in which the Central Committee had acted. See also the account of two party dissidents, Gérard Molina and Yves Vargas, *Dialogue à l'intérieur du Parti communiste français* (Paris: François Maspero, 1978), pp. 59-66.

26. See, "Les socialistes et la force de frappe," in *Le Nouvel Observateur*, 30 May 1977, and the article by Jacques Huntzinger, "A la recherche d'un compromis nucléaire," in the Socialist Party weekly, *L'Unité*, 3-9 June 1977.

the two parties brought into the open the considerable differences that separated them.

According to the press reports, the executive committee of the PS met on 23 July and raised a number of objections to the PCF proposals. In particular, the socialists were concerned whether the reference to national independence and the "tous azimuts" strategy would involve breaking all cooperative ties with the allies and adopting a neutralist orientation. If the response were affirmative, the PS could only reject it, but in any case, the terminology employed was objectionable because it raised doubts about the maintenance of France's alliances. Moreover, the PS criticized the conception of "collective responsibility" for the use of nuclear weapons as impractical and rejected the idea of a promise of "no first use" of nuclear arms because it would destroy the strategy of deterrence, given the distribution of forces in Europe.[27]

These disagreements were exacerbated after 26 July by Mitterrand's proposal to submit the question of maintaining the nuclear force to a referendum. Even though they admitted on the day after the second meeting of the working group that such a referendum would require a change in the constitution, the socialists still clung to their proposal, while the communists insisted that the idea of a referendum did not remove the need to formulate "a good policy of national defense." In point of fact, fundamental differences separated the two parties, and it soon became clear that the hesitations of the PS reflected Mr. Mitterrand's skepticism about France's nuclear capability. In an interview with "TF 1" on 27 July, the First Secretary of the PS was to declare that, "Personally, I am not convinced that the French nuclear force can play a deterrent role. . . . I only believe in arrangements; that is, I do not believe in total autonomy in matters of defense. I am afraid that if one reasons in any other way one arrives at a sort of nuclear Maginot line. The renunciation of nuclear weapons—that is our goal; negotiation is our method."[28] From that point on, the talk became tougher. The same day Mr. Fiterman, who led the communist delegation to the talks on updating the Common Program, announced following a meeting of the PCF politburo that, "there would be no agreement on an updated program if the leaders of the PS do not make a clear and irrevocable commitment on this question [of defense policy]. . . . The referendum cannot be used to avoid the immediate and pressing necessity for a clear commitment. . . ."[29]

All of the proposals elaborated by the working group between 17 May and 29 July had to be approved by the leaders of the three leftwing parties in mid-September, but on the defense questions agreement was limited to the

27. *Le Monde*, 26 July and *Le Figaro*, 27 July, 1977.
28. *Le Figaro*, 28 July and *Le Monde*, 29 July 1977.
29. *Le Monde*, 29 July 1977.

maintenance of the nuclear force pending the achievement of general disarmament. On the missions to be assigned to the nuclear force the differences in outlook were striking. Whereas, Mr. Mitterrand declared that he did not believe in the value of an autonomous French nuclear force and that someday the problem of defense would have to be faced at the European level, Mr. Marchais had replied that "in the present circumstances, the atomic 'force de frappe' remains the only valid deterrent and that the Communist Party is resolutely opposed to any new European defense community." As far as the independence of the nuclear force was concerned, according to the PFC, that did not imply neutrality and "did not in any way contradict the fact that France remains a member of the Atlantic Alliance, even if we think that eventually we should reach the goal of liquidating all military blocs."[30]

The polemics and exchanges of accusations continued right up until the meeting of the party leaders which was scheduled for 14 September. In a statement to "TF 1" on 3 August, Mr. Marchais declared bitterly that by proposing a referendum on nuclear policy Mr. Mitterrand had harmed the Left. Another communist spokesman, Mr. Leroy, for his part, shared the views expressed by *Le Figaro,* which saw in the idea of a referendum "a smokescreen around the socialists' uncertainties on matters of defense."[31] Moreover, Mr. Marchais judged the socialists' reticence "incomprehensible" after the agreements which had been reached on the "tous azimuts" strategy— a proposition which Mr. Loncle of the MRG immediately characterized as an abusive interpretation of the agreement. Mr. Miterrand replied in an interview published in the Socialist daily *Le Matin* (8 August 1977), in which he reproached the PCF for having qualified its acceptance of nuclear weapons with reservations about no first use, no anti-city strategy, and collective decision-making so that it ended up devoid of any deterrent effect. The following day, Mr. Marchais, writing in *l'Humanité,* gave a more precise interpretation of his idea of a "tous azimuts" deterrent and attempted to focus the divergencies between the two parties on the affair of the referendum.[32] But when *Le Monde* published on 10 August the text of the agreement entered into on 28 July on the updating of the chapter of the Common Program relating to "Disarmament and National Defense" the controversy broke out anew, with each of the parties imputing to the other the respon-

30. Interviews of George Marchais on "Antenne 2" as reported in *Le Figaro,* 29 July 1977 and *Le Monde* 30 July 1977. Mr. Kanapa had been even more explicit in an article in *L'Humanité* on 25 July: "To deprive our country of the only deterrent force at its disposal would lead . . . very quickly to placing it under the American umbrella. We want no protectorate. . . . Sovereign independence is . . . a vital necessity."

31. *L'Humanité,* 5 August 1977. See also the Mitterrand's reply in *Le Matin,* 8 August.

32. *Le Monde,* 10 August 1977. See also the statement of Defense Minister Yvon Bourges in *Le Monde* 11 August and *Le Figaro* 10 August 1977.

sibility for leaking the information to the press and contesting the accuracy of what was revealed. The explanations furnished by the leaders of the two principal leftist parties make it possible to assess the scope of their differences.

1) The referendum, according to the communists, made no sense; while the socialists felt that such a procedure followed directly from the principle that "the final decision should belong to the people of France."[33]

2) The communists envisioned a form of deterrence "tous azimuts" while the socialists saw in that strategy the manifestation of a dangerous neutralism. However, Mr. Marchais did spell out in an interview with radio station "France-Inter" on 10 August, that he was using the term in its gaullist sense. According to him, General de Gaulle was supposed to have said in a speech delivered on 29 January 1968 to the *Centre des Hautes Etudes Militaires,* "Our strategy must be 'tous azimuts' to show clearly that France should be able to defend herself against anyone." It was that conception that the communists supported, he said, and the General Secretary remarked ironically on the contradictions surrounding Mr. Mitterrand's worries about the missiles aimed at capitalist countries while he was quite comfortable about those pointing toward a socialist country.

3) Concerning the matter of collective decision-making on the use of nuclear weapons, Mr. Marchais had explained that there could be no question of giving any sort of veto power to four or five people who could be consulted. Thus, the collegial decision would not deprive the "force de frappe" of its deterrent value. The socialists thought differently.

4) The communists had conceded that the anti-city strategy would be maintained so long as the countries that possessed nuclear weapons had not agreed on "a strategy which was aimed not at cities nor at populations but at military bases." On this point the original differences had been surmounted. But the communists persisted in thinking that an agreement on no first use of nuclear force was compatible with the practice of a strategy of deterrence. The socialists estimated that such an engagement on the part of France could permit the Soviet Union to impose its will on her without needing to have recourse to nuclear weapons, given the imbalance of conventional forces in Europe.

33. In a statement to *Le Monde* on 11 August, Mr. Charles Hernu indicated that a Government of the Left would only have recourse to the referendum procedure in the case that disarmament negotiations failed. "Then it would be appropriate to consult the French people on whether we should unilaterally disarm our country," he said. The general tenor of the agreements said to have been reached on 28 July was revealed in *Le Monde,* 10 August 1977. An anonymous commentator let it be understood that the three party leaders could stipulate at their summit meeting in September whether the referendum in question would bear on the multilateral disarmament treaty which the Government of the Left had committed itself to try to negotiate.

These differences were not smoothed out during the meeting of the three party leaders in September and it is clear that the disagreements on defense questions were an important element in the breakup of the talks on the updating of the Common Program.[34] Later on, the Communist and Socialist Parties, although protesting their desire to reach an agreement, continued to display their divisions and after the adoption of a resolution on defense by the national convention of the PS on 8 January 1978, the divorce became final. In the electoral campaign of March 1978, each of the principal Leftist parties relied on its own party program as it appealed to the voters. The communists used an "updated Common Program" which gave a prominent place to their propositions, but that also mentioned the initiatives of the socialists and left radicals on which there had been consensus.[35] The socialists, on the other hand, had come to an agreement on a compromise formula which took into account the nuclear force while awaiting the possibility of giving it up in favor of a general disarmament. The tactical agreement between the parties which was reached following the first round of the legislative elections did not include even the slightest allusion to the litigious questions of defense and foreign policy; the only things mentioned were "the initiatives taken to progress along the path of general disarmament."[36]

The Limits of Consensus

The electoral defeat of the Left Union and its disintegration immediately after the balloting was over, together with the breach which subsequently opened between the three parties that made up the Left Union, have led to the *de facto* abandonment of the Common Program. Even though it is now a dead letter, the negotiations over updating the Program are indicative of the extent to which the views of the PS and the PCF on questions of French defense and national security have evolved. The unilateral renunciation of nuclear weapons and of the strategy of deterrence, formerly considered to be an essential article of the Opposition's program, was once again called into question in the course of a long process of self-examination marked by tergiversations within the PS and by a sudden turnabout on the part of the PCF. But if the communists' support for the idea of national defense based on a minimum deterrent capability and the implementation of a "tous azimuts"

34. The persistence of disagreements on defense policy was illustrated by the contradictory reports of the summit meeting given by Francois Mitterrand to "Europe 1" on 28 September and by Jean Kanapa in *L'Humanité* on 30 September. See also the commentary in *Le Monde,* 1 October 1977.

35. *Programme commun de gouvernement actualisé. Introduction de Georges Marchais* (Paris: Editions Sociales, 1978).

36. *Le Monde,* 15 March 1978.

strategy was clear and unambiguous, once the Central Committee had decided to change directions, the socialists' acceptance of the nuclear force was arrived at in an atmosphere of confusion and was hedged about with reservations. The most important of these were the doubts expressed by Mr. Mitterrand, the First Secretary of the PS, who had admitted that he did not believe in France's capability to mount an autonomous defense and had indicated that alliances offered greater security.

In fact, the main problem for the socialist leadership was to reassure their own militants, who were not on the same wave length as the experts on the party's defense committee, and who had been made uneasy by the absence of any democratic debate within the PCF prior to the Central Committee's decision in favor of the nuclear force. At the outset, the change in attitude by the PCF had caught the PS by surprise; the socialists could not modify their positions so easily and had to contend with an anti-nuclear opposition group which developed with its ranks. The national convention on defense issues that met in Paris on 7-8 January 1978 was specifically designed to allow the PS to surmount the divisions that had emerged by finding some middle ground between the principle of renouncing nuclear weapons and the need to maintain them during a transition phase pending a general disarmament. In addition, if there was no question of reintegrating France into NATO, neither was there any wish to give up the possibility of participating in the elaboration of alliance strategies or of playing an active role in the defense of Europe.

The draft resolution on defense matters that had been adopted by the political bureau of the PS on 9 November 1977 attempted to synthesize the different points of view of the several factions. It insisted on the need for disarmament, set out as a goal the renunciation of nuclear weapons, and reasserted the party's fidelity to the mutual defense pact constituted by the Atlantic Alliance. The resolution also reflected the conceptions of the CERES group which was concerned to preserve the French capability for autonomous action to prevent Europe from being turned into a nuclear battleground, but the recognition of the necessity for nuclear weapons as a means of implementing such a policy was left in the shadows. Upon close examination, this text appeared to have been less the "definition of an authentic defense policy than the proclamation of a strategy of disarmament, accompanied by a continual reference to French membership in the Atlantic camp."[37] However, some socialists judged it to be still too soft on nuclear weapons and they introduced an amendment that sought to halt their development and to proceed unilaterally toward "the denuclearization of the national territory"

---

37. See the article by Jacques Isnard, "L'imbroglio," *Le Monde,* 8-9 January 1978.

by abandoning the Mirage IV bombers, the Pluton missiles (tactical nuclear weapons) and the land-based ballistic missiles on the plateau of Albion. In an effort to block this maneuver, the CERES presented a manifesto entitled: "For an Independent Defense: The Necessary Condition for Implementing the Common Program."[38]

During the period immediately preceding the national convention the spokesmen for the various groups within the party had worked overtime providing the newspapers with a stream of articles expressing their views. From the outset of the convention, it became clear that the anti-nuclear forces had the wind in their sails and they sought to modify the draft resolution in a way that reflected their theses. At the end of a confused debate and after a battle over a series of amendments presented by the CERES and by the anti-nuclear faction, the PS finally adopted a compromise text dealing with the questions of defense and security.[39] Although a number of questions remained unanswered, the party leadership considered the debate closed. Outside observers could not help but wonder, however, what line the PS would follow in the event that it had to exercise power. At least four tentative conclusions can be suggested:

1) The text adopted by the socialists' national convention hardly helped at all to clarify what sort of defense policy a Government of the Left might apply. The draft resolution proposed by the party leaders was itself an attempt to compromise irreconcilable positions and it obviously reflected the proposals that had been submitted to the executive committee in November 1976. The amendments that were added certainly did not lend greater coherence.

2) The CERES was violently attacked by the *rapporteur*, Mr. Jean-Pierre Cot, who charged it with "nationalism," the same fault which had been imputed to the PCF a few days before the convention,[40] and all the amendments proposed by the CERES were rejected.

3) The anti-nuclear advocates forced the leadership to accept some of their amendments, such as the decision to sacrifice the Mirage IV aircraft and the missiles on the plateau of Albion on the altar of disarmament.[41] The only

38. The texts submitted to the national convention were published in a supplement to the PS monthly, *Le Poing et la rose,* No. 65, November 1977.

39. The final resolution was published in *Le Poing et la rose,* No. 67, January 1978. The proceedings of the convention were reported in the press on 9 January and even the newspapers that were oriented toward the Left expressed reservations about the conduct of the session. See, for example, the articles of Michel Field in *Le Quotidien de Paris* and Jean-Pierre Mithois in *Le Matin.*

40. See, *La lettre de l'Unité,* 6 January 1978.

41. The final resolution affirmed that, "The willingness to reconsider the Mirage IV aircraft and eventually the missiles on the plateau of Albion would constitute a concrete gesture that would permit us to launch a diplomatic offensive of great scope." It stipulated

element of the nuclear force that would be maintained at full strength was the missile-launching nuclear submarines, and they would be retained only until a disarmament agreement would make it possible to give them up. Although the convention refused to adopt the statement that, "the possession of nuclear weapons was inconsistent with the realization of socialist objectives," the opponents of nuclear weapons did obtain agreement to insert into the final resolution a paragraph which noted the "crisis of the concept of deterrence" in a world where the number of powers that possess nuclear weapons is increasing and where the boundary between nuclear and conventional weapons is becoming blurred. At their insistence, the PS finally committed itself to create the conditions that would permit an alternative to nuclear defense within five years.

4) The PS maintained a certain measure of ambiguity about its defense policy even though the First Secretary of the party had declared that the gaullist heritage had to be accepted. In fact, this acceptance was hedged about with conditions such that nuclear deterrence lost its credibility. Moreover, some commentators remarked on the similarities between the views of Mr. Mitterrand and those of Mr. Giscard d'Estaing, both of whom had expressed doubts about the effectiveness of an autonomous defense and placed their faith above all in the solidity of France's alliances. In this regard, the very firm intervention of Mr. Mitterrand against an amendment proposed by the CERES only added fuel to the controversy over the persistence of "Atlanticism" within the PS. The CERES had demanded that, "France not allow itself to be drawn into the path of a harmonization of our strategy with that of the United States in Europe, notably by reinforcing its conventional military capabilities in conformance with the wishes of the Pentagon. . . . It would rule out any doctrine for the use of our forces that could lead them to participate automatically in a forward battle in the heart of Europe." Mr. Mitterrand demanded that the convention vote against that amendment "without hesitation," and it was defeated.

If the PCF spoke out more clearly on matters of national defense and seemed to have accepted nuclear deterrence without reservation, should one credit the communists with a coherent program on these issues? In the first place, on one might wonder about what might have motivated the Communist Party, which had adamantly opposed nuclear weapons ever since the Stockholm appeal of 1950, suddenly to become the strongest supporter of a French nuclear force whose illusions and risks it had for so long denounced.

---

that the renunciation of nuclear arms would not be undertaken except within "the conditions of the global disarmament strategy of a Government of the Left." This formulation is less clear-cut than that contained in the original draft resolution of the leadership in which the abandonment of the manned aircraft and the surface-to-surface ballistic missiles "obviously remains subordinated to the effective advance of the [disarmament] negotiations."

Moreover, it was argued that from now on the nuclear force was the only instrument of an independent defense because the powers that be had neglected the development of the conventional forces, which were no longer able to fulfill that mission.

In that form the argument is specious and casts doubt on the sincerity of the communists' acceptance of the logic of deterrence. Indeed, it would appear that they considered nuclear weapons a second best alternative in the absence of a strong conventional army. However, no one ever explained what sort of policy in respect to conventional weapons would have made it possible to do without nuclear arms. But it is clear that even with greatly increased firepower French conventional forces could never have any deterrent effect against a major power equipped with atomic weapons. In addition, if one admits that the conventional military forces have declined over the years, is still remains to be seen against what sort of threats the PCF judged them to be inadequate. Is the determining factor in this respect the assymmetry in the balance of forces between the Warsaw Pact and NATO or the increase in the strength of the *Bundeswehr?*

Although the PCF proclaimed its attachment to the Atlantic Alliance, it was singularly undisturbed about the threat posed by the Soviet Union and its allies to Western Europe, except to accuse those who mentioned it of being anti-Soviet. On the other hand, for several years past it had insisted on the dangers of "German-American collusion to ensure the triumph of imperialism." It is probable that the economic importance of the Federal Republic and the growing influence that it exercises in European and Atlantic councils had incited the French communists to want to preserve the nuclear weapons which differentiate the military policy of France from that of her German ally and which provide a measure of insurance against any interference from the state that possesses the strongest conventional military force in Western Europe. Furthermore, maintaining the national nuclear deterrent would tend to put the brakes on any temptation towards Atlantic integration and would interfere with the creation of a European defense community. Thus, foreign policy considerations no doubt influenced the PCF decision in favor of nuclear weapons and their use within the framework of a "tous azimuts" strategy. It is not surprising that this initiative raised questions within the PS where some feared a shift toward armed neutrality and a rupture of France's international commitments.[42]

The ambiguities surrounding the PCF's defense policy also were in evidence when it came to the way in which the party defined the concept of deterrence. To be sure, the "tous azimuts" strategy in the gaullist sense of

---

42. In an article that appeared shortly after the rupture of the talks on updating the Common Program, Jacques Huntzinger saw in the foreign policy of the PCF the main reason for its choice of "an autarkic national defense." According to him, the Communist Party had

the term would not have aroused so many controversies if the communists had not also announced that, "the determination of targets and the aiming of the launchers will be reviewed as a consequence." On the other hand, who could help but doubt the deterrent capability of a middle power that abandoned an anti-city strategy and confided the responsibility for using nuclear weapons to a committee. As Mr. Joël Le Theule pointed out, "any other strategy than an anti-city strategy would require a panoply of weapons which is beyond our reach, and to rely on a committee composed of a number of people to decide on the use of nuclear weapons would impose delays that an aggressor probably would not allow us."[43] We know that the PCF changed its mind on the abandonment of the anti-city strategy and attempted, although without great success, to convince the experts that it was possible to adapt the principle of collegial decision making to the exigencies of manipulating nuclear weapons within the framework of a strategy of deterrence.[44] Finally, it considered that the agreement on no first use of nuclear weapons, proposed by the Warsaw Treaty Organization in November 1976, was not incompatible with the practice of deterrence. Yet it is obvious that any such engagement would weaken the defensive capability of the country confronting an adversary powerfully armed with conventional weapons and would deprive it of a decisive incentive against any aggression.

Lastly, the aims of the PCF program were not at all in keeping with the means which were allocated for their implementation. In effect, the party was proposing to upgrade substantially the status of the military, to reinforce the conventional units and to modernize the nuclear forces, while all the time letting it be understood that the costs of those operations would not exceed the available resources and that there would be no great enlargement of the budget nor any increase in the proportion of the national income allocated to defense. In support of these arguments, communist spokesmen pointed to the savings that were going to be realized from the application of the Common Program (the nationalization of the armaments industry, for example), but it is scarcely likely that such expedients would have sufficed to cover the new expenses involved in implementing the defense policy of the PCF.

The conflicts over national defense between the partners of the Union of the Left led the PCF and the PS to refine their ideas about these matters, but

not opted clearly for the Western camp and remained in the middle of the stream. See, "La politique étrangère du P. C. F.," *Le Monde,* 2-3 October 1977.

43. Joël Le Theule, "Les ambiguités de la politique de défense du P.C.F.," *Le Monde,* 29 July 1977. Ambassador François de Rose expressed a similar point of view in "Indépendance on neutralité," *Le Monde,* 20 July 1977.

44. See the *proposition de loi* on national defense, *Journal Officiel, Assemblée Nationale,* Document No. 511, 23 June 1978, pp. 6-14.

they did not lead them to define a common position. The two parties did indeed come to recognize the reality of nuclear weapons and they did attempt to integrate them into their global strategy, but their proposals were too discordant to permit any agreement about how national defense should be organized and collective security assured. To tell the truth, their impassioned polemics on defense reflected different foreign policy preferences which were only alluded to, but which seemed to underlie the positions defended by both the socialists and the communists. In this respect, former Prime Minister Couve de Murville could not resist pointing to the tie between the vicissitudes of the Union of the Left and those of detente between the United States and the Soviet Union. Should one then deduce a connection between the actions or the positions taken by the leaders of the two parties and the policies of Washington or Moscow? Mr. Couve de Murville was inclined to think so and he declared "purely and simply that the Socialist Party is turned toward the United States and the Communist Party toward the Soviet Union," and that these opposite leanings explain their profound disagreement on the position of France "faced by these two giant rival-accomplices who seek to dominate and everywhere they split the allegiances of others between themselves."[45] Thus, the adherence of the PCF to the international communist movement and the European and Atlantic options of the PS would have constituted a major obstacle to the formulation of any unified defense policy for the Left and it seems probable that those parties will not be able to surmount their differences so long as the European continent remains divided between two antagonistic systems.

Within Europe as it exists today, the most realistic defense policy for France remains the one that was defined by General de Gaulle. It implies the freedom to decide about the use of military force, cooperation with France's allies and the recourse to the use of nuclear weapons to preserve her vital national interests. By denying the possibility of an autonomous French defense, Mr. Mitterrand stands in opposition to that philosophy. By advancing the "tous azimuts" strategy, the PCF is closer to de Gaulle's position, but it espouses a conception of defense that is scarcely credible in the event of an East-West confrontation. As far as nuclear weapons are concerned, if all the political parties now support them, that unanimity does not mean that they have arrived at a national consensus on the military and political role which those weapons are to be assigned. In that respect, the debate remains wide open and is not likely to end any time soon.

45. Maurice Couve de Murville, "La gauche face aux grands problèmes nationaux," *Le Monde,* 6 October 1977.

Recent Developments in Strategic Doctrine

D. BRUCE MARSHALL

It is particularly appropriate, in the case of France, to begin an examination of defense policy with a discussion of strategic doctrine, because such doctrine provides both a definition of the threats to vital national security interests and a plan to meet those threats. It is both an overview of the specific situation confronting the nation and a logically derived plan for organizing, equipping and training the forces which bear the responsibility for national defense.

The French case is particularly interesting for several reasons: First, because France is the only one of all the middle powers that seeks to play an independent role which is not confined to a single region of the globe. By contrast, Britain is heavily dependent on the United States for the maintenance of its nuclear capability, while the other major industrial states either lack nuclear forces altogether or, like India, lack the ability to develop them on a scale adequate to seriously threaten one of the superpowers. Even China, which has some nuclear capability, apparently lacks the delivery systems necessary to mount a credible deterrent or to act outside of her immediate border regions. Next, France has sought to retain the ties that link her to the rest of Western Europe and the Atlantic Alliance while developing a capacity for independent action and has not sought neutrality, but rather has attempted actively to encourage changes in the international distribution of power that would promote greater stability and increased security for Europe as a whole. In this role, French official and unofficial specialists have advanced telling criticisms of the existing NATO strategies for European security. Finally, having ended her role as a colonial power, France nevertheless maintains an extensive network of contacts and commitments with the former colonial countries and with other states of the Third World and seeks to develop cooperative relations with them that will tend to diminish the likelihood of serious international conflicts in regions such as Africa, the Middle East, the Mediterranean and Latin America.

By examining the French vision of the present international security system and the role they seek to play within it, it should be possible not only to understand more fully the priorities which they have established and thus anticipate their actions more accurately, but it may also be possible fruitfully to contrast their experience with that of other middle powers in a period when the domination of the international system by the two superpowers appears to have diminished somewhat.

Major Elements of French Strategy

The central idea underlying French strategic doctrine is summed up in the theory of "proportional deterrence" which holds that a state with relatively limited nuclear capabilities can deter a much larger nuclear power (as well as any non-nuclear power, of course) with a high degree of probability under most circumstances, because deterrence is thought to depend on the relative value of the alternative outcomes of a nuclear clash, not on the relative size of the nuclear forces to one another. This theory rests on a number of assumptions: First, the creation of nuclear weapons and long-range missiles is thought to have fundamentally altered politico-military relations by rendering all states vulnerable in the face of a threat of nuclear attack. Second, the U.S. nuclear guarantee does not necessarily protect Europe against an attack from the East because the U.S. cannot be expected to use its central strategic weapons systems against the USSR unless the American homeland is struck first; to do so would invite immediate retaliation on the U.S. Third, the growing nuclear parity between the two superpowers makes the possible use of NATO tactical nuclear forces less likely to be attempted because the danger of escalation is excessive, and, likely to be unsuccessful because the USSR is gaining superior capability. Fourth, the geographic separation of France from the central European front, while narrow, is nevertheless clearcut enough so that an attack on Germany is not necessarily an attack on France. Finally, the political position of France is fundamentally different from that of Germany, since it has no outstanding claims on any part of the Soviet bloc, nor does it pose a threat to any vital Soviet interests. Hence, in a crisis situation, the separate French nuclear force contributes to the stability of the regional deterrent by complicating the calculations of a potential attacker, and if deterrence were to fail, it still could induce an attacker to forego the destruction and occupation of France by threatening substantial destruction of the industrial and population centers of the opponent's homeland.[1]

---

1. The best general treatment of the development of French nuclear strategy is to be found in Lucien Poirier, *Des Stratégies nucléaires* (Paris: Hachette, 1977).

Thus, the French strategy plays upon the asymmetrical costs and benefits to a potential nuclear opponent of pressing an attack on Western Europe to the extreme of over-running the "sanctuary" defined by French national territory at the cost of massive damage to his own homeland. The force structure initially derived from this general doctrine embodied a radical separation between the nuclear and conventional components and gave clear priority to the strategic nuclear force (FNS). By 1972, according to the figures set forth in the *White Paper on National Defense* issued by the Ministry of Defense, the FNS consisted of 36 Mirage IV aircraft capable of carrying nuclear weapons of approximately 100kt; 18 land-based ballistic missiles with a range of 330km capable of delivering 150kt warheads; and two nuclear powered submarines capable of launching 16 missiles each armed with M2 warheads of approximately 450kt each and able to travel 2500km.[2] This force was regarded as sufficienty varied, mobile, and invulnerable to constitute a meaningful deterrent, and plans were made for its continued development both in numbers and in quality.

Alongside the FNS, the conventional forces were divided into two units. The "maneuver force" had the task of opposing an attacker at the subnuclear level, forcing him to concentrate his forces and to give the government time to assess its options before resorting to a nuclear response. The addition of tactical nuclear weapons to the conventional armory was seen as a way to strengthen the defensive capability of the ground forces and to signal the imminent approach to the strategic nuclear threshold if an enemy persists. The other conventional component, the Territorial Defense Forces (DOT) were redesigned to defend the nuclear installations and, together with the *Gendarmerie,* to police the country in case of infiltrations or sabotage. These forces were designed not to wage a limited, conventional war—which in any case was beyond the capability of France—but to guarantee that the FNS would survive to perform its deterrent role.

During the subsequent years, the FNS has been further strengthened by the addition of two nuclear submarines, with a third to become operational in 1979. It also is being equipped with longer range missiles (3000km) and increased payloads (500kt), improved land-based missiles with similar characteristics and more modern aircraft capable of carrying air-borne missiles. Additional qualitative improvements are currently under development which will give France a new generation of missiles (the M4) with multiple warhead capability and longer range (4000km), and plans are well advanced for a new generation of nuclear submarines.

2. *White Paper on National Defense,* Vol. 1, 1972, Ambassade de France, Service de Presse et d'Information, New York.

At the time when President Giscard d'Estaing took office in 1974, France possessed both a significant deterrent capability and a doctrine that sought to integrate the various components of the national armed forces into a force posture which seemed to official spokesmen to ensure that France would not be drawn into any continental battle against her will and that the survival of the national "sanctuary" would be relatively secure against a nuclear threat and totally secure against any conventional attack.

A number of ambiguities remained, however, about critical points in the French doctrine, particularly concerning the articulation of conventional and nuclear forces, the role of tactical nuclear weapons, and the contribution that France could make to regional or global security efforts. Several factors tended to cast doubt on whether the French strategy could be implemented. On one hand, some critics raised questions about the financial feasibility of the FNS for the long term, particularly in view of the high costs of research and development, additional infrastructure such as better surveillance capabilities and communications networks, and the mounting costs of weapons production for a limited market. Others pointed to political restraints arising out of the disappearance of a strong national leader such as de Gaulle whose reputation for independent action gave credibility to the threat of nuclear retaliation, and the relatively ambiguous national consensus on defense policy that seemed to restrict the possible actions of a future president who would not enjoy the same popular sanction as de Gaulle. The other chapters in this section examine some of these restraints.

More serious, from the point of view of the coherence of French doctrine, were a number of other international developments. First, the rapid expansion of nuclear missile technology, especially in the aftermath of the 1972 SALT I interim agreement, increased the risk that more accurate weapons might easily eliminate the land-based components of the FNS, while improvements in detection and the installation of ABM sites required greater attention to penetration aids and larger numbers of warheads to maintain the capability of the French force, although because it sought only to threaten urban population centers, improved guidance mechanisms were less vital than increased payloads, and longer range missiles. The latter were particularly important as a means of improving the effectiveness of the submarine launched systems which were to be equipped with the M4 missile capable of travelling 4000km and delivering 3-7 warheads totalling about 1mt. The rapid expansion of Soviet missile technology and the continued pursuit of bilateral agreements between the U.S. and the USSR on offensive strategic weapons also raised the possibility that Europe might find itself more exposed to conventional threats from a larger and still growing conventional force in the hands of the Warsaw Pact. The growing imbalance of conventional forces in Europe accentuated two basic ambiguities in the French doctrine. First, it increased the likelihood that early use of tactical nuclear weapons would be required to halt a conventional attack in force on the NATO positions, thereby rekindling the debate about the efficacy of tactical weapons as the "testing" device envisioned by the French strategy. More importantly, however, it also reopened the question of how French doctrine, which was oriented to the protection of specific French territorial interests, could be related to NATO actions in order that France might contribute to the security of Europe as a whole and to the fulfillment of broader goals of the Atlantic Alliance of which France was still a member. Finally, the Middle East war of 1973, mounting tensions in the Horn of Africa, where French forces were engaged in maintaining the security of the Territory of the Afars and Issas, and continuing local conflicts in the Chad and along the borders of the former Spanish Sahara among Mauretania, Algeria and Morocco, reinforced the awareness that the nuclear deterrent could not safeguard French interests and maintain her commitments in regions of the world outside of Europe.

The New Debate

This combination of international developments in fields as disparate as nuclear technology, the balance of global forces between the U.S. and the USSR, the European regional conventional balance, and local conflicts in other areas, all coincided during the years after 1972 to provoke a continuing debate about the nature of French strategy which was very different from the argument over whether or not to build a national deterrent that had dominated the 1960s. At issue in the 1970s was the adequacy of the doctrine that had been elaborated to deter a direct attack and to enable France to defend her interests if deterrence were to fail.

The participants in that debate were a varied assortment of active and retired military officers with widely different backgrounds in French and NATO posts. The most influential among them were Colonel Marc Geneste, an associate of General Beaufre in the Institute for Strategic Studies and a frequent contributor to the journal, *Stratégie;*[3] Commandant Guy Brossolet, the author of a very provocative *Essai sur la non-bataille* which appeared in 1975,[4] and General Pierre-Marie Gallois, probably the foremost French critic of NATO military strategy and the author of a series of studies that sought to explicate the significance of the superpowers actions for the future of French strategy.[5]

---

3. A brief overview of Marc Geneste's general view of French strategy can be found in English in *Orbis,* vol. 19 (Summer 1975), No. 2.

4. Guy Brossolet, *Essai sur la non-bataille* (Paris: Ed. Belin, 1975).

5. See, in particular, Pierre-Marie Gallois, *Stratégies de l'Age nucléaire* (Paris: Calmann-Levy, 1960); *Les Paradoxes de la Paix,* 1967 and *La Grande Berne,* (Paris: Plon, 1975).

Geneste's main concern was to explore the implications for French strategy of the rapidly emerging nuclear parity between the U.S. and the USSR which threatened to neutralize the central nuclear weapons systems of both sides and leave Europe open to greatly increased threats from the imbalance of conventional forces which greatly favored the countries of the Warsaw Pact. In an important essay, "Triomphe de la défensive"[6] he argued for the restructuring of French forces around tactical nuclear weapons in order to deny a quick victory in case of a conventional attack, thereby re-establishing the continuity of risk that escalation would result. Hence, deterrence could be preserved.

Brossolet perceived the impossibility for France, given her very limited resources, to wage a conventional battle in Europe, but he discounted the prospect of tactical nuclear exchanges as well, since they involved unacceptable risks of escalation and in any case were destined only to serve the very limited role of identifying the nuclear threshold. By contrast to Geneste, he proposed a reorganization of French forces into small, highly mobile units armed with precision-guided munitions and backed by helicopters and heavy armament which would form a network of defensive positions 120km deep along a front running across the entire northern part of France from the Channel to Switzerland. Tactical missile units would be separated from the conventional forces to ensure that they were available only for the deterrent role, and it was the prospect of becoming ensnarled in an impenetrable web of strongly armed defenses that was expected to render the prospect of a quick victory improbable, and hence to reinforce the deterrent effect.

In Gallois' view, both the preceding analyses were faulty because they failed to credit the potential enemy with the intelligence to understand what was being prepared, they underestimated the means at his disposal, and they misunderstood the nature of the objective. Early in 1976, Gallois published *L'Adieu aux armées,*[7] another in a series of vigorous polemics against the failure of the government to draw the logical conclusions from the changes taking place in the relations between the two superpowers. In it he argued that Geneste's thesis is invalid because the probable enemy is much better equipped with tactical nuclear weapons than France or the NATO allies, whose nuclear forces are controlled by the U.S. and, therefore, are likely not to be used at all. Hence, an assailant would have the option of resorting to tactical weapons to wipe out the smaller forces arrayed against him. Indeed, it might be enough merely to threaten their destruction to bring about a surrender. Still more plausible was some other less violent form of action that

6. *Stratégies,* No. 39, 1975.

7. Pierre-Marie Gallois, *L'Adieu aux armées* (Paris: Editions Albin Michel, 1976).

would render tactical weapons entirely useless. Similarly, Brossolet's proposal, although based on a clear insight into the weakness of the established doctrine which linked conventional and nuclear weapons, did not offer a coherent response, because it assumed that the enemy would play according to rules that were not in its favor. Moreover, the notion of a "test" of an opponent's intentions appeared unnecessary to Gallois, since no sane leader would contemplate an invasion of a country that possessed nuclear weapons for any other purpose than to destroy it completely. Taking hostages or chipping away a piece of territory—Brossolet mentions the Ile de Yeu or Corsica as possible targets—makes no sense at all in the face of a potential nuclear riposte.

The heart of Gallois' argument, to which he returns again and again in this, as in his earlier works, is that in the nuclear age, France has a specific role to play which is defined by her continental position and the limited resources at her disposal to defend the security of that position. If she is attacked, she will have no other recourse but to retaliate massively against an attacker. Hence, there is no need to "test" the opponents intentions. Once the frontier is crossed their intentions are obvious. Neither is it possible for France to contribute to the battle for Europe with conventional forces, for to do so would only weaken France without in any way affecting the outcome of the battle whose result is foreordained, in any case. Given her geographic position and the nature of her capabilities, France inevitably faces an "all-or-nothing" choice in the event an enemy attacks her borders. The only way to improve her security is by improving the size, capability and control of the nuclear forces in order to deter such an assault. However, in his view, effective deterrence requires drastic changes in the structure of the armed forces, beginning with a reinforcement of the strategic nuclear component. Despite official claims, the FNS is not yet "sufficient" and must be constantly modernized, for example, by improving access to reconnaissance satellites and by increasing the number and capabilities of the submarine fleet and the land-based missile units. To carry out such a program requires abandoning the mass army of conscripts, building a professional force of specialists, and concentrating expenditures where they can be cost-effective rather than dispersing them over a wide range of armaments that contribute nothing to deterrent capability.

The Policy of Giscard d'Estaing

For a number of political reasons not directly related to this debate, President Giscard d'Estaing began soon after assuming office in 1974 to shift the emphasis in French defense policy away from nuclear weapons and to reinforce the conventional component. In a series of press conferences and television interviews as well as other official declarations during 1974 and 75, he expressed concern over the weakness of French conventional forces and indicated that France's security interests in Europe and in other regions such as the Mediterranean and Africa were suffering because of the priority given to the nuclear deterrent.[8] These concerns were presented in a speech to the Institute de Hautes Etudes de Défense Nationale on 1 June 1976 in which Giscard took issue with prevailing doctrine and with its critics.[9]

After endorsing the purpose of maintaining "autonomy of decision" and recognizing that the continued existence of the nuclear force was essential for the future, he indicated that he considered the present level of the FNS "sufficient" for the needs of deterring an attack that in any case seemed very improbable. Consequently, he objected that the existing strategic doctrine left France in an "impasse" unable to respond to other, more immediate threats arising from the many varied sources of instability in the modern world which ranged from disrupted communications links to local disorders in areas of special concern. He also questioned the political consequences of the reliance on the FNS without a strong conventional force to support it, because it left the government facing an "all-or-nothing" choice at the outset of any conflict. Finally, since nuclear deterrence could only secure French national territory, it left French interests inadequately protected in the region between the Iron Curtain and the French border where geographical contiguity seemed to rule out a narrow definition of security interests.

Hence, the proposal to strengthen conventional forces was intended to serve several purposes. First, it was thought that it would contribute to the credibility of the deterrent because it would ensure the continuity of risk and avoid creating an "impasse" where aggressive actions would not warrant nuclear retaliation. Second, by increasing the means at the President's disposal, France could play a more active role in the wider European theater, particularly in "complex situations" which might arise and in which the behavior of some other states—presumably meaning the U.S.—might be impossible to predict. Under those conditions, France could function as part of "a single military ensemble" within a larger area of the continent, not just within the confines of the national "sanctuary." Finally, improved conventional forces would permit France to act outside of Europe to protect specific commitments and to influence future events, as for example, by providing a limited military force to stabilize the situation in Lebanon, as was proposed by Giscard during his trip to the United States in May.

---

    8. See the press conferences of 24 October 1974, 4 March 1975, 25 March 1975, 30 October 1975, the interview with "Antenne 2," on 12 November 1975. In *Politique Etrangère de la France*. Paris: Ministère des Affaires Etrangères, (cited hereafter as *PEF*).
    9. *Défense Nationale*, July 1976, pp. 5-20, especially pp. 13-17.

To serve these ends, Giscard proposed to restructure the ground forces into larger units capable of engaging in "battle," a word he chose explicitly to emphasize their conventional mission. The surface navy was to be reequipped and the Air Force provided with a new generation of Mirage 2000 intercepters. The clear intent of this effort was to give France a capability to intervene in areas where French interests were less directly involved than on the European continent. In those areas, as he explained, "the conflicts that have occurred since the end of the Second World War never involved the use of the nuclear forces, or even the probability of their use."[10]

The "loi de programmation 1977-82" spelled out the same ideas in detail and also made clear that the acquisition of new conventional forces had to be conducted within the limits set by the military budget, as Giscard had indicated during his news conference of 24 October 1974. Inevitably, that involved stretching out the planned expansion of the nuclear force, and in particular abandoning a third missile unit for the land-based forces, and cancelling the sixth nuclear submarine, at least pending completion of studies on a new generation of vessels and improved missiles.[11]

To add to the speculation, the Chief of the General Staff, General Guy Mery, published an article in the journal, *Defense Nationale,* which appeared the same day and discussed in more detail the conception of a French role in the "forward battle" for Germany.[12] They reflected the sentiments expressed also in the preamble to the *Rapport* on the Loi de Programmation 1977 published the previous month in which it was argued that "territorial integrity" was a necessary, but not a sufficient condition of national security, since the latter, depends directly on the balance of forces within Europe. Thus it was argued, "It would be illusory indeed to hope that France might retain anything more than a diminished sovereignty if its neighbors came to be occupied by a hostile power or simply to pass under its control. The security of the whole of Western Europe is, therefore, essential to France."[13] While the government remained very discreet about precisely what actions might be contemplated, these declarations seemingly were intended to suggest a greater willingness on the part of France to play a role during peacetime in a joint European defense effort so as to hasten the political process of integration. General Mery, therefore, rejected the course of action recommended by Gallois, which placed virtually total reliance on nuclear deterrence to protect the "sanctuary" within France's borders, partly for military reasons, but also for political

10. *Ibid.,* p. 14.
11. Gérard Vaillant, "Chronique" in *Défense Nationale,* July 1976, pp. 145-50.
12. Guy Méry, "Une armée pour quoi faire et comment?" in *Défense Nationale,* June 1976, pp. 20-8.
13. *Ibid.,* p. 22.

reasons, because it made it impossible for France to play a role in the shaping of a future European entity, and called into question the significance of France's continued membership in the Atlantic Alliance and the Western European Union.

In the months that followed these initiatives, the debate over strategic doctrine came to focus more clearly on two issues: the relative importance of nuclear and conventional forces, in particular of tactical nuclear weapons, and the geographical limits within which these arms would be deployed or where their use was contemplated. The latter issue was the central theme of a particularly lucid analysis by General Lucien Poirier, at that time the Research Director of the Fondation pour les Etudes de Défense Nationale and formerly a member of the Centre de Prospective et d'Evaluation which drafted the original studies that served as the basis for the elaboration of the deterrence strategy. Poirier pointed out that the new version of the doctrine enunciated by Giscard and Méry was predicated on a *political* judgment regarding the consequences of geographical contiguity: France could not avoid suffering the consequences of a conflict that involved its neighbors in Western Europe. From this assessment of current conditions, however, they inferred that a single, continuous military strategy was required to meet the security needs of the entire region. But in so doing they failed to recognize that, in Poirier's words, "The *contiguity* of strategic spaces did not signify their *continuity;* that is to say, an identification such that one might in practice consider that the defense of the first circle [the national territory] was so much a part of the second circle [the rest of the European region] as to dissolve itself within it."[14] That conclusion was open to question on two counts, Poirier argued; first, because it assumed that France would necessarily be implicated in any European conflict even if it were the result of "some hasty action by one of our allies"—which was one of the fears that had led General de Gaulle to end French participation in NATO. But if that were the case, then there would be no point in pretending that France enjoyed "autonomy of decision" to start with or in devoting great effort to constructing a nuclear deterrent, since there really was no freedom of action.

Giscard's language left unspecified the nature, timing, extent and circumstances under which French support for Germany or the Atlantic Alliance might be forthcoming, and in that sense he did not commit France anymore than de Gaulle had done. However, by the emphasis he placed on the element of the "battle" with conventional and tactical nuclear weapons, and by the reference which General Mery made to "enlarging the sanctuaries," a number of serious confusions were injected into the strategic doctrine that seriously

---

14. Lucien Poirier, "Le Deuxième Cercle" in *Le Monde Diplomatique,* July 1976, p. 22.

compromised its deterrent effect. The notion of a contiguous space giving rise to a continous strategy tended to reverse the relationship between the security of the national territory [the first circle] and that of the regions lying outside [the second circle]. Instead of deciding on external actions because they would contribute to deter an opponent from attacking the homeland, the implication was that the deterrent would be employed beyond the frontiers. But that was simply not a credible position, as General Mery himself recognized when he questioned whether the national will would exist to use nuclear force after the rest of Europe had been devastated.[15] Therefore, he felt it was necessary to posit French participation in a single "military ensemble" capable of winning a war within the contiguous European military space.

But it was precisely this point, which, in Poirier's view, undermined the credibility of the French strategic doctrine as it had been stated up to that time, because it implied that France would join its resources to those of the other allies in a battle that was bound to require tactical nuclear weapons; but in that process, it was bound to invite nuclear retaliation against its own territory. At the same time, given its very modest resources, there was little likelihood that the French contribution would greatly affect the outcome of a major confrontation in which the total power of the Soviet tactical nuclear armament would be committed. In short, by amalgamating into a vague generalization about deterrence an action whose outcome depends mainly on the power of the U.S. in Europe—a region far from its own borders and where it retains a large measure of discretion about the forces that might or might not be committed—and the action open to France, whose homeland is immediately threatened by any such action, looses sight of the requirements of "deterrence of the strong by the weak."[16]

Given the strategic discontinuity between the two regions, it is still possible to contribute to the deterrence of an attack in both, but it requires different policies. A weak nuclear state can only deter a much stronger nuclear state if it reserves its strategic forces for the single purpose of riposting against an assault on the homelands. It also must preserve enough conventional forces to be capable of defending its strategic installations and to oppose an initial resistance, with the possible use of tactical nuclear weapons to indicate that the threshold of central war is at hand. Beyond that, if there are other conventional forces available, there is no reason why they cannot be committed to other actions, assuming that national interests are directly served. To think that such alternatives in any way remove the necessity for an

---

15. *Défense Nationale,* June 1976, p. 27.
16. Poirier, "Le Deuxième Cercle," p. 23.

"all-or-nothing" choice when the homeland itself is directly threatened, however, is to misunderstand the nature of nuclear deterrence.

Poirier therefore concluded that, "The real problem lies in establishing practical measures to unite changing circumstances with enduring continuities; an egoistic defense of the citadel with the great adventure out beyond the castle walls. . . . As long as nuclear weapons retain their power to instill terror in the eyes of peoples and governments, the second circle will never become simply a prolongation of the first. To act beyond [the castle walls] it is necessary to leap over the moat, not to fill it in!"[17]

Another, more impassioned response to the shift in government outlook came from General Gallois who detected the "renunciation of a France defended in favor of a Europe protected."[18] Reviewing the same chain of events and statements noted earlier, Gallois stressed the political dimension of Giscard's concerns and speculated on the outlook of the general staff and the careerist interests of the professional military. The substance of his objections, however, is very close to Poirier's, with the critical difference that he places much greater importance on avoiding *any* involvement in the collective defense of Europe—an undertaking which he views as doomed to fail because of the asymmetries that have been allowed to develop in the strategies and capabilities of the Warsaw Pact and NATO. Thus, he views with great alarm any tendency to commit French forces beyond the defense of the hexagon, especially since the progress of the nuclear forces themselves is falling further behind schedule each year as a result of the diversion of funds to the maintenance of a large and expensive conscript army and to the refurbishing of the surface navy without regard to the new missions that it must fulfill. In his opinion, the more France seeks to employ military means outside the framework of deterrence, the greater will be her objective dependence on other, more powerful allies and the less her "autonomy of decision." Hence, instead of worrying about military actions to influence events in Africa, the Mediterranean or elsewhere—except for some small detachments stationed in French overseas territories for peacekeeping duties—Gallois argues that it is more vital to reduce to a minimum those areas of continuing dependence such as with respect to surveillance satellites and radars, to move ahead as rapidly as possible with technological development of the deterrent forces, and above all, to strengthen the submarine and land-based missiles components of the FNS.

17. *Ibid.*
18. Pierre-Marie Gallois, *Le Renoncement,* (Paris: Plon, 1977).

The Return to Orthodoxy

It would appear that the French authorities took to heart a number of the criticisms advanced by General Gallois, General Poirier and others during the summer and fall of 1976. The Minister of Defense, M. Yvon Bourges, reasserted the determination of the government, "not only to maintain but to develop [the FNS]." Insisting on the originality and autonomy of the French deterrence doctrine, he nevertheless muddied the waters by linking conventional deterrence with nuclear deterrence and presenting the strengthening of conventional forces mainly as a reinforcement of nuclear deterrence because they enabled the country to meet subversive actions aimed at wearing down the deterrent forces [*grignotage*] and undermining economic and financial capabilities.[19]

The Prime Minister, Raymond Barre, gave greater emphasis to the priority of the nuclear deterrent in remarks to the IHEDN in September[20] and in his declaration of general policy to the fall session of Parliament he repeated the assertion that the government's policy remained firmly within the lines set forth by General de Gaulle and President Pompidou. Further, he stressed the increase in the defense budget as an indication that both nuclear and conventional forces would be kept at the required level of quality. On that occasion he also noted that France remained committed to the Atlantic Alliance, then at its 25th anniversary, but he emphasized that there was no question of her returning to the joint military organizations since, "One can only be alone when one must take the supreme responsibility."[21] The Defense Minister again addressed the IHEDN on November 15th and reaffirmed that, the nuclear risk cannot be shared—"for France, deterrence can only be national."[22] Speaking to the same body in March 1977, General Mery carefully avoided any reference to "enlarging the sanctuary" created by French nuclear weapons. Instead, he insisted on the exclusively deterrent role of tactical nuclear weapons as well as strategic weapons, and rejected any idea of a gradual escalation of combat from conventional to tactical nuclear to strategic weapons. If they were to be used in combat, Mery envisioned "the brutal use in large numbers of our TNW in the course of a clash must have

19. Speech of M. Yvon Bourges, Minister of Defense, 9 July 1976, *PEF,* 1976, 2, pp. 26-7.

20. Raymond Barre, Speech to IHEDN, 14 September 1976, *PEF,* 1976, 2, p. 9, and *Le Monde,* 15 September 1976.

21. Speech of 5 October 1976, *PEF,* 1976, 2, pp. 55-6.

22. Cited by Gallois, *Le Renoncement,* p. 272.

above all a political significance. . . . The military effectiveness remains secondary by comparison with the demonstration of our political will."[23]

During the same speech Mery also strongly criticized some of the views that had been circulated by younger officers who took up the idea of conducting a continuing battle with small tactical nuclear weapons on the grounds that it would impose on France exactly the sort of combat that the deterrent strategy was designed to prevent.[24]

On June 18, 1977, the Prime Minister spoke out in a visit to the ground forces at Camp Mailly where he again reviewed the logic of deterrence. Insisting that the existing FNS was "sufficient" and that it would be kept at an effective level, subject to the overall limits of the effort that can be devoted to that purpose, he went on to declare, "From now on, our instrument of defense is, in effect, strictly defensive and deterrent; it will be utilized, if by some dreadful misfortune it must be, only when the very life of our country is at stake, and no consideration of any sort can turn us away from the search for maximum deterrent efficiency; that is to say, from that which reduces to a minimum the chance that this terrifying instrument will ever really have to be used."[25] Unfortunately, after this clear and unambiguous explanation which seemed to bring the government's position back into line with the established doctrine—if not entirely with the wholehearted reliance on strategic nuclear deterrence favored by Gallois—Barre proceeded to offer a definition of French "vital interests" that rekindled many doubts. Thus, he maintained, "this conception of deterrence applies to the defense of our vital interests, that is to say, essentially to our national territory, the heart of our existence as a nation, but also to its approaches, that is, to the territory of our neighbors and allies. Because it is obvious that if those territories, except for ours, were to fall into the hands of an aggressor, our days would inevitably be counted. In the same manner, if a conflict broke out on one of those territories, it would not take very long, given the distances involved, for it to overflow into ours."[26] Moreover, Barre also repeated the government's commitment to action beyond the confines of the hexagon in defense of "historic and economic interests," expecially in the Mediterranean and in Africa. Finally, with respect to these areas removed from the central theater of operations, he indicated that the possibility of tactical nuclear weapons being included in the armory of the forces destined

23. Méry, Speech to the IHEDN, March 1977.

24. For example, see: Phillippe Debas, *L'Armée de l'Atome* (Paris: Editions Copernic, 1976).

25. Speech of Prime Minister Barre at Camp Mailly, 18 June 1977, *PEF*, 1977, 2, pp. 94-8.

26. *Ibid.*, p. 97.

to act on the high seas and outside the country was not out of the question, but that these weapons would be used, if at all, only in extreme situations and against strictly military targets.[27]

Hence, it is apparent that the French government had taken to heart some of the criticisms of specialists such as Gallois and Poirier, but that the basic questions that disturbed those writers remained largely unresolved. The scope of deterrence remained clouded by the suggestion that it might be interpreted to cover allied territory as well as French territory. Alliance cooperation was similarly confused by the identification of geographical conditions and political ambitions with strategic realities. Simultaneously, a growing debate about tactical nuclear weapons was stimulated by the American decision to develop so-called "neutron bombs" for use in Europe which overflowed into the French internal debate further confusing the question whether tactical weapons should be strictly reserved for deterrent purposes, or whether they also offered a possibility for France to participate more effectively in combat either within or outside of Europe.

Several further observations by the Chief of Staff of the Armies speaking to the IHEDN again in April 1978 reinforce the conclusion that confusion still abounds regarding the direction that the French government intends to move in its evident desire to gain more flexibility and greater capacity to deal with immediate issues without compromising France's deterrent posture or its alliance commitments. Citing the historic ties between France and Africa and the evident economic interests that link France to the newly independent countries of that continent, General Méry declared that France was prepared to assist some African countries with military aid and in extreme cases would consider direct action. But initiatives that he recognized depended on the continued development of better means of transportation, as the intervention of French forces in Shaba province of Zaire dramatically demonstrated.

The future role of the Navy received special attention, and in that context, Mery indicated that the deterrent mission of the Navy was now clearly primary. As for the future, the highest priority was given to increasing the technical capabilities of the nuclear submarine force by pressing forward the plans to modernize the five existing submarines, to enable them to fire the more powerful M20 missile. That step is expected to be completed around 1980. At that time, the M4 missile capable of delivering multiple warheads over a 4000km range is due to become available. While he stopped short of announcing a decision to proceed with the construction of the sixth nuclear submarine, which is to be of a new generation with significantly improved capabilities, it was clear from the context of Méry's comments that the matter was receiving very serious attention.

27. *Ibid.*

Finally, with respect to land-based missiles, Méry also noted that the French were interested in substituting more maneuverable missiles for the increasingly vulnerable fixed missiles and for the Mirage bombers that are due to be retired from service beginning about 1985. Perhaps a French variant of the cruise missile or a different type of mobile or semi-mobile missile might give an improved deterrent effect he argued. Similarly, the tactical missiles [Pluton] would eventually be replaced by more flexible launchers that can fire at longer range. In the same context, Méry evoked the question of the "neutron bomb" which he considered important mainly because he thought that it could reinforce deterrence, "insofar as it gives greater military effectiveness by enabling one to fire closer to ones own troops, and by enlarging the zone within which the weapons can be used without too many risks for the population."[28] While he thus confirmed the interest that also has been shown by other French military figures for miniaturized tactical weapons, Mery nevertheless discounted any intention to acquire large numbers of such devices that might lead to engagements in a "nuclear battle" where France inevitably would find itself heavily outnumbered.

Mery's speculations concerning the role of tactical nuclear weapons were subsequently disavowed by the Elysée,[29] but they made it clear that there was important support within the military staff for the acquisition of so-called "mini-nukes," even if the doctrinal implications of that move had not been fully examined. More recently, M. Jacques Cressard, the *rapporteur* for the Finance Committee of the National Assembly responsible for the 1979 defense budget, referred to the combat role which he saw "neutron weapons" playing for the NATO alliance in the face of a substantially superior conventional force of the Warsaw Pact. Cressard concluded, "To abandon the neutron bomb would seem, under the present circumstances, to be giving up providing the forces of the Atlantic Alliance with an anti-tank capability susceptible of compensating for the superiority of the Soviet Union in conventional forces."[30] The Ministry of Defense promptly issued a statement clarifying the Government's view and insisting that if the Soviet Union possessed the military capability for a massive surprise attack on Western Europe, as described by M. Cressard, there were, nevertheless, compelling political restraints which it was felt made such an option "impossible for

28. General Méry, Speech to the IHEDN, 3 April 1978, *Défense Nationale,* June 1978, pp. 17-44. The official government position was stated by Admiral Lannuzel, Chief of Staff of the Navy on 24 April 1978 in a speech to the IHEDN, extracts of which were later published in *Défense Nationale,* October 1978, pp. 31-38.

29. See also, Admiral P. Lacoste, (former commandant of the Ecole supérieure de guerre navale), "Problèmes contemporains de politique et stratégie navale," *Ibid.,* pp. 47-48.

30. *Le Monde,* 14 October 1978.

them to exploit."[31] It may be significant, however, that the Government's statement made no mention of neutron weapons. In any case, the Communist Party was quick to question whether M. Cressard had been charged by the President of the Republic with preparing public opinion to accept the utility of neutron bombs for French security?" The possibility that France might employ neutron weapons in a combat situation had grave implications for national security, it was emphasized, because it would create, "a serious risk of seeing any conflict open the way to veritable nuclear war. [Hence,] the security of the country itself would be put in danger."[32]

The Parliamentary debate on defense policy which occurred on June 15, 1978 also provided a further demonstration that, despite the affirmation of priority for a policy of deterrence, there remain important areas of uncertainty, and even confusion, about precisely what such a strategy implies. For example, M. Bourges asserted that, "Defense is not in any way a negative or passive notion." Moreover deterrence, he insisted, "did not meet all the needs of defense" because an opponent might attack indirectly, or by proxy in a manner that did not justify nuclear retaliation such as by resorting to "threats of envelopement, seizure of hostages, in short, to actions which in a general way would tend to harm us, but without touching our vital interests."[33] Thus, it appears clearly that the government's position was moving in the direction of the "flexible response" doctrine of NATO, despite the protestation of the Gaullists who insist that such a doctrine can only undermine the credibility of the deterrent.

How effective the latter have been in maintaining doctrinal orthodoxy is difficult to judge, but it seems clear from the statements of General Bigeard and Pierre Messmer, during the defense debate[34] and the public criticisms voiced by Michel Debré, Joël Le Theule, and Jacques Cressard, among many others, that the RPR was determined to force a reversal of the decision to postpone the sixth nuclear submarine and to include funds for its construction in the 1979 budget. That effort ultimately succeeded when the Elysée announced on 25 September that 220 million francs had been added to the program authorizations for 1979.[35] However, since the total cost of the new submarine, including the more powerful missiles, is estimated to run to approximately 2 billion francs, excluding missile development costs, that

31. *Le Monde*, 15 October 1978.
32. *L'Humanité*, 14 October 1978.
33. Bourges, J. O., A. N. Débats Parlementaires, 15 June 1976, p. 2946.
34. *Ibid.*, pp. 2953-56, 2959-61.
35. *Le Monde*, 27 September 1978. An ajoining excerpt from *La Lettre de la Nation* quoted P. Charpy as stating that the issue of the sixth nuclear submarine was the only one on which the RPR was prepared to break with the Government.

amount seems more a gesture of intentions than a guarantee of achievement, particularly since the pressures to reduce the overall budget deficit (now estimated at 30 billion F) is likely to mount over the next several years.

Conclusion

What can one conclude from this rapid review of recent developments in the debate on the form and content of French strategic doctrine? First, it seems evident that the direct challenge to the priority of nuclear deterrence which was quite evident in Giscard's and Mery's speeches of 1976 has been abandoned, and it seems appropriate to speak of a return to orthodoxy to the extent that the government now recognizes the necessity of strengthening the FNS and is prepared to commit resources to that task—as evidenced by the decision to proceed with construction of the sixth nuclear submarine.

In the process of articulating its strategic doctrine, however, there remain serious ambiguities of two sorts: 1) the relationship between strategic nuclear forces and conventional forces is muddied by a force structure based on large battle formations and by the continued insistence on maintaining a conscript army far larger than needed to protect the FNS, but too small and too ill-equipped to be effective in a conventional conflict. 2) The identification of vital interests has also become obscured in the effort to avoid creating an impasse that would force the government immediately to confront an all-or-nothing choice, so that it is no longer totally certain just what level of threat might provoke a resort to nuclear weapons. In this respect, the speculation about "taking hostages" and "going around the deterrent," together with notions such as "popular deterrence" tend to weaken the credibility of the French deterrent posture.

More seriously, however, two other elements also seem to be causing increasing confusion. One one hand technological developments in nuclear weaponry, particularly the proliferation of smaller warheads and more accurate delivery systems, have caused legitimate concern about the increased vulnerability of the existing FNS components. But they have also incited a continuing controversy over the role of tactical nuclear weapons. In the eyes of some observers, these new weapons reinforce the defense against superior conventional forces and reinforce the deterrent effect by assuring a continuity of risk. Others argue, with greater logic in the view of the present author, that a country with the limited resources available to France cannot match the tactical nuclear potential of the probable adversary; hence, any resort to such weapons in a battle situation would involve monumental risks of immediate escalation. It is understandable that military men should be fascinated by the possible uses of exotic weapons, such as the neutron warhead, the cruise missile, or PGMs; however, given the severe constraints imposed by the French military budget and the political difficulty, at least for the short term, of altering the force levels to sharply reduce manpower costs, it is hard to see how investments in such techniques can do anything but weaken the capabilities of the FNS.

A third element which also seems to lend confusion to the current French doctrine is the extent to which forces essential to the effective operation of the deterrent might be committed to the pursuit of extra-metropolitan goals. The Giscard administration's desire to defend French interests beyond the frontiers, both in Europe and in other regions where traditional links are still strong (such as the Eastern Mediterranean and Africa) or where important economic interests are at stake (as in the Persian Gulf and the Indian Ocean) are perfectly understandable. The question is whether, to the extent that such policies rely on the manipulation of military force, they are consistently evaluated to ensure that they do not undermine the independent deterrent capability.

Such evaluations are, of course, matters of judgment and the factors that must be considered are both complex and changeable. Nevertheless, the manner in which the government has intermixed the concern for exterior interests—however legitimate—and the essential requirements for deterrence, lends substance to the objections of critics like General Gallois who are convinced that "in attempting to do too much, France will fail to do what is essential." And while Gallois may underestimate the extent to which the government has taken into account the objections of its gaullist critics—and particularly those that he himself has lavished upon them—he seems, nevertheless, to be on very solid ground in objecting that President Giscard d'Estaing and his advisers have not made "the right choice" in respect to strategic doctrines. For, as he recently observed, "The Government subscribes to ambitions which, in the world as it is, cannot be ours! In so doing, it sacrifices the security of the metropole and the contribution that France eventually might make to the construction of Europe to the chimera of a foreign policy based on armed force."[36]

The primary problem for France is to reconcile the requirements for maintaining a credible deterrent against nuclear intimidation and foreign intervention with the preservation of other important, although clearly less vital, interests. In that context, and given the exposed geographical position

---

36. In a private communication to the author, June, 1978. See also his article, "The Future of France's Force de Dissuasion," *Strategic Review* (Summer 1979): 34-41.

which she occupies, a strategic doctrine which emphasizes flexible responses seems singularly inappropriate—no matter how appealing it may seem for political reasons. On the contrary, the "politico-strategic insularity" of France imposes on her the necessity of tailoring initiatives beyond the metropole to perserve the freedom of action on which the deterrent depends. Above all, it depends on enunciating a doctrine that leaves no doubt about the conditions under which an opponent must expect to confront the choice of abandoning his attack or suffering an appalling wound. The best that can be said, is that the current debate has not yet produced a doctrine of such clarity.

Naval Policy Outside of Europe

STEPHEN S. ROBERTS

French naval policy, as outlined by senior naval officers and informed observers, is in many ways similar to French defense policy. In particular, the navy's views on strategic nuclear deterrence and the defense of metropolitan France are the logical maritime equivalent of those of the Army, Air Force, and Ministry of Defense. However, in the area of defense policy outside Europe, French naval writings go further than those of the other services or the ministry. The naval writers have defined an additional threat, "indirect strategy," that they feel France faces overseas, and they have adapted French deterrence theory in an effort to respond to it.

The term "indirect strategy" was originated by the noted French strategist General André Beaufre.[1] It is one of two components of this concept of "total strategy," the other being "direct strategy." Direct stategy is the achievement of a decision (or of deterrence) by primarily military means, while "the essential feature of indirect strategy is that it seeks to obtain a result by methods other than military victory."[2] Beaufre's clearest definition of indirect strategy is as follows:

> Indirect strategy is . . . the art of making the best use of the limited area of freedom of action left us by the deterrent effect of the existence of nuclear weapons and of gaining important and decisive victories in spite of the fact that the military resources which can be employed for the purpose must, in general, remain strictly limited.[3]

1. General André Beaufre, *An Introduction to Strategy* (New York: Praeger, 1965), p. 108.
2. Beaufre, *An Introduction to Strategy,* p. 108.
3. Beaufre, *An Introduction to Strategy,* pp. 109-110.

There are two aspects of this definition that are worth underlining. The first is that an actor's resources can be limited either because he is deterred from using them or because he does not possess them. Indirect strategy is thus for use by the weak as well as by the deterred. The second is that, the more complete nuclear deterrence becomes, the more prevalent indirect strategy will become. Since we have practically reached what Beaufre calls "nuclear paralysis," we can expect indirect strategy to be the dominant form of action in today's world.[4]

Beaufre outlines two types of maneuvers that can be used in indirect strategy, each of which uses a combination of direct (military) action and indirect (psychological) action. The first consists of "nibbling" away at the enemy's weak point by quick, limited military actions separated by periods of negotiation. This he calls the "piecemeal" or "salami" maneuver. The second consists of the use of prolonged conflict combined with a psychological offensive to erode or wear down the enemy's will to resist. In this "erosion" or "weariness" maneuver, the military objective is not to win but simply to hold out without losing until the enemy gives up. The example of "nibbling" that Beaufre cites most often is Hitler's actions in Central Europe between 1936 and 1939, while his "erosion maneuver" is clearly an effort to describe the wars of national liberation since 1945, especially those inspired by the ideas of Mao Tse-tung.[5]

Beaufre published these ideas in three books between 1963 and 1966.[6] While they have had considerable impact on French thinking, his concept of indirect strategy was not immediately incorporated into official statements of French policy. It was only in the past 4 to 5 years, with the increasing activism of the Soviet navy, the development of strong regional states and, above all, the shock of the 1973 oil crisis, that the notion of indirect strategy has attracted wide attention in France. Navy spokesmen have been particularly prominent in adopting Beaufre's concept and modifying it to meet the new circumstances.[7] In its revised form this concept now also appears in statements of the Ministry of Defense, notably in recent speeches of Yvon Bourges.[8]

4. Beaufre, *Deterrence and Strategy* (New York: Praeger, 1966), p. 145.

5. Beaufre, *An Introduction to Strategy*, pp. 113-120.

6. Beaufre, *An Introduction to Strategy;* Beaufre, *Deterrence and Strategy;* Beaufre, *Strategy of Action* (London: Faber and Faber, 1967).

7. Particularly prominent Navy writers were Admirals Joire-Noulens and de Joybert (Chiefs of Staff of the Navy) and Vice Admirals Schweitzer and Wolff (Major-Generals of the Navy). These posts equate roughly to our CNO and VCNO.

8. For example, Bourges' speeches to the Institut des Hautes Etudes de Défense Nationale on 15 November 1976 and 11 October 1977: "La Politique Militaire de la France," Dossier d'Information no. 51, Service d'Information et de Relations Publique des Armées (SIRPA), Paris, January 1977, pp. 6-7; "Indépendance Nationale," *Armées d'Aujourd'hui,* November 1977, pp. 6-7.

Navy spokesmen, following Beaufre, distinguish between two strategies open to France's enemies: "direct strategy" and "indirect strategy."[9] In today's world, direct strategy used against France would consist of overt armed aggression against French territory, especially in Europe. France's nuclear deterrent force was designed to counter this strategy, and navy spokesmen agree with Beaufre that this force, coupled with the nuclear balance between the two superpowers, makes the use of direct strategy anywhere in Europe extremely unlikely. If war in Europe did occur, it would probably result from indirect causes: an accident, disruption of the East-West military balance, or the spread of conflicts that start outside Europe. The navy spokesmen also agree with Beaufre's contention that the more complete nuclear deterrence becomes, the more prevalent indirect strategy will become. Since we have practically reached what Beaufre calls "nuclear paralysis" in Europe, we can expect indirect strategy outside of Europe to become the dominant form of action in today's world, both for major powers and for lesser powers.[10]

Of the two forms of indirect strategy described by Beaufre, the one that concerns the French navy is the piecemeal approach. (The French clearly hope that Algeria was the last large-scale war of national liberation that they will have to face.) In the navy's view the main threat is an enemy "nibbling" away at French interests one by one when he is afraid or unable to attack France directly. He would alternate local thrusts with calls for negotiation and conciliation, in an effort to find the point of least resistance and test the will and ability of France to resist.[11] At first he would try to choose forms of action that were either covert or non-violent and which therefore could not easily be characterized as aggression. He would choose as his initial targets interests which appeared of marginal importance, even if they were not. The enemy would subsequently have the choice of proceeding to more overt forms of violence if resistance was weak, or of continuing his piecemeal attacks until their cumulative effect brought France to her knees.

Indirect strategy is of particular concern to the navy, since if feels it is most likely to be exercised at sea. Naval forces can easily be moved at sea to

---

9. A main navy spokesman on indirect strategy is Admiral Joire-Noulens. See his "Reflexions sur les missions de la marine," *Armées d'Aujourd'hui,* July 1975, especially p. 29; "Problemes operationnels et financiers de la marine nationale," *Défense Nationale,* October 1975, pp. 5-22; "Quelle marine et pour quoi fair des le temps de paix," *Défense Nationale,* July 1976, pp. 21-42. See also Admiral Marc de Joybert, "Cassandre bleu marine," *Défense Nationale,* June 1974, pp. 9-14.

10. Joire-Noulens, "Quelle marine," pp. 22, 27; Vice Admiral Marcel Wolff, "Politique de defense et politique navale," *Défense Nationale,* May 1976, p. 55.

11. "Marine et defense de la France," *Revue Maritime,* March 1977, p. 229. This article is by a group of former attendees of the Institut des Hautes Etudes de Défense Nationale (IHEDN) and is referred to hereafter as IHEDN, "Marine et défense."

interfere with commerce, intimidate an opponent or protect a friend. Claims to territorial waters, to economic zones at sea and to the right to impose environmental regulations can give a pretext for harassing or interrupting traffic in straits and in coastal waters and for appropriating resources on the sea bed.[12] Covert military actions are also possible at sea. A recent French CNO pointed out that nuclear submarines are capable of sinking merchantmen at sea, selecting them according to departure point, transit route, or arrival point, without revealing the submarines' nationality and making their government subject to retaliation.[13] Another way to avoid retaliation is to instigate attacks by a small littoral power using fast patrol boats or land-based aircraft. Finally the deployed naval forces of the superpowers (possibly based in the Third World) and the navies of littoral states are capable of limited overt military action, which could also be part of an indirect strategy.

Indirect strategy would be of little importance to France were it not for the fact that it can endanger vital French interests without triggering France's strategic deterrent. Indirect strategy owes its popularity to the fact that the piecemeal attacks that make it up can all be kept small enough so that a strategic nuclear response to any one of them would not be credible. For example, an attack on a few merchant ships would probably not arouse sufficient public sentiment to justify a nuclear response.[14] On the other hand, France has realized that some of her interests that are vulnerable to indirect strategy are truly vital to her survival. It thus becomes possible for indirect strategy to "turn the flanks" of the French strategic deterrent by nibbling away at these vital interests until the cumulative damage brings France to her knees.

France has traditionally had numerous political and cultural interests overseas, but, while these are important, none of them, as they exist today, is regarded as vital. On the other hand, recent events have made her acutely aware that her economic interests overseas, which are highly vulnerable to indirect strategy, are indeed vital to her survival.[15]

---

12. Joire-Noulens, "Quelle marine," pp. 21-22; G. Mouline, "Des missions, une marine," *Cols Bleus,* 19 June 1976, p. 14; Gen G. Méry (Chief of Staff of the Armies), "Une armée pour quoi faire et comment?" *Défense Nationale,* June 1976, p. 21; Joire-Noulens, "Problèmes operationnnels," p. 10; Rear Admiral H. Labrousse "La route du pétrole peut-elle être coupée?" *Défense Nationale,* October 1976, p. 29.

13. Joybert, "Cassandre bleu marine," p. 12. See also Philippe Veyrard, "Quelques aspects de l'évolution des menaces et de leurs parades," *Défense Nationale,* November 1974, p. 18.

14. Vice Admiral Jean Schweitzer, "La marine dans l'océan Indien," *Armées d'Aujourd'hui,* November 1976, p. 33.

15. Joire-Noulens, "Réflexions," p. 29; "Problèmes opérationnels," pp. 10-11; Bourges, "Politique militaire de la France," p. 7.

Politically, France has the obligation to protect her overseas departments and territories in the West Indies, off Newfoundland, and in the Indian and Pacific Oceans. These are all small specks of land, but they fly the French flag and have recently gained new importance due to the declaration of a 200-mile economic zone around all French territory. France has also accepted extra-European obligations by signing defense agreements with some of her former West African colonies. In addition France has made it known that "de-facto solidarity" could cause her to participate, if asked, in the defense of other former colonies with which she does not have formal agreements.[16] France also wants to be able to participate in peacekeeping operations under the auspices of international organizations, and she wants to be able to protect French nationals overseas wherever the necessity may arise.

The French also claim that the diffusion and welfare of French culture abroad is a French national interest. This has been a recurrent theme in French history, and today it serves to make French interests greater than they might otherwise be in certain parts of the world, notably West Africa and the southwest Indian Ocean. Cultural affinity could help bring about France's involvement in these areas under the guise of "de-facto solidarity."

France has always had economic interests overseas, but only recently has it become widely agreed that they are vital to her survival. Traditionally agriculture played a large role in the French economy and made her self-sufficient in many areas. Since World War II, however, France has experienced a remarkable economic boom that has greatly increased the relative importance of her industrial sector. This has brought great rewards but has also greatly reduced her self-sufficiency, since she does not have within her own borders either the energy resources, raw materials or markets needed to support her industrial economy.[17] The French defense community was slow to see the significance of this change—these economic interests did not figure at all in the 1972 White Paper on National Defense, which mentioned only French overseas political interests.[18] In 1973, however, the shock of the oil embargo accompanying the October War and the subsequent rise in oil prices made everyone aware of the vulnerability of France's energy supplies. 99% of France's oil and 73% of her overall energy supply come from abroad, as does 63% of the minerals used in her industry.[19] More recent controversies,

---

16. Bourges, "Politique militaire de la France," p. 6.

17. Joybert, "Cassandre bleu marine," pp. 11-12; Joire-Noulens, "Réflexions," p. 28; Joire-Noulens, "Quelle marine," p. 7; Veyrard, "Quelques aspects," pp. 16-17.

18. Joire-Noulens, "Problèmes opérationnels," p. 11; "White Paper on National Defense," French Embassy, New York, 1972, vol. 1, p. 8. (This is an official French translation of "Livre blanc sur la défense nationale," vol. 1, Cedocor, Paris, 1972.)

19. Bourges, "Politique Militaire de la France," p. 7; Bourges, "Indépendance Nationale," p. 7.

including debates over the Law of the Sea, have drawn attention to other essential resources overseas and the means by which they are brought to France. France also depends on traffic in the other direction—her exports provide her with the funds she needs to pay for her oil and other supplies.

Senior navy spokesmen and others now argue that overseas interests are truly vital for France's economic health and standard of living, and that France could be brought to her knees in three months or less if her overseas connections were cut, even if her land frontiers were never crossed.[20] Admiral Joybert, then Chief of Staff of the Navy, wrote in 1974 that France's nuclear deterrent force had transformed her into a mighty citadel but that "one can always reduce by famine, and without firing a shot at it, an impregnable fortress."[21]

France's economic interests overseas are vulnerable in three places: the foreign countries that supply France with oil and raw materials and buy her products, the trade routes along which these materials travel to and from France, and the economic zones at sea where resources can be found in and under the water.

The producing countries, either on their own or at the instigation of a cartel or a superpower, could do great harm to France by imposing arbitrarily high prices or by shutting down production. France would be equally hurt if political instability, civil disorders or a war in the producing country obstructed production. This situation is aggravated by the fact that a few individual states and cartels have a near monopoly over several natural resources that are vital to France.

The French navy is even more concerned about the vulnerability of these supplies on the trade routes. 75 to 80 percent of France's imports travel by sea, and 70% of her oil travels on one long, vulnerable trade route, the one around the Cape of Good Hope.[22] The possible actions against these routes have already been mentioned—they include legal restrictions, covert attacks by submarines or forces of littoral proxy states, or limited but damaging overt attacks. Such attacks could put enormous pressure on France and Western Europe—one writer argues that the loss of even a few supertankers could cause the suspension of the oil traffic and a serious energy crisis in Western Europe.[23]

20. Joybert, "Cassandre bleu marine," p. 12; A. Loest, "Pour une fois, écoutons Cassandre," *Revue Maritime,* Jan-Feb 1975, pp. 80-92; "Programmation militaire pour les années 1977-1982," Law no. 76-531 of June 19, 1976, Assemblée Nationale, Textes d'Intérêt Général, no. 76-139, Paris, 1976, p. 3, (hereafter referred to as Law 1977-82).

21. Joybert, "Cassandre bleu marine," p. 11.

22. Joire-Noulens, "Quelle marine," p. 26; Schweitzer, "La marine dans l'Océan Indien," p. 32; Mouline, "Des missions," p. 13.

23. Labrousse, "La route du pétrole," p. 30.

France's interests in the wealth in and under the seas could also prove of major importance to her. France followed the lead of other states and declared a 200 nautical mile economic zone around her territories, including those overseas, in 1976. Due to France's possession of numerous small isolated islands, this has raised her area from 550,000 to 11,000,000 square kilometers and raised her rank among coastal states from 53rd in area to 3rd.[24] She has already begun searching for oil off Metropolitan France and the Indian Ocean island of Kerguelen, and she also hopes to find manganese nodules off her Pacific Islands. France also draws much wealth from areas not under her control: her fishing fleets work the Dogger and Grand Banks among others, and she has oil survey crews at work around the world. France needs to protect her potential riches at sea from rapacious exploitation by others, and she must protect her own legitimate interests in regions not under her sovereignty.[25]

The French do not feel that they are alone in being economically vulnerable to indirect strategy outside Europe. They feel that the other major industrial powers, including the superpowers, are all more or less dependent on overseas resources. The result is that the world is now engaged in a subtle competition in which powers, acting on their own or through interposed smaller states, are trying to gain control of these resources (or deny them to their rivals) by any means that will not lead to the use of strategic nuclear weapons. The French feel that the stakes in this competition are truly enormous—the wealth of the whole world outside Europe, North America and Russia—and that the redistribution of this wealth could lead to the establishment of a new world balance, despite the fact that the nuclear stalemate prevents use of direct strategy. The dangers of this situation are further increased by the number of Third-World states, the instability of many of them, the proliferation of armaments, and the increasing economic interdependence of nations. The result is that the world is in a state of permanent crisis and the interests of France and her friends are in continuous jeopardy. The French want to be able to protect their own interests in this dangerous world and also participate in the formation of the new balance, and they have made this a primary mission of their non-strategic forces.[26]

Having defined the threat of indirect strategy and the interests that are vulnerable to it, we turn to the strategy that the French navy has adopted to

24. Joire-Noulens, "Quelle marine," p. 25; Speech of Admiral Lannuzel (Chief of Staff of the Navy), March 16, 1977, *Cols Bleus*, April 2, 1977, p. 7; Wolff, "Politique navale," p. 949.

25. Schweitzer, "La marine dans l'Océan Indien," p. 32-34; Jacques Perrot, "Le développement océanologique et la France d'Outre-Mer," *Défense Nationale*, February 1975, pp. 23-40.

26. Vice Admiral Marcel Wolff, "Politique navale," *Revue Maritime*, August-

counter it. The French realize that in a world populated by two superpowers and a number of strong regional powers, some located at great distances from France, she does not have the ability to respond with brute strength. (In any case, this might not be an appropriate response to certain kinds of indirect attack.) Instead she has turned to her version of deterrence theory in an effort to develop a defensive strategy "for the weak against the strong."[27]

French deterrence theory of the 1960s generally resembled the U.S. doctrine of massive retaliation, which called for a massive nuclear strike as the reaction to any aggression. In the 1960s both the U.S. and France turned away from this doctrine due to its "all or nothing" character—it was simply not credible that a nation would respond massively (and presumably absorb a counter strike) in a minor case of aggression in which its central interests were not at stake.[28] The U.S. responded to this problem with the doctrine of "flexible response," which calls for oppressing each threat with the lowest level of force capable of containing it. This allows for a response to any threat, but, in an effort to raise the nuclear threshold, it also calls for the use of conventional warfighting against all but the most massive aggression. France could not afford to buy large conventional forces or to fight a long conventional war, and she has therefore rejected flexible response.

The French have tried to develop an equivalent to flexible response which, instead of countering each threat with an appropriate amount of force, counters it with an appropriate deterrent. France plans to respond initially to aggression with a "coup d'arret"—a swift, sharp move at a level of violence appropriate to that used by the aggressor.[29] The purpose of this move is not to defeat him militarily but to show him that France has the resolve to defend her interests, that the aggression has been detected, and that France has the ability to inflict severe pain on an aggressor. Hopefully a prompt "coup d'arret" would nip the aggression in the bud or "kill the chicken in the egg" before it gets too big for French forces to handle. If the aggressor defies this warning and confirms his aggressive intent by overriding French resistance at this level of violence, France would increase the level of violence (or, pre-

---

September 1976, pp. 943, 949; Mery, "Réflexions sur le concept d'emploi des forces," *Défense Nationale,* Novembler 1975, pp. 17-19; Méry, "Armées pour quoi faire," p. 13; IHEDN, "Marine et Défense," p. 229; Law 1977-82, pp. 3-4; D'Allières, "Rapport fait au nom de la commission de la défense nationale et des forces armées sur le projet de loi portant approbation de la programmation militaire pour les années 1977-1982," Assemblée Nationale, no. 2292, Paris, May 13, 1976, vol. 1, pp. 4-5.

27. IHEDN, "Marine et défense," p. 226.

28. Bourges, "Politique militaire," p. 10. An example of the earlier French doctrine is General Ailleret, "Opinion sur la théorie stratégique de la 'flexible response'," *Défense Nationale,* August-September 1964, pp. 1323-1340.

29. IHEDN, "Marine et défense," p. 229.

ferably, put the aggressor in a position where he had to do it) until he realized that the price he had to pay to reach his objective had become exorbitant and he backed down.[30] In short, France would deter her opponents by showing her readiness and willingness to ascend an escalatory ladder, the top rung of which, in her case, is a strategic nuclear force. Hopefully the fact that the last rung in the ladder is nuclear catastrophe would give actions on the lower rungs sufficient deterrent value to cause the opponent to back down even if the French forces that were confronting him were not strong enough to defeat him militarily.[31]

The original version of this concept of deterrence was first published in 1969 by General Fourquet, then Chief of Staff of the Armies, as the basis for France's response to a direct strategy applied in a European theater.[32] However, the fact that it allows for an almost unlimited variety of possible actions (not necessarily violent) in response to threats means that it is also capable of responding to the subtleties of indirect strategy.[33] It has therefore become the basis for French crisis management. The French feel that military forces can contribute to crisis management in two non-violent ways: through their mere existence and through their manipulation. If these fail, the French are prepared to escalate to combat in a further effort to deter their opponent.[34]

Military forces can help crisis managers by their mere existence, either in general or within reach of a specific region. The presence of forward-deployed forces, either permanent or periodic, shows French political, economic, and military power and emphasizes the interest France has in the region in which the units are deployed. It also gives solid evidence of her determination to protect her interests in the region.[35] Presence forces can also help forestall aggression before it starts by friendly actions such as port calls, disaster relief, etc., designed to reinforce alliances and promote good will between France and the nations in the area.[36] The French place considerable emphasis on the importance of a continuing "presence" of forward-deployed conventional forces as a means for deterring indirect strategy.

Presence forces can make a more intense non-violent contribution to crisis management if they are properly manipulated during crises. Maneuver-

30. IHEDN, "Marine et défense," p. 232.

31. Bourges, "Politique militaire," p. 10; IHEDN, "Marine et défense," pp. 232, 236, 240; Bourges, "Dissuasion et forces nucléaires stratégiques," Dossier d'Information no. 48, SIRPA, Paris, August 1976, p. 8.

32. General M. Fourquet, "Emploi des différents systèmes de forces dans le cadre de la stratégie de dissuasion," *Défense Nationale*, May 1969, pp. 757-767.

33. IHEDN, "Marine et défense," pp. 232-233.

34. Méry, "Réflexions," pp. 20-21; Law 1977-1982, p. 6.

35. Joire-Noulens, "Quelle marine," p. 23.

36. Schweitzer, "La Marine dans l'Océan Indien," p. 33; "La Marine," *Forces Armées Françaises*, March 1974, p. 32.

ing these forces increases their deterrent effect by making more clear the connection between their presence and specific French diplomatic objectives. Techniques often used include placing presence forces on alert, moving them closer to the crisis area, and reinforcing them.[37] Even if not reinforced, presence forces on the scene may have the capability of resolving a local crisis through fast action before it can spread. It they do not, they can help deter an aggressor by introducing uncertainty into his calculations. They can deny him the possibility of "nibbling" without risk—even very small forces can be manipulated so as to force him to make his act of aggression overt. They can be used to show him that France is watching him and knows what he is doing. They can also provide Paris with the information it needs to manage the crisis.[38]

The ways in which naval forces can be manipulated in response to indirect strategy are limited only by the imagination of commanders—each threat is likely to lead to a different response. The French have given several examples of ways even weak naval forces can respond constructively to specific threats that might be part of an indirect strategy. One problem encountered during the October 1973 Middle East War was that merchant ships would not enter the danger zone declared by the belligerents, primarily because their insurance would not cover them there or would do so only at exorbitant rates. In 1973 the danger zones did not block any important French trade routes, but, if they had, the navy could have taken operational control of these ships, accompanied them through the zone, and thus minimized their insurance problems.[39] A more serious problem would arise if French shipping were directly threatened by another power. In this case the navy could again take operational control of French merchantmen and assign them routes distant from the usual ones so as to conceal them in the vastness of the sea. In areas such as straits, where only one route is feasible, the navy could use its few ships as escorts. Any action against an escorted French merchantman would thus automatically be escalated to an action against a French warship, which would be much more serious politically and might deter the action altogether.[40]

If these non-violent military actions coupled with diplomacy fail, the next option is actual combat. This option could be used in an effort to resolve

37. Law 1977-1982, p. 6; Méry, "Réflexions," p. 20; Joire-Noulens, "Quelle marine," p. 24.

38. IHEDN, "Marine et défense," p. 234; Joire-Noulens, "Quelle marine," p. 23.

39. Schweitzer, "La Marine dans l'Océan Indien," p. 33; Wolff, "Politique navale," p. 948.

40. Schweitzer, "La Marine dans l'Océan Indien," p. 33; Labrousse, "La route du pétrole," p. 32.

the crisis directly by force, but it is much more likely in the French case that combat will be regarded as a continuation of deterrence by other means. Following the principle of deterrence referred to above, France would use her forces to force the conflict up the escalatory ladder until the aggressor backs down. The French speak of several tactics they would use in combat: riposte, retaliation, and a combination of these.

Riposte consists of a direct parry against the enemy and refers to the situation in which French forces would be strong enough to confront him directly and defeat him on the battlefield. The French would certainly use this when feasible; but they feel that, due to the limited strength and size of their forces, they cannot count on it.

Retaliation (*retorsion*) might be used when riposte was not possible. It consists of striking the aggressor hard, not at the point of aggression, but where he is most vulnerable. It is a deterrent act, designed to show the enemy the French will to resist, her ability to harm her opponent, and her ability to escalate the level of violence if necessary. Its objective is to induce him to reconsider the advisability of his aggression. It is a tactic of the weak which uses shock to compensate for lack of strength, and in theory could be a brutal affair. It requires skillful and imaginative management on both the political and military levels. Speed and surprise are necessary, and it is essential that the retaliating country have justice squarely on its side.[41]

Against a determined opponent, riposte and retaliation would be used together in climbing the escalatory ladder. French plans for war in Europe call for confronting advancing Warsaw Pact forces with significant resistance by conventional and tactical nuclear forces, while the more mobile French forces launch retaliatory strikes on the enemy's flank or in his rear. The level of violence would be progressively increased until the enemy backed down or was unambiguously confronted with the threat of a strategic nuclear strike.

France has made it clear that she regards some of her overseas interests (especially her SLOCs) as vital, and in principle the same tactics could be applied overseas. The only difference is that France's strategic nuclear deterrent might not be usable against aggression in the Third World. French policy is far from clear on this subject (the matter appears still to be under debate) but there are indications that France might use tactical nuclear weapons in a conflict outside Europe, either as a warning shot or as the ultimate form of retaliation.[42]

Current French doctrine assigns tactical nuclear weapons two functions: to do substantial harm to the enemy's military capabilities in the theater, and

41. IHEDN, "Marine et défense," pp. 235-236.
42. *Défense Nationale*, June 1978, p. 171.

to serve as a penultimate deterrent that will confront him unmistakably with the prospect of a strategic nuclear strike. Due to the escalatory nature of the use of tactical nuclear weapons in Europe and due to France's limited resources, French doctrine discourages the use of these weapons in isolated warning shots or in any conflict not directly involving the territorial security of metropolitan France.[43]

It has been suggested, however, that these obstacles to the use of tactical nuclear weapons are greatly reduced at sea and that the sea is the optimum environment for their use. There is, for example, practically no danger of collateral damage to civilian populations—this could be interpreted as meaning that the danger of uncontrollable escalation would be reduced. In the context of a crisis outside Europe, even a single tactical nuclear warning shot would have an extremely high impact, both as a diplomatic signal and as a means of retaliation.[44]

Current discussions refer only to the use of these weapons in conflicts involving other countries whose naval forces also have tactical nuclear weapons. The French feel that possession of these weapons is required to give their naval crisis-management forces credibility against nuclear-armed opponents, and will help offset the inferiority in numbers of French forces. They are currently equipping both of their aircraft carriers with tactical nuclear weapons. Current French naval tactical nuclear weapons are gravity bombs, although there is talk of developing air- and sea-launched tactical nuclear missiles.[45]

Currently, French defense policy calls for basing French defenses at all levels of violence on deterrence. This deterrence is achieved by demonstrating to potential opponents France's readiness and willingness to ascend an escalatory ladder which consists of three main sections:

1. French forces would first mark France's determination not to let certain limits be passed. They do this through peacetime presence and maneuvers.

2. If war breaks out, French forces would force the aggressor to pay an excessive price for his covetousness (through retaliation and escalation) in an effor to persuade him to renounce his enterprise. (If possible, of course, they would stop him by riposte).

43. IHEDN, "Marine et défense," p. 236; Paul-Marie de la Gorce, "Marine et armée nucléaire tactique," *Armées d'Aujourd'hui,* October 1977, p. 6; "White Paper," pp. 13-14.

44. IHEDEN, "Marine et défense," p. 236; Joire-Noulens, "Quelle marine," p. 36; Veyrard, "Quelques aspects," p. 19; J. Geriville-Réache, "La France et la défense militaire," *Défense Nationale,* October 1974, p. 105. Jacques Isnard states in *Le Monde,* November 28, 1978, p. 20 that France would consider use of naval tactical nuclear weapons against military targets in order to bring an end to a crisis or local war, and calls this doctrine "the Indian Ocean Strategy."

45. Joire-Noulens, "Quelle marine," p. 36; Veyrard, "Quelques aspects," p. 19.

3. If the war goes badly, the strategic nuclear deterrent constitutes an ultimate threat designed to enable France to escape an unconditional surrender imposed by force.[46]

The existence of the strategic nuclear deterrent at the top of the ladder is the basis for the credibility of the whole structure—the fact that it is directly linked to actions further down the ladder will hopefully give these actions sufficient deterrent value to stop the conflict before it reaches the nuclear level.

The navy has four missions, three of which are directly connected to this strategy. These four missions are:

1. Participating in nuclear deterrence (i.e., providing and protecting the SSBN force)

2. Maintaining surveillance over and, if necessary, defending the maritime appoaches to France

3. Retaining at sea and overseas the freedom of action that is needed

4. Participating at sea in the tasks of public service (i.e., non-military Coast Guard functions).[47]

The first two of these cover the participation of the Navy in France's deterrent strategy in Europe. The third, "retaining at sea and overseas the freedom of action that is needed" is the one that covers action outside of Europe. "Freedom of action," according to Beaufre, is the ultimate objective of all strategy.[48] Since France has no expansionist aims, "freedom of action" means in her case having available the widest possible range of responses to aggression, in particular to indirect strategy. The navy has implemented its mission of action outside Europe in three ways. It has set up a worldwide crisis management organization that allows close control of forces overseas by political authorities in Paris, it provides presence forces permanently stationed overseas, and it has intervention forces capable of being sent from France in case of special need.[49]

The Navy has designed its peacetime operational command structure so it can respond to crises anywhere in the world. It has divided the world into

---

46. IHEDN, "Marine et défense," p. 240, also 232-233.

47. This list of missions is from M. Crespin, "Avis présenté au nom de la commission de la défense nationale et des forces armées sur le project de loi de finances pour 1977," Défense, Tome VI: Section Marine, Assemblée Nationale, no. 2532, Paris, October 12, 1976, vol. 6, pp. 8-11. A slightly different version is in G. Mouline, "Des missions, une Marine," *Cols Bleus,* June 19, 1976, p. 8.

48. Beaufre, *An Introduction to Strategy,* p. 110; Beaufre, *Deterrence and Strategy,* pp. 56-57.

49. Joire-Noulens, "Quelle marine," p. 29.

seven zones: the North Sea, the North Atlantic, the Mediterranean, the Indian Ocean, the Pacific, the West Atlantic and Caribbean, and the South Atlantic. Each of these is assigned to the senior naval commander in the zone. Of the four non-European zones, the Pacific and Indian Ocean are under specially designated flag officers who have fleets of roughly 10 ships each while the other two are under commanders of the French naval shore facilities in the zones. These zone commanders are responsible for keeping track of events in their zones and controlling the operations of naval forces there. During crises their actions are in turn controlled by the Chief of Staff of the Armies who in turn reports to the civilian government. During routine periods this control is delegated to the Chief of Staff of the Navy.[50]

Naval presence is an essential part of the French response to indirect strategy, but there are severe limitations on the French ability to carry it out. France has few ships, her budget does not permit many long deployments, and she has few support facilities overseas. The result is that she cannot maintain overseas on a permanent basis forces sufficient to cope with crises. Instead she maintains token forces in her overseas zones during routine periods and attempts to anticipate crises and reinforce her forces where their psychological impact and military capabilities are most needed. This reinforcement capability is demonstrated during routine periods by periodic overseas cruises (especially in the Indian Ocean) by small task forces (usually two destroyers) drawn from the Atlantic and Mediterranean fleets. French deployments are proportioned according to French interests and political objectives in a region as well as to the potential crisis level. Aircraft carriers are only sent if the situation is particularly grave or if the French President has a particularly strong diplomatic signal that he wishes to transmit. The most recent case of this was the deployment of a carrier to the Red Sea during Djibouti's transition to independence.[51]

If presence forces fail to deter a crisis, France would send larger forces with the capability to intervene, either at sea or ashore. Recent African crises have involved the use of nonnaval intervention forces (notably transport aircraft and airborne troops), but the navy also has a substantial intervention capability which, it feels, is far less dependent on support facilities and far more capable of sustained operations than other forms of intervention.

In the case of a crisis at sea the navy could respond with whatever type ship was most appropriate: submarines, surface combatants, minesweepers, etc. If projection of force ashore was required, the navy would probably turn to its two aircraft carriers. One of the carriers would be quickly converted to a

50. Wolff, "Politique navale," pp. 952-953; Joire-Noulens, "Quelle marine," p. 24.
51. IHEDN, "Marine et défense," p. 234. On the base problem see Joire-Noulens, "Quelle marine," pp. 28, 30.

helicopter assault ship, while the other would act as an attack carrier, providing air cover for the naval force and tactical air support ashore. A typical French naval intervention force might consist of the following:

- One carrier with 40 fighters and attack aircraft escorted by 6 to 8 AAW and ASW ships.

- One carrier rigged as a helo assault ship, one dock landing ship and several tank landing ships. This force could land and support ashore 2,300 men from the Navy's commando force and the Army's marine infantry, along with 250 vehicles including a squadron of AMX-30 light tanks.

- A logistic force, consisting of two tankers and two repair ships.[52]

Some of the escorts might also carry small commando groups of 20-30 men. If supplies or troops in excess of these carried in the task force were required, the navy would organize a sealift using chartered merchantmen.

The navy's ability to intervene varies according to the geographic region involved. The French have decided that they must maintain their primary naval intervention capability (including the two carriers) in the Mediterranean, since it is an unstable region where both direct and indirect strategy could do great harm to France.[53] This disposition has the advantage of putting the carriers within reach of the area outside Europe that is of greatest importance to France—the Indian Ocean. (They could also reach West Africa if necessary, although this has not occurred.) Elsewhere French naval crisis management forces would be smaller, but they would still be capable of limited combat actions, patrol of sea lanes, and support actions such as providing technical military assistance or war supplies.[54]

The weakest point in the French navy's overseas strategy from the French viewpoint appears to be the defense of the sea lanes. French writers have repeatedly stated that France cannot do this alone, and that she would need allies. They believe, however, that any crisis affecting the sea lanes will affect all of Western Europe and the United States, and they seem to expect that the allies would be there when needed.[55]

French naval policy outside Europe thus consists of the use of deterrence against the threat of indirect strategy using both presence forces and inter-

52. Joire-Noulens, "Quelle marine," pp. 27-28.
53. Bourges, "Politique militaire," p. 6; Joire-Noulens, "Quelle marine," pp. 22-24; Joire-Noulens, "Problèmes opérationnels," p. 12.
54. Méry, "Armées pour quoi faire," p. 15; Méry, "Réflexions," p. 20.
55. Law 1977-1982, p. 7; Méry, "Armée pour quoi faire," p. 15; Méry, "Réflexions," p. 21; Joire-Noulens, "Quelle marine," p. 28; Joire-Noulens, "Réflexions," p. 28; Joybert, "Cassandre bleu marine," p. 12; Labrousse "Route du pétrole," p. 29; Mouline, "Des missions," p. 14; "White Paper," pp. 13-14, 26; Admiral Marc de Joybert, "Transports maritimes et défense," *Défense Nationale,* April 1973, pp. 33-34.

vention forces. Navy writers fear that an enemy could use an indirect strategy to "turn the flanks" of France's nuclear deterrent and defeat France through a deliberate series of small actions against vital French interests outside of Europe, especially her supplies of oil and raw materials. The navy, with its ability to operate worldwide, is the logical counter to this threat; but, due to its limited resources, it would have to base its actions on the use of escalation as a deterrent. Possible actions include non-violent crisis-management techniques, riposte, retaliation, and perhaps ultimately the use of tactical nuclear weapons. The French navy maintains presence forces, intervention forces, and a crisis management organization which it hopes will enable it to respond to indirect strategy anywhere in the world.

Looking into the future, it seems that this policy will endure, although the means for executing it may change. The need to protect French territories overseas, the economic zone around them, and the supply of oil and other raw materials all seem to ensure that France will continue to maintain a naval presence overseas (especially in the Indian Ocean) regardless of any political changes that may occur in Paris. However, the disappearance of the aircraft carriers in the 1990s could cause some changes in the navy's intervention capabilities. Some indication of future French capabilities may be gleaned from the fact that the French are already talking of the retaliatory potential of nuclear submarines outside Europe,[56] the possible equipping of surface combatants with nuclear-tipped cruise missiles,[57] and the construction of specialized helicopter assault carriers.[58] It appears that deterrent action against indirect strategy will be a major role of the French navy well into the 21st century.

56. Joire-Noulens, "Quelle marine," p. 28; Jean Bertaux, "Surprendre et frappe—les sous-marines d'attaque," *Armées d'Aujourd'hui*, May 1976, pp. 50-51.

57. Joire-Noulens, "Quelle marine," p. 36; Veyrard, "Quelques aspects," p. 36.

58. This ship, the PA-75 (formerly PH-75) is best described in Jean Labayle-Coubat, *Combat Fleets of the World, 1976/77*, (Annapolis: Naval Institute Press, 1976), p. 84. This ship was to have been begun in 1975, but is currently scheduled to be laid down in 1982.

Index